The
Development and Chronology
of Chaucer's Works.

The
Development and Chronology
of Chaucer's Works.

BY

JOHN S. P. TATLOCK, Ph.D.

ASSISTANT PROFESSOR OF ENGLISH IN THE
UNIVERSITY OF MICHIGAN.

GLOUCESTER, MASS.
PETER SMITH
1963

PREFACE.

THIS book was begun as an examination into the received chronology of all Chaucer's works, with a view to ascertaining how much of it is sound. There appeared on examination so many unworked corners, so much unused evidence, and so many of what seemed to the writer "vulgar and common errors," that weighing and expounding of old material had to give large place to destruction and construction. The work expanded so much that it became necessary to disregard most of the minor poems, and to discuss only those works a decision as to which was necessary to other decisions, and those on which the prevalent opinion seemed most erroneous or on which the most new light could be thrown. So the book does not profess to be exhaustive, or to afford anything except the essential elements of a general scheme. But neither has its purpose been merely to give the results of wholly original research ; rather by all means available, and to the extent of the writer's ability, to ascertain, advance, and present the *status quo* of our reliable knowledge as to when and how Chaucer's principal works came to be written. This statement is made in order to anticipate the possible criticism that some sections contain little or nothing that is new. Sometimes the purpose of the book has required long investigation and restatement of earlier opinion, with the result simply of confirming it ; yet this does not seem labour and space thrown away, for thorough confirmation of earlier guesses or brief statements is of the nature of an addition to knowledge.

It may be proper to state here that the writer has nearly ready for publication another volume, on the evolution of the *Canterbury Tales*, and is only awaiting complete information as to the arrangement, and some readings, of the numerous manuscripts in private hands in various parts of Great Britain. In this second book he hopes to throw some new light on the supposed nine groups of tales, on the arrangement of the poem, and on the questions whether and how far Chaucer revised it, whether and how far he published it during his lifetime, and finally how it came into the shape in which we find it in the manuscripts. In particular he has made a thorough collation of MS. Harleian 7334 with ten of the most important others, with a view to discovering whether its peculiarities are due to corrections made by the poet himself.

In conclusion, the writer is glad to express a strong sense of obligation to others. First of all, to the two most distinguished living Chaucer scholars, the Rev. Professor Skeat and Dr. Frederick J. Furnivall. Without the great edition produced by the former, with its invaluable commentary, any sound work on Chaucer must be far more difficult and less extensive ; without Dr. Furnivall's prolonged and self-sacrificing labours on the manuscripts it must be impossible. All accurate philological and historical, which implies also all sound literary, study of Chaucer had its new birth, after Tyrwhitt, in two events, the publication in 1862 of Professor Child's *Observations on the Language of Chaucer*, and Dr. Furnivall's launching of the Chaucer Society in 1868. To him, as representing it, I am bound again for its liberal dealing with this book. We may hope, after the recent second renascence of fruitful study of Chaucer, that oftener than ever the society dedicated to him will perform its trentals in his memory. With the passing away of the older generation of German Chaucerians, such as ten Brink and Zupitza, Anglo-Saxons on both sides of the Atlantic are showing more interest in the father of their poetry.

But I have other and still more personal obligations. The material on which is based my treatment of the two versions of the *Troilus and Criseyde* is mainly the unpublished work of Professor W. S. McCormick, of Edinburgh ; which, since it was done for the Chaucer Society, I have had Dr. Furnivall's authorization to use. To Professor George Hempl, of Leland Stanford University, I return thanks for handing over to me unpublished work of his own on the same subject. I have often been indebted to Dr. George L. Hamilton, of the University of Michigan, and to his wide knowledge of mediæval literature. To Professor George L. Kittredge, under whose supervision in Harvard University much of this work was done, my obligations are not easy to express ; in particular, whatever merit there may be in my manner of treating the two versions of the *Troilus* is due to him. I have been bound to him for proposing and making the way plain for an undertaking which seemed at first a trifle audacious ; for his keen insight and his inexhaustible liberality, with which all his pupils are so familiar ; and above all for what I can only call the education of my point of view.

INTRODUCTION.

THE early history of Chaucer criticism illustrates the pseudo-classical indifference to everything except literary right and wrong, and later the curiosity about the past which came in with romanticism and the serious attempt to understand it which came with the beginnings of the modern scientific spirit. Till the last quarter of the eighteenth century there was scarcely any non-æsthetic Chaucer criticism, and since the reign of Elizabeth there had been a tendency not to take him very seriously under any aspect. Some of the early editors showed more discernment than others as to the works which they accepted as canonical, and that was all. Even Warton's treatment of the poet (1778), which marks the transition, was mainly descriptive and appreciative ; he did a large amount of re-search on the sources, but nothing on the chronology and development of Chaucer's literary work, and he wholly disregards them in his account of the poet. A worthy and thorough Chaucer criticism began with Thomas Tyrwhitt's edition of the *Canterbury Tales* (1775-8). Although his work was chiefly on them, and although he did little on the subject of chronology, his other results have frequently so important a bearing on it, and his taste and judgment were so admirable, that he deserves to head the list of critics. But he needs no praise of mine ; every later editor and critic who deserves the name has been glad to honour him.

For further noteworthy advances we have to wait nearly a century. But during the last forty years, to say nothing of numberless mono-graphs and articles, mentioned in their proper places in the present work, some dozen books have treated Chaucer's literary evolution and chronology with system and more or less independence, or have made other wide and general contributions to an understanding of the subject. Passing over the work of Henry Bradshaw,[1] former librarian of Cam-bridge University, important in other directions than that of chron-ology, we come to the most influential book ever written on the subject, Bernhard ten Brink's *Chaucer Studien*,[2] the starting-point of systematic work on Chaucer's development. To it are due the division of his literary life into periods and a good part of the dates usually accepted. It never reached the subject of the *Canterbury Tales*, and many of its results are unreliable ; but its value is permanent. Ten Brink's second book

---

[1] See *Memoir of Henry Bradshaw*, by G. W. Prothero (London, 1888), pp. 212–25, 346–59, etc. ; and *Collected Papers of Henry Bradshaw* (Cambridge, 1889), pp. 102–48.

[2] *Chaucer. Studien zur Geschichte seiner Entwicklung und zur Chronologie seiner Schriften, von Bernhard ten Brink: erster Theil* (Münster, 1870) ; the second part never appeared.

which bears on the subject is his *Geschichte der Englischen Litteratur*,[1] where he deals fully with Chaucer, and (guardedly) with his chronology.

The work of Dr. Frederick J. Furnivall on Chaucer-chronology is less important than his work in other directions. The *Temporary Preface to the Six-Text Edition of Chaucer's Canterbury Tales*[2] deals chiefly with the construction, interpretation, and manuscripts of the poem. The *Trial Forewords to My "Parallel-Text Edition of Chaucer's Minor Poems"*[3] deals at some length with the dates of a few poems, and more summarily with those of all; but Dr. Furnivall offered little new and reliable evidence.

Mr. F. G. Fleay, in his small *Guide to Chaucer and Spenser*,[4] discusses chronology and the like. His manner is primitive and amateurish, but sometimes not a little suggestive. In particular he has some premature but laudable conjectures as to the development and arrangement of the *Canterbury Tales*, and also on the order in which they were written.

The next book to be mentioned is Dr. John Koch's *Chronology of Chaucer's Writings*.[5] His most important contribution to Chaucer chronology is the date 1381–2 for the *Parliament of Fowls*, which he had announced many years before.[6] The *Chronology*, though a convenient *résumé* of earlier views, was less illuminating and judicious than might have been desired.

In 1892, in his *Studies in Chaucer*,[7] Professor Thomas R. Lounsbury waged vivacious war against prevalent misapprehensions, endeavoured to put the poet in his proper relation to literary history, and incidentally collected a large amount of known facts and added not a few new ones. The value of the work, great though it is, cannot always be called proportionate to its bulk, and at times it shows a tendency to represent Chaucer as a modern exiled among barbarous ancients. It rarely deals with chronology directly, but it is indispensable to any student of Chaucer's literary evolution.

Mr. A. W. Pollard, in 1893, contributed to a series of *Literature Primers*[8] one on *Chaucer*; in 1903 he republished it, with slight changes. This is another, and especially convenient, summary of earlier work, treated with justifiable conservatism, but with many modifications and additions.

Professor W. W. Skeat, in the great *Oxford Chaucer*,[9] deals with the

[1] Berlin, 1877; second edition, edited by Alois Brandl, Strasburg, 1893 English translations (respectively) 1883 and 1896.

[2] Chaucer Society; London, 1868.

[3] *Ibid.*, 1871.

[4] London and Glasgow, 1877.

[5] Chaucer Society; dated 1890, but evidently not published till 1892, since he refers to ten Brink's death.

[6] In *Englische Studien*, I. 288; reprinted in the Chaucer Society *Essays*, pp. 400–9.

[7] Harper and Bros., New York; 3 volumes.

[8] Published by Macmillan and Company.

[9] *The Complete Works of Geoffrey Chaucer*, Oxford, 1894; 6 vols., with a supplementary one (1897).

chronology of all Chaucer's works. He accepts nearly all the results of ten Brink, Koch, and other writers, and in many cases simply repeats (without needed revisions) what he had himself published in his earlier editions of parts of Chaucer's writings. He is not always careful of consistency, and frequently draws conclusions without full examination of the evidence. The greatest value of his edition lies in its notes and indices. In his *Chaucer Canon* [1] he gives a conjectural chronological table.

Dr. F. J. Mather, in a school-edition of *The Prologue, the Knight's Tale, and the Nun's Priest's Tale, from Chaucer's Canterbury Tales,*[2] has given us an interesting and valuable study of Chaucer's literary development. Since he embodies the latest results, some of them his own, and has gone at the whole matter afresh in a critical spirit, his book has more significance than its unpretending form would suggest.

The editors of the excellent *Globe Chaucer* [3] have generally expressed themselves on the subject of chronology. They are always judicious and sometimes original. The most important work is that by Mr. Pollard and Professor McCormick.

Among recent work most important of all, Professor J. L. Lowes has thrown much new light on the chronology of Chaucer's middle period in two long articles in the *Publications of the Modern Language Association of America.*[4] I am able to accept by no means all his conclusions, which depart widely from earlier views, but his new facts, the product of careful and penetrating investigation, are an addition to Chaucer knowledge of high and permanent value.

Finally, Professor R. K. Root has just published, after most of the present work was in type, the best handbook on Chaucer yet written.[5] It is an excellent guide to understanding and appreciation, and a good, though rather conservative, *rationale* of chronology and the like.

It may be convenient if I give a condensed summary of previous opinion as to the dates of Chaucer's principal works. It may strike a reader that later in this book some changes are suggested where hitherto there has been notable unanimity of opinion. But this unanimity sometimes ceases to be impressive when one sees on what slight grounds of evidence it has been based.

[1] Oxford, 1900; see pp. 154-5.
[2] Boston, 1899.
[3] *The Works of Geoffrey Chaucer,* edited by Alfred W. Pollard, H. Frank Heath, Mark H. Liddell, and W. S. McCormick ; London, 1901.
[4] Vol. xix. pp. 593-683; vol. xx. 749-864. His conclusions are summarized on pp. 860-4 of the second article.
[5] *The Poetry of Chaucer,* Boston, 1906.

Romance of the Rose.

Extant text not genuine; Chaucer's
translation about 1377–80 (ten
Brink).

Extant translation not genuine;
Chaucer's translation 1366–7 (?)
(Koch).

Not genuine, "with the possible
exception of" Fragment A
(Kittredge).[1]

Doubtful if any of the extant text
is genuine; Chaucer's version
"early in life" (Mather).

Fragment A (only) genuine; very
early (Skeat).[2]

Fragment A may be genuine, B
not, C possibly (Liddell).[3]

Extant text probably not genuine;
Chaucer's version early (Pollard).

Fragment A genuine, B not, C
perhaps; done in youth (Root).

A B C.

(?) 1367 (Furnivall).
About 1373 (ten Brink).
(?) 1368 (Koch).
Before 1373 (Mather).
Very early (Skeat and Root).
1369 or a little later (Heath).
Before 1380 (Pollard).

Complaint to Pity.

(?) 1367–8 (Furnivall).
Probably 1370–2 (ten Brink).
(?) 1373–4 (Koch).
Before 1373 (Mather).
1372–3 or later (Skeat).
1369–71 (Heath).
Before 1380, perhaps after 1372
(Pollard).
Very early (Root).

Book of the Duchess.

1369 (Furnivall, Mather, Skeat).
1369–70 (ten Brink, Koch, Pollard,
Root).
Soon after 1369 (Heath).

Complaint of Mars.

(?) 1375 (Furnivall).
1379 (Koch).
1387–1400 (Mather).
(?) 1379 (Skeat).
After 1378–9 (Heath).
"Probably towards 1380"
(Pollard).

Boethius.

(?) 1376 (Furnivall).
About 1381 (ten Brink).
(?) 1377 (Koch).
1373–8 (Mather).
1377–81 (Skeat).
Rather early (Liddell).
1380–3 (Pollard).
About 1382–3 (Lowes).
About 1380 (Root).

Troilus and Criseyde.

(?) 1382 (Furnivall).
1380–81 (Koch).
1378–81 (Mather).
1379–83 (Skeat).
1380–3 (Pollard).
Perhaps 1383–5 (Lowes).
Not far from 1380 (Root).

House of Fame.

(?) 1384 (Furnivall).
1384 (ten Brink, Mather).
1383–4 (Koch, Skeat, Pollard).
Begun some years before 1383;
finished after the *Troilus* (Heath).
About 1379 (Lowes).
1378–85 (Root).

Parliament of Fowls.

(?) 1374 (Furnivall).
1382 (ten Brink, Koch, Mather,
Skeat, Heath, Pollard, Lowes,
Root).
About 1375 (Hales).[4]

Anelida and Arcite.

(?) 1375–6 (Furnivall).
Not long after 1390 (ten Brink).

---

[1] *Harvard Studies and Notes*, I. 65.
[2] I ordinarily quote Skeat from his *Chaucer Canon*, and others from their latest
expression of opinion.
[3] The views of Professors Liddell and Heath are quoted from the *Globe
Chaucer*.
[4] *Dict. Nat. Biogr.*, x. 164.

(?) 1383–4 (Koch).
1378–81, after *Troilus* (Mather).
1372–7 (Skeat).
About 1380 (Pollard).
Before 1382 (Lowes).
Soon after 1380 (Root).

Palamon and Arcite.

After 1374 (ten Brink).
(?) 1375–6 (Koch).
About 1381 (Mather).
Shortly before 1385 (Pollard).
About 1382 (Lowes).
About 1380–2 (Root).

Legend of Good Women.

(?) 1385, the *Prologue;* the rest
    probably at various times
    (Furnivall).
1385 ; G-*Prologue* "hardly before
    1393 " (ten Brink).[1]
1384–5, the *Prologue* and some of
    the *Legends ;* 2nd *Prologue,* 1385
    (Koch).
1385 (Mather).
1385–6 (Skeat).
1384–5 (Pollard).
F-*Prologue,* 1386 ; *Legends* about
    1379 and later ; G-*Prologue,* 1394
    (Lowes).
1385–6 (Root).

Canterbury Tales begun.

(?) 1386 (Furnivall).
About 1390 (ten Brink).
1385 (Koch).
Probably 1387 (Mather).
1386 (Skeat).
After 1385 (Pollard).
1387 (Root).

General Prologue.

(?) 1388 (Furnivall).
(?) 1385 (Koch).
1387 or later (Mather).
1386 or later (Skeat).
After 1385 (Pollard).

Man of Law's Tale.

1390 or soon after (ten Brink).
(?) 1386–7 (Koch).
1385–1400 ; possibly earlier
    (Mather).
1373–7 (Skeat).
1370–80 (Pollard).
Before 1390 (Root).

Melibeus.

1386–7 (Koch).
1373–8 (Mather).
1372–7, revised later (Skeat).
After 1385 (Pollard).

Monk's Tale.

(?) 1386–7 (Koch).
1373–8 (Mather).
1369–73 (Skeat).
1373–80 (Pollard).
Early (Root).

Physician's Tale.

About 1388 (ten Brink).
(?) 1386–7 (Koch).
After 1382–5 (Skeat).
After 1385 (Pollard).
Before 1387 (Root).

Clerk's Tale.

About 1388 (ten Brink).
(?) 1386–7 (Koch).
1385–1400 (Mather).
About 1372–3 (Skeat).
1373–80 (Pollard).

Second Nun's Tale (" Life of St. Cecelia ").

(?) 1373 (Furnivall).
About 1373 (ten Brink).
(?) 1373–4 (Koch).
Shortly after 1373 (Mather).
1369–73 (Skeat).
1370–4 (Pollard).
1373–4 (Root).

[1] *Engl. Stud.*, xvii. 20.

CONTENTS.

xiii

The Development and Chronology of Chaucer's Works.

CHAPTER I.

THE *TROILUS AND CRISEYDE*.

§ 1. *The Two Versions.*

THE first suggestion that there are two genuine versions of Chaucer's *Troilus and Criseyde* was made by Dr. Furnivall, who in the Chaucer Society's *Parallel-Text Print of Chaucer's Troilus and Criseyde* (London, 1881, p. 195) indicates that a certain difference among the MSS. as to arrangement may be due to the poet himself. Professor W. S. McCormick, in a paper read before the London Philological Society, Dec. 6, 1895, and briefly reported in the *Academy*, Dec. 21 (no. 1233, p. 552), supported the idea with greater definiteness, and illustrated it by eleven printed pages containing five or six hundred various readings from the sixteen MSS. and Caxton's and Thynne's editions.[1] When he wrote his introduction to the *Troilus* in the *Globe Chaucer* (London, 1901, pp. xli–xliii), he had come to believe in three versions, each represented by one of the three families into which he regards the MSS. as falling; the second containing "more than one partial revision," and the third being "a later copy, either carelessly corrected by the author, or collated by some hand after Chaucer's death." His introduction to the *Troilus* MSS., announced by the Chaucer Society in 1894 as at press, in which he may be expected to deal with the whole subject more authoritatively than any one else can do, has never appeared, and he has nowhere in print defended or even expressed his views in any detail.[2]

[1] He indicates cases where one reading is nearer than another to the Italian or Latin original.
[2] The probability of a revision is recognized also by Dr. F. J. Mather (*Furnivall Miscellany*, p. 309; Chaucer's *Prologue*, etc., Boston, 1899, p. xix); by Dr. G. L. Hamilton (*The Indebtedness of Chaucer to Guido*, New York, 1903, p. 149); as well as by Dr. John Koch in his review of the *Globe Chaucer*, *Engl. Stud.* xxvii. 12 (cf. *Chronology*, p. 36).

That Chaucer should at some time or other have revised the *Troilus* is far from being improbable *a priori*, even though revision was not his custom.[1] Of his longer poems it is the most carefully studied and the only completed one, a work on which he must have spent some of his closest meditation, so mature that he could never have grown beyond it, as he grew beyond some of his other works. He shows solicitude about the purity of its text (as we say now) in book V. 1793-8, and in the lines to Adam. It seems highly natural that when it befell his scrivener to write *Troilus* anew, Chaucer should not always have allowed him quite to reproduce the old copy.

The question cannot be wholly settled till the relations of the MSS. are clearer than they are now, but a strong probability can be established by the use of Professor McCormick's table of variants already mentioned, and of the seven MSS. published by the Chaucer Society.   I have been fortunate also in being able to refer to certain unpublished researches of Professor Kittredge's on the relations among the MSS.

It is necessary first to discuss the principal MSS. concerned.   It is impossible to construct a genealogy for them, but their relations have been sufficiently determined to insure fairly reliable results. These MSS. are the following :

Ph—Phillipps 8252	Jo—St. John's Coll., Cambridge [4]
H$_4$—Harleian 2392	Cp—Corpus Christi Coll., Camb.[4]
Gg—Cambridge, Gg. 4. 27 [2]	H$_1$—Harleian 2280 [2]
H$_2$—Harleian 3943 [3]	Cl—Campsall [2]

Ph is a late MS., and (according to Skeat) not of much value; [5] H$_4$ is a late, not very correct, paper MS. ; H$_2$ does not seem to be very good.   Jo is called by Skeat "a fair MS., perhaps earlier than 1450"; Cl, written on vellum before 1413 for Henry V. while Prince of Wales, he pronounces one of the best, derived from a still better ; Cp is also an excellent MS., fairly early, and probably once in the possession of John of Gaunt's granddaughter, Anne Neville, Duchess of Buckingham ; H$_1$ Skeat considers third

---

[1] The revision of the *Prologue* to the *Legend of Good Women* I shall try to show later was due to a peculiar reason.
[2] In *A Parallel-Text Print of Chaucer's T. and C.* (Ch. Soc., 1881).
[3] In W. M. Rossetti's parallel-text edition of the *T. C.* and the *Filostrato* (Ch. Soc., 1873).
[4] In *Three More Parallel-Texts of C.'s T. and C.* (Ch. Soc., 1894).
[5] See his *Chaucer*, II. lxvii. ff. ; and his *Piers Plowman*, II. lxx.

best. The first four MSS. in the table Professor Kittredge says are proved to belong at least in part to the same family of MSS. by common corruptions which unite them by twos and threes. But the relations of all the MSS. are very complicated, and were frequently disturbed by contamination.[1] The only sure footing in this quagmire, but a very satisfactory reliance, is the almost complete agreement of the three last excellent MSS., two of which seem to have been once in the possession of members of the royal family. This group I shall call (2); the other five, though, singly or several at once, they often agree with (2), may be grouped as (1). It should be added that Ph is McCormick's main reliance for his first version; the next four he assigns partly to the first and partly to the second redaction; and the last three wholly to the third.[2]

The most important various readings are those where one alternative is distinctly nearer than the other to the Italian original, of which I give some ten from McCormick's lists:

I. 111.   With chere and vois ful pitous, and wepinge,   Ph, H_2
             E con voce e con vista assai pietosa

             With pitous vois, and tendrely wepinge,   Gg, Jo, (2)

II. 734–5.   Men loven women al this toun aboute;   Ph, H_2, Gg
             Be they the wers? why, nay, withouten doute.
             Io non conosco in questa terra ancora
             Veruna senza amante, e la più gente
             . . . . *s'innamora* . . .
             E come gli altri far non è peccato.

             Men loven wommen al biside hir leve,
             And whan hem lyst namore lat hem leve. H_4, Jo, (2)

IV. 57–9.   To Priamus was yeve at gret requeste   Ph, H_2, (2) [3]
             A tyme of trewe, and tho they gonnen trete
             Hir prisoneres to chaungen, moste and leste.
             Chiese Priamo triegua, e fugli data;
             E cominciossi a trattare infra loro
             Di permutar prigioni quella fiata.

---

[1] As is abundantly proved by McCormick's tables; and cf. *Globe Chaucer*, p. xli. The contamination, it seems to me, may sometimes have taken place as follows: a scribe with a good verbal memory, having already copied the poem once or more from one redaction, when he came to copy it again from another, might easily at times insert the older reading which he chanced to have in mind. In various Chaucer MSS. there is good evidence that the scribes did become familiar with Chaucer's poetry at large. But this sort of contamination would be quite impossible to trace.

[2] For full information on the MSS. see Skeat II. lxvii. ff. and *Globe*, xli. f.

[3] This is the only case where (2) has what looks like an earlier reading. See p. 11 below.

> But natheles a trewe was ther take
> At gret requeste, and tho they gonnen trete
> Of prisoners a chaunge for to make.   H₄, Jo

IV. 246–8. His eyen two, for piete of herte,
  So wepen that they semen welles tweye;   Ph, Gg
  The heighe sobbes . . . .   H₂, Jo, (2)
  I miseri occhi per pietà del core
  Forte piangeano, e parean due fontane . . .
  Gli alti singhiozzi . . .

  His eyen two, for pitee of his herte,
  Outstremeden as swifte welles tweye;   H₂, Jo, (2)
  Therwith the sobbes . . .   Gg¹

IV. 258. That wel unnethe the body may suffyse   Ph, Gg
  Che'l capo e 'l petto appena gli bastava

  That wonder is the body may suffyse   H₂, Jo, (2)

IV. 736–763. Lines 750–6 immediately after 735, and 750 reads: "The salte teres from hir ȳen tweyne," with other important variants in 747, 752, 757, 762–3,—Ph, Gg, Jo. Order and readings as in Skeat—H₂, (2). (The first order is Boccaccio's, but the second agrees better with 735.)

IV. 882. As he that shortly shapeth him to deye.   (1)
  Il qual del tutto in duol ne vuol morire

  For verray wo his wit is al aweye.   (2)²

IV. 1214. And he answerde, "Herte myn, Criseyde," Ph, Gg, Jo
  A cui il disse: "Dolce mio disiro,"

  And he answerde, "Lady myn, Criseyde," H₂, H₄, (2)³

IV. 1218. And he bigan conforte hir as he mighte.   Ph, Gg, Jo
  Come potea . . . *La confortò.*

  And he bigan to glade hir as he mighte.   H₂, (2)⁴

V. 923–4. I wil be he to serve yow myselve,   H₂, Gg, Jo
  Ye, lever than be king of Greces twelve.
  . . . *assai degno amadore* . . . *io sarei desso,*
  Più volentier che re de' Greci adesso.

---

¹ The other reading is probably the only genuine one, for this seems to occur in but one MS.; Ph has "the sobbes," which may be the middle term between the two readings.

² This line may be inferior in itself, but it greatly improves the grammatical construction. Cf. the curious punctuation which McCormick, who keeps the first reading, finds necessary in the *Globe* edition.

³ "Herte myn" occurs in 1216; hence the change.

⁴ "Hir to glade" occurs in 1220, so the variant may possibly be a scribe's blunder.

I wol be he to serven yow myselve
Ye, lever than be lord of Greces twelve. (2)

These cases are only about half of those given by McCormick, though they are the most striking. It can hardly be doubted that at any rate most of these variations are due to Chaucer; and therefore that the second set of readings, in which he departs from his original, are the later.

A number of cases may be noted where a change seems to have been made in the interest of ancient and especially pagan colouring:

III. 188–9. Withouten honde, me semeth that in toune,
For this miracle, I here eche belle soune.[1] H_2, Gg, Jo
For this merveille . . . (2)

III. 705, 712. *Seynt Venus* in one line or the other in every MS. of (1). *Blisful Venus* in both lines in (2).

IV. 299–301. Ne never wil I seen it shyne or reyne, Ph, Gg
Ne hevenes light; and thus I in derknesse
My woful lyf wil enden for distresse.
But ende I wil, as Edippe,[2] in derknesse
My sorwful lyf, and dyen in distresse. H_2, Jo, (2)

IV. 644. But any aungel tolde it in thyn ere. Ph, Gg, Jo
But-if that Jove tolde it in thyn ere. H_2, (2)

These last two changes are certainly Chaucer's own, and if version (2) is later than (1), so are the others, for the change from mediæval to ancient colouring could hardly be due to a scribe.[3]

In a large number of cases some stylistic reason is evident for the change from (1) to (2).

I. 640. Ne no man wot what gladnesse is, I trowe, (1)
Ne no man may be inly glad, I trowe, (2)
(Four other words in *-esse* occur just before and after.)

[1] This is the earliest occurrence, so far as I can find, of an impressive circumstance common later in ballads and folklore. Probably Chaucer derived it from some ballad or popular romance now lost. Cf. the ballad of *Sir Hugh of Lincoln*, Child's *Ballads*, III. 244; and *ibid.*, I. 173, 231; III. 235, 519.

[2] Troilus is speaking; but we may notice that one of Criseyde's favourite books was the *Siege of Thebes* (II. 84).

[3] There is just one case of the opposite kind. In II. 115 (1), except Jo, reads "Ye maken me by Joves sore adrad"; (2) and Jo read "By god, ye maken me right sore adrad." The change would be a strange one for Chaucer to make; and since "god" occurs twice in the two preceding lines, it may be due to the scribe.

II. 1210.   Now for the love of god, my nece dere,   Gg, Jo
             Now for the love of me, my nece dere,   H₂, (2)

(The second is more Pandaresque ; not likely to be due to a scribe.   Cf. II. 290.)

III. 256.   Thou wost thyselven what I wolde mene.   (1)
             Al seye I noght, thou wost wel what I mene.   (2)

III. 269.   For never was ther wight . . . That ever wiste H₄,Gg,Jo
             For that man is unbore . . .   Ph, H₂,(2)

III. 672.   Than is it tyme for to gon to reste.   H₄, Jo
             So go we slepe, I trowe it be the beste.   H₂, Gg, (2)

III. 677.   And alwey in this mene whyle it ron.   H₄, Jo
             And evere mo so sterneliche it ron.   H₂, Gg, (2)

IV. 638.   Pandare answerde—" Of that be as be may." Ph, Gg, Jo
            "Why, so mene I," quod Pandare, "al this day." H₂,(2)

IV. 1097.   Canst thou not thenken thus in thy disese ? Ph, Gg, Jo
            Lat be, and thenk right thus in thy disese.   H₂, (2)

(No less than seven rhetorical questions have come just before.)

IV. 1138–9. So bittre teres weep not thurgh the rinde Ph, Gg, Jo
             The woful Myrra, written as I finde,

             So bittre teres weep not, as I finde,
             The woful Myrra thurgh the bark and rinde. H₂, (2)

Cf. also the following passages, which make in the same direction : II. 1399, IV. 165–6, IV. 560 (cf. 567, 570), IV. 581 (cf. 580), IV. 696–8.

In other cases, though the motive for the change is less obvious, it is difficult not to attribute it to Chaucer.

III. 501–3. Som epistle . . . That wolde . . . wel contene   H₄, Jo
             An hundred vers . . .

             Neigh half this book . . .   H₂, Gg, (2)

III. 568.   And she on game gan him for to rowne   H₄, Jo
             Sone after this to him she gan to roune   H₂, Gg, (2)

III. 1436–42.
             Thou dost, allas ! to shortly thyn offyce,   H₄, Jo
             Thou rakel night, ther god, maker of kynde,

    For thou dounward thee hastest of malyce,
    [Thee for thyn haste and thyn unkinde vyce] H_2 Gg, (2)
    Thee curse and to our hemi-spere bynde,
    [So faste ay to our hemi-spere bynde] H_2, Gg, (2)
    That never-more under the ground thou wynde!
    For thurgh thy rakel hying out of Troye
    [For now, for thou so hyest out of Troye,] H_2, Gg, (2)
    Have I forgon thus hastily my joye. H_4, Jo

IV. 789–90. . . . the feld of pitee . . . Ther Pluto regneth Gg, Jo
        „   „   „   „   That hight Elysos H_2, (2)

IV. 828–9. Myn eem Pandare of Joyes mo than two   Ph, Jo
            Was cause causing first to me Criseyde.

            Pandare first of Joyes mo than two
            Was cause causing unto me Criseyde. H_2, (2)

Cf. also III. 543, 668; IV. 1093, 1113.

There are three important passages, the omission of which in
some MSS. is strong additional evidence for more than one redaction. The first is Troilus' hymn to love at the end of book III.
(1744–1771), from Boethius. The second is Troilus' long soliloquy
(IV. 953–1085) on free-will, also mostly drawn from Boethius.
The third is the account of the ascent of Troilus' soul to heaven
(V. 1807–1827), drawn from the *Teseide* of Boccaccio. A particularly significant fact is that they were all three omitted in MS. Ph,
and in somewhat the same list of other MSS.

Troilus' hymn to love is absent from MS. Harl. 3943, and
inserted later (which means the same thing) in MS. Ph; in all
other MSS. and early editions it seems to have been present from
the first. Boccaccio at this point (III., st. 74–89) puts a very long
hymn to love into Troilus' mouth, the first six stanzas of which
Chaucer used to form the greater part of the proem to this book of
the *Troilus*. Troilus' hymn to love in Chaucer, therefore, is not
from Boccaccio, but is a versification, with a slight rearrangement,
of Boethius, II., metre 8. The song is not at all likely to have
been cut out by the scribe, and cannot possibly have been omitted
accidentally. Its absence is a clear sign of incompleteness, for the
context runs (in MS. Hl. 3943,[1] III., ll. 1743, 1772–3):

        And þan he wold syng in þis manere.

        In al þe nedis for þe tounys werre
        he was & ay þe ferst in armys dight.

    [1] See W. M. Rossetti, parallel-text edition, 167–8.

The first of these lines translates the end of the stanza just preceding the song in Boccaccio, and the second translates the first
of the stanza just following it.   It is clear, therefore, that Chaucer
omitted Boccaccio's song for the obvious reason that he had just
used the first part of it ; and that he allowed some MSS. of the
Troilus to go into circulation before he added the substitute.
Such carelessness on his part is not unparalleled in the *Canterbury
Tales.*[1]

The second of the three passages, IV. 953–1085, is wholly
omitted in MSS. Harl. 2392 (H_4) and Harl. 1239,[2] omitted all
but the last stanza[3] in Gg, which hereabouts agrees with (1), and
added later in Ph ; it is present in Harl. 3943 (H_2), Johns and (2).
In the first place, it is important to notice that the passage forms
a complete unit; every stanza in it (except the last) is Boethian and
scholastic, and its length and subtlety form a strange break in
Troilus' passionate despair.[4]   It is hardly likely that so long and so
unified a passage would have been omitted by a scribe.   Secondly,
the continuity of the context is better without it.   In line 947
Pandarus finds Troilus alone in the temple, yet seems to be stand-

[1] It may be asked whether the present proem, or such part of it as is from
Boccaccio, may not have originally stood as Troilus' song.   Internal evidence
is much against such a view.   The first three lines of stanza 6 are fairly closely
translated from the Italian, yet the last four lines are spoken by the author in
his proper person, and cannot possibly have been in Troilus' mouth ; so also
stanza 7, which is not, however, from the Italian.   At first sight MS. Rawl.
Poet. 163 ("not a very good copy," according to Skeat, II. lxxiv.) seems to
suggest that the proem was lacking in Chaucer's first copy, for this MS. (only)
omits the proems to books II.–IV. (see W. S. McCormick, pp. 296–300 of *An
English Miscellany Presented to Dr. Furnivall*, &c., Oxford, 1901).   But this
argument is quashed by two considerations.   In the first place, this MS. has,
in its proper place, Troilus' hymn from Boethius, so the absence of the proem
is certainly not due to its use elsewhere.   Secondly, the proem to book IV.
we can hardly doubt was written continuously with books III. and IV., for
all three correspond to consecutive parts of the Italian ; stanza 93 of Boccaccio's third book is rendered at the end of *T. C.* III., the proem to IV.
includes most of the 94th and last stanza, and book IV. of Chaucer begins
with Boccaccio's next stanza (IV. 1).   If the absence of the proem to IV.
from MS. Rawl. cannot be due to its absence from Chaucer's first version
neither can it well be argued that its omission of those to books II. and III.
is.   The absence of these proems, therefore, is a sign of lateness, not of earliness ; so much so, in fact, that it seems to me probably due to the scribe,
not to Chaucer.   But on this matter, as on so many others, we must defer to
Professor McCormick's views, when they shall be expressed.
[2] Printed in *Three More Parallel-Texts*.   In this part of the poem it
generally agrees with (1).
[3] This clearly belongs with what precedes, for 1080 ("wost of al this
thing the sothfastnesse") refers to the philosophical disquisition, not to the
amorous lament in 950–2 : so also does 1084 ("Disputing with himself in this
matere").
[4] Cf. Lounsbury, *Studies*, III. 374–5.

ing at the door during the whole of this discourse, for he does not come in till 1085 ; these two lines almost contradict each other.[1] Another piece of evidence that the rest of the poem underwent revision, and that during it this passage was added, is that the only variants in it noted by McCormick are four trivial ones clearly due to the scribes (957, 958, 989, 1064) ; this makes 1 variant to 33 lines, but elsewhere in book IV. according to McCormick's tables there are about 1 to 11 lines, including some very significant changes.[2]

A wholly different consideration which distinguishes this passage from the context is the rhyme-usage, as to which, by the kindness of Professor George Hempl, I am able to present some information gained by him. Excluding this passage, the impure ō : ǭ[3] rhyme occurs, to 1000 lines, 3 times in book I., 2 in book II., $\frac{1}{2}$ in book III., and not at all in books IV. and V. ; but in these 133 lines it occurs twice (1035–6, 1072–4). He also points out that the cheap rhyme-words in accented -inge (or -ing, participle or verbal noun) occur, to 1000 lines, 18 times in book I., 11 in II., and 4 in III.– V.[4] ; but in this passage they occur no less than 11 times (986–7, 989–91–2, 1014–15, 1016–18, 1075–6)—more than twenty times as often as they should according to what is usual in book IV. The force of this last argument is somewhat weakened, to be sure, by the fact that such a discourse as that of Troilus naturally contains an unusual number of abstract nouns in -inge. But the two points together certainly distinguish the passage sharply from its surroundings.[5]

[1] Pandarus is named in both 1085 and 1086. If the lines had been written consecutively the repetition would probably have been avoided.
[2] To this bit of evidence cf. a parallel in L. G. W., p. 119 below.
[3] Cf. ten Brink, Chaucers Sprache und Verskunst (Leipzig, 1899), p. 191 ; but cf. p. 23.
[4] I. e. only 4 times to every 1000 lines in book IV., excluding this passage.
[5] Since all this evidence shows that Chaucer became more fastidious as to his rhymes during the composition of T. C., it may suggest to some that this passage must have been written before the greater part of the poem ; it may seem as if we had here another example of Chaucer's "economy" (to use Professor Koeppel's word) in putting pieces of old cloth into a new garment. But this is more than doubtful. The first two and the last stanzas were certainly written for T. C., and the others, with their plentiful use of the pronoun I, have the appearance of being. I doubt very much if any thoroughly consistent uniformity or development in rhyme-usage or metrical-usage can be made out in Chaucer's poetry ; and there does not seem to be any a priori reason why it should be. I am not ignorant that others take a vehemently opposite view, and that Shakspere's practice has been pleaded as a parallel ; but Shakspere's metrical development was part of a widespread, traceable and easily explicable national evolution in versification. On all this cf. Lowes in Public. Mod. Lang. Assoc., xx. 811–12.

It can hardly be doubted, therefore, that Chaucer added this passage when the poem had been some time in circulation. Most readers will agree that it was no great improvement. At times it is impressive and beautiful, and recalls part of the *Complaint of Mars* and Palamon's fine lament in the *Knight's Tale*, but enough has already been said of its unsuitability to the " lewed " Troilus in a mood of despair. This is not the only case where Chaucer appears as a careless or injudicious reviser. It should be added that there is nothing surprising in the inclusion of this passage in one or two MSS., such as the Johns, which otherwise in this book follow the first redaction ; for the passage was one sure to interest the serious-minded reader, and therefore to be copied in where it did not belong (as we can see happened in MS. Phillipps). In a case like this, omission is more significant than insertion.

The passage from the *Teseide* (V. 1807–1827) is absent from MSS. Harl. 3943 (H$_2$) and 2392 (H$_4$), and added later in Phillipps ;[1] MS. Gg, which in this book generally agrees with Ph, breaks off before this point. The passage is present in Johns and (2). It can hardly be doubted that this, too, is a later insertion. The passage contains unsympathetic erudite conceits, brought from afar, and forces apart two lines (1806, 1828) which are consecutive in the *Filostrato ;* we may wonder a little that Chaucer should put it in at any time, but his doing so is more intelligible when the poem had grown somewhat cold to him.[2] It is true that other passages at the end indicate some sort of revulsion of feeling on Chaucer's part ; but a Christian transcending of a worldly poem, a sense of the futility of earthly happiness, which a mediæval man might easily draw from the *Troilus*, is not the same thing as a rather meretricious piece of that paganism which Chaucer expressly disclaims a little later (1849–55). In the other cases the Middle Ages were simply calling back one of their children who was escaping from them. Without this passage the course of thought is decidedly better ; as things are, " Swich fyn hath, lo, this Troilus " (1828), " in this

---

[1] It is highly interesting to note that the later insertion of these three passages in MS. Ph show that it belonged to a really scholarly admirer of the poet. We have here an example of something like collation in the fifteenth century.

[2] Koch thought (*Engl. Stud.*, I. 271) it was put in on first writing because Chaucer considered Boccaccio's account of Troilus' death too brief ; later, he thought it first appeared in a second version (*Chronology*, p. 36). Cf. also A. W. Pollard, *Chaucer : The Knight's Tale* (London, 1903), p. 116. Lowes takes a more favourable view of the addition (*Publ. Mod. Lang. Assoc.*, xx. 847).

wyse he deyde " (1834), have to go back twenty or thirty lines for
their explanation, and after his cheerful flight and scorn of those
who wept for him it is a little odd to return to the pathos of his
death.[1] Considering, then, that the passage is a unit, of different
source from that of its context, that it is lacking in at least three
related MSS., some of which also lack the Boethius passages, and
that such a passage is less likely to have been omitted by a scribe
where it once was than to have been inserted where it was not,—
this passage, too, is a strong argument for revision.

It may be taken as proved, I think, that we have at least two
versions of the *Troilus*.[2] And almost all the evidence that bears
on the question of priority has indicated that the version contained in (2), MSS. Corpus, Campsall, and Harleian 2280, is the
later; it is the farther from the Italian, and the better. Disregarding the fact that this version omits I. 890–6 and IV. 708–14,
admirable and even essential stanzas which must have been omitted
by oversight,[3] I find just one case worth mentioning where the
reading of (2) looks like the earlier, the striking one recorded above
on pp. 3, 4.[4] A few cases like this and those in the note may be

---

[1] Similarly ten Brink (*Chaucer Studien*, pp. 60–1) ; I agree with Koch that
some of his other arguments are not so good (*Eng. Stud.*, I. 270). I defer till
later a discussion of the idea that this passage is part of the *débris* of a
stanzaic *Palamon and Arcite* (see pp. 49–51).

[2] It is suggestive to compare the clearly genuine character of these revisions
with the insignificant various readings on which Prof. R. K. Root bases his conjecture that Chaucer revised the *Parl. of Fowls* (see *Journ. of Germ. Philol.*,
V. 189–193), and Prof. J. B. Bilderbeck that he revised the first six *Legends of
Good Women* (*Chaucer's L. G. W.*, London, 1902 ; pp. 34–42) ; or to compare them even with the peculiarities of MS. Harl. 7334 of the *C. T.*, which
I believe are not due to Chaucer. Cf. my preface, p. v. The genuineness of
the revisions is further suggested by the fact that nearly all that I have
recorded (many of McCormick's variants may be scribal) are in books III.
and IV. Evidently Chaucer took most interest in the more intense parts of
the story.

[3] The former passage is known only in three MSS., all belonging to the first
version (McCormick, in the *Furnivall Miscellany*, p. 300).

[4] There are three other possible cases. "Or that the god ought spak " (Ph,
H_2, Gg : III. 543) introduces more variety than "Er that Apollo spak " (Jo,
(2) ; cf. 541, 546). In V. 436, MSS. H_2, Gg, Jo, and Hl 1239 have it that
Sarpedon was "ful of heigh largesse " ; (2) says he was "ful of heigh prow-
esse " ; the Italian has "d'alto cuore," while the stanza dwells on his hospi-
tality. But the first reading is doubtful English, and is very likely a scribe's
blunder. In V. 1502–4, where the reference is to the *Thebaid* of Statius, IX.
497–539, 867–907, the reading of Gg and Jo is slightly more faithful to the
Latin (though it shows less familiarity with it), than that of Ph, H_2, and
(2). [Note here an important case where Ph agrees with (2) against others of
(1). See below.] But when the reference is to another work than the general
source of the poem accuracy is ambiguous in its testimony, and the second
reading is better in other ways. Obviously nothing can be based on these
cases.

accounted for in so many ways that they do not weaken perceptibly the conclusion that the version consistently represented by the second group of MSS. is the later.

Professor McCormick,[1] as has been said above, believes that the versions which we have been discussing are the second and third in point of time, and that from the second may be extracted a first. This opinion is much more difficult to deal with by evidence, so it is important to realize that the burden of proof is heavy upon one who holds it.[2] The evidence accessible at present seems to me to be anything but favourable to the idea of a third version. In the first place, though it is quite true that we should not expect many cases of three genuine readings for one passage, it would be natural that in some cases Chaucer should not have satisfied himself even in his second version. Now there are no cases where a third reading carries conviction of its genuineness; and only twice can a third reading which occurs in more than one MS. possibly be considered.

II. 737–8. . . . he able is for to have . . . the thriftieste
    That womman is, so she hir honour save. Ph, H$_2$, Gg
    As ferforth as she may hir honour save.   H$_4$, Jo
    To ben his love, so she hir honour save.   (2)

III. 458–9. Lest any wight divynen or devyse
    Wolde in this speche . . .   Ph, H$_2$, Gg
    Wolde on this thing . . .   H$_4$, Jo
    Wolde of hem two . . .   (2)

In the first passage the second reading is probably corrupt, and in the second the first. In neither is there any evidence for a third edition.

The only other satisfactory evidence would be a MS. which should consistently embody it, as group (2) constantly represents a version different from that best represented (according to McCormick) by MS. Camb. Gg; which should be nearest of all to the Italian, and which should sometimes agree with the second version and not with the third, and sometimes differ from both, and should never follow the third only. These demands are exacting, of course, but an approximation to them would be necessary in order to carry conviction. Some such MS. McCormick appears to think

---

[1] *Globe Chaucer*, p. xli.
[2] Many little slips in the *C. T.* and elsewhere show that Chaucer was not much in the habit of even reading his own poetry.

we have in Phillipps, and at the very beginning of his table we
seem to find confirmation of his opinion. It can hardly be doubted,
as we have seen already, that

"With chere and vois ful pitous, and wepinge " (I. 111)

was Chaucer's original translation of

"E con voce e con vista assai pietosa,"

and that he made a later improvement in

"With pitous vois and tendrely wepinge ";

now the first reading occurs only in Ph and H$_2$, which agree
closely throughout this book, and the other MSS. of (1) agree with
(2). But this, so far as I can discover, is absolutely the last evidence of the sort; there is no other significant case in which Ph is
closer to the Italian than our last version, where the Gg MS. is not
just as close.[1] Moreover, the Ph MS. seems, on the testimony of
Professor Skeat[2] and Professor Kittredge, unlikely to deserve
the importance which Professor McCormick attaches to it; it is
late and very corrupt, and appears to be at the end of a long descent;
it would be not a little strange if this MS. alone should preserve
the first version intact. But the most ruinous charge against MS.
Ph is that several times during book III. and elsewhere (among
others, in some of the passages quoted above) it switches over and
agrees with (2), the Corpus-Campsall group, which throughout,
McCormick says, represents the third version, while his second group
(Johns, etc.) differs from both. This on his theory is absolutely
inexplicable[3]; it can indicate just one thing—that in book III., at
least, Ph is derived or corrected from some MS. of group (2). But
if in practically all significant variations, Ph follows MSS. now of
my group (1), now of (2), what becomes of its independence, of its
testimony for a version different from both ?[4]

[1] The omissions or later insertions in Ph (already treated) are not peculiar
to it.
[2] See his *Piers Plowman*, II. lxx.
[3] The possible suggestion that Chaucer might have taken an uncorrected
copy of the first version as a basis for the third, which would therefore at times
follow the first and not the second, is negatived by the extraordinary
solicitude which he shows for the text of the poem.
[4] A further argument against the primatial position which McCormick
assigns to MS. Ph is to be found in the peculiarities of MS. Rawl. Poet. 163,
which he has thoroughly collated, and which his tables show to agree usually
with (1), though it sometimes switches over to (2). In his article in the *Furnivall Miscellany* (pp. 296–300) he shows that it contains at the very end of book
II., between 1750 and 1751, a genuine stanza found nowhere else. Professor
McCormick believes that it is misplaced ; but it seems to me that its insistence

The whole subject is immensely complicated; to say that the poem underwent one thorough revision all at one time may possibly be too simple an explanation. All that I have said must be regarded as submissive to Professor McCormick's further communications. But meanwhile it seems certain that Chaucer produced two versions, and fairly certain that he produced only two.[1]

As to the date of the revision, it is impossible to be very definite and certain, but it seems natural that some years should have elapsed between. There is one small, but perhaps respectable and certainly curious, piece of evidence in the two versions as to the date of the second. In book IV., 596–7, MSS. Ph, Gg, Jo, Harl. 1239 and Harl. 4912 (all belonging, apparently, to version I.) make Pandarus say to Troilus, while urging forcible detention of Criseyde in Troy,

> " It is no rape in my dom ne no vice,
> Hir to withholden that ye loven most," [2]

---

that Criseyde shall be merciful affords a perfectly logical connection with what precedes, and connects as well with what follows as 1750 does. It seems much less likely to have been added in this MS. than to have been omitted in the others, probably by a very early scribe. The MS. omits I. 890–6, no doubt by accident, and (as we have seen) the entire proems to books II., III. and IV. The presence of the unique stanza, and perhaps one or two of its other peculiarities, would put Rawl., and not Ph, in a peculiar position ; of which, again, it will be deprived by the fact that it agrees with three-quarters of the authorities in omitting the admirable (and indeed indispensable) lines I. 890–6, and in containing the song of love from Boethius. So we are farther than ever from having a MS. which consistently embodies Chaucer's first version. Is not the cruelly kind answer to the puzzle that which McCormick elsewhere shows must so often put the textual critic out of his misery : namely, contamination ? The more one studies the MSS. the clearer it becomes that Chaucer was not the only person who cared about the purity of his text. In the fifteenth century there were more fastidious and critical readers than we always realize. In a graphic passage of the preface to the second edition of the *C. T.* (quoted by McCormick elsewhere) Caxton tells how one of his customers protested against the incorrectness of the first, and supplied him with a better copy.

[1] The next thing we may hope for is a parallel-text edition of the two versions, which perhaps could be produced with a fair amount of accuracy.

[2] It is worth noting that here is a clear case where *rape* means *forcible detention* or *removal*. It is high time that the more disagreeable interpretation of the incident to be mentioned were dismissed for good to the Limbo of Vanities. Chaucer's own father was abducted—"rapuerunt et abduxerunt" (*Life Records*, 1900, p. ix.) ; and in 1387 the thief was set to catch a thief— Chaucer was on a commission to inquire into the abduction of an heiress, of which exactly the same verbs are used (*ibid.*, p. 270). On the frequency at the end of the fourteenth century of this sort of abduction and forced marriage, see S. Armitage-Smith, *John of Gaunt*, pp. 350–1. If the worse interpretation were the true one, is it conceivable that Chaucer would have adopted such a beginning to the *Wife of Bath's Tale* (D, 888), a beginning confined to his version of the story ? Cf. also Furnivall's *Trial Forewords* (Ch. Soc., 1881), pp. 136–44, for the law bearing on the subject.

for which the other and later authorities, (2) and Harl. 3943, read,

"It is no shame unto you ne no vice" . . .,

certainly weaker and less appropriate. We ought to be able to discover some reason for the change. Now it will be remembered that on May 1, 1380, one Cecelia Chaumpaigne executed an instrument of release to Chaucer, " de raptu meo." [1] It may be not quite fanciful to suggest that when in the course of revision Chaucer came to this passage, a recent disagreeable incident sprang before his mind, and even at the cost of substituting an inferior phrase he seized the opportunity of removing the reminder from his own and his friends' sight. He can hardly have been proud of the episode, and had probably suffered in his pocket.[2] If this suggestion is allowed some weight, it indicates 1380, or somewhat later, as the date of revision, which fits admirably (as will be seen later) with the evidence as to the date of first composition.[3]

§ 2.   *The Date.*

The date of the original writing of the *Troilus and Criseyde* has always been a good deal of a problem, and it cannot be said to be settled yet. In 1903 I showed [4] reason to believe that the poem was mentioned by Gower in his *Mirour de l'Omme*, in a passage (5245–56) which it seemed then could hardly have been written later than 1376, but which may probably date from about 1377.[5] This early date has recently been argued against briefly by Professor John Koch,[6] and more at large by Professor J. L. Lowes.[7]

---

[1] See *Life Records of Chaucer* (Ch. Soc., 1900), pp. 225-7.

[2] The force of this conjecture is not destroyed by the fact that he allowed the verb *ravisshe* to stand in IV. 530, 637 and 643, and in V. 895, and the noun *ravisshynge* in I. 62 and IV. 548 ; for the two forms of the word are so different in appearance and connotation that they would not necessarily be closely associated ; *rape* inevitably suggests the *raptus*, not so *ravisshe*. [Cf. such a use of the verb as in *T. C.*, IV. 1474 and *N. P. T.*, 4514 ("So was he ravisshed with his flaterye").] Moreover, Chaucer may not have been earnest enough in his antipathy to undertake so many further changes.

[3] I shall show later that the insertion of the *Teseide* stanzas can hardly have been done later than the writing of the *Knight's Tale* (which I hold to be practically identical with the *Palamon*). The revision, therefore, must have considerably antedated the *Prologue* of the *Legend*, 1386. See pp. 74–5 below.

[4] In *Modern Philology*, I. 317–324. I need hardly repeat the criticism of previous conjecture there given.

[5] For a full discussion of the date of the *Mirour* I must refer to Appendix A, pp. 220–5.

[6] *Engl. Stud.*, xxxvi. 140–41.

[7] *Publications of the Mod. Lang. Assoc. of America*, xx. 823–33.

The objections of the former seem to me not difficult to meet. He thinks the period from 1373[1] to 1376 too crowded by the *St. Cecelia,* the *Palamon* and the *Boethius.* But there is not the least necessity for putting the first and last here,[2] and the best possible reason, as we shall see later, for not putting the *Palamon* here and for not believing that any part of the *Troilus* was derived from that poem. The idea that the word *comedie* in *Troilus,* V. 1788, implies prevision of the *House of Fame* or the *Parliament of Fowls* I tried to show in this very article is groundless ; as also the gratuitousness of the idea that the epithet " moral " applied to Gower in V. 1856 must refer to any of his longer poems. " We may reasonably suppose that he was born about the year 1330 or possibly somewhat later ; "[3] are we to suppose that at the age of forty-five he had written nothing or shown no traits of character that would have earned him such an epithet from a personal associate as well then as ten years later ? Happily we are coming to realize Chaucer less as a literary phenomenon and more as a man ; were not his relations with Gower rather personal than literary ? Nor can I see that four or five years is too short a time for such modifications in the *Troilus* of Boccaccio's conception as Dr. Koch mentions. Altogether, therefore, he does little but reiterate, without developing, the arguments which I tried to refute at the beginning of my article. He suggests that Chaucer was writing the *Troilus* but had not yet finished it in 1376. But he does grant that Gower's reference is to Chaucer's poem.

Lowes' discussion demands more extended treatment. His arguments against my interpretation of the passage in Gower it will be more convenient to treat later ; first I shall consider his arguments in favour of a late date, that which he suggests being 1383–5.[4] One matter which bears on the date of the *Troilus* is its relation with the *Legend of Good Women.* Lowes adopts[5] and develops ten Brink's view of a close chronological relation between them. The matter can be discussed here only by anticipating some points in my discussion of the later poem. He declares (p. 821) that "the immediate occasion of the Prologue was manifestly the stir caused

[1] May, not November (as Koch says, ignoring Mather's rediscovery of the date) ; see my article, p. 319.
[2] On the *Boethius,* see p. 34 below.
[3] G. C. Macaulay's *Gower,* IV. xxix.
[4] *Public. of the Mod. Lang. Assoc.,* xx. 861.
[5] *Ibid.,* pp. 819–23.

by the publication of the *Troilus*," but I believe a very good case can be made out for a different view. The God of Love reproaches the poet (322–35) [1] with enmity to him and his servants, with hindering them by his " translacioun," and with having " translated the Romaunce of the Rose," and having said as he " liste " of Criseyde. The *Romance of the Rose*, the translation *par excellence*, is at least as prominent in this passage as the *Troilus*, and so also in Alcestis' defence (362–72, 441). Therefore there is nothing in these references to make one suppose that the *Troilus* had just been published, any more than that the *Romance of the Rose* had just been. But what is more important, I hope to show later strong reasons for believing, as Lowes does not, the orthodox view that not only is the F-Prologue an elaborate compliment to the queen, but that the whole *Legend* may have been written at her request. She landed in England in December, 1381, a girl of fifteen, who almost certainly knew no English, and it would be some years before she would be familiar with Chaucer's poetry. It seems to me that the language of the *Prologue* is at least as consistent with the view that she had just become familiar with his poetry and urged him to a more gallant manner towards women, as with the view that it is the product of a supposed general sensation produced by the first publication of the *Troilus*. [2]

Of Lowes' arguments for a late date for the *Troilus*, there remain two—the fact (pp. 820–821) that the end of it seems to suggest prevision of the *Legend of Good Women*, and its excellence and maturity (833–840). As to the second, I have nothing to say against his fine analysis of some of the virtues of the poem; assuredly, he says none too much of its vigour of characterization, its artistic mastery and its skill in dialogue and in episode. But I do deny his conclusion. In the first place, to an extent which is seldom realized, and which deserves much fuller treatment than this, the merits of the *Troilus* are due to the *Filostrato*. To my mind the latter is quite as good a poem ; it is better proportioned, and its characterization, if less complex and attractive, is most natural. Again, I see no difficulty in believing that the powers evinced by the

---

[1] I shall here assume that version F (" B ") of the *Prologue* is the earlier, a view which Lowes has done so much to establish. If G (" A ") were the earlier, it would not matter in this connection.

[2] The use in *L. G. W.* of three stanzas from the opening of the *Filostrato* (discovered earlier by Lowes ; cf. his article, pp. 822–3) of course is not surprising, since Chaucer owned a MS. of that poem, and implies no necessary chronological connection of *T. C.* with *L. G. W.*

Troilus were developed within a few years of Chaucer's introduction
to Italian literature. It is possible to misunderstand the Italian
influence on Chaucer; what it did for him, it seems to me, was to
open the sluice rather than to fill the reservoir. He had long
been a mature man, and, what we do not always remember, familiar
with the greatest poets of the Romans. Till he went to Italy, what
he lacked was a poetic form, and the ability to assimilate the
influence of the ancients; he had had hitherto only the *trouvère*
manner of the French. The *Trecentisti* were in part an intermediary between him and the ancient and higher ideal of poetic
style, they performed (if so humble a metaphor may be allowed)
the function of the plant between the mineral and the animal. I
see no reason why under a keen stimulus the poet should not
have rapidly overtaken the man, why Chaucer could not do at
thirty-five what he could do at forty-three. Any number of
other poetic biographies will bear me out.[1] As to the particular
qualities which Lowes dwells on, it seems to me they would be
almost as sudden in appearing at the latter age as the former,
for I cannot possibly believe that the *Palamon and Arcite* and
the *Legends* preceded the *Troilus*. Again and again *a priori*
arguments of this kind have burst before a piece of evidence.
May I say that I have become gradually but firmly convinced that
Chaucer's literary manner after 1372 depended far less on the time
of life when he was writing than on the character of his subject?
This is a highly important point, to which I shall have to return
repeatedly in treating the *Canterbury Tales*. It will account for
the inferiority of the *House of Fame* and the *Parliament of Fowls*
to the *Troilus*. Therefore I cannot feel that the excellence of the
Troilus is an argument against an early date.

The most striking point which Lowes makes, it seems to me, is
the foreshadowing of the *Legend* in *Troilus*, V. 1772–85; Chaucer
wishes he might write of Penelope and Alcestis, and warns women
against false men.[2] There is nothing surprising in the occurrence of
this passage in the *Troilus;* even without the *Legend* it would not

---

[1] Lowes at times well illustrates Chaucer's procedure by Tennyson's.
May not the rapidity with which Chaucer responded to the Italian stimulus
be paralleled by Coleridge's sudden poetic growth under the influence of
Wordsworth? Both he and Chaucer were impressionable poets, and it seems
to me that their rapid growth was exquisitely natural.

[2] Lowes, pp. 820–1. As to the *comedie* in line 1788, Lowes and I both
show thoroughly that it cannot be made to imply any particular plan
(*P. M. L. A.*, xx. 855; *Mod. Philol.*, i. 318).

"have seriously puzzled any one for a moment" (to borrow Lowes' own language from where it is less in place, p. 828, note); and there is nothing unlikely in Chaucer's having vaguely foreseen the *Legend* years before he wrote it. If it was written at the queen's suggestion, this passage at the end of the *Troilus* may have been what made her think of such a reparation for "the Rose and eek Criseyde." At any rate, I cannot think for an instant that this passage can be weighed against the evidence for an early date; to which we may now turn.

Two considerations point to a fairly early date for the *Troilus*, earlier certainly than 1385, the date which Lowes assigns it. To begin with, it is well known that Chaucer is very fond of his own words, and constantly repeats favourite or convenient phrases or lines. I shall later have to point out very many cases of this. Now the present *Knight's Tale* is connected with the *Troilus* on the one hand, and the *Legend of Good Women* on the other, by a large number of such repetitions, as I shall show later, which seem to indicate for the original *Palamon and Arcite* a position between the two.[1] The absence of such parallels between the *Troilus* and the *Legend* is very striking, considering their frequent parallels to other poems. Except for the passage in the *Troilus* which foreshadows the *Legend*, and for one or two expressions which are paralleled in the *Knight's Tale* as well (which therefore was probably the transmitter), I find only two common to the *Troilus* and the *Legend*. *T. C.*, IV. 15, is almost the same as *L. G. W.*, Prologue G, 265 :

"For how (How that) Criseyde Troilus forsook."

But here, it will be seen, the parallel is in the prologue which we shall see is surely the later, dating from about 1394. *T. C.*, III. 733–4, is parallel to *L. G. W.*, 2629–30 :

"O fatal sustren, which, er any clooth
Me shapen was, my destene me sponne;"

"Sin first that day that shapen was my sherte,
Or by the fatal sustren had my dom."

But most of this is paralleled in the *Knight's Tale*.[2] Considering,

---

[1] See pp. 76–8 below, in my chapter on the *Teseide* poems. The value of this evidence is recognized by Skeat, though it makes against his chronology (iii. 394), and by Mather (*Furnivall Miscellany*, p. 308).

[2] "That shapen was my deeth erst than my sherte" (1566). For the rest, *T. C.*, III. 1282 = *Kn. T.*, 3089 = *L. G. W.*, Prol. F, 162. In the passage

then, the closeness of the *Knight's Tale* in phraseology to the *Troilus* and to the whole *Legend of Good Women*, it is very striking that there should be almost no parallels between the two latter. It certainly makes against the view[1] that the *Troilus* was written close to and between most or all the individual legends and the *Prologue* of the *Legend of Good Women;* that the legends were written about 1380, the *Palamon* about 1382, *Troilus* 1383–5, and the *Prologue* of the *Legend* in 1386.[2] So far as this evidence has value, it seems to indicate an order of things like that which I arrive at by other methods : *Troilus* (revised later),[3] *Palamon*, *Legend of Good Women.*

But there is one more piece of evidence against Lowes' date for *Troilus*, and somewhat in favour of mine. Skeat points out that it is mentioned and frequently quoted in the *Testament of Love*,[4] once attributed to Chaucer, but really by Thomas Usk.[5] I need not repeat all the instances of borrowing which Skeat mentions in his notes;[6] the important passage is where Usk openly refers to Chaucer and the *Troilus*. The discourse between the author and Love (in close imitation of that between Boethius and Philosophy) has been on divine foreknowledge and human free-will.

" ' I wolde now (quod I) a litel understande, sithen that [god] al thing thus beforn wot, whether thilke wetinge be of tho thinges, or els thilke thinges ben to ben of goddes weting, and so of god nothing is ; and if every thing be thorow goddes weting, and therof take his being, than shulde god be maker and auctour of badde werkes, and so he shulde not rightfully punisshe yvel doinges of mankynde.'—Quod Love, ' I shal telle thee, this lesson to lerne.

---

which foreshadows *L. G. W., T. C.*, V. 1780–1 = *L. G. W.*, Prol. F, 486 (G, 476) ; 1782 = 2546 ; 1785 = 2387.

[1] Lowes, *P. M. L. A.*, xx 860–62.

[2] This date we may gladly accept.

[3] I may also recall the date, 1380 or shortly after, which I have suggested for the revision, which will throw the original writing far back ; the earlier we put the latter, the more natural is the thorough revision. It must be recollected that revision was far from being Chaucer's custom. The only other known case, that of the *Prologue* of *L. G. W.*, was due to a very special cause, as I believe we shall see ; as we shall also see that *P. A.* was probably altered only at the beginning and the end.

[4] See the Supplement to Skeat's *Chaucer*, vii. 1–145. Practically all the knowledge we have of this work is due to Skeat, to whom my treatment of it is indebted at every step.

[5] On the authorship, see *Skeat*, VII. xx. It may be remembered that the attribution of the *T. L.* to Chaucer, and a misinterpretation of it, were responsible for a particularly absurd part of the " Chaucer Legend " (cf. *e. g.* Hales, in *Dict. Nat. Biogr.*, x. 162, and Lounsbury's *Studies*, i. 188–90).

[6] As a possible addition, cf. III. 9, 89–90 with *T. C.*, V. 1856–9, and see p. 23, note.

Myne owne trewe servaunt, the noble philosophical poete in Eng-
lissh . . . he (quod she), in a tretis that he made of my servant
Troilus, hath this mater touched, and at the ful this question
assoyled. Certaynly, his noble sayinges can I not amende ; in
goodnes of gentil manliche speche, without any maner of nycetè of
storiers imaginacion, in witte and in good reson of sentence he
passeth al other makers. In the boke of Troilus, the answere to
thy question mayst thou lerne.' " [1]

As Skeat points out (with less conviction than seems to me in
place), the reference is to *Troilus*, IV. 953–1085, the passage
already discussed at large, where Troilus soliloquizes on the question whether God's foreknowledge interferes or not with man's
free-will. Now the interesting thing is that, as we have seen,
this passage came in on the revision. Therefore Chaucer's revised
version of the *Troilus* was known to Thomas Usk.

The question as to the date of the *Testament of Love* may be
answered with certainty and exactness.[2] Usk refers to events of
1384 in London in a manner much more certain and detailed even
than Skeat points out. According to Malverne,[3] John Northampton, who in 1383 had been mayor for two years, was very severe
toward the fishmongers, who had charged excessive prices, and
thereby for a time he won popular applause ; but by extending the
same austerity toward other trades he awoke discord and alienated
his former friends, insomuch that, when he came up for re-election,
after a stormy campaign Nicholas Brembre was put in his place.
But the two factions so failed to agree, and the validity of Brembre's
election was so doubtful, that the royal authority seems to have
been necessary to secure the office to him. He at once undid the
work of his stern predecessor, and restored their liberties to the
fishmongers. Shortly after this Northampton caused disturbances
in London, was accused of provoking sedition, and was arrested
and imprisoned by the King in Corfe Castle. Brembre, however,
laboured to calm the tumults against Northampton, and to promote
peace. Usk was arrested about July 20, 1384, and induced to
betray Northampton's secrets and bring accusations against him ;
these Northampton denied, declared Usk a false ribald, and defied
him to single combat. Subsequently other leading citizens were

---

[1] III., ch. 4, ll. 241–9, 253–9.

[2] Here I am simply enlarging on and confirming what Skeat has done. See
VII., xxii. ff.

[3] Pp. 29–31, 45–51 (Malverne's continuation of Higden's *Polychronicon*,
Rolls Series, vol. ix.).

arrested and accused ; of all this, Malverne says, the incensed fishmongers were the cause. In October, 1384, when Brembre came
up for re-election, great precautions were taken to avoid a recurrence
of such disturbances as those of his first election.

Usk's account, the vaguely expressed version of a personal enemy
of Northampton, perfectly agrees with this.[1] After dwelling on how
much he has desired the peace of the city, he says he had been enticed
into a faction which attempted to abate the evils of extortion, but
really meant to make things disagreeable for leading citizens who
disapproved of the present misgovernment. This faction and its
"governour," after he had been put out in a " free eleccion," pre-
tended that the latter had been invalid, and raised a great disturb-
ance. Usk himself was imprisoned until he should reveal what he
knew for the benefit of the commonweal, even if it involved
betraying his "owne fere." He justifies himself for this action,
but later he was accused of bearing false witness against his
master,[2] and offered to substantiate his statements by single combat.[3] The neatness with which Usk's slightly cryptic account
corresponds to the facts proves that it cannot have been written
before 1384.

But we may go farther, and say that it must have been written
later yet, after Chaucer's *Legend of Good Women*, with which it
certainly shows familiarity. The following parallels, especially the
first, seem conclusive.[4]

" Certes, I wot wel, ther shal be mad more scorne and jape of
me, that I, so unworthily clothed al-togider in the cloudy cloude
of unconninge, wil putten me in prees to speke of love, or els of
the causes in that matter, sithen al the grettest clerkes han had
y-nough to don, and (as who sayth)[5] gadered up clene toforn hem,
and with their sharpe sythes of conning al mowen, and mad
therof grete rekes and noble, ful of al plentees, to fede me and many
another. . . . And al-though these noble repers, as good workmen
and worthy their hyre, han al drawe and bounde up in the sheves,
and mad many shockes, yet have I ensample to gadere the smale
crommes. . . . Yet also have I leve of the noble husbande Boëce,
al-though I be a straunger of conninge, to come after his doctrine,

---

[1] *Testament of Love*, bk. I., ch. 6, especially ll. 53–6, 76–89, 93–107,
117, 130–50, 188–91.
[2] He had been confidential secretary to Northampton.
[3] I. 7, 10 ; II. 4, 116.
[4] *T. of L.*, I., Prol., ll. 94–114. Most of these parallels are pointed out by
Skeat.
[5] This phrase shows that the passage is a conscious reminiscence ; it will be
seen how he plays with the idea (and mixes the metaphor).

and these grete workmen, and glene my handfuls of the shedinge
after their handes ; and, if me faile ought of my ful, to encrese my
porcion with that I shal drawe by privitees out of the shocke."

> " Allas ! that I ne had English, ryme or prose,
>   Suffisant this flour to preyse aright !
>   But helpeth, ye that han conning and might,
>   Ye lovers, that can make of sentement ;
>   In this cas oghte ye be diligent
>   To forthren me somwhat in my labour,
>   Whether ye ben with the leef or with the flour.
>   For wel I wot, that ye han her-biforn
>   Of making ropen, and lad awey the corn ;
>   And I come after, glening here and there,
>   And am ful glad if I may finde an ere
>   Of any goodly word that ye han left " (F, 66–77).

" Hast thou not rad how kinde I was to Paris, Priamus sone of
Troy ? How Jason me falsed, for al his false behest ?" (*T. L.*, I. 2,
91–3 ; Love is speaking to the writer).

> " Thou rote of false lovers, duk Jasoun ! . . .
>   Ther other falsen oon, thou falsest two ! " (1368, 1377).

Jason swore to Medea that he

> " Ne sholde her never falsen, night ne day." [1]

" And nere it for comfort of your presence, right here wolde I
sterve " (I. 3, 119–120; he is addressing Love). [2]

> " For, nadde comfort been of hir presence,
>   I had been deed, withouten any defence " (F, 278–9).

We shall later see reason to agree with Professor Lowes that the
Prologue of the *Legend* can hardly have been written before 1386,
and to believe that the poem can hardly have been published till
1387. Hence the *Testament of Love* cannot have been written
before that date.

On the other hand, it cannot have been written later than the
early part of 1388, for the very good reason that in March of that
year Usk was executed.[3] The previous year seems to be indicated

---

[1] Line 1640. These seem to be the only cases where *falsen* is used in
L. G. W.

[2] Cf. also *K. T.*, 1398. *Test. of Love*, III. 7, 36–9, affords a parallel to
L. G. W., 735–6 ; but it is more closely paralleled in *T. C.*, II. 538–9.

[3] Pointed out by Skeat, VII. xxiii. He was sentenced March 4 ; Malverne, p. 169. Yet Skeat " suspects " (p. 473) that Usk copies from Chaucer's
Astrolabe, which Skeat himself (and everybody else) dates 1391 (cf. *Chaucer*,
III. 352) ; and assures us (p. 458 ; cf. p. xxvii.) that Usk quotes the C-text
of *Piers Plowman*, which Skeat dates 1393. In neither case can I see the least
internal probability of copying.

by the complete silence of the work as to Usk's final imprisonment
and peril. At the end of 1387 the Duke of Gloucester and his
party succeeded in turning the tables on Richard and his supporters,
among whom were Sir Nicholas Brembre and Usk, now sub-sheriff
of Middlesex.[1] Though we hear nothing of Usk till February, some
of his party were accused as early as November 14, 1387. Now
Usk has his own affairs much on his mind; in his Prologue he
says, " this book shal be of love " (81–2), yet he has a great deal
to say of the bygones of 1384, and seems greatly concerned as to
what people think of his conduct in the Northampton affair, and
very anxious to vindicate his reputation from the charge of false-
hood and treachery. Is it credible that he should utterly ignore
this new great danger?[2] Working backwards, therefore, as well
as forwards, we arrive at 1387 as the date of the *Testament of
Love.*

We find, then, that Chaucer's revised version of the *Troilus*
was known to Usk in 1387.[3] If, as Lowes thinks, the first version
was not finished till 1385, is not this rather quick work? So

[1] Malverne's continuation of Higden, IX., 106–8, 115–16, 118, 134, 150–1,
169; cf. also Walsingham's *Historia*, II. 173. The former of course was
the ex-mayor, and Chaucer's former colleague at the custom-house. On his
execution, cf. also Gower, *Cron. Tripert.*, I. (Macaulay, IV. 318).

[2] Skeat thinks (p. xxii.) that he was in prison while he was writing the
latter part of the work, because in speaking of the events of 1384 he mentions
being for the " firste tyme enprisoned" (II. 4, 103–5); but obviously he may
have been in prison twice in the first connection, or once later for some unknown reason. His first chapter (*e. g.* ll. 14–17, 36–48) talks much of prison,
but, as Skeat says, this is doubtless because he is imitating the prisoner
Boethius, and is meant metaphorically; for it is here that the allegorical fiction begins. In the Prologue, where he speaks directly in his own person, there
is not a hint of such a thing. Nor can I see any reason to believe, with Skeat,
that he was ever involved with the Lollards. His old associates, whom he has
abandoned, were doubtless the Northampton faction, and the meaning of
" Margaret " is too vague to be made to imply a recent reconciliation with the
Church.

[3] The *Testament of Love* borrows rather extensively also from the *House of
Fame.* In a few passages it suggests *Kn. T.*, but that is not at all likely to have
been seen by Usk, or to have been published before his death. *T. L.*, bk. I.
ch. 3, ll. 13–14 suggests *Kn. T.*, 951; I. 3, 120 suggests 1398 (but cf. also
L. G. W., F, 278, cited above). Other parallels to *Kn. T.* are paralleled also
in *T. C.* or *L. G. W.* With *T. L.*, I. 1, 70 (the sentence that follows shows it is
meant as a quotation) and III. 1, 137 cf. *Kn. T.* 3089, *T. C.*, III. 1282, *L. G. W.*
(F) 162; and with *T. L.*, III. 7, 50 cf. *Kn. T.* 1838 and *T. C.*, V. 1433. In
a good many other passages, some of which Skeat mentions and some not,
T. L. recalls various other scattered parts of the *C. T.* But after considering
every one, I am convinced that there is no evidence of borrowing, nothing
like as much as there is in the case of *L. G. W.*, or even *Kn. T.* Yet Skeat
sometimes announces the borrowing without ever considering whether the
thing is possible, or whether the borrowing may not have been on Chaucer's
part.

extensive and minute a revision of a poem originally so finished as
the *Troilus*, it seems to me, implies the passage of a number of
years. But all this agrees perfectly with the date 1377 for the
original completion and 1380 or later for the revision.

A very early date for the *Troilus and Criseyde* is indicated by
Lydgate's manner of speaking of it.[1] In the *Falls of Princes*, in
a long list of Chaucer's works which is roughly but rather strikingly
chronological,[2] the *Troilus* stands first and is attributed to the poet's
youth :

> " In youthe he made a translacion
> Of a boke whiche called is Trophe
> In Lumbardo tonge, as men may rede and se,
> And in our vulgar, long or that ye [he] deyde,
> Gave it the name of Troylous and Cresseyde."

In the *Troy-Book* he speaks of Chaucer's

> " book of Troylus and Cryseyde
> Which he made longe or that he deyde." [3]

Fifteen years would not be so very long before he died, and
youth in the fourteenth century certainly did not extend to the
middle forties. The probabilities I think are distinctly in favour
of the view that Lydgate knew Chaucer personally, and he certainly
knew him well by hearsay.[4] The list in the *Falls of Princes*
shows very considerable intimacy with Chaucer's literary history,
and I see no reason why a good deal of weight should not be attached
to Lydgate's testimony. It is striking that he says nothing about
the time when any other of Chaucer's works was written. Perhaps
the world had not even then got through marvelling at the precocity
of such a work from an almost unknown poet. It is certainly noteworthy that the evidence derived (as we shall see) from Chaucer's
friend and contemporary Gower, and the direct testimony of his
chief admirer and disciple Lydgate, should agree so perfectly on an
early date for the *Troilus*.

[1] The point developed here was first made (I believe) in my article in
Modern Philology, i. 324, note.
[2] See Lounsbury, *Studies*, i. 419–422 ; Morris' *Chaucer* (London, 1891), i.
79. The list, in order, is *T. C.*, *Boethius*, *Astrolabe*, "*Ceix and Alcion*," *B. D.*,
R. R., *P. F.*, *Origen upon the Magdalen*, *Book of the Lion*, *A. A.*, *Mars*,
L. G. W., *C. T.*, *Melibeus*, *Cl. T.*, *Monk's T.*, small lyrics. The *Troilus* is also
first in the list of Chaucer's works in the certainly genuine Retractations at
the end of the *Pars. T.* : *T. C.*, *H. F.*, *L. G. W.*, *B. D.*, *P. F.*, *C. T.*, *Book of
the Lion*, small lyrics.
[3] See Rossetti's edition of the *T. C.* and the *Filostrato* (Ch. Soc.), p. x.
[4] Cf. Schick, *Temple of Glas*, xci. f. The *Falls of Princes* was written
about 1430–8, and the *Troy-Book* about 1412–20 (*ibid.*, cxii.).

Up to this point it seems to me temperate to say that we have found no reliable evidence in favour of a late date for the *Troilus*, especially for so late a date as 1385 ; and evidence of no little value in favour of an early, even a very early, date. It will be all clinched if we can be sure that the poem was referred to as early as 1377. The passage in Gower's *Mirour de l'Omme* which seems to mention the *Troilus* is as follows (ll. 5245–56) :

> " Au Sompnolent trop fait moleste,
> Quant matin doit en haulte feste
> Ou a mouster ou a chapelle
> Venir ; mais ja du riens s'apreste
> A dieu prier, ainz bass la teste
> Mettra tout suef sur l'eschamelle,
> Et dort, et songe en sa cervelle
> Qu'il est au bout de la tonelle,
> *U qu'il oït chanter la geste*
> *De Troÿlus et de la belle*
> *Creseide*, et ensi se concelle
> A dieu d'y faire sa requeste."

Koch admits that the reference here is to Chaucer's poem. This, however, Professor Lowes does not do, and with much thoroughness and ingenuity he tries to discover many loopholes of escape from the inferences which I have drawn from the passage.[1]

First of all, he thinks that the *geste de Troylus et de la belle Creseide* of which Sompnolent dreams may have been the *Filostrato*. But consider that Gower knew no Italian, and was writing for people ignorant of both Italian and Boccaccio ; I do not ask what point there would have been in referring to the latter, but how could it ever have occurred to him, even if he had heard Chaucer speak of the poem, to make in so off-hand a manner a remark so unintelligible ? Is it impertinent to ask whether a modern preacher would rail at his parishioners for staying at home on Sunday to read the last Sherlock Holmes story or the works of a novelist of Paraguay ? Obviousness and popularity are necessarily implied in Gower's remark. This and the apparently rather humble station of Sompnolent are what suggest that the poem is in English ; Lowes' suggestion that by the same token Cato and other ancients

---

[1] *Public. Mod. Lang. Assoc.*, xx. 823–33. The reason why Gower's editor, Mr. Macaulay, did not recognize the allusion to Chaucer's poem is no doubt that by the received chronology it greatly antedated it ; the fact that he did not was my reason for ignoring his remark in my article (cf. Lowes, p. 824). The priority in recognizing the allusion rests with Hamilton.

quoted in the *Mirour, by the author*, should be in English rather surprisingly ignores the point. Moreover, Lowes does not seem to see the world of difference in naturalness between a poet referring, for a particular reason, to a little-known work by himself, as Chaucer and Froissart[1] do, and making a recondite allusion where a familiar one is to be expected. It seems to me the possibility that the reference is to Boccaccio ought to be eliminated.

Lowes' next attempt is to weaken the presumption that the allusion is to an independent poem of some length, rather than to a mere episode, by paralleling it with Froissart's references in *La Prison Amoureuse* to the " tréttiés," or " livret," " de Pynoteüs et Neptisphelé." [2] But there is no parallel whatever ; not only is the latter work one by himself, but the poet *as a character in the Prison* writes the " livret," and the later references to it are by him and another character *in the story*. The "gest of Troylus and of the fair Creseyde," it still seems to me, certainly implies an independent work of some length.[3]

Lowes argues (p. 829) that Sompnolent's meditation should hardly be on so tragic a story as Chaucer's completed version. This seems a little fine-drawn, and at any rate will prove to be an argument rather in favour of my view. No version of the story is known which is any less tragic than Chaucer's. Boccaccio's great innovation and success,[4] in which of course Chaucer follows him, is the account of the courtship and happiness of Troilus. Benoît and Guido give no account of the story except reminiscently at the time when the exchange of Briseida for Antenor is arranged ; in Benoît the prominent thing (though not treated very seriously) is the grief of Troilus and the fickleness of Briseida. Moreover, if there is any inappropriateness in Gower's allusion, does not this suggest that there was some special reason why he made it ? And what more natural than that his friend had just been writing the story ? Gower was not so sensitive an artist, and the allusion is not so much dwelt on, that this inappropriateness was very likely to strike him ; but it does seem that the story was not likely to have occurred to him unless for some special reason. If it cannot be called tactful to represent Chaucer's poem as a favourite with such a person as Sompnolent,

---

[1] All that Froissart does in the *Paradys* is to mention, among a large number of heroes and heroines, some of those of his own *Méliador* (cf. *Engl. Stud.*, xxvi. 330). Lowes refers also to *L. G. W.*, F, 420-1.

[2] Scheler, I. 257-78, 286-340.

[3] Cf. Lowes, p. 826.

[4] Cf. Koerting, *B.'s Leben und Werke* (Leipzig, 1880), 584-5, 587.

this hardly conflicts with the impression we get elsewhere of
Gower's personality ; witness his remarks about Chaucer's "daies
olde" at fifty or so.   Perhaps the moral Gower somewhat disapproved of the *Troilus*, even though it was dedicated to him.

The fact that it was Boccaccio and Chaucer who made the story
of Troilus and his lady-love prominent, and its insignificance all
over Europe before or apart from their influence, must never be lost
sight of, and is of high importance in weighing probabilities in this
case.   It was probably Boccaccio's relations with "Fiammetta"
that led him to select this episode from the Troy story, enormously
expand it, and in a measure make its heroine a warning to his own
lady.[1]   While Troilus is very prominent all through Benoît's and
Guido's works as a warrior, the mention of his lady and his *amour*
are at very little length, and do not even form a unified episode ;[2]
yet Lowes seems (p. 833) to entertain the idea that the *geste* which

---

[1] Cf. Koerting, *B.'s Leben und Werke*, p. 585 ; W. Hertzberg, *Jahrbuch
der deutschen Shakspere Gesellschaft*, vi., 196, 199.   Cf. also Schofield, *Engl.
Lit. from the Conquest to Chaucer*, 291–2.

[2] In Benoît, Briseida is "termed 'la pucele'" in verse 12977. . . . . The
loves of Troilus and Briseida are not described at length, nor the various
vicissitudes of them notified : but, now that the lady is to leave Troy, Benoît
informs us that she and Troilus are deeply enamoured. . . . Her monologue
[as to the final capture of her heart by Diomed] . . . ends at verse 20330 ;
and, though the poem goes on to the formidable number of 30108 lines, we
hear henceforth no more of her, nor of Diomed as related to her, nor (save in
one instance soon afterwards) of Troilus in the character of her deserted and
incensed lover.   It will thus be perceived that, in the Briseis narrative of
Benoît, the more substantial subject-matter is the Briseida-Diomed amour, to
which the Briseida-Troilus amour forms rather the proem ; whereas, in the
Chryseis narrative of Boccaccio and Chaucer, the main interest by far centres
in the Cryseyde-Troilus amour, to which the Cryseyde-Diomed amour forms
but the sequel, and, even in that connection, is but little developed except
in so far as it wedges the iron into the soul of Troilus" (W. M. Rossetti,
Troilus and Filostrato, Ch. Soc., p. vi.).   In both Benoît and Guido the
account of Briseida is scattered in some four or five spots over the whole middle
of the work.—In the *Laud Troy-Book* (E. E. T. S., 1902–3, ed. Wülfing),
which was probably written about 1400 (see *Engl. Stud.*, xxix. 3–6, 377–8,
396), but which shows no knowledge of Chaucer's poem (the only, and a
very insufficient, ground for dating it earlier), the episode is disposed of in
about 60 lines (9060–90, 10365–6, 13437, 13543–64) out of 18664, much
more briefly than in Guido, the source.   In the "*Gest Hystoriale*" *of the
Destruction of Troy* (E. E. T. S., 1869 and 1874, ed. Panton and Donaldson),
it occupies about 200 out of over 14,000 (7886–7905, 8026–8181, 8296–8317,
9942–9959 ; cf. 10306) ; the author refers (8053–4) to Chaucer's poem for
more particulars.   In the *Troy-Book* the story is first mentioned when
Diomed sends Troilus' horse to the heroine, and in the *Gest* when she is
exchanged for Antenor.   In the fourteenth-century *Seege of Troye* (ed. Wager,
1899), a greatly condensed poem of 1922 ll., Troilus is frequently mentioned,
but his lady and his *amour* never.   It is the *Seege* and the *Gest* that Miss
Kempe refers to in her rather vague statement in *Engl. Stud.*, xxix. 3.
There is not a single poem in English which mentions the love-story, and
which can plausibly be dated before Chaucer's *Troilus*.

Somnolent dreams he hears sung[1] may have been a few scattered passages in Guido's Latin prose !

Furthermore, in works other than those which tell their story, though Troilus is not infrequently mentioned as a brave warrior, I find only one reference to him as a lover (by Froissart), and no reference at all to the heroine, earlier than Chaucer's *Troilus*, in any language.[2] In the fifteenth century I find several references in French to the heroine and the *amour;* when we find that the *Troilus and Briseida*,[3] a French prose translation of the *Filostrato*, was written at the very end of the fourteenth or early in the fifteenth century,[4] is not the inference obvious that the rise of the love-story to prominence was largely due to this ?[5] And when we find

---

[1] Cf. Chaucer's address to his poem (V. 1797), "red wher-so thou be, or ellee songe"; and (II. 56) "As I shal singe, on Mayes day the thridde."

[2] Therefore to Lowes' question (p. 828, note), "Supposing Chaucer's *Troilus* never to have existed, would such a reference as Gower's, on the basis of known relations of the other versions of the story, have seriously puzzled any one for a moment ?"—to this question I answer *Yes*.

[3] Or "Creseide" or "Brisaide."

[4] See Moland et d'Héricault, *Nouvelles Françoises*, p. ci. There are six MSS. in the Bibliothèque Nationale alone (*ibid.*, p. cxxxiv.). Benoît's work was written about 1165, and Guido's in 1287.

[5] The following are the only references I find to Troilus and Criseyde outside the works which tell their story. I. Troilus as a warrior is mentioned :— 1! In *Partenopeus de Blois*, I. p. 6 (ed. Crapelet, twelfth century; he is barely mentioned among five Trojan knights; Hector is dwelt on). 2. In *Floriant et Florete*, p. 32 (ed. Francisque-Michel; thirteenth century; barely mentioned). 3. In *Anseïs de Cartage*, l. 1653 (*Stuttg. Lit. Ver.*, thirteenth century). 4. In *Chronique Rimée de Ph. Mouskes*, I. 289 (ed. de Reiffenberg; A.D. 1243; Troilus with others used as a simile for bravery). 5. In 1249 the German Albertus Stadensis wrote a Latin poem in distichs, in the proem of which he says, "Liber est Troilus ob Troica bella vocatus." It does not, however, deal with Troilus particularly, and apparently never mentions his love affair, but is a mere paraphrase of Dares (see G. Koerting, *Boccaccio's Leben u. Werke*, p. 589; W. Hertzberg, *Jahrbuch d. deut. Shaks. Gesellsch.*, vi. 181). 6. In *Escanor*, ll. 15698-9 (ed. Michelant: about 1285; he is barely mentioned). 7. By Deschamps, IX. 91 (*Soc. Anc. Textes;* about 1381; barely mentioned among ancient warriors). 8. By Georges Chastellain, VII. 424 (ed. Kervyn de Lettenhove: C. died 1475; mentioned among many others). I may add Malory, *Morte d'Arthur*, XX. 17; bare mention among ancient heroes, probably due to Malory himself; the numerous other fifteenth-century English references it is needless to collect. II. Troilus or Criseyde, or both, are mentioned as lovers by:—1. Froissart, I. 29 (ed. Scheler: before 1370; Troilus is barely mentioned, but heads a list of lovers; cf. Lowes, p. 825, who makes too much of this single instance). 2. Jean le Seneschal, p. 203 (*S. A. T. F.*; about 1389; "Troÿluz," lover of "Brisaÿda"). 3. Charles d'Orléans, p. 307 (ed. Champollion-Figeac; lived 1391-1465, and often alludes to the Troy-story; three lines on Troilus); p. 120 (not 126, as Dernedde says; speaks of the beauty of "Criséis, de Yseud et Elaine"; the editor says, p. 427, "lisez Briséis"). 4. Alain Chartier, p. 734 (Paris, 1617; lived about 1392-1429; Troilus barely mentioned; "Briseyda," who broke faith with him, appears among a number of faithless ones). 5. *René of Anjou*, III. 111-112 (ed. Hawke; born 1408; T. is mentioned between Paris and Diomed, among many lovers; loved "Grisade"

that Gower, after this first reference in the *Mirour*, makes many
other such, in the *Vox Clamantis*, in a *balade* and in the *Confessio
Amantis*, never mentions Troilus but as a lover, and always spells
the heroine's name with a *C*, is not the inference still more justifiable
that the prominence of the story with Gower, as with fifteenth-century English writers, was due to Chaucer? The most interesting case
in Gower is a reminiscence of the passage in the *Mirour* (*C. A.*,
IV. 2794–7); when Genius examines the Lover as to the sin of
"Sompnolence," he proves himself innocent by showing his constant
readiness to please his lady :

> "Or elles that hir list comaunde
> To rede and here of Troilus,
> Riht as sche wole or so or thus,
> I am al redi to consente."

The reference here, of course, is to Chaucer's *Troilus*, which
there cannot be a doubt that Gower knew well when he wrote the
Confessio. Yet we are asked to believe that the precisely similar
reference in the *Mirour* is to some poem unknown to Gower's
readers (or else to us), or else to a few scattered bits lost in a long
poem, or (worse yet) in a Latin prose work.[1]

I hardly think it can be said, then, that the argument "that
Gower's reference is to Chaucer's *Troilus*, rests in the last analysis
on a single letter, the initial *C* of the heroine's name" (Lowes, p. 826).

---

or "Grisayde").——Most of the references in this note are derived from
Robert Dernedde's *Ueber die den altfranz. Dichtern bekannten epischen
Stoffe aus dem Altertum* (Erlangen, 1887), pp. 122–3 ; I owe the reference to
Dr. G. L. Hamilton. No doubt the list could be extended, but after some
search I find no more. Neither T. nor C. is mentioned, *e. g.*, in Petrarch's
Trionfi (ed. Appel), where many such are ; she is never mentioned by
Deschamps nor (so far as I can find) by Froissart, and he only once by each
(as noted above). No other references are to be found in the ninety volumes
of the *Soc. des Anc. Textes*, or in Langlois' *Table des Noms Proprcs*. I find
Criseyde mentioned in no manner anywhere else ; but of course I have not
collected fifteenth-century English references.

[1] Troilus and Criseyde are frequently mentioned by Gower. The earliest
case appears to be that in *M. O.* The next, pointed out to me by Dr.
Hamilton, is in *Vox Cl.* (soon after 1383), VI. 1325–8, where the faithful
T. and Medea are paired off against the fickle Jason and "Crisaida." In one
of the French *balades* (XX. 20 ; probably late) he speaks of T. as supplanted
by Diomed in the love "du fille au Calcas." In *C. A.* (finished 1390) among
examples of supplantation he quotes the case of Agamemnon, Achilles, and
"that swete wiht" "Brexëida," and then directly "Criseïda," Troilus and
Diomed (II. 2451–8) ; twice again, similarly, of "Criseide" and the other
two (V. 7597–7602 ; VIII. 2531–5 ; the story of "Criseide douhter of Crisis,"
is told in V. 6433–75). It is worthy of remark that there is no significant
change in his manner of mentioning the lovers, which suggests that he had
had no accession to his information since the first reference.

But this is still a strong argument. We must not assume, it is true, that Chaucer was the innovator in this spelling; not only in one fourteenth- and two fifteenth-century MSS. of Guido does her name appear as *Criseida* or *Griseida*,[1] but in one fifteenth-century MS. *C* has replaced *G* even in the *Filostrato*.[2] At the same time, it is not unlikely that Chaucer did substitute the less unfamiliar, and perhaps more agreeable, *C* for *G*. But the main point is that the form with *G*, and therefore that with *C*, is due only to Boccaccio; without him, Troilus' mistress would everywhere have been called *B*riseida,[3] which seems to have been, outside Chaucer's and Gower's poems, the universal form in England in the fourteenth century.[4] The spelling of Gower and Chaucer alike is due to the influence of Boccaccio. Through which of them is it more likely to have entered England ?[5] But it is not only the initial in Gower's spelling which indicates Chaucer's influence. Gower's form is French, with a final -*e*, *Creseide*. The name appears in Chaucer MSS. under various French forms, among which, though *Criseyde* is perhaps the commonest, Gower's form is often found I find the final -*e* nowhere else except in those who write under Chaucer's influence and two or so other post-Chaucerian writers.[6]

---

[1] See Morf, in *Romania*, xxi. 101, note 1. See also G. L. Hamilton, *Chaucer and Guido*, 134–5.

[2] *Cryseida* is the form in a MS. of the Marquis de Santillane's library ; see *Bibliothèque de l'École des Hautes Études*, Fascicule 153, p. 328 (pointed out to me by Dr. Hamilton). So in old printed editions (Hertzberg, *Jahrb. d. deut. Sh. Ges.*, vi. 197) ; and cf. Koerting, *Boccaccio*, 569. The form with a *C* is the commonest in the French translation (cf. Lowes, p. 827) ; otherwise with a *B*.

[3] This is true, so far as I know, of all the documents. But the Italian Armannino, who ignores the love-story, in speaking of the Homeric "Brisseida" and "Crisseida," says that, according to some, the latter was the daughter of Calchas (see Gorra, *Testi Inediti*, p. 555).

[4] To balance the substitution by a reader, under Chaucer's influence, of *C* for *B* in two passages in the *Laud Troy-Book* (cf. Lowes, 828), the *Gest Hystoriale*, which directly mentions Chaucer's *Troilus*, preserves only the form with *B* as I pointed out in my article (p. 323, note ; this will correct Miss Kempe, *Engl. Stud.*, xxix. 5) ; and the only MS. of the *Filostrato* in the British Museum (Addit. 21246, early fifteenth century) has *Briseyda* three times at the beginning, though elsewhere it always has *Griseyda*.

[5] Lowes' suggestion (828–9) that the *C* may have been substituted by Gower's scribe after the poem was written of course cannot be disproved ; but, especially since the work was not a popular and much-copied one, and this MS. (as Lowes admits) was almost certainly "written under the direction of the author," the suggestion can be allowed little weight. Lowes refers to my "tacit assumption" that the reading is Gower's, not the scribe's ; if we did not make the tacit assumption that the MSS. represent the author's words, where should we be in the study of mediæval literature ?

[6] The fifteenth-century, or post-Chaucerian fourteenth-century, French version of the *Filostrato* has commonly *Creseide ;* probably influenced by

In English, German, Norse, French and Latin, in Benoît and Guido alike, the regular form is *Briseida* or *Brisaida*.[1] Chaucer seems to have been the first to use the *-e*, of course for the sake of the rhyme. The combination of the initial *C* with the final *e*, apart from Chaucer and Gower and those who owe it directly to them, seems to be found only in some MSS. of the post-Chaucerian French translation of the *Filostrato*. Are we to look upon the occurrence of one and the same very unusual form in the works of two friends within a very few years as a coincidence?

So all the evidence looks in the same direction. We have seen that if the reference is not to Chaucer's poem the spelling with *C——e* is surprising; and that the occurrence of the reference at all is more than surprising. Lowes must battle against the coincidence of the two surprises. I must say that the more I investigate *Troilus* literature the more I am struck by the improbability that Gower's reference is to any work but Chaucer's.

But now Professor Lowes, who has as many holes to start to as the Wife of Bath's mouse, suggests that, even if Gower's reference is to Chaucer's poem, it may not have been made as early as 1376 (the extension of the limit to 1377 will not matter here).[2] He appeals (p. 830) to that forlorn hope, a possible interpolation in the *Mirour*. For this proposal I cannot see the slightest justification, or the slightest reason to believe that there are interpolations anywhere in the *Mirour*. Lowes' argument that the passage which mentions the *Troilus* looks like an interpolation is fallacious. Gower says earlier (5179–84), it is true, that Somnolent will not get up in the morning, and leaves the labour of prayer to the nun and the friar; yet he says here that he goes to sleep at the morning service in church. But Gower says expressly that this is when he *has* to go, on a high festival (5245–8).[3] Therefore there is no means of escape

---

this, the fifteenth-century René of Anjou has *Grisade, Grisayde;* the *Gest Hystoriale,* which appeals to Chaucer, has (rarely) *Bresaide, Breisaide* (usually—*said*); a late fifteenth-century MS. of an Old French version of Guido has *brisade* (Brit. Mus., Royal 16. F. ix.). I find no other cases.

[1] With the variants *Brescida, Breyseyda, Brisayda, Briseida, Briseyda, Brixeida, Brixeyda, Bryseida, Prixaida* (quaintly, in a German version), *Breiseida, Breiseidä, Breisida* (these three in a Norse version). I find no other forms (except for *Brisade* in one late version, as noted above) after a thorough search in the British Museum, including seven early printed editions, twelve MSS. and five MS. translations of Guido, and one MS. and two modern editions of Benoît. The occasional occurrence of *Briseide* as a genitive or dative form in Guido's Latin seems to have misled Hertzberg (p. 210). A MS. of Guido in the Harvard Library has *Briseida, Briseyda.*

[2] I refer again to Appendix A, pp. 220–5, on the date of Gower's *Mirour.*

[3] For similar passages cf. 5557–68, 5617–28.

from the conclusion that the reference to the *Troilus* in the *Mirour* must have been written not later than soon after the death of Edward III. Altogether, therefore, Professor Lowes' whole long and ingenious argument seems like piling very numerous feathers into one scale to outweigh a lump of lead in the other. It is seldom in literary investigations that we have stronger evidence than we have here for the view that Chaucer's *Troilus* was mentioned not later than 1377.

After this exhaustive study of the evidence, the conclusion I reach, then, is that the *Troilus and Criseyde* was written at the very beginning of the period when Chaucer was under Italian influence. And after all, why not? He had returned from Italy by May 23, 1373,[1] after an absence of six months, during which he doubtless read much Italian, including very likely the *Filostrato* and *Teseide*.[2] On his return, having once learned Italian, is it not natural that he should plunge with zeal into the study of Italian literature? Not till over a year later, June 8, 1374,[3] was he appointed Comptroller of Customs, and during the interim, adorned by several benefactions and payments from the king, he may probably have enjoyed much well-earned leisure at court,[4] with his books and pen. After his responsible mission to Italy, he would surely not be worked very hard as Esquire of the King's Chamber. In the office of Comptroller there is not the least reason to believe that Chaucer was overworked; I have showed elsewhere, and Koch admits, that his supposed lamentations in the *House of Fame* are not such at all.[5] As one turns over the pages of the *Life Records* for this period he sees indications that Chaucer's life was financially comfortable, and broken in upon by no public commissions until 1377 and the very end of 1376. With perhaps a year of leisure, followed by two years and a half or so of routine work, and another year only partly spent abroad, is there anything unreasonable in supposing the *Troilus* to have been produced at this time?[6]

[1] *Life Records*, pp. 183–4.
[2] Mr. Karl Young (*Mod. Philol.*, iv. 169–77) makes out a good case for Chaucer's showing familiarity also with Boccaccio's *Filocolo* in the *Troilus*, especially book III.
[3] *Life Records*, p. 191.   [4] Cf. *Life Records*, p. 185.
[5] *Mod. Phil.*, i. 326–7; *Engl. Stud.*, xxxvi. 142.
[6] Koch believes the best conclusion to be that Chaucer was engaged on the *T. C.* in 1376, but did not finish it till several years later (*Engl. Stud.*, xxxvi. 140–1). Gower's reference implies somewhat widespread familiarity with it. It is not quite impossible, perhaps, that familiarity might have

Chaucer chronology so hangs together that I can hardly avoid briefly discussing the position of the translation of *Boethius*. For previous opinion I may refer to my introduction. It is hardly necessary to say that it must have been written before 1387, since it is constantly used in Usk's *Testament of Love*, which we have found reason for dating in that year. No other evidence on the date has ever been found except its relation to Chaucer's original works, in which the philosopher is frequently borrowed from,[1] especially and remarkably in *Troilus*. All the critics have therefore put it immediately before the *Troilus*, sometimes overlapping, a position which, since they all assign a rather late date to the latter, means that the date for the *Boethius* has ranged from 1373 to 1383, or even later, but has always been later than the first Italian journey. When we find that from the date of the *Troilus* to the end of Chaucer's life Boethius' views were never far from his thoughts, and influenced all his speculations and even his turns of phrase, and when we find that in the *Book of the Duchess* the influence is all second-hand, through Jean de Meun, we seem justified in concluding that (in 1369) he was not yet familiar with the Roman philosopher, and certainly that he had not translated his work. The extraordinary familiarity with it shown in the *Troilus* justifies the belief that, when he wrote that poem, he had already studied and translated it. But of course there is no reason in the world why this should not have been done before he went to Italy ; and since the *Troilus* itself is enough to fill the succeeding years, it very probably was. We may therefore with some confidence date the translation of *Boethius* about 1370–2.

CHAPTER II.

CERTAIN MINOR POEMS.

§ 1. *The House of Fame.*

I CAN hardly avoid briefly discussing the date of the *House of Fame*, since it has a necessary bearing on that of the *Troilus*. But

---

been gained for the poem in certain circles by author's readings and the like, before it was wholly finished. But Gower's remark is infinitely more naturally interpreted as implying that when it was made the completed poem was spreading abroad and exciting every one's interest. And the other arguments for an early date are not affected by this bare possibility.

[1] Skeat very conveniently gives the cases ; II. xxviii.–xxxvi.

I have little that is new or certain to offer, and prefer to leave a detailed discussion of the problems connected with it to one or two other writers at present engaged upon it. Three much-debated points, in particular, I shall dismiss in a few words. All attempts to read a subtle personal or general allegory into the poem seem to me worse than futile. Subjective allegory is "wholly alien from Chaucer's realistic, unspeculative genius" (to quote Professor Francis T. Palgrave).[1] Renascence allegory is sometimes obscure, inconsistent and ambiguous, because frequently a side-issue and used (as Professor Courthorpe says) for purposes of decoration; mediæval allegory is clear and intellectually consistent. An allegory which does not fairly well explain itself I think had best be ignored; and this no one can maintain the *House of Fame* does. As to the relations between the *House of Fame* and the *Divine Comedy*, it seems to me that while the relation of this poem to Dante is far closer than that of any other,[2] it is entirely improper to call it an imitation of the *Divine Comedy*, and unlikely that Chaucer foresaw it in that light. Therefore Chaucer's aspiration, at the end of the *Troilus*, "to make in som comedie" (V. 1788), there is no reason to take as alluding to Dante's title, nor any reason to see here an allusion to the *House of Fame*. If an absolutely sufficient explanation of the "comedie" passage is the desire for a cheerful subject,[3] what right have we to read anything else into it? Therefore, though the older interpretation would make in favour of my view that the *House of Fame* was written soon after the *Troilus*, all these points mentioned above may be rejected as chronological arguments.

My chief reason, of course, for dating *Fame* after *Troilus* is that the early date which I have assigned the latter makes it quite impossible to put between it and Chaucer's first Italian journey a poem so long and showing such familiarity with Dante as the *House of Fame*. There are other reasons also, and this order of things is the orthodox one, but I must first discuss the arguments

---

[1] *Nineteenth Century*, xxiv. 345.

[2] Besides the parallels pointed out by Rambeau (*Engl. Stud.*, iii. 209–268) and Cino Chiarini (*Di una imitazione inglese della D. C.*, Bari, 1902; reviewed by F. N. Robinson, *Journ. of Compar. Lit.*, N. Y., i. 292–7), 1063–81 may be suggested by the apparition, in the *Paradiso*, of the souls in the appropriate celestial spheres, though they are actually present in the Empyrean.

[3] Cf. Lydgate's way of speaking of Chaucer's poems — "My mayster Chaucer with his fressh commedies" (Skeat, III. 431); cf. also my article in *Modern Philology*, i. 318, which seems slightly to understate the matter; and Lowes, *Publ. Mod. Lang. Assoc.*, xx. 855.

of Professor Lowes,[1] the only writer who has defended the contrary opinion. His view is required by the fact that he believes the *House of Fame* to have preceded the *Legend of Ariadne*, the latter to have preceded the *Palamon*, and that to have preceded the *Troilus*. I have already tried to refute the last point, and shall later try to do the same for the second. It only remains to mention his auxiliary arguments.

He quotes the suggestion that *H. F.*, 1391-2 looks as if it had preceded *T. C.*, IV. 659-62. In attributing "partriches winges" to Fame, Chaucer clearly mistakes Virgil's "*pernicibus* alis" for "*perdicibus*"; while in the *Troilus* Fame flies through Troy, more properly, with "preste winges." But Lowes seems to me to deprive the argument of all weight by showing that the latter passage closely translates the *Filostrato*, which has "prestissim' ale." If Chaucer thought Virgil wrote "perdicibus" or "perdicum," in quoting the passage why should he think of "pernicibus" or of "prestissime" or of "preste"? Nor will it do, especially in considering mediæval literature, to assume that the incorrect impression always precedes the correct one.

Lowes seems also to believe that the fact that Chaucer here uses the 8-syllable couplet rather points to a time before the *Troilus*,[2] though he fully grants the skill with which Chaucer uses it. His argument is not quite clear; but, aside from the fact that he himself believes Chaucer to have returned to the 7-line stanza from the 10-syllable couplet, and that a somewhat similar return here is not surprising, he himself has also, with great justice, dwelt on the impropriety of drawing hard and fast lines as regards Chaucer's use of metres. I believe that many scholars, in their zeal for chronological evidence, have been too much inclined to make Chaucer's style vary rather with epoch than with subject. For this humorous and almost jaunty *tour de force*, what verse could be more appropriate than the 8-syllable couplet? Why did not Chaucer write Sir Thopas in heroic couplets?[3]

---

[1] *Publ. Mod. Lang. Assoc.*, xx. 819, 854-60.

[2] Professor Heath holds this view for the first part of the poem (*Globe Chaucer*, xliii.).

[3] One other argument for putting *Fame* before *Troilus* may be anticipated. The eagle in 630-40 commends Chaucer for his faithfulness to love:

> "ever-mo of love endytest,
> In honour of him and preysinges,
> And in his folkes furtheringes,
> And in hir matere al devysest,
> And noght him nor his folk despysest."

But to turn now to arguments in favour of putting the *House of Fame* after the *Troilus and Criseyde*. One reason, it seems to me, as ten Brink points out, is the appearance of "Lollius" (1468) among the historians of the Trojans. It seems idle to discuss further Chaucer's reason for attributing Boccaccio's works to this shadow of a name, but twice in the *Troilus* he does so.[1] If he invented an author named Lollius as a mere piece of mystification, he surely did not do so before he wrote the *Troilus;* and in any case it is certain that to his readers the reference would be quite unintelligible unless the *Troilus* was known to them. Another reason advanced by ten Brink[2] is that certain parallel passages in the two poems suggest that the *House of Fame* followed the *Troilus*. *H. F.* 1–65 is surely a reminiscence of *T. C.*, V. 358–85, rather than *vice versa ;* Pandarus' discourse on dreams grows out of the situation in the *Troilus*, and is partly drawn from the *Filostrato*, while the passage in the *House of Fame* is a mere prelude, and looks greatly like an expansion of the other.[3]

As to arguments based on the style and subject of the *House of Fame*, they seem to me void of conclusiveness; but they certainly do not make particularly in favour of an early date for the poem. Indeed, Lowes does not believe that they do, but rather devotes himself to disproving the contrary. The *House of Fame* may be, it is true, a poor piece of work, and show a lamentable falling off in design, substance

---

The *Troilus* is represented in the *Legend of Good Women* as utterly cynical and anti-amorous. Then does not this passage sound as if Chaucer had just been writing more conventional love-poetry rather than such a poem as this ? The answer to this possible objection is that the language of the God of Love in *L. G. W.* is greatly exaggerated for the purposes of the poem ; probably, as I shall try to show later, because Chaucer had been reproached for having represented the female sex in an unfavourable light. If any one wishes to see how far from cynicism Chaucer's *Troilus* really is, let him compare it with the Shaksperian treatment of the same theme. The faithfulness and sufferings of its hero are rather dwelt on than the pathetic inconstancy of its heroine ; and fully four-fifths of the poem are as amorous as possible. One little point more : at first sight one might expect a mention of Troilus and Criseyde among the seven faithless couples in 388–426 (cf. *P. F.*, 291 ; *Against Women Inconstant*, 16) ; but among these it is always the man who is faithless.

[1] I. 394 ; V. 1653. In the former case, of course, the fact that he really quotes a sonnet of Petrarch does not signify ; unless it strengthens the view that "Lollius" is a hoax.

[2] *Studien*, p. 121.

[3] It is natural that Pandarus should dwell only on ill causes of dreams ; in *H. F.* Chaucer does the same, though the dream which follows is pleasant. Cf. especially *H. F.* 30 with *T. C.* V. 360 (directly from Boccaccio), 15–17 with 362 and 371, 41–2 with 365–8, 21–22 with 369–70, 25 with 370.

and style from the *Troilus*.   Yet it has one quality which indicates
great maturity, especially in a mediæval poet—freedom.   It is not
merely that as regards source it is among the most independently-
imagined of Chaucer's narrative poems.   It shows a general freedom of self-expression, of informal and roguish humour, combined
with remarkable composure and poise ; in this poem he has left the
French house of bondage far behind.   This seems to me more suggestive of a late date than the want of symmetry and method in the
poem suggests an early one.   It was in the *Troilus*, it seems to me,
that Chaucer became emancipated.   Boccaccio both stimulated his
growth and was (if I may say so) the cocoon that protected it.   The
House of Fame followed his emancipation.   My conclusion is that
the necessity which I have found of following the usual view in
putting the *House of Fame* after the *Troilus* is an easy, plausible,
and well-supported necessity ; and that the auxiliary arguments in
favour of this view are much more convincing than those on the
opposite side.

On the exact date there is no very reliable evidence.   Ten Brink
suggests[1] that since it is Jupiter that sends the eagle to Chaucer, the
adventure may have taken place on a *dies Jovis*, a Thursday, which,
since it was December 10 (ll. 63, 111), indicates 1383.   The
year 1377 would do as well, by the way.   But from whom should
an eagle come if not from Jupiter, and who is more likely to send
a dream than the father of gods and men ?   And is not this a case
where such a subtlety would be lost if not announced ?   The
microscopic symbolism of Dante must not be attributed to Chaucer ;
and even Dante, where particularly subtle, commonly gives a hint.

The extreme limits are June, 1374, and February, 1385, as ten
Brink points out,[2] the dates when Chaucer received his custom-
house appointment and was relieved of his duties there by the
appointment of a deputy ; though he cannot be said to complain
of his clerical duties, it is clear that his life is one of routine office-
work (652–60).[3]

There is a somewhat striking parallel between the *House of Fame*
and Gower's *Mirour de l'Omme*.   Fame, according to Chaucer, is
quite unaccountable in giving or withholding her favours,

[1] *Studien*, pp. 150–1.   [2] *Ibid.*, 114.
[3] If we needed any proof that the work was published by 1387, we should
have it in the fact that it is extensively quoted in Thomas Usk's *Testament of
Love*, written doubtless in that year.   Cf. p. 24 above, and *Skeat*, VII. xx.,
xxvi. f. and notes.   I add *T. L.* I. 6, 198 = *H. F.* 2088–2109 ; II. 3,
111–15 = *H. F.* 269–72.

> " Right as hir suster, dame Fortune,
> Is wont to serven in comune " (1547–8).

She sends for Eolus to be her trumpeter :

> " And bid him bringe his clarioun,
> That is ful dyvers of his soun,
> And hit is cleped Clere Laude,
> With which he wont is to heraude
> Hem that me list y-preised be :
> And also bid him how that he
> Bringe his other clarioun,
> That highte Sclaundre in every toun,
> With which he wont is to diffame
> Hem that me list, and do hem shame " (1573–82).

Gower, after discoursing on emperors, Alexander especially, apostrophises Fortune, and continues :

> " Fortune, tu as deux ancelles
> Pour toy servir, si volent celles
> Plus q' arondelle vole au vent,
> Si portont de ta court novelles ;
> Mais s'au jour d'uy nous portent belles,
> Demein les changont laidement :
> L'une est que vole au noble gent,
> C'est Renomée que bell et gent
> D'onour les conte les favelles,
> Mais l'autre un poy plus asprement
> Se vole, et ad noun proprement
> Desfame, plaine de querelles.
> Cist duy par tout u sont volant
> Chascune entour son coll pendant
> Porte un grant corn, dont ton message
> Par les paiis s'en vont cornant.
> Mais entrechange nepourqant
> Sovent faisont de leur cornage,
> Car Renomé, q'ier vassellage
> Cornoit, huy change son langage,
> Et d'autre corn s'en vait sufflant,
> Q'est de misere et de hontage :
> Sique de toy puet estre sage
> Sur terre nul qui soit vivant " (22129–52).

No parallels to either passage have ever been pointed out, and the case for borrowing between the two poets is always especially strong because of their mutual relations. We know that Chaucer used the *Mirour* in the *Prologue* to the *Canterbury Tales*. As to which was the borrower here, the probability seems rather strong

that it was Gower. Like Chaucer, he dwells on the capriciousness
of the trumpeters, and departs from his original scheme and re-
lapses into Chaucer's by forgetting all about Desfame and making
Renomée use both horns ; and by making the transaction consist
not in conferring a good or ill lot in life, but in proclaiming good or
ill moral fame. Gower's last six lines or so distinctly suggest that
he was the borrower.

In Appendix A the date of the *Mirour* is discussed. This passage
I should date about 1379. Is there not, then, some evidence
here that the last part of *House of Fame* was somewhat known
by 1379? In that case it and the whole middle part of the *Mirour*
were in hand during the same time, and the *House of Fame*
was finished about two years after the *Troilus*, a highly probable
conclusion. This evidence should not be insisted on, but tentatively there is no objection to about 1379 as the date when the
House of Fame was completed.[1]

---

[1] We may notice then that there is no objection to believing it was
begun directly after the *Troilus* was finished, and (if we wish) that the date
1377 for its beginning is as well indicated by ten Brink's astrological method
as 1383. *H. F.* 130–9 seems to be the original of *K. T.*, 1955–66, which is
not from the *Teseide*, as Skeat erroneously says in his note on the former passage ; the source of the idea he shows may be in Albricus Philosophus,
Koeppel thinks (*Anglia*, xiv. 233–8) that the *Parliament of Fowls* shows
signs of borrowing from Boccaccio's *Amorosa Visione*. This may be doubted,
but the *House of Fame* certainly does, as is shown by him and also by Professor C. G. Child (*Mod. Lang. Notes*, x. 379–84). If one grants the influence on *P. F.*, since these are the only poems which do show this influence, a
date not far from 1381 is suggested for *H. F.* Professor Heath believes he
finds evidence that book III. was written some years after I. and II. (*Globe
Chaucer*, xliii., f. ; cf. Lowes, *P. M. L. A.*, xx. 860, n., who disposes of his
argument as to a change of tone.) Some of his arguments seem to me without value, but there are certainly some suggestions of an important change
of plan during the composition of the work. In the invocation at the beginning of book III. Chaucer seems to be more conscious than before, as
Heath points out, of the informality and sketchiness of his verse. But
besides this, in the first part of the poem, Fame has the Virgilian sense of
Rumour, and what Chaucer is to learn at her house is wholly about love
(673–99, 701–6, 713–24, 782–6, 817–21, 848–52, 879–83, 1025–83). At the
very beginning of book III. Fame acquires the mediæval and modern sense
of Renown (1136–9) ; that she is " goddesse of renoun and of fame " is expressed in 1312–3, 1320–3, 1405–6, and elsewhere, and this seems to be the
point of introducing the harpers, trumpeters, and minstrels (1197–1258).
The idea of Rumour does not recur till Chaucer has left the house of Fame
and come to the revolving twig-house (1920 ff.) ; here, in a somewhat *ex post
facto* way, Chaucer makes her a goddess of Fame in the sense of Rumour
(2110 ff.) ; love, which was to have been the subject of Chaucer's news, is
mentioned very casually in the house of Fame (1739–62) ; he does not seem
to care very much about it (1889), though there is promise of some love-tales
when the poem breaks off (2143). All this might be held to indicate a lapse
of time between books II. and III.—A few analogues to one of the folk-lore
elements in *H. F.* may be pointed out—the revolving-house. It is found in

§ 2. *The Parliament of Fowls.*

The greatest service which Dr. John Koch ever performed for Chaucer chronology was the identification, in 1877, of the eagles in the *Parliament of Fowls* with Anne of Bohemia and her various suitors.[1]   The date 1381-2 at which he arrived has been accepted, I believe, by every one who has written since that date, except Professor Hales,[2] and has proved to be one of the two pivotal and unshaken dates in the chronology of all Chaucer's poems.   It may be worth while, however, to give a few more particulars.

As early as the spring of 1377, when Richard was ten years old, at the wish of Edward III. there were conferences between French and English commissioners, of whom Chaucer himself was one, regarding a marriage between the heir-apparent and Princess Marie of France.[3]   After the death of his grandfather the young king's guardians continued the matrimonial negotiations.   Early in 1378 Chaucer was again a member of a commission for the same purpose.[4]   The negotiations, however, fell through.   Early in 1379, Bernabò Visconti, Lord of Milan, anxious to ally himself by marriage with royal houses, sent to Richard II. proposing a marriage between him and his own daughter Caterina;[5] and may we not conjecture, by the way, that this was not unconnected with the visit to his court a few months before, in 1378, of Chaucer,

---

the O.F. romance of *Perceval le Gallois* (tr. by S. Evans, *The High History of the Holy Graal*, J. M. Dent, 1898 ; vol. ii. p. 21) ; in two Welsh works and one Latin (John Rhŷs, *Studies in the Arthurian Legend*, Oxford, 1891 ; pp. 301, 302, 326) ; and in the eleventh-century *Voyage de Charlemagne* (ed. E. Koschwitz, 1880, in Foerster's *Altfranz. Bibl.*, vol. ii.; ll. 354-91).   In at least three of these cases, including the last, the turning-house is adorned with images which blow real trumpets, just as the house of Fame is in Chaucer (1193 ff.).

[1] See *Engl. Stud.*, i. 287-9 ; English version (enlarged) in *Essays on Chaucer* (Ch. Soc.), pp. 400-9.

[2] *Dict. Nat. Biogr.*, x. 164 ; *The Bibliographer*, i. 37-9.   Professor Hales argues that the poem is too poor to be so late.   Few persons, I think, will agree with him in either point.   He also argues, but unconvincingly, that Chaucer may have known Italian before his first journey to Italy.

[3] Froissart, in *Life Records* (Ch. Soc.), pp. 203-4.

[4] *Life Records*, pp. xxviii., 219, 230.

[5] On March 18, 1379, Richard appointed a commission to treat on the subject (Rymer's *Foedera*, London, 1709 ; vol. vii., 213).   See also Thomas Walsingham, II. 46, and Theodor Lindner, *Geschichte des deutschen Reiches unter K. Wenzel* (Braunschweig, 1875), i. 117 ; C. Höfler, *Anna von Luxemburg*, in *Denkschriften d. Wiener Akad.*, *Phil.-Hist. Cl.*, xx. 127-8.   The latter long and valuable essay (pp. 89-240) deals rather with Richard II., Wyclif and general contemporary history than particularly with Queen Anne.

who had so recently been a matrimonial commissioner, though
his ostensible purpose this time was military?[1] The advances
of the Visconti were finally rejected.   The first intercourse
between Richard and the King of the Romans, Wenceslas,
was on May 20, 1379, when the latter took the initiative in
treating with the former as to the recognition of Urban VI. as
the legitimate pope.[2]   About the same time, according to Froissart,[3]
there was much deliberation about Richard's marriage.   In June,
1380, commissioners were appointed to treat of a marriage between
Richard and Anne, Wenceslas' sister, and December 20 Richard
announced that he had chosen her.[4]   At Epiphany, 1381, pleni-
potentiaries met in Flanders to arrange the conditions ; January 23,
1381, Anne in her own person appointed ambassadors to treat ;
and early in May it was agreed that she should be received by
the English envoys on Michaelmas next.[5]   She actually landed
at Dover about December 18, 1381, and was received with great
enthusiasm ; the marriage took place January 14, 1382.[6]

It was peculiarly natural that poetic notice should have been
taken of all this by Chaucer, who had so recently been concerned
in at least one of the earlier matrimonial negotiations of Richard.
It is also interesting to observe how he manipulates the material.
Anne's two tentative childish betrothals, which occurred when she was
five and seven years old, are brought down and made contemporary
with that to Richard, for literary reasons and in order to compliment
him.   Chaucer's courtiership and tact go further, in representing the
affair as purely a matter of love on the part of the suitors, and the
choice as purely on the part of the *formel* eagle ; in reality, we can
hardly doubt that on the German side the choice was mainly on
the part of Anne's king-brother and empress-mother, and that the
chief exercise of choice was on the English side.   The *Parliament*

[1] *Life Records*, p. 218.
[2] Höfler, p. 127.
[3] *Chronicles*, tr. by Johnes (N.Y., n.d.), p. 258 ; vol. ii., ch. 43.
[4] See Lindner, I. 118 ; Höfler, 128-9.   She was born May 11, 1366, so
was a few months older than Richard.   According to Höfler, she had already
been twice betrothed ; once to Duke William of Baiern-Holland, in 1371 ; and
in 1373 to a son of the Landgraf Frederick of Thüringen.   See also F. M.
Pelzel, *Lebensgeschichte des Königs Wenzeslaus*, 1788, which is Koch's
authority and seems to be Höfler's.
[5] Höfler, 131-2 ; Lindner, 118-9 ; Walsingham, i. 452 ; Rymer's *Foedera*,
vii. 290, 295, 301.   Later, her coming was deferred (Rymer, 334 ; October 28).
[6] Höfler, 136, 156 ; Wallon, *Richard II.*, i. 116 ; cf. J. L. Lowes, *Mod.
Lang. Notes*, xix. 240-3.

of Fowls was certainly an excellent beginning for friendly relations between the middle-aged poet and the girl-queen.

Can we narrow the date down any further than Koch has done? Since the decision was not made till the very end of 1380, the early part of 1381 is the earliest probable date. But Pollard and Koch[1] choose the early summer of 1382. The former believes that " royal marriages were too likely to be broken off for poets to hymn them prematurely "; but is this true of betrothals of fairly mature people, which had advanced as far as this had done by the middle of 1381? The other argument is a highly ingenious one. Chaucer invokes Venus to aid him,

> " As wisly as I saw thee north-north-west,
> When I began my sweven for to wryte " (117–8).

The planet Venus obviously can never be in quite that quarter, so Koch feels the need of emendation to *west-north-west*, though all the MSS. read *north-north-west* (or *north-west*); the planet can be visible in such a position only in the summer or late spring, and with the assistance of two astronomers Koch finds that the only otherwise possible years which fulfil this condition are 1380 and 1382.[2] Since he believes the former to be too early, he accepts the latter. But it seems to me that any argument which depends on an emendation and a slightly cryptic interpretation is to be very doubtfully received, if at all; and there are arguments against this date which seem to me almost conclusive. The ending of the Parliament is a clever treatment of a somewhat flat situation : the other fowls mate, to be sure, and the poem ends with a beautiful lyric, but after all the main characters are left in suspense, "unto this yeer be doon." Chaucer missed a chance for a striking, complimentary and pompous climax, such as every mediæval reader would have expected. A date before the wedding seems to me so clearly suggested that, if regard must be paid to this astronomical evidence, 1380 would seem to me more likely than the summer of 1382, when the pair had been married nearly six months. As to the time of year, the selection of St. Valentine's Day was made so inevitable by the conditions of the fable that there is no justification

---

[1] *Ch. Primer*, pp. 50, 90 ; *Chronology*, p. 38.
[2] Any mathematically-accomplished student who wishes to attempt the task of verifying these results will find the astronomical wherewithal in *Astronomical Papers* (Washington, 1898), vol. vi., pp. 271–382.

for the assigning the poem to that date.[1] We can hardly come nearer the truth, therefore, than that 1381 is the probable date.[2]

---

[1] As late as May 6, 1381, Anne was expected to arrive by Michaelmas, September 29 ; but the wedding actually occurred just about a year from the original decision. This may possibly suggest that the poem was written in the latter part of the year. Mather's opinion agrees pretty well with mine; he puts the poem between Anne's arrival in England and the wedding, *i. e.*, between December 18 and January 14 (*Furnivall Miscellany*, p. 305, note).

[2] An attempt has been made by Dr. R. K. Root to prove that Chaucer revised *P. F.* Miss E. P. Hammond, in her valuable paper on *The Text of Chaucer's "Parlement of Fowles"* (*Decennial Publ. of Univ. of Chicago*, 1903, vol. vii., pp. 3–25 ; see pp. 8–9), gives fifty various readings by which the MSS. are divided into two main groups, which she calls A and C. She points out "the marked decrease in group divergences after line 250," and the fact that "the text of the A archetype was probably nearer to the ultimate original verbally." The latter point she bases partly on the fact that line 221 is nearer the Italian in A than in C. (She might have said the same of 238 ; see Skeat, I. 70, for the Italian.) Now Dr. Root, in his review of Miss Hammond's paper (*Journ. Germ. Phil.*, v. 189–93), supports the view that these divergences show deliberate corrections made in the ancestor of A, stopping at 250 ; he marks with asterisks most of the fifty various readings, which seem to him "reasonably clear examples of emendation." He asks "who is this skilful reviser ?"; and rather than believe that the falling off at line 250 in the number of changes is due to the fact that "an inventive and poetical" scribe passed on the task to "a sober, accurate" one, he would have it that Chaucer corrected at leisure this occasional poem which had perhaps been composed in a hurry. His *a priori* arguments seem hardly valuable. There is not the least evidence of haste in the ending of the poem, which can hardly be called abrupt, except in comparison with the dawdling start, and the character of which I have shown to be due probably to another cause. The appeal to Chaucer's revision of other poems is also unfortunate. I shall show later that the revision of *Kn. T.* was probably slight, and certainly was not a "complete reworking" ; and that that of the prologue to *L. G. W.* was due to a particular and unique cause ; and we shall see that Chaucer conspicuously neglected revision in some of the *Canterbury Tales.* I hope to show also elsewhere that the peculiarities of MS. Harl. 7334 of *C. T.*, which look infinitely more like author's revisions than those here, are probably due to a scribe. The genuine revisions in the *Troilus* make these various readings in the *Parliament of Fowls* look like the merest petty scribal variations. Of the 45 various readings before line 251 given by Miss Hammond and Dr. Root I find none that suggest to me revision by Chaucer, few or none that suggest anything like deliberate revision by any-body, and none that may not quite well be scribal blunders in C ; in the following 19 lines I think the C MSS. certainly are corrupt, and their readings cannot possibly be due to Chaucer.

3	69	135	221
5	70	178	229
43	72	194	234
55	107	209	238
64	110	215	

I grant cheerfully Dr. Root's postulate that Chaucer was a conscious literary artist ; that is why I do not think the C readings can be due to him.

CHAPTER III.

POEMS DEPENDENT ON THE *TESEIDE.*

§ 1. *The Palamon and Arcite : its Original Metre.*

THE *Teseide* of Boccaccio is used in four of Chaucer's extant poems : the *Knight's Tale* in the *Canterbury Tales* is a condensed adaptation of it ; the *Troilus* derives from it (as we have seen) a passage at the end (V. 1807–27) and a small one earlier (V. 1, 8–11) ; most of the description of the temple of Venus in the *Parliament of Fowls* (183–294) is from the *Teseide ;* and in *Anelida and Arcite* a good deal of the first seventy lines is from it.[1] It must also have formed the entire basis of a work of which all our certain knowledge is derived from the mention of it in the *Legend of Good Women* (Prol. F, 420–1 ; G, 408–9). Alcestis, it will be remembered, is mentioning those of Chaucer's works which speak well of women or of love, with a view to moderating the God of Love's indignation, and among these works, she says, is one on

> "al the love of Palamon and Arcyte
> Of Thebes, thogh the story is knowen lyte."

It is impossible that this can refer to the *Anelida*, a mere abortive fragment which never mentions Palamon, and in which Arcite appears not as a lover but as a roving and heartless flirt.

That the passage cannot refer to the *Knight's Tale* exactly as it stands is equally clear, since in places it is directly adapted to the *Canterbury Tales*, which can hardly have been fully conceived when the passage was written ; but there has been a strong tendency among scholars to regard the *Palamon and Arcite* as having been widely different from the *Tale*, though for this view the evidence has always been, to say the least, very insufficient. Tyrwhitt (I. clxxii.) suggested that " it is not impossible that at first it was a mere translation of the Theseida of Boccace." Other early Chaucer scholars, down to 1870, were divided in opinion.[2] It was ten Brink, in his distinguished *Chaucer Studien*,[3]

---

[1] It has lately been proved that the *Legend of Ariadne* shows the same influence ; but it hardly extends to verbal borrowings, and, I believe, comes through *Kn. T.* rather than directly (see J. L. Lowes, *Publ. Mod. Lang. Assoc.*, xx. 802–18, and pp. 122–5, below).

[2] On the views of Sandras, Hertzberg, Ebert and Kissner, see ten Brink's *Studien*, pp. 39–48.

[3] Münster, 1870 ; pp. 39–69.

who set up the highly ingenious theory that Chaucer not only largely altered the *Palamon* in adapting it to the Knight, but that he originally wrote it in the seven-line stanza ; and that the longer of the *Teseide* passages in the *Troilus* and those in the *Anelida* are fragments of this earlier version. The former he thinks (p. 61) may have been put in tentatively by Chaucer, or carelessly by his scribe, and the survival of the latter may be due to an attempt to preserve parts of the original poem which he did not require for the revised form of it (p. 56). The *Parliament of Fowls* he believes (p. 128) was written before the *Palamon* was finished, and therefore that the *Teseide* passage there was never in the *Palamon*.[1]

The almost universal acceptance which this theory has found must be due largely to the authority of the prominent scholar who proposed it. Dr. John Koch defended and developed it in an article in the first volume of the *Englische Studien ;*[2] he regarded the *Teseide* passages in all three of the stanzaic poems as part of the *débris* of a *Palamon and Arcite* deliberately broken up before the *Knight's Tale* was conceived. Ten Brink's theory, and usually Koch's modification of it, was accepted by Dr. Eugen Kölbing,[3] by Mr. A. W. Pollard,[4] by Professor Skeat,[5] and by many others, and to this day may be called the orthodox view.[6] Only three writers, to the best of my knowledge, have expressed themselves against it ; at the time of writing his introduction to the *Canterbury Tales* in the *Globe Chaucer*, Mr. Pollard had changed his views, and rejected the theory ;[7] Dr. F. J. Mather argues against it ;[8] and finally Professor J. L. Lowes agrees with them in rejecting it.[9]

---

[1] Cf. also his *Hist. Engl. Lit.* (London, 1893), ii. 63–72 (German version, Strassburg, 1893, ii. 65–74).
 [2] Pp. 249–93 (1877) ; translated in the Chaucer Society's *Essays*, 357–400 ; cf. also his *Chronology* (1890), p. 30.   [3] *Engl. Stud.*, ii. 528–32.
 [4] *Chaucer Primer* (London, 1893), pp. 76–7.
 [5] III. 389–90 ; cf. his *Prioress' Tale* (Oxford, 1893), pp. xvi.–xvii. But in 1900 he seems to have held it with less conviction (*Chaucer Canon*, p. 57 ; yet cf. p. 154 !).
 [6] Assumed, *e. g.*, by Koch (by implication, *Engl. Stud.*, xxxvi. 140), Dr. R. K. Root, *Journ. of Engl. and Germ. Philol.*, v. 193, and Professor W. P. Ker, *Essays on Mediæval Literature* (1905) p. 96.
 [7] Though not decisively (pp. xxvi.–xxvii.). He rejects it with horror in his *Knight's Tale* (1903), p. xviii., and in the 1903 edition of his *Primer*.
 [8] In his *Chaucer's Prologue* (1899), xvii.–xviii., and in a paper on *The Date of the Knight's Tale* in the *Furnivall Miscellany* (*An English Miscellany Presented, etc.*, 1901), pp. 301–13.
 [9] *Publ. Mod. Lang. Assoc.*, xx. 809 ; he refers to Mather, and to the present discussion (then of course unpublished).

The capital errors in the stanza-theory seem to me its enormous *a priori* improbability, and its needlessness.   The evidence for it, which might perhaps be respectable if the theory in itself were either plausible or serviceable, breaks down at once if these mistakes are recognized.   In fact, the longer one ruminates on the theory and its consequences, and the more carefully he examines the evidence, the more inconceivable does it become.   At the risk of being intricate and long-winded, it is worth while to try once and for all to destroy it.

Why should Chaucer have wished to transpose a poem of thousands of lines from stanzas into couplets?   The heroic couplet may be on the whole a finer and more useful form of verse than the rhyme-royal; but Chaucer was very far from abandoning the latter even after he had begun writing in the former, and for a poem like the *Knight's Tale* the stanza would have been perfectly suitable. Such a proceeding would be strange in any one, and would require strong evidence for its proof.   A writer might well wish to withdraw a short poem in order to develop it, but such destructive treatment as is postulated here is unparalleled, so far as I know, in ancient or modern times.   But Chaucer especially was not a man to be easily brought to spend trouble on a detailed and vexatious task to gain no great advantage; on the whole, he took his poetry with a lack of constant seriousness that is in part characteristic of the Middle Ages and in part of himself, and his willingness to leave things unfinished and unrevised (even where revision would seem imperative) may be proved by a mere reference to the *Anelida,* the *House of Fame,* the *Astrolabe,* the *Legend,* and the *Tales* of the *Shipman,* the *Squire,* and the *Second Nun.*   It is true that he revised the *Troilus* and the *Prologue* of the *Legend;* but these revisions must have been largely done by merely altering earlier MSS., and they left the metre untouched, which is the point at issue and makes all the difference.

The supporters of the stanza-theory of course have felt the need of discovering some motive for Chaucer's supposed procedure. Ten Brink's explanation is very curious—that the poem was published and failed (*Studien,* p. 64).   If the possibility of such a suggestion may ever be denied, it may here.   It is difficult to imagine the failure of anything in the Middle Ages, and as nearly as we can reconstruct in fancy the supposed stanza-poem out of the *Teseide,* the *Knight's Tale,* and the *Troilus,* it would have had an

interest, a sweetness and a brilliance which would have been likely
to make it one of the most successful of his works.   Moreover, the
changes which he would have made would have been far too subtle
to weigh much with a mediæval audience ; except a change in the
direction of brevity, which in the Middle Ages was not deemed
a virtue at all.   Again, those who have criticized the theory [1] have
raised the pertinent question whether, if the poem had circulated
enough to have failed, it could have been withdrawn so completely
that Chaucer would have cared to use it again in a new form,
and that no MS. of it should have come down to us.   This
explanation is to be rejected without qualification. [2]

Dr. Koch [3] gives a different reason for the suppression of the
earlier form of the poem.   He thinks it was never published, and
was transformed not because Chaucer preferred the couplet to the
stanza, but because it was written in the sentimental and pathetic
tone of the *Teseide* and was inharmonious with the maturity of the
Troilus, earlier than which he assumes that it was written.   His
only evidence for this belief is not a little curious—that there is no
other discoverable reason why Chaucer should have rejected the
earlier poem.   This explanation is more extraordinary, if possible,
than the other.   The *Teseide* is not sentimental, and neither are

[1] Pollard (*Globe Ch.*, xxvi.) ; Mather (*Miscellany*, 307) ; and even Koch,
who accepts it ; he thinks there was only one MS., which was never published
(*Engl. Stud.*, i. 281).   Ten Brink thinks there were only a few (p. 65).

[2] It has sometimes been thought to be countenanced by the fact that
Alcestis says "the story is knowen lyte."   This is not the view of ten
Brink, Koch, or Skeat, but even Tyrwhitt made the suggestion (I., clxxii.).
Another probably false explanation of her remark is offered by ten Brink
(p. 64) and Skeat (III. 306), and approved by Pollard (*Kn. T.*, xiv. f., note)—
that Chaucer is alluding to Boccaccio's statement in the introductory epistle
to Fiammetta or in the opening of the poem (I. 2), that it is an ancient
story known to few.   But this was not true after Boccaccio had written his
poem, still less if Chaucer's poem had been published.   Why should Alcestis
echo Boccaccio's language, and why should she say *though* ?   The remark
seems useless and senseless unless it means just one thing, that though she
wished to make the most of all Chaucer's creditable performances, she
doubted whether the fact that he had written such a poem had reached Love's
ears (or those of Chaucer's readers).   So thinks Koch (p. 282).   The most
natural reason for such a doubt is that the poem had not yet been published.
If it had been written only shortly before, as we shall later find other reasons
to believe (cf. pp. 76–80), there are several possible reasons for its still being
withheld, much the most probable of which is that it was not quite finished.
Any apparent strangeness in Alcestis' mention of an unpublished work is fully
explained by the fact that she is raking in everything she can find to
Chaucer's credit.   Is not this more likely than that she should mention a
work which Chaucer in vexation had been rending asunder ?   (Cf. Pollard,
Globe Ch., xxvi.)

[3] *Engl. Stud.*, i. 279–83.

the passages from it in these two poems. But Chaucer was not indisposed to sentiment at any time in his life, and the *Knight's Tale* itself contains affecting passages which are not in the *Teseide* (*e.g.*, 1281–1333).

Then if we cannot believe that Chaucer had the failure or the immaturity of the *Palamon and Arcite* to induce him to recast it in a new form, the plausibility of the stanza-theory is reduced to the utmost tenuity.

The stanza-theory is no more useful than it is probable. There is not the slightest difficulty in accounting for the presence of stanzas from the *Teseide* in the *Troilus*, the *Parliament*, and the *Anelida*. When Chaucer had become familiar with the poem, and before he had resolved to translate it, why should he not take from it a brilliant description for the second poem and an imposing opening for the third ? [1] And even though we may regard the addition of

---

[1] Pollard seems to feel some difficulty in the use of the same passages in the *Anelida* and the *Kn. T.* But there is none if the former was abandoned before the latter was begun.—Chaucer had been more or less familiar with the *Teseide* since shortly after his first journey to Italy. Besides the more important quotations discussed above, I am not the first to point out the borrowing of *T. C.*, V. 1, 8–11 from *Tes.*, IX. 1 and II. 1. *Parl. of F.*, 176–82 may be another borrowing. One more, quite as clear, is more curious. In three passages Chaucer shows that he understood Helicon to be a spring.

> "Ye sustren nyne eek, that by Elicone
> In hil Parnaso listen for to abyde" (*T. C.*, III. 1809–10).

(Rossetti, *T. C. and Fil.*, p. 169, attributes this to *Tes.*, I. 1, but he seems to be mistaken. He is clearly unjustified also in attributing the first part of the stanza to *Tes.*, I. 3.)

> "Be favorable eek, thou Polymnia,
> On Parnaso that, with thy sustres glade,
> By Elicon, not fer from Cirrea,
> Singest with vois memorial in the shade " (*Anelida*, 15–18).

(Cf. "Parnaso Cirreo," *Tes.*, VIII. 57. In the passage of the *Teseide* which Skeat mentions as the source of this, Boccaccio refers to the "monte Elicona," but the passage presently to be quoted must also have been in Chaucer's mind.)

> "And ye, me to endyte and ryme
> Helpeth, that on Parnaso dwelle
> By Elicon the clere welle " (*H. F.*, 520–2).

This has always been explained as due to Dante :

> "Or convien ch' Elicona per me versi " (*Purg.*, XXIX. 40).

(So Skeat, III. 254. Scartazzini adduces a somewhat similarly ambiguous line from Virgil (*Aen.*, VII. 641). Note that Chaucer always uses the Italian form for Parnassus; even in *Frankl. Prol.*, 721, though that passage is supposed to be imitated from Persius. Cf. p. 165 below.) A comparison of these passages with one in the *Teseide* will show, I think, that Boccaccio's error was the source of Chaucer's :

the passage in the *Troilus* as no great improvement, it is no easier to
explain it as a purple patch taken from an old garment.[1] New or
old, Chaucer would not have put it in unless he liked it, and it is
a poor compliment to him and a very forced conclusion to say that
he used the verses because he had them.[2] To infer a thousand
stanzas from two or even twenty seems very rash. The theory explains just one real difficulty. The *Prologue* to the *Legend of Good
Women* has usually been considered as Chaucer's first essay in the
heroic couplet,[3] and the God of Love's permission to " make the
metres "[4] of the legends as Chaucer pleased (F 562) has been interpreted as the proof of this and as the inauguration of a new metre,
new not only to Chaucer but to all English poetry. Frankly, this
is the most obvious explanation of a rather odd remark. But
other explanations are possible. When Chaucer wrote the *Prologue*[5]
he may have intended to use various metres in the legends, as later

---

" Vedeasi appresso superar Pitone,
E quindi sotto l'ombre graziöse
Sopra Parnaso presso all' Elicone
Fonte seder con le nove amorose
Muse, e cantar maestrevol canzone " (XI. 63).

The error was, first and last, somewhat widespread. It is explicit in the notes
to the Dante passage by Dante's own son and by another Florentine of the
fourteenth century (*Petri Allegherii* . . . *Commentarium*, p. 503 ; *Com-
mento* . . . *d'anonimo Fiorentino*, II. 475) ; perhaps both were misled by
Dante. Deschamps, in his *balade* to Chaucer (No. 285 ; *Soc. Anc. Textes*, ii.
139), exhorts the English poet to give him an authentic draught "de la fon-
taine Helye." The error occurs also in a letter of Boccaccio's (Corazzini, *Le
Lettere di Boccaccio*, p. 195). Later, Skelton makes the same blunder (*Philip
Sparrow*, l. 610), and so does Spenser (*Shep. Cal.*, April, 41–2) ; both, no
doubt, were misled by Chaucer. In spite of the frequency of the error,
Boccaccio was probably Chaucer's blind guide, as is partly shown by the fact
that they two only (except the Dante commentators) represent Parnassus and
Helicon as being close together. In reality they are some thirty miles apart.

[1] Cf. ten Brink, *Studien*, pp. 60–2.

[2] The idea that Chaucer used up fragments of cast-off poems in this manner
has been advanced in another connection—to explain the presence of bits
translated from Pope Innocent's *De Contemptu Mundi* in the *Man of Law's
Tale*. Ten Brink, who held this view in the case of the *Palamon*, in this
latter case rejected it with mockery (*Engl. Stud.*, xvii. 22). Dr. Emil Koeppel
characterizes Chaucer's supposed procedure by the gentle word " economy,"
and pleads ten Brink's own example for holding the view in the second case
(*ibid.*, p. 197; cf. Herrig's *Archiv*, lxxxiv. 410 ff.). Skeat holds the
" economy " view in both cases (cf. pp. 181–2 below).

[3] The very subversive views of Professor Lowes on this matter will be
discussed later (see p. 125 below).

[4] MSS. Pepys and Add. 9832 read " Make thy matere (the maters) of hem
as the lest (ye liste)."

[5] It will appear subsequently that version F (" B ") is the earlier ; the line
is omitted from the other version.

in the *Canterbury Tales*. Better still, if the *Palamon* was unfinished, and if it had not yet gone abroad among his readers, so far as they were concerned the decasyllabic couplet was a new metre, and it was by no means old to Chaucer. Therefore, though it is difficult not to regard this line as an allusion to a metrical innovation, the innovation need not have been made in this poem.[1]

This exhausts the *a priori* considerations, and it seems temperate to say that direct and weighty evidence would be required to over- throw the strong presumption against the stanza-theory. Such evidence does not exist; on the contrary, there is important evidence on the other side. And first let us examine the supposed *Palamon* passages in the three stanzaic poems for indications that they were not originally meant for their present positions, indica- tions which might be expected to appear on careful scrutiny. We may seek them, but we shall not find them. But suggestions that the two longest never occurred in any other English poems we shall find. Dr. Koch asks[2] why, if Chaucer took these passages directly from the *Teseide*, he did not more completely fuse them with their present surroundings. As to the passage in the *Troilus* (V. 1807– 27), whatever lack of harmony there may be between it and its context is entirely explained by the fact that it came in on the revision.[3] The passage in the *Anelida* is perfectly fused; if it seems to us partly superfluous, this may be because the poem is frag- mentary. As to that in the *Parliament*, it is difficult to imagine any fusion more perfect. In fact, examination will show, I think, that if Chaucer took these two longer passages from the *Palamon* he made a largely unnecessary revision of them.

In the *Anelida and Arcite* lines 1–21, 36–9, and 50–70 are (partially) from the *Teseide*, but ten Brink[4] regards the whole of the first ten stanzas (lines 1–70) as derived from the *Palamon*, with certain changes. Now the first stanza contains a very warlike invocation of Mars, Bellona and Pallas, though the *Teseide* (I. 3) invokes Mars, Venus and Cupid. It is not at all likely that the more martial invocation stood in the *Palamon*, which if anything

---

[1] So Dr. Mather suggests (*Furnivall Miscellany*, 312).
[2] *Engl. Stud.*, xxvii. 3.
[3] If the *Troilus* passage ever stood in the *Palamon*, Chaucer must have rewritten the first line (in the Italian, XI. 1, "Finito Arcita colei nominando, La qual nel mondo più che altro amava"); no other change would have been necessary, and there is no internal evidence for either opinion.
[4] Pp. 56–8.

must have been less warlike than the *Teseide ;*[1] the *Anelida*, on the
other hand, begins in a more warlike style than the *Knight's Tale*,
and since it breaks off with Anelida's vow of sacrifice and visit to
the temple of Mars, the indications are that it was to continue
in that style. Therefore the stanza must have been revised ; yet
needlessly, for love is prominent enough in the *Anelida* to render
Boccaccio's invocation perfectly suitable.[2] As far as this evidence
goes, then, it indicates that these stanzas were never in the *Palamon*.
It may possibly be thought that the fact that some of them have no
obvious connection with the story which follows suggests that they
were not written for it ; but if the poem had been continued a
connection presumably would have appeared, and we certainly
ought to abandon the idea that Chaucer put them in for no better
reason than to preserve them.[3]

The description of the temple of Venus in the *Parliament* (183-
294) is taken from a passage which stands later in the *Teseide* (VII.
51-66) than in the *Knight's Tale ;* the prayer which Palamon offers
just before the tournament becomes personified as a kind of nymph,
who, before presenting herself to the goddess, visits and inspects the
actual abode of Venus at Mount Cithaeron ; in the *Teseide* the
oratories built by Theseus are not described at all. The first-
personal verbs in the *Parliament* (" I saw," etc.) are therefore
third-personal (" vide," etc.) in the Italian. Ten Brink (p. 128)
thought this passage so thoroughly fitted to the *Parliament* that it
could not have stood in the *Palamon*. Koch,[4] however, disagreed,
and his view is accepted by Skeat (III. 390) ; it may therefore be

[1] As ten Brink admits (p. 62). *Kn. T.* omits the first book of the *Teseide*,
on the wars of Theseus with the Amazons. Ten Brink is not quite fair in
saying, " wir haben nicht den geringsten grund zur vermuthung, dasz der
kriegsgöttin in Anelida and Arcite ein gröszerer spielraum zugedacht war als
in Palamon and Arcite " (p. 57).
[2] Other changes which must have been made are in ll. 11, 21 (probably),
48-9, and 67-70, as ten Brink admits (pp. 57-8) ; and it must be remembered
that changing one line of a stanza may involve changing much more.
[3] Kölbing (*Engl. Stud.*, ii. 528-32) points out verbal resemblances between
A. A. and *Kn. T.* (to which I may add *A. A.* 182 = *Kn. T.* 2397), where
there is little or nothing in the *Teseide* to correspond, and thinks they indicate
that *Kn. T.* is done over from an earlier stanzaic version. But if *A. A.* was
written and abandoned before *Kn. T.* was begun, these reminiscences are
natural enough. Mather bases on *A. A.* an argument different from mine
against the stanza-theory (*Miscellany*, p. 307). He points out that " it stops
abruptly with the promise of a description of the temple of Mars, a description
which, according to the theory, lay ready in *Palamon*. It is strange that
Anelida should end where it required only a little copying to carry the story
scores of lines further." Cf. Pollard, *Primer*, p. 80.
[4] *Engl. Stud.*, i. 249, 261-2.

said that the prevalent form of the stanza-theory puts this passage in quite the same category as the other two.   Now I think it may be shown by something like a *reductio ad absurdum* that if it ever was in the *Palamon* it must have been very much more extensively rewritten than Dr. Koch thinks, yet that this rewriting was largely needless ; and therefore that it never was in the *Palamon*.

I agree with him that Chaucer is not at all likely to have adopted in the *Palamon* what he calls " diese etwas gezwungene und unnatürliche darstellungsweise " (p. 261) of personifying the prayers and conducting them to the actual dwellings of the deities. When we consider what liberties Chaucer takes with the *Filostrato* and the *Teseide*, how his treatment of his sources always tends to the rational and the simple, and how his sense of the incongruous was as much greater than Boccaccio's as his reverence for precedent was less, it becomes allowable to disbelieve that Chaucer would have adopted so frigid a conceit.   Moreover, in the description of the temple of Mars in the *Knight's Tale*, which belongs by hypothesis in the same category, there is not the slightest indication that from the first he did not appropriate Boccaccio's description to the shrine erected by Theseus in his theatre ; yet this passage is one of the few longer ones which follow the *Teseide* closely, with many lines almost literally translated, a fact which certainly makes against the supposition that such changes were made as would be involved in getting rid of the personified prayer.   Therefore the indications are that in neither case was it personified.   Finally, certain phrases in the description in the *Parliament* are distinctly inconsistent with the personification.   We should have to believe that Chaucer attributed to the young woman who represents the prayer strong views on the subject of decorum, or else pleasure in beholding the thinly-veiled beauties of Venus :

> " The remenant wel kevered to my pay
> Right with a subtil kerchef of Valence,
> Ther was no thikker cloth of no defence " (271–3).[1]

After describing Venus, the poet says (departing from his original),

> " thus I leet hir lye,
> And ferther in the temple I gan espye " (279–80),

singular conduct on the part of a prayer addressed to the goddess ;

---

[1] " E l'altra parte d'una
Veste tanto sottil si ricopria,
Che quasi nulla appena nascondia " (*Tes.* VII. 65).

he then goes on with a part of the description which in the *Teseide*
immediately precedes the description of the goddess. This change
of order has no apparent motive, and certainly would not have been
made if the prayer figured in the account. It is not legitimate
to plead that in fitting the stanzas to the *Parliament* Chaucer made
such gratuitous alterations as these in a passage that would have
served perfectly well unaltered. It seems certain, then, that the
prayers were not personified in the supposed stanzaic *Palamon*.

Yet if this passage was taken from that poem it is equally clear
from internal evidence that the prayers were personified. Unless
very extensive changes have been made, *some one* filled a prominent
part in the description, and in a perfectly impersonal romance who
could it have been if not the prayer? In the 112 lines such
expressions as "herde I," "saw I," occur no less than fourteen
times; and, what is still more striking, five phrases imply motion
on the part of the observer.[1]

Dr. Koch thinks the former set of phrases are entirely paralleled
in such phrases as "ther saw I," which occur five times in the
84 lines of the temple of Mars passage in the *Knight's Tale*,
and five times in the 38 lines of the temple of Diana passage.
But if we take them in conjunction with the indications of motion
(entirely absent from the passages in the *Tale*), it becomes clear
that we have all the difference between a vividness due to poetic
transport and a deliberate case of what rhetoricians sometimes call
description by means of narrative. In order to make this quite
unmistakable it is necessary to pause to account for these phrases
in the *Tale*. Koch thinks that their absence[2] from the temple of
Venus passage in the *Tale*, and their presence in the Mars and
Diana passages, and in the temple of Venus passage in the *Parliament*, shows that the latter three passages are all derived from the
Palamon. I think a perfectly satisfactory explanation is the
following. Having written an original[3] description of the temple

---

[1] "Ther I fond" (242), "as I wente" (253), "fond I" (261), "thus I leet
hir lye" (279), "ferther in the temple I gan espye" (280). All but the third
contain rhyme-words.

[2] He points out, however, "maystow se" (1918 ; see Koch, 260). Mather
(*Miscellany*, 304) suggests that Chaucer may have been a poor enough Italian
scholar to mistake *vide* for *vidi*. This explanation will hardly do, for no one
could have failed to see that the observer of the temple was the personified
prayer. He also makes the suggestion, given above, that the use of the first
person is merely a licence for the sake of vividness.

[3] For no other reason that I can conceive than that he had already written
P. F. ; see p. 78 below.

of Venus for the *Palamon* (which I believe was substantially identical with the *Knight's Tale*), he returned to the *Teseide* for the temple of Mars, which in the *Tale* comes next.   In reading the account in Boccaccio he felt the vivid effect of the repeated *vide*, and by a licence not unusual in poetic description he reproduced it, of course by verbs of the first person ; and then carried it through his original account of the temple of Diana, which follows.   It appears, therefore, that the conditions in the *Tale* and in the *Parliament* are not parallel.

So we have accomplished a *reductio ad absurdum.* If the description in the *Parliament of Fowls* has not been considerably altered from its original form, the prayer at first must have been personified and had the experiences indicated. But both probability (as Koch admits), and evidence, oppose the idea that the prayer was personified. Therefore if this passage occurred in the *Palamon* it must have been considerably altered before it was put into the *Parliament.* But every one of the alterations was unnecessary—whether or not the personified prayer appeared in the first form, the passage would have served quite well unchanged (except for the person of the verbs) ; and, considering the extent to which Chaucer must have been affected by the sin of Accidia while he was using up fragments of this devoted poem, a sin in reality not unknown to him, it is very unlikely that he would have made these alterations. Some of them would have involved more trouble than recasting couplets into stanzas.

The upshot of our examination of the supposed *Palamon* passages in the *Troilus*, the *Anelida* and the *Parliament* is about this :— There is not a shred of evidence that a single line of them ever appeared in an earlier English poem, and there is strong evidence that the two longest of them did not. If this conclusion does not destroy the stanza-theory, at the very least it disposes of the conjecture that there may be any evidence in these passages to favour it.   Now since these passages are practically all the evidence which the theory has, and considering the enormous burden of proof which rests upon its advocates, it is not difficult to see where we are coming out.

But there is a whole set of evidence yet to be examined, which is to be derived from a minute comparison of the *Knight's Tale* and the *Teseide*, with a view to discovering if there is anything to show whether an English poem in stanzas intervened.   It is

necessary to begin with three postulates, supposing the *Palamon
and Arcite* to have been written in stanzas. The first is that
Chaucer used the *Palamon* as the basis for the *Knight's Tale*,
and did not produce a quite new poem directly from the
Italian; probably every one would grant this without cavil,
as Kölbing,[1] ten Brink,[2] and Koch[3] do. The second postulate is that though it is not impossible that Chaucer might once
in a while refer again to the *Teseide*, it is illegitimate to suppose
that he did do so often or in any particular case, for once he had
drawn his material from the *Teseide* and put his own interpretation
on it, there is no reason why he should regard Boccaccio's form of
the story, or keep it open before him during the revision.
Finally it is ten Brink's opinion[4] that in general "berechtigen uns
die fragmente [des angeblichen stanzäischen Palamon und Arcite]
wohl zu der annahme, dasz hinsichtlich der treue der übersetzung
und des äusseren umfanges derselben zwischen Palamon und Arcite
und der Teseide ein ganz ähnliches Verhältnisz bestanden habe wie
rwischen Troylus und Cryseyde und dem Filostrato." If the stanza-
theory is correct, this is an opinion which it is quite improper to
deny,[5] and it has always been granted. That it is therefore
entirely fair to use the *Troilus* as a test for some of the evidence
derived from comparing the *Knight's Tale* and the *Teseide* is my
third postulate. It is highly important that these postulates
should be clearly seen to be a necessary consequence of the
stanza-theory, for it is by their means that I shall attempt to
reduce it to an absurdity—to show that if they are a necessary
consequence of it, the theory is wrong.

This evidence will show that there are no vestiges of stanzaic
structure in the *Knight's Tale* at points where, if the theory is
correct, it must necessarily appear on careful scrutiny. The
evidence may be divided for convenience into three classes : that
which deals with the actual number of lines taken from the
Teseide ; that which deals with possible traces of the beginning
and end of the stanza; and that with passages where the *Tale*
closely follows the *Teseide* for at least several lines. For the first
two classes it is necessary to have a table of the lines in the *Tale*

---

[1] *Engl. Stud.*, ii. 529–31.   [2] *Studien*, pp. 56, 61, 65.
[3] *Engl. Stud.*, i. 277–8.   [4] *Studien*, p. 63.
[5] Except that we can hardly suppose the *Teseide* to have been expanded as
much as the *Filostrato* was. Ten Brink cannot have meant that.

derived from the *Teseide*, arranged according to the position in the Italian stanza of the lines from which they are translated. Such a table will be found in Appendix B.[1]

Much of my evidence is based on the following considerations. The last four lines of a seven-line stanza without change form two couplets, and a whole stanza may be resolved into couplets by the omission of the 2nd line, and perhaps some adaptation of the 1st and 3rd. This statement may easily be tested ; of the 16 *Teseide* stanzas in the *Parliament of Fowls*, such a transformation would be perfectly easy in about 10, and of the 156 stanzas in book I. of the *Troilus* it would be perfectly easy in about 86. I include here only cases where the 2nd line is easily dispensable in sense as well as form. There is no reason to believe the supposed stanzaic *Palamon* to have been so much longer than the *Knight's Tale* that Chaucer must have generally used a more heroic treatment, and could not have used this device most of the time ; the *Teseide* is a very profuse poem without vivid psychological interest, and it is quite certain that from the first he would have greatly condensed it. And my representation of Chaucer's procedure should not be regarded as crude or trivial. No poet can escape the technical conditions of his art; no poet would disdain a simple method of preserving his own good work. Especially would a sometimes impatient and easily-satisfied poet like Chaucer, who had a particular fondness for his own words,[2] have welcomed a device which would save time and trouble, and ensure the preservation of bits of this unhappy poem for which he would still cherish a certain tenderness.[3] But whether, thus at close quarters, the stanza-theory begins to look absurd, let others decide.

First we will consider the frequency with which the various lines of the Italian stanza occur in the *Knight's Tale*.[4] Here the important premise must be made that, when *ottave rime* are translated into seven-line stanzas, in a general way an Italian line passes

[1] Pp. 226–230 below. Book I. of the *Troilus*, which contains 1092 lines, is enough for purposes of comparison, for it follows the *Filostrato* closely.

[2] As is shown by the very large number of phrases which appear in his works more than once.

[3] There is a curious illustration of the ease with which the opposite change can be made (from couplets into stanzas) in the spurious prologue to the *Franklin's Tale*, composed out of the true *Merchant's Epilogue* and *Squire's Prologue* (see *Six-Text*, Introd., p. 54).

[4] The total number of lines due to the Italian is valueless as evidence. According to my count, it is 498 out of 2250 (22%); in the *Troilus* (according to Rossetti, p. iii.) it is 2583 out of 8246 (31%).

over into a line of the same position in an English stanza; in the *Troilus*, book I., $\frac{3}{4}$ of the Italian 8th lines translated (35 out of 47) correspond to English 7th lines, $\frac{7}{8}$ of the Italian 2nd lines (56 out of 64) correspond to English 2nd lines, and $\frac{13}{14}$ of the Italian 1st lines (64 out of 69) correspond to English 1st lines. A cursory inspection of Mr. Rossetti's edition of the *Troilus* and the *Filostrato* in parallel columns also will show at once that the first and second parts of an Italian stanza correspond respectively to the first and second parts of an English stanza. Now by hypothesis the same conditions should hold for the stanzaic *Palamon and Arcite*.

The 504 Italian lines which appear in the *Knight's Tale* are distributed in the Italian stanza as follows:

1st lines, 98 (19%).		5th lines, 56 (11%).
2nd „ 80 (16%).		6th „ 44 (9%).
3rd „ 69 (14%).		7th „ 55 (11%).
4th „ 47 (9%).		8th „ 55 (11%).

For the *Troilus* the figures are these:

1st lines, 69 (16%).	5th lines, 47 (11%).
2nd „ 64 (15%).	6th „ 45 (10%).
3rd „ 59 (14%).	7th „ 53 (12%).
4th „ 51 (12%).	8th „ 47 (11%).

In degree of frequency the eight lines stand in the following order:

> *Knight's Tale* 1, 2, 3, 5, 7–8, 4, 6;
> *Troilus and Criseyde* . . . . 1, 2, 3, 7, 4, 8–5, 6.

The closeness with which these results agree is obvious; but so far from favouring the stanza-theory, this fact makes strongly in favour of the view that the *Tale* was made directly from the *Teseide*. Here I take issue with Dr. Koch.[1] I maintain that, if

---

[1] Who says (*Engl. Stud.*, I. 277–8): "Die betreffenden stanzen der Teseide sind in der Knightes Tale gerade so behandelt wie in den siebenzeiligen strophen, in denen er Boccaccio's gedichte übersetzt hat. Er überträgt nämlich möglichst genau die ersten zeilen jeder stanze—insoweit er sich überhaupt an sein vorbild halten will—kann dies aber (einmal wegen der schwierigkeit des versmasses; zweitens, weil er ja 8 zeilen des originals in 7 eigene zusammenzieht) nicht immer für den rest durchführen, und lässt daher häufig die mitte weg, um dann öfter wieder die letzten zeilen wörtlicher wieder zu geben. Genau diese behandlungsweise finden wir in den stellen der Kn. T., welche mit strophen der Teseide correspondiren. In den von mir citirten versen ergibt sich das verhältniss der nach art der siebenzeiligen strophen bearbeiteten stanzen zu denen, deren anfang unberücksichtigt geblieben ist etwa = 5 : 1; ganz so im Troilus, soweit er von Mr. Rossetti mit dem Filostrato verglichen ist." Dr. Koch clearly misinterprets his facts.

Chaucer wished to translate a whole Italian stanza, it would make little difference whether he was putting it into stanzas or couplets, at least so far as concerns the presence in the English version of this or that Italian line.   In either case, a falling off in frequency of occurrence is most natural at the middle of the stanza, for that is where the diffuseness of the *ottava rima* especially shows itself; not only are the beginning and end of the stanza the strategic points,[1] but the freshness of the rhymes there gives the poet a freedom which he has not in the 4th, 5th, and 6th lines.   Therefore the agreement between the two poems does not *favour* the stanza-theory.

But further examination of these lists I think will reveal evidence which is absolutely destructive of the stanza-theory.   We have seen that the last four lines of a 7-line stanza are much easier to take over into a couplet-poem than the first three, and also that in general the last part of an Italian stanza corresponds to that of an English stanza. If the stanza-theory is correct we ought to find in the *Knight's Tale* the Italian lines 5–8 as compared with lines 1–4 much better repre- sented than they are in the *Troilus*.   But the opposite is the case ; in the *Troilus* they are 192 to 243 (44%), and in the *Tale* 210 to 294 (only 42%).

Most important of all, since it has been shown how easily and how often a 7-line stanza may be transformed into couplets by omitting the second line, it would be very surprising if this line should not suffer considerably during the transformation ; a fact which would be instantly betrayed in the *Knight's Tale* by a falling off in the number of Italian 2nd lines represented, about $\frac{7}{8}$ of which we have inferred would have passed over into 2nd lines in the English stanzas.   Yet on consulting the list we see not only that the Italian 2nd lines are the most numerous of all, except the 1st, but also that their percentage of the whole number of Italian lines represented is higher than in the *Troilus* (16% to 15%).   Therefore the very closeness with which the figures for the *Knight's Tale* agree with those for the *Troilus* is a very strong argument against the stanza-theory.   If our postulates are sound, I think it disproves it.

I come now to the lines which are closely translated, and there- fore must have stood practically the same in the *Palamon :*

---

[1] The Italian final couplet has a summary, epigrammatic character that tends to preserve it ; the very rhymes are sometimes carried over into the *K. T.* (1625–6, 2371–2, 2445–6).

1st lines, 26 (27%).		5th lines,	7 (7%).
2nd „ 20 (21%).		6th „	4 (4%).
3rd „ 8 (8%).		7th „	17 (18%).
4th „ 9 (9%).		8th „	5 (5%).

The testimony of these figures is the same as that of the others. Though on the stanza-theory we should expect lines 5–8 to be much more numerous than 1–4, there are only 33 of them against 63 (34%); and Italian 2nd lines are more fully represented than any others except the 1st.[1]

The second class of evidence deals with possible traces of the beginnings and ends of the original stanzas. In the nature of the case, as will appear, it is less satisfactory and conclusive than that which has just been presented. But it bears out the other, and I trust will make my refutation of the stanza-theory more well-rounded.[2]

One characteristic of Chaucer's treatment of the couplet is the frequency with which a strong pause, marking a striking period in the thought, breaks the couplet at the end of the 1st line. If the stanza-theory is correct, we should find this characteristic rather unusual in the *Knight's Tale;* since in a stanzaic poem, as one may see by a glance at the *Troilus,* practically all such pauses come at the ends of stanzas, and we have seen reason to believe that the last four lines of the stanzas would in large measure have been carried over into the *Tale* unchanged. Therefore there should be a very striking contrast between the *Knight's Tale* and Chaucer's other poems in the heroic couplet as regards this break in the middle. Below will be found a table in which the comparison is

---

[1] Another point connected with these may be mentioned here. The omission of the 2nd line of an English stanza would leave lines 1 and 3 (perhaps slightly altered) as a couplet; this ought in many cases to be betrayed by couplets in the *Knight's Tale* formed out of Italian 1st and 3rd lines. This actually happens four times out of a possible 80 or so. (See 1893–4, 2011–2, 2393–4, 2831–2. Four other cases are not to be counted, because the Italian 2nd line is fully included in one or both of the English lines.) But not only is it natural enough in any case to find this happening occasionally, but in every one of these passages a good reason is apparent; the Italian 2nd line is unimportant, it sometimes partly survives in one of the English lines, and often the whole translation is exceedingly distant.

[2] It may perhaps be asked if older stanzas show at all by the presence in the *Tale* of blocks of 6 or 8 lines; there are not enough such to be significant. Another similar matter may be mentioned. Four times in the 1092 lines of *T. C.,* I., one Italian stanza is expanded into two English; in the *Tale* (more than twice as long) one Italian stanza makes 11 or 12 lines only three times, always where Chaucer is very closely following his original. This is not offered as evidence, but merely to dispose of a possible conjecture.

made.   For the pauses which come at the end of the first line, and for those at the end of the couplet, I have borrowed from Shak-sperian metrical criticism the terms "run-on" and "end-stop."   I have made two lists, one of which includes all the breaks in the sense which seem really considerable, the other (in order to secure as much objectivity as possible) only the ends of paragraphs.[1] The poems selected for comparison are as miscellaneous as possible in character and probable date.[2]

	ALL BREAKS IN SENSE.		PARAGRAPHS.	
	Run-on.	End-stop.	Run-on.	End-stop.
Squire's Tale	·63	·37	·50	·50
Sumner's Tale ...	·58	·42	·56	·44
Legend of G. W. ...	·51	·49	·47	·53
L. G. W., Prol. G. (A)...	·49	·51	·59	·41
Pard. Prol. and Tale ...	·46	·54	·39	·61
L. G. W., Prol. F. (B)...	·44	·56	·46	·54
Knight's Tale	·40	·60	·30	·70
Physician's Tale ...	·39	·61	·25	·75
Wife of Bath's Tale ...	·34	·66	·31	·69
C. T. Prologue	·31	·69	·31	·69
Franklin's Tale... ...	·27	·73	·17	·83
Wife of Bath's Prol. ...	·26	·74	·21	·79

[1] As marked in Skeat's small edition; all his paragraphing is included in the second case, but a few cases in which he seemed to paragraph wrongly are disregarded in the first.

[2] Some time after these tables were compiled, Mr. Pollard expressed the hope that some such study might be made (*Knight's Tale*, 1903, p. xx.). But he will see that the prospect is not very encouraging for "metrical tests" of chronology.   Cf. also Lowes, *Publ. Mod. Lang. Assoc.*, xx. 811–12. It will be easily seen by looking at these figures that they cannot be used, as at first one might have fancied, as a test of dates.   *Sq. T.* and *Sumn. T.* on the one hand, and *W. B. P.* and *Frankl. T.* on the other, all of which are certainly late, stand at opposite ends of the list, and the *Legend of Good Women* and the *Prol.* of the *C. T.*, which I am convinced are nearly contem-poraneous, are also a long way apart.   In Chaucer's case there is not the same reason as in Shakspere's for a steady metrical development.   Nor does the character of the poem seem to determine the proportion.   It seemed at first as if it might, for in *Pard. T.* and *C. T. Prol.*, when the actual narrative begins and the more epigrammatic descriptions and moralizings stop, the propor-tion of run-on couplets rises.   But this is at once outweighed when we notice that *W. B. P.*, the most colloquial poem Chaucer ever wrote, is quite at the bottom of the list.   In *Romania*, xxiii. 1–35, there is an important article by Paul Meyer which deals with this fracture in the Old French couplet.   According to him, Chrétien de Troyes was the first important poet to break up the couplet in this way, and it was largely due to his influence that this great improvement in narrative verse became common.

It may seem at first as if this table contained but little evidence against the stanza-theory ; but certainly the position of the *Knight's Tale* is very far from being as peculiar as that theory requires.   In the all-breaks list (the more important) it is the seventh of twelve, with 40% of run-on couplets as against extremes of 63% and 26% ; in the paragraphs list it is ninth of twelve, with 30% as against 59% and 17%.   It is less than the average to the extent of 8% in the latter list and 2% in the former.   When, once more, we consider the conditions under which the transformation from stanzas into couplets would naturally have taken place, this is certainly a considerable argument against the stanza-theory.

We may look at this matter from the converse side, and inquire whether the English representatives of Italian 1st and 8th lines are more apt than we should otherwise expect to follow or precede (respectively) a full stop.   It will be remembered that, to judge from the *Troilus*, $\frac{13}{14}$ and $\frac{3}{4}$ of these two lines (respectively) would have been the first and last in English stanzas.   In the *Troilus*, book I., only three stanzas do not end in a full stop (numbers 25, 104, 106).   It would be rather strange, therefore, if in a couplet poem reconstructed from a stanzaic a very large majority of these lines did not show this evidence of their earlier history. On the other hand, in a poem taken directly from one in the *ottava rima*, unless it were condensed more and quite otherwise than the *Knight's Tale* is, we should expect full-stops before and after these lines (respectively) considerably oftener than not, simply because the first and last lines of the Italian stanza introduce and conclude periods in the thought.   The actual figures are these :   of the representatives of Italian 1st lines, 53 follow a full stop and 45 do not ; of the representatives of Italian 8th lines, 30 precede a full stop and 25 do not.   Considering the ease with which the last part of the stanza could have been transferred unchanged, these latter figures are amazing if the stanza-theory is right.   In both cases the figures make distinctly against it.

Just one more such test may be given.   Since the Italian first and last lines would almost always have become the first and last (respectively) in the English stanza, and since the last in an English stanza is the second in a couplet, and the first follows a complete couplet, and, therefore, would naturally form the first line in the next (if the stanzas were transformed as we have supposed), the representatives in the *Knight's Tale* of Italian 1st and 8th lines ought to be almost always respectively the first and second in their couplets. If the stanza-theory is incorrect, we should expect this to be so usually, for the reasons indicated in the last paragraph; but to nothing like the same extent, since in a translation into couplets the Italian stanza is not transformed into a similar unit. A quick way of ascertaining how often this is the case is to notice when the numbers of representatives of Italian 1st lines are odd, and those of representatives of Italian 8th lines are even.[1] For the first line the figures are 33 even to 65 odd, and for the last 14 odd to 41 even. These figures are pretty much what we should expect if the stanza-theory is not correct, and harmonize well with the results of the last test.

So much for attempts at finding the supposed original stanzas in outline; they certainly have not been successful. It is apparent that in the nature of the case this class of evidence could not be as striking as the first, but it has added some little weight to the negative argument.[2]

For the third class of evidence we may examine passages several lines long which are close to the Italian and therefore would have occurred, in much the same shape, in the *Palamon and Arcite*. Here, if anywhere, the supposed stanzaic form ought not to escape careful scrutiny and comparison with the original. First, I give the one passage which comes nearest to harmonizing with the stanza-theory, and then two or three which most strongly refute it. In a note I shall refer to about twenty more such cases, almost all of which are hostile to the theory.

And if ye wol nat so, my lady swete,	E se t'è grave ciò ch'io ti dimando
Than praye I thee, to-morwe with a spere	Far, fa'che tu nel teatro la spada
That Arcita me thurgh the herte bere;	Primaia prendi, ed al mio cor forando,
	Costrigni che lo spirto fuor ne vada
	Con ogni vita il campo insanguinando;
	Chè cotal morte troppo più m' aggrada,
Thanne rekke I noght, whan I have lost my lyf,	Chè non sarebbe senza lei la vita,
Though that Arcite winne hir to his wyf (2254-8).	Vedendola non mia, ma sì d'Arcita (VII. 49).

---

[1] If an Italian line is rendered by more than one English line, in the one case of course we should look at the first English line and in the other at the last.

[2] One or two attempts, hardly worth describing in detail, to find vestiges of the rhyme-scheme of the *ottava rima* end in the same way.

These five lines form a unit, and might easily have been transformed from a stanza by the omission of two lines, before and
after the third ; yet it is difficult to fancy what the first of these
two lines could have been.[1]

The following three passages are strongly opposed to the stanza-
theory :

For from his feet up to his brest was
come
The cold of deeth, that hadde him
overcome.
And yet more-over, in his armes two
The vital strengthe is lost, and al
ago.
Only the intellect, with-outen more,
That dwelled in his herte syk and
sore,
Gan faillen, when the herte felte
deeth,
Dusked his eyen two, and failled
breeth (2799-2806).

La quale in ciascun membro era
venuta
Da' piedi in su, venendo verso 'l
petto,
Ed ancor nelle braccia era perduta
La vital forza ; sol nello intelletto

E nel cuore era ancora sostenuta
La poca vita, ma già sì ristretto

Eragli 'l tristo cor del mortal gelo,

Che agli occhi fe' subitamente velo
(X. 111).

Obviously this passage, if any, would have formed a stanza, but
so far from its first part showing any signs of alteration, it is rather
nearer the original than the latter part.

And after this, Theseus hath y-sent
After a bere, and it al over-spradde
With cloth of gold, the richest that
he hadde.
And of the same suyte he cladde
Arcite ;
Upon his hondes hadde he gloves
whyte ;
Eek on his heed a croune of laurer
grene,
And in his hond a swerd ful bright
and kene.
He leyde him bare the visage, on the
bere,
Therwith he weep that pitee was to
here (2870-8).

El fece poi un feretro venire
Reale a sè davanti, e tosto fello
D'un drappo ad or bellissimo fornire,

E similmente ancor fece di quello

Il morto Arcita tutto rivestire,

E poi il fece a giacer porre in ello

Incoronato di frondi d'alloro,

Con ricco nastro rilegate d'oro
(XI. 15).

The case here is exactly the same. Considering that there are
scarcely any other passages which correspond so nicely to an Italian
stanza, these two are striking.

Duk Theseus, with al his bisy cure,
Caste now wher that the sepulture
Of good Arcite may best y-maked be,
And eek most honurable in his de-
gree.

Quinci Teseo con sollecita cura
Con seco cerca per solenne onore
Fare ad Arcita nella sepoltura ;
Nè da ciò 'l trasse angoscia nè
dolore,

---

[1] The other cases least inharmonious with the stanza-theory are 1999-2010
(= *Teseide*, VII. 34), 2011-6 (= VII. 35), 2334-8 (= VII. 91.)

And at the laste he took conclusioun,
That ther as first Arcite and Palamoun
Hadden for love the bataille hem
    bitwene,
That in that selve grove, swote and   Ma pensò che nel bosco, ove rancura
    grene,
Ther as he hadde his amorous desires,   Aver sovente soleva d'amore,
His compleynt, and for love his hote
    fires,
He wolde make a fyr, in which   Faria comporre il rogo dentro al
    thoffice   quale
Funeral he mighte al accomplice   L' uficio si compiesse funerale
    (2853–64).   (XI. 13).

For several reasons this could hardly have formed two stanzas, or been expanded from one. Other similar cases I relegate to a note.[1]

The outcome of the examination of these passages is that in one or two of them there is nearly as much appearance of stanzaic form as could be expected or as there is against it ; but that in almost all of them, if the stanza-theory is correct, Chaucer must have taken the most extreme pains to obliterate vestiges which would have been apparent only on the minutest search. Whether this seems natural for any poet, especially a mediæval poet, I will not say ; but I am quite certain that it is not like Chaucer. The result here harmonizes perfectly with those which have been gained by other methods.

This concludes my discussion of the stanza-theory. If it has been no less convincing than it has been tedious, I shall be satisfied. My tests, taken together, with all deference to the memory of ten Brink and to later scholars, I think show that the stanza-

[1]
905–15 =	II. 26.	2314–21 =	VII. 84.
1048–55 =	III. 10.	2322–5 =	VII. 85, 1–6.
1975–80 =	VII. 31.	2349–57 =	VII. 89.
1981–3 =	VII. 32, 1–3.	2371–8 =	VII. 23–24.
2221 6 =	VII. 43, 2–8.	2410–18 =	VII. 28.
2238–43 =	VII. 46.	2423–34 =	VII. 39–40.
2244–50 =	VII. 47.	2561–4 =	VII. 14, 1–4.
2275–80 =	VII. 71.	2843–6 =	XII. 6, 1–3,
2289–96 =	VII. 74.	3017–26 =	XII. 7.
2307–10 =	VII. 81, 1–4.		

(In line 2411, by the way, it looks as if Chaucer had mistaken *compagnone* for *compagnia ;* Arcite would be more likely to dedicate to Mars the arms of his former comrade and present enemy than those of his own followers.) Most of these passages might well be disregarded, but exhaustiveness makes the proof more conclusive. Every passage is given here or earlier in which the Italian offers guidance and which could reasonably be thought significant. I certainly have tried to treat the stanza-theory generously throughout, yet I have found nothing which is not perfectly natural if that theory is incorrect. The evidence which the passages in this note add to the main discussion is :—In favour of the theory, nothing ; against it, a considerable quantity of indications, singly small, but in the mass rather effective.

theory is as destitute of evidence in its favour as it is of probability.
Granted (and they do grant it) that Chaucer would have used his
older version as the basis of the *Knight's Tale*, if not one sign of it
can be discovered even where concealment would be equally difficult
and unnecessary, I think the stanza-theory may be regarded as
disproved.

§ 2. *The Knight's Tale: How Far Altered.*

We come back, therefore, to the position of Tyrwhitt and other
early scholars,[1] since if the *Palamon* was not written in stanzas
it must have been written in its present metre. All we know
is that a poem on the subject of "all the love of Palamon and
Arcite of Thebes" was written before the *Legend of Good Women*,
and that such a poem exists as the *Knight's Tale*. The question
next arises whether in its first form it was practically the *Knight's
Tale* as we have it, or whether it has undergone considerable
revision and abbreviation. That some slight changes must have
been made of course all are agreed. A passage near the beginning,
lines 889–892, which allude to the pilgrims and the supper, must
be new, and probably the whole paragraph 875–892. At the end
there is nothing which must be new except the very last line, a
benediction on the "fair company:" yet the ending is so brisk and
succinct that it gives countenance to my belief that the poem was
never finished in its original form and that the whole present
ending was made for the *Canterbury Tales*. Elsewhere I find not
the least indication of adaptation or alteration.

It will probably be felt, however, that there are some grounds for
believing that the poem was originally much longer than now. There
is a certain force in the analogy of the *Troilus*;[2] if in translating
one poem of Boccaccio's Chaucer made it half as long again, it might
seem a little strange that he should reduce another to one-fifth.
Yet on examination this argument loses most of its force. In the
first place, consider the dissimilarity of the *Troilus* and the *Knight's
Tale*. The one is a study of the human heart, with only so much
incident as is necessary to keep it working and changing, a study on
which Chaucer poured out all his interest and sympathy, and which

[1] Cf. Ebert (1862), *Jahrbuch für rom. u. engl. Litt.*, iv. 95; Kissner
(1867), *Chaucer in seinen Beziehungen zur ital. Litt.*, p. 59.
[2] So ten Brink, *Studien*, 43–4; Kissner, *l. c.*, p. 59. Cf. Mather (*Furnivall
Miscellany*, p. 312, note), one or two of whose arguments against this objection
agree with mine.

it is evident that he regarded as his great work. The *Teseide*, like
the *Knight's Tale*, is a brilliant romance of picturesque incident,
with little and weak emotional interest, the sort of thing which
also appealed to Chaucer, in a more superficial way, which he would
be instantly moved to condense, and of which he would more
readily tire. That he even tired somewhat of the *Troilus* I think
there is evidence in the abruptness with which both Troilus and
Criseyde disappear.[1] What is more natural than that, after working
long on one poem of Boccaccio's, within a few years he should turn
to another by this same poet whose style he admired, a poem which
he had known for years and had already quoted from ; but that
from the start he should condense it ? While the *Filostrato* has
only about 5700 lines, the *Teseide* has nearly 10,000. As it is, the
Knight's Tale is by a good deal Chaucer's longest single poem
except the *Troilus*.[2]

The general similarity in style between the *Knight's Tale* and
most of the *Canterbury Tales* may appear to some readers a reason
for thinking it largely transformed from its early form. But, to say
nothing of what I believe to be the fact, that Chaucer's style after
1373 varied rather with his subject than with the date, we must
remember that it is a question of only a few years in any case, and
in general what a man can do at forty-five or fifty he can do at
forty or forty-five. If it is a better poem than the *Legend of Good
Women*, this is because Chaucer threw himself into it with greater

---

[1] It clearly prolonged itself beyond his expectations. He meant to finish it
in the fourth book, as he himself announces (IV. 26–8). The contrast in the
ratio between the earlier and later parts of the *Troilus* and of the *Filostrato* is
very striking. *T. C.*, I.–IV. contain 6370 ll. ; *Fil.*, I.–IV. (which exactly
correspond) contain 3688 ll. *T. C.*, V. has 1869 ll., and *Fil.*, V.–IX. (which
correspond) have 2016 ll.

[2] One who compares the *Knight's Tale* with the *Teseide* will frequently
wonder at the good passages which Chaucer omits (some of them are collected
in Appendix C, pp. 231–3), and will perhaps wonder if their absence from
the *Tale* is not due to revision. But if it has been shortened this was
certainly done by small omissions all through ; the longest passage which he
omits, book I., dealing with the war of Theseus with the Amazons, is so
remotely connected with the rest of the poem that he doubtless omitted it
from the first (as ten Brink and apparently Koch believe ; *Studien*, 62–3 ;
Engl. Stud., i. 282). Chaucer must have had too much taste to cut
out these good touches ; why did he not reduce as well (or instead) a considerable number of needless and disproportionate couplets and longer passages
which an attentive reading will discover in *Kn. T.* ? I may mention the first
150 ll. or so, or such a speech as Theseus' at the end (2987–3066), which is of
about the same length as its original in the *Teseide* ; such a couplet as 2087–8,
or the passage where Theseus decides on a site for Arcite's funeral-pyre (2853–
64). There are some bits in the *Knight's Tale* which are distinctly verbose.

interest ; he really cared but little for the Romans and Greeks,[1] and
in a retelling of the stories of Ovid and the others, with their pale
unintelligible background and the impossibility of making them
over to suit himself, he had no chance to do his best work.   Even
as it is, not a trait of character or style appears in the *Knight's Tale*
that is not also in the *Legend of Good Women ;* fresh love of nature,
occasional levity, humour, satire, his own "favourite line," "Pitee
renneth sone in gentil herte" (*L. G. W.*, F, 503 ; *K. T.*, 1761), and
a remarkable number of other correspondences in expression (which
will be mentioned later).   It can hardly be supposed that Chaucer
would have altered the *Palamon* quite completely ; yet these
characteristics run all through the *Knight's Tale*.   The one legitimate deduction which I think we may draw from all these facts
is that the poem in its first form was written only shortly before
the *Canterbury Tales* and the *Legend ;* of which suggestion more
hereafter.

   Dr. Koch discovers another evidence of revision : " Die schil-
derung des Marstempels trägt so sehr das gepräge einer überarbei-
tung, dass es kaum einem zweifel unterliegen kann, dass auch dieses
stück ein—wenn auch durch das verschiedene versmass mehrfach
modificirter—theil der früheren redaction des Palamon und Ar-
citas ist."[2]   Of the only two of his points which need be mentioned
here, one (the use of the first person in the description) has been
dealt with already ; the other is the fact that Chaucer seems to
confound the portraiture on the wall of Theseus' oratory with the
real temple of Mars in Thrace.   But Dr. Koch seems to forget that
the inconsistency is no greater in the *Knight's Tale* than it
would have been in any form of the *Palamon* which we can
postulate ; for he himself does not believe that Chaucer ever represented the real temple as visited by Arcite's personified prayer.
Furthermore, is not such an inconsistency far more likely to occur
in an unrevised poem than to have survived revision ?   It is easy
enough to explain.   Wishing to preserve as much as possible of
Boccaccio's imposing and terrible description, he conceived on the
walls of the oratory pictures of both the outside and the inside [3] of
the Thracian temple, and even of the designs with which it was

---

[1] Of course the people in *Kn. T.* are Greek only in name.
[2] *Engl. Stud.*, i. 258 ; cf. 258–61.   This point is one of the more unintelligible parts of an unintelligible theory.
[3] " Al peynted was the wal, in lengthe and brede,
        Lyk to the estres of the grisly place " (1970–1).

" istoriato " (VII. 36).   He even went so far in vividness as to
describe the storms, the shaking of the temple and the shrieking,[1]
partly perhaps because he was carried away himself.   This is not
scientific but poetic description, and is simply carrying a little
further the sort of imagination which we find in Keats' *Ode to a
Grecian Urn,* and even in Chaucer's original description of the
shrine of Venus, where broken sleeps, sighs and oaths are painted
on the wall.[2]   The passage I think has no bearing on the question
of revision.[3]

[1] 1979-80, 1985-6, 2004.

[2] *Kn. T.,* 1920-4.   There is a much worse example of the same sort of thing
in the *House of Fame,* mentioned earlier ; after describing the niches and
statues on the outside of the palace, Chaucer goes on :

> " Ther herde I pleyen on an harpe
> That souned bothe wel and sharpe,
> Orpheus ful craftely " (1201-3).

[3] Dr. Koch sees evidence of a confused text in three small passages in this
description.   "Shippes hoppesteres "(2017) has been satisfactorily explained
(see Skeat, V. 80-1).   The connection with Mars of such undignified figures
as "the barbour, and the bocher, and the smith " is due to the usual
mediæval identification of the pagan god with the planet and its astrological
relations.   Finally, Koch objects to the lines

> " The sleere of him-self yet saugh I ther,
> His herte-blood hath bathed al his heer ;
> The nayl y-driven in the shode a-night " (2005-7) ;

he suggests an impossible emendation ("The housbond slain by his wif ")
which is modified and approved by Skeat (V. 80).   It would be extraordinary
to mention the driving of the nail after the flow of blood, and the emendation
would destroy the force of the allusion in 2007, for Sisera was not the husband
of Jael.   The passage is perfectly simple if we divide it into two images, of
which the first suggested the second.   There are, however, certain real
internal inconsistencies in the *Kn. T.,* all due to careless treatment of the
original (and more likely to occur in an unrevised than in a revised work).   In
2355-7 Diana says to Emily :

> " The fyres which that on myn auter brenne
> Shul thee declaren, er that thou go henne,
> Thyn aventure of love,"

although the performances of the fire have already been described (2334-40) ;
here Chaucer has kept the future tense of the Italian, though he has reversed
the order (*Teseide,* VII. 89, " vedrai" ; cf. 91-2).   In 2858 ff. Theseus cuts
down the grove and makes Arcite's pyre and tomb on the scene of the sylvan
combat, regardless of the fact that he had previously erected a vast and
sumptuous theatre on the same spot (1862) ; here Chaucer has followed the
Italian in the later instance and not in the earlier.   Finally, Theseus speaks of
Arcite's "cosin and his wyf " (3062), though Emily had not married Arcite ;
in the *Teseide* she had already done so.   An apparent blunder in 2046 is due
only to Skeat's punctuation ; the line looks not forward but back, and should
be followed by a period.   Professor Liddell (*Chaucer's Prol., etc.,* N.Y. 1902,
p. 169) says that the promise in line 2039, "Suffyceth oon ensample in stories

One bit of internal evidence tends to disprove the idea of extensive revision. After mentioning Theseus' following Pirithous to hell, Chaucer says (1201):

"But of that story list me nat to wryte."

Nobody has doubted that the *Second Nun's Tale*, mentioned in the *Legend of Good Women*, and written, by an "unworthy son of Eve," to be read, was taken over unchanged into the *Canterbury Tales*. Is not the case nearly as good for the story of Palamon and Arcite, also mentioned in the *Legend of Good Women*, also written for readers, and only known to have been adapted for the *Canterbury Tales* at the beginning and the end?[1]

But the strongest argument against much alteration of the *Palamon* is that of probability and Chaucer's usual practice. In the *Second Nun's*, *Shipman's* and *Merchant's Tales* (as we shall see later) Chaucer neglected very necessary revisions. The revision of the *Prologue* to the *Legend* I shall try to show was due to a very special cause. It is a fair presumption that Chaucer avoided needless trouble in adapting the *Palamon* for the Knight. There is no reason or evidence for the belief that the original form of the poem was different from the present, or that if it had been Chaucer would have felt called on to alter it. The indications are therefore very strongly in favour of the practical identity of the *Palamon and Arcite* with the *Knight's Tale*.

§ 3. *The Knight's Tale: The Date.*

All this is a long preamble to a discussion of the date of the

---

olde," is not fulfilled; but Julius, Nero and Antonius, who have been spoken of a little way back, answer very well to the "slayn or elles deed for love," and the "oon ensample" no doubt refers vaguely to them. Dr. Mather (*Furnivall Miscellany*, 303, n.) suggests "error or negligence" in 2914-5; but is not this a not very violent case of metonymy, paralleled only five lines below (2919)? The peculiarity of the passage is accounted for by the fact that Chaucer has transferred to the pyre the language which Boccaccio uses of the grove which was cut down to make it (XI. 18, 19); an example of Chaucer's rather lax style of translation.

[1] The point was first noticed by Holthausen (*Anglia*, viii. 453), who, however, did not see the full bearing of it,—"bei der umarbeitung hat der dichter unachtsamer weise dies überbleibsel der ersten redaktion stehen lassen;" and by Dr. Furnivall (*Temp. Pref.*, "corr. and add."). It should be noted that in the prologue to *Melibeus* (2153-4) Chaucer speaks of the "tretis lyte After the which this mery tale I wryte," a similar oversight, which perhaps weakens the argument a little.

Knight's Tale,[1] but it is all essential to the subject, and has already thrown considerable light on it. I shall try to show that the tale was written between the *Troilus* and the *Legend*. A position after the *Troilus* has been assigned it hitherto only by Pollard[2] and Mather,[3] simply because almost everybody else has held the stanza-theory.[4] A later date than that of the *Troilus* can hardly be denied if my date for the latter is accepted, since (among other reasons) it is impossible to put two such long and elaborate poems as the *Troilus* and the *Knight's Tale* between 1373 and 1377. The most important argument for the inverse order is that of Professor J. L. Lowes,[5] whose opinion that the *Troilus* was written just before the *Legend* involves the priority of the *Knight's Tale*. I have already endeavoured to dispose of his arguments for this position for the *Troilus*. It remains to meet those for the priority of the *Knight's Tale*.

Lowes first points out the curious fact that it is on the 3rd of May that Pandarus[6] has a particularly sharp attack of love, and that Palamon escapes from prison;[7] and very naturally believes that one case must be due to the other. That the choice of this date was made first in the *Knight's Tale* he thinks is shown by the supposed facts that there is no reason for it in the other case, but that here it is "an essential part of the carefully calculated scheme of days and astrological hours on whose every step explicit emphasis is laid in the poem." Now Lowes' argument may be made to refute his own view. In the first place, the date in the *Knight's Tale* can be shown to be perfectly arbitrary, and not at all an essential part of the scheme. The essential parts are the hours, and the days of the week, which are wholly independent of the days of the month, and this is the only point where a day of the month is mentioned. Aside from the improbability that Chaucer's whole scheme was already devised at this point in the poem, where it first

---

[1] Hereafter this term may be used interchangeably with *Palamon and Arcite*.
[2] Apparently ; see *Globe Chaucer*, p. xxvii.
[3] *Furnivall Miscellany*, p. 309 ; *Chaucer's Prol.*, etc., p. xvii. He thinks, for no very clear reason, that Chaucer put the *Teseide* passages into the revised *T. C.*, and into *P. F.*, after "the plan of *Palamon* (*Knight's Tale*) was complete" (*Prol.*, etc., xix., note ; cf. 102, n. Cf. also *Misc.*, 309, 310, 312).
[4] Cf., *e. g.*, Koch, *Chronology*, p. 30.
[5] *Publ. Mod. Lang. Assoc.*, xx. 841–54.
[6] *Ibid.*, xx. 842–3 ; Lowes says *Troilus*, by a slip.
[7] *T. C.*, II. 56–63 ; *Kn. T.*, 1462–8. The detail is in neither original. Cf. Pollard, *Knight's Tale*, p. 89.

begins, there is absolutely no reason whatever why he should have
chosen this date unless it came into his head for some outside
reason.[1]   But for the selection of this date in the *Troilus* there is a
reason, though a homely one.   The passages in the *Tale* and the
Troilus run thus :

> " It fel that in the seventhe yeer, in May,
> The thridde night " . . .
> . . . . " it so betidde
> As I shal singe, on Mayes day the thridde."

It should not be thought a criticism unworthy of a great poet if I
suggest that Chaucer chose the word *thridde* for the sake of the
rhyme.   There are a large number of such cases in Chaucer's
poetry, and some fairly important ones, as Lowes himself points
out only thirteen pages later.[2]   If Professor Lowes will pardon
me, I will sum up my argument in his own words ; " if in one
of the poems the employment of the third of May is directly
dependent upon certain exigencies of the treatment of the material
itself, while in the other its relation to the story is wholly accidental, we may be practically certain that the instance which grows
out of the requirements of the story came first, and that it naturally
enough suggested the other."

Lowes argues (pp. 850–2) that the character of Boccaccio's two
poems would make it likely that Chaucer should translate the
Teseide before the *Filostrato*.   The former may well have been a
part of his first introduction to Italian literature,[3] but that he would
translate it first does not at all follow.   Lowes' argument that " an
earlier attraction to the *Teseide* than to the *Filostrato* is what we
should naturally expect," because the interest of the former is in
superficial narrative and of the latter is in profoundly human feeling,—this argument, I say, seems to me a little odd.   We must once
more remember that the man Chaucer at his first going into Italy
in 1373, at the age of thirty-three or so, must have been far more
mature than the poet Chaucer who had written the *Book of the
Duchess* only a few years before.   Surely Dr. Lowes would not say
that he who was capable not more than at most ten years later of
writing the *Troilus* must have been at first more attracted to the lesser

---

[1] See pp. 81, 82 below for a fuller treatment of this scheme and its value for
dating *K. T.*

[2] See p. 855, where he refers to *T. C.*, V. 1788, 1797 ; *L. G. W.*, F, 328.

[3] We have seen that he shows familiarity with it even in the first version
of the *Troilus ;* cf. p. 49 above.

poem. It seems to me that to a man of his age and tastes—consider
that his two greatest character-creations are of women, Criseyde and
the Wife of Bath,—the *Filostrato* would have appealed especially
and at once. Moreover, it would have seemed a less enormous
task, and his experience with the *Romance of the Rose* had probably already taught him the uncertainties in beginning on a poem
of great length. He would have begun to work on the *Filostrato*
with no intention of expanding (I have already pointed out that
he meant to finish the *Troilus* in the fourth book). After his
experience with the *Troilus*, it is not surprising that he greatly
condensed the *Teseide* from the first.

Nor do I find any more convincingness in Lowes' argument
(pp. 852–4) that the style and manner of the *Troilus and Criseyde*
and of the *Knight's Tale* would make the latter the earlier. I
must say again what I have said elsewhere, that Chaucer's style and
manner, after his return from Italy, it seems to me depended very
much more on the character of the poem he was writing than upon
the period,[1] though the former often depended on the latter. It
seems to me that the argument from style is a very, very dangerous one. He treated the *Teseide* freely because he wished to
condense that excellent but lengthy poem ; yet he made less change
in its characterization [2] than in that of the *Filostrato*, because the
characters are less important and naturally interested him less.
Lowes himself lays great stress elsewhere on the fact that the
centre of gravity in the *Troilus* is psychological; why should a
brilliant romance of incident be expected to compete with it in
regard to characterization ? Was *A Winter's Tale* written before
Hamlet ? Dr. Lowes thinks we should hesitate to put Emily and
Arcite and Palamon and Theseus later than Criseyde and Pandarus. But there is no reason why we should confine ourselves to
comparing the *Troilus* with Chaucer's other Boccaccian poem.
How about Dorigen and Aurelius and Arviragus ? How about
Canacee and Griselda and Constance ?[3] Lowes' argument, if carried
to its logical conclusion, would make the *Troilus* the last of
Chaucer's long poems. Lowes' comparison of the *Troilus* to the

---

[1] Cf. what ten Brink has to say (*Studien*, p. 44) in reply to a remark of the
usually judicious Kissner (*Chaucer in seinen beziehungen zur ital. lit.*, p. 65).
[2] But he did make a rather striking change in the characters of the cousins ;
see Appendix C, pp. 231–2.
[3] I hope to show later good reason for the belief that the *Tales* of the *Clerk*
and the *Man of Law* are late poems.

Knight's Tale in regard to the idea of fate expressed in it, and to its greater suggestiveness, I think may be answered in the same way. How *could* the *Knight's Tale* have been treated in the same manner as the *Troilus and Criseyde* ? Which is more suggestive, *Hamlet* or *A Winter's Tale* ? These considerations which Professor Lowes adduces, it seems to me, have no argumentative value whatever.

Lowes [1] hardly does justice, I think, to the argument from the presence in book V. of the *Troilus* (ll. 1807–27) of the stanzas which describe the flight of Troilus' soul to heaven, for which in the *Knight's Tale* Chaucer makes a rather flippant substitution (2809–15). It is natural to see, as almost all critics do see, a parallel here to Chaucer's insertion in the *Knight's Tale* of an inferior and original description of the temple of Venus, because he had already used Boccaccio's description in the *Parliament of Fowls*. The best explanation of the peculiar character of the passage in the *Knight's Tale* about Arcite's soul, in which Chaucer professes utter ignorance as to what became of it, is that he is gently mocking at Boccaccio.[2] It is hard to believe that he not only used but went out of his way to fit into a later poem a passage which he had rejected with something like contumely from an earlier, unless there shall prove to be a very striking contrast in fitness between the two cases. This Lowes seems to think exists, but I cannot see it. The *Troilus* is a much more thoughtful and skeptical poem than the *Knight's Tale ;* why should this skeptical attitude toward the other world appear so spontaneously in the latter rather than in the former ? If this is why Chaucer omitted the passage from the *Tale*, it is doubly odd that he put it into the *Troilus ;* but if he had already used it in the *Troilus*, the gently joking manner of its analogue in the *Knight's Tale* seems quite intelligible. The striking thing is that he should omit the whole passage in the *Knight's Tale*, though, however inharmonious some parts of it might be with what precedes or follows,[3] parts of it would do perfectly well, and though before and after it he is following the *Teseide* closely. The *Knight's Tale* is much less realistic and contains much more of the supernatural than the *Troilus*. I cannot but feel that the stanzas would be a little

---

[1] Pp. 843–7.

[2] For Lounsbury's strange opinion that Chaucer is here expressing "agnostic" views, see his *Studies*, ii. 513–15. A still different interpretation is that of Dryden in the *Palamon and Arcite*.

[3] Cf. Pollard, *Knight's Tale* (Macmillan), p. 116.

out of place in either poem ; if he had once weighed them and found them wholly wanting, it is passing strange that he used them later.   Therefore the indications are that the *Troilus* was not only written, but also revised before the *Knight's Tale* was written.[1]

A more forcible argument for the priority of the *Troilus* seems to me to be that from metre.   If Chaucer had been familiar with the possibilities of the couplet, it seems to me hard to believe that he would have written such a poem as the *Troilus* in the melodious, but difficult, wordy and languid stanza.[2]   Lowes thinks otherwise.[3] But it is one thing that Chaucer should return later to this sweet, romantic and half-lyric form of verse for such poems as the *Tales* of the *Prioress*, the *Clerk*, and the *Man of Law*, and quite another to imagine his returning to it for one of his great realistic and dramatic creations, for which the simplest and most flexible of mediums would be the most suitable, for which he might well have used blank verse if he had known it; as well revive the seven-line stanza in the *Wife of Bath's Prologue*.   Far be it from me to underestimate the skill with which he uses it in the *Troilus*, but I am sure that Chaucer would have felt at once that the other form would have been more suitable ; just as Shakspere and Dryden, though they may have been sensible that they could write good dramatic dialogue in the ten-syllable couplet, came to prefer the simpler and freer blank-verse.   When Lowes argues that though Chaucer had already written the *Knight's Tale* in couplets, he had not shown its potentialities for presenting dialogue and shifting moods, and that therefore for the arduous task of the *Troilus* he returned to the more familiar instrument, I believe he is misled by a metaphor.   We have already seen that it is merely the presence of the second line which distinguishes the stanza from three couplets.   This line completely alters the effect of the stanza and adds very considerably to its difficulty ; but hardly makes it a different instrument.   An accomplished pianist might well hesitate to perform in public on the organ, but why should

---

[1] Cf. p. 15 above.

[2] Koch (*Engl. Stud.*, xxvii. 3–4) uses the metrical form and free treatment of the *Tale* as an argument against putting it early in its present shape.   Of course his conclusion is that the original form was very different ; if this is not so, he gives unintentional support to the view expressed above.   (He is unjust to Pollard in implying that he puts it before *T. C.* ; cf. *Globe Chaucer*, p. xxvii.)

[3] Pp. 847–50.

a poet who felt himself thoroughly at home in the stanza distrust his own ability to manipulate it with the second line gone? This seems to me to attribute extraordinary diffidence to Chaucer, especially if he had already written over a thousand admirable couplets in the *Knight's Tale*. Even supposing he had written none, and supposing it might take him longer to produce a satisfactory passage in a new form of verse than in the old, with the same exacting taste and judgment the final result should be as satisfactory in the one as the other. But, more important yet, Lowes makes a rather curious oversight; he tells us that when Chaucer began the *Troilus* the stanza was an instrument " whose stops he knew from its lowest note to the top of its compass," while the couplet was a " less tried medium." Yet, even if we accept Lowes' very late date for the *Troilus*, 1383–5,[1] the only poems, so far as we know, which Chaucer had then written in the stanza were the *Parliament*, the *Second Nun's Tale*, the *Complaint to Pity*, a part of the *Complaint of Mars* (perhaps), the *Anelida*, and a few short poems— at most perhaps 1800 lines; yet the *Knight's Tale*, as it stands, contains 2250 lines, and surely nobody can deny that it shows far more mastery than these stanza-poems do, especially in the sort of manner required in the *Troilus*. Yet Dr. Lowes would have us believe that Chaucer felt very much more at home and self-confident in the more difficult and less-used [2] form of verse.

To the best of my belief this disposes of all the evidence which Professor Lowes adduces. It seems to me, therefore, even apart from the very early date for the *Troilus* which I have defended, that the probabilities are strong that the *Knight's Tale* followed the *Troilus*. We may now consider certain other arguments on the date of the *Knight's Tale*.

A clear indication that the *Knight's Tale* comes between the *Troilus* and the *Legend* may be found in the very large number of similar or identical phrases and lines in the *Tale* and one or the other of these two poems.[3] It is well known that in almost every one of Chaucer's poems there are reminiscences of the phraseology of others; it is clear that he had a vivid verbal memory, and had not

---

[1] Pp. 860–1; a date later than that proposed by any other writer.

[2] If we accept Lowes' opinion that most of the Legends were written before the *Kn. T.*, the disparity is far greater. And even if we then should add the *Clerk's* and *Man of Law's Tales* to the opposite scale, the disparity is still almost exactly the same as at first.

[3] Cf. Pollard, *Kn. T.* (1903), p. xii.

the least objection to using a good thing twice. In each of these poems there are such links to a number of Chaucer's other works, but those between the *Knight's Tale* and the other two are so much more numerous that it is fair to allow them considerable significance. It has been made plain, I trust, that they cannot be explained as having come in when the poem was being adapted to the *Canterbury Tales.* Since the passages are too numerous to quote in full, I merely give the references, first of those mentioned by Skeat,[1] then of some which I add. Those in parentheses are the less important; those marked with a † are due to originals which are in the *Teseide* or the *Filostrato* but are not close enough to have suggested the English expression; a ‡ indicates that the Italian is very close.

Kn. T. and *T. C.*	*Kn. T.* and *L. G. W.*
(925 = 4, 2)‡	(1035–6 = 2425–6)
†1010 = 4, 627	(1196 = 2282)
(1047 = 2, 112)	(1302 = 866)
1101 = 1, 425–6‡	1502 = 1204
[2] 1133 = 1, 674	1566 = 2629
(1155 = 5, 332)†	1761 = 503 (F), 491 (G)
[3] 1167–8 = 4, 618†	(2235 = 2132)
(1401 = 4, 865)†	†2602–20 = 637–53
(1500 = 2, 112)	
1509 = 2, 920	
1566 = 3, 733–4	
1838 = 5, 1433	
2449 = 4, 1456	
‡(3042 = 4, 1586)	

	873–4 = 1210–1
	1057 = 937
1462–3 = 2, 56 [4]	†1060 = 1962
(1809 = 4, 1567)	1164–6 = 1186–7
‡(2203 = 2, 503)	(1333 = 2604)
‡2406 = 1, 21‡ [5]	†1403–6 = 2046–7
†2529 = 4, 1086 (also 1079)	1423–4 = 1070–1
2991–3 = 3, 1762–4	(1531 = 1167)
3089 = 3, 1282	‡2506 = 1208
	2565 = 635
	3089 = 162 (F)

---

[1] III. 394, and in the notes on the passages. Cf. *Notes and Queries*, 4th Series, IV. 292. Only *Kn. T.* 1566 and 3089 are paralleled in both the other poems.

[2] For a little note on this line, see Henry Hinckley in *Mod. Lang. Notes*, xiii. 461–2.

[3] Skeat says 1163 (wrongly ; III. 394).

[4] See p. 72 above.

[5] The line in the *Teseide* is : " Io il diletto, e tu n' abbi l' onore " (VII. 27) ; in the *Filostrato :* " Tuo sia l' onore, e mio si sia l' affanno " (I. 5). The latter looks like the original of both Chaucer's lines. It is worthy of remark that in the more striking cases above where the Italian has suggested a line in *K. T.* or *T. C.*, it is in the *Filostrato*—an argument for the priority of the *Troilus.*

Some of these parallels are small, a few are due to Boccaccio or *Le Roman de la Rose*, or are proverbial, and one or two are (rather rare) idioms. But the important thing is their number,[1] which is far greater than that of parallels between any others of Chaucer's poems. Another striking fact is that there are hardly any such parallels between the *Troilus* and the *Legend ;* of the few which exist, two are in the *Tale* as well.[2] It seems fair to say that these parallels suggest for the *Knight's Tale* a position between the *Troilus* and the *Legend*.[3]

A date after the *Troilus* will also be necessarily involved by the early date which I have assigned the latter; we can hardly crowd anything long between Chaucer's first return from Italy and the commencement of the *Troilus*. This gives 1377 as the earliest possible date for Chaucer's working on the *Knight's Tale*. But on other grounds it will be necessary to put it much later than this.

In the first place, it must come after the *Parliament of Fowls*, since there is no longer any possible reason for thinking that the *Teseide* passage there ever stood in the *Palamon*. However it may be with the passage about Arcite's death, it is quite inconceivable that in the *Palamon* Chaucer should have substituted an original description of the temple of Venus for the far superior imagery of Boccaccio, unless he had used that in an earlier poem.[4] Hence we derive 1381 as the earliest possible date for the *Knight's Tale*.

For this there is some confirmation in the style of the poem,

---

[1] It should be remarked also that two-thirds of them are in contexts which are fairly close to the *Teseide ;* this in further answer to the possible conjecture that they came in on revision, which I have shown other reasons for disbelieving.

[2] See pp. 19, 24 above.

[3] Skeat, who of course holds the stanza-theory, sees the force of some of these parallels between the *Troilus* and the *Tale*, and makes the rather curious comment : "This tends to shew that the Knightes Tale (rather than the original Palamon and Arcite) was written not very long after Troilus ; rather in 1386 or 1387 than in 1388 " (III. 394). Cf. *Notes and Queries*, 4th Series, iv. 292, for his earlier view. Dr. Mather also (*Furnivall Miscellany*, p. 308) says : "Somewhere near *Troilus* it must surely go, for the two poems agree notably in thought and in expression." But neither of these two writers pays any attention to the correspondences between the *Knight's Tale* and the *Legend of Good Women*, which seem entitled to equal consideration.

[4] On this point I must strongly disagree with Dr. Mather (*Furnivall Miscellany*, p. 310). It is striking that for this new description he turned in part to a passage in an earlier poem of his own, the *House of Fame ;* the description of Venus (1955–66) is expanded, but otherwise almost word for word, from *H. F.*, 132–9. In his note to the latter, Skeat erroneously speaks of the former as from Boccaccio.

which instantly links it to the *Legend of Good Women* and
especially the *Canterbury Tales*, rather than to Chaucer's earlier
works; the good judgment, the keenness, the aptness, the rapid
alternation of humour and pathos, the general certainty of touch.
The poem contrasts even with the *Troilus*, and resembles most of
the *Canterbury Tales*, in its condensation and vigour and speed.
Though the *Troilus* is a greater poem, to me at least it seems less
artistic and finished, and less marked by most of the qualities just
mentioned than the *Knight's Tale*.[1] There are also certain favourite
phrases in the *Tale* which occur again and again in Chaucer's later
poems, and seldom or never in the earlier.   The phrase "gentil
herte" (*Kn. T.*, 1043, 1761, 1772) does occur in the *Troilus* (IV.
1674); but it is much commoner later.[2] Chaucer's "favourite
line,"

" Pitee renneth sone in gentil herte,"

occurs only in *Knight's Tale*, 1761; *Legend*, F, 503 (G, 491);
Merchant's Tale, 1986 ; *Squire's Tale*, 479 ; and in a close variant
in *Man of Law's Tale*, 660.[3] Again, no locution is more characteristic of Chaucer's later style than such elaborate phrases as "by
aventure or sort or cas," which I have elsewhere shown to be
probably due to reminiscences of Dante.[4] They occur only in the
Canterbury Tales, and of the six cases which I have noted, two are
in the *Knight's Tale*.

A similar date is indicated by two probable contemporary references in the *Knight's Tale*.   Saturn, among the results of his male-

---

[1] For a different view cf. Kissner, *Chaucer in seinen beziehungen zur ital.
literatur*, p. 65 ; and cf. ten Brink, *Studien*, p. 44.
[2] *L. G. W.*, 503 (F), 491 (G) ; *M. L. T.*, 660 ; *Melib.*, 2832 (the Latin has
"ingenui animi," the French "gentil cuer"), *Merch. T.*, 1986 ; *Sq. T.*,
452, 479, 483.
[3] Professor Liddell (*Chaucer's Prol., etc.*, p. 167) says : "This seems to
have been a proverbial expression"; but it seems more likely to be a favourite
invention of Chaucer's own. Mr. Paget Toynbee (*Journ. Compar. Lit.*, i.
351) announces the line as a translation of Dante's "Amor che a cor gentil
ratto s'apprende" (*Inf.*, V. 100). But the only phrase which the two lines
both have is very common, in Italian, in French and (as we have just seen)
in Chaucer. Professor Francis Palgrave had already announced this supposed
borrowing in 1888 (*Nineteenth Century*, xxiv., 349). [In Mr. Toynbee's article
just quoted, in which he conveniently collects most of Chaucer's borrowings
from Dante, he attributes (as Cary had done) *L. G. W.*, 2638 to *Inf.*, VII.
64 ; but he exaggerates the similarity by reading *gold* for *gode*, the only reading in the nine printed MSS. On this line cf. *W. B. T.*, 1064–5.]
[4] See *Modern Philology*, iii. 372. Such cases as *N. P. T.*, 4291, *Kn. T.*,
1242, 1506, 1516 (not mentioned there), less striking and Dantesque, are
certainly commoner in *C. T.* than elsewhere.

ficent influence, mentions " the cherles rebelling " (2459); we can
hardly avoid seeing a reference to the peasant revolt of June, 1381,[1]
since the introduction of the item (founded on nothing in the
Italian) before that date would be difficult to account for. Professor
Lowes, in a thorough and judicious article,[2] throws light on
both the date and a puzzling line in the poem. " The tempest at "
Hippolyta's " home-coming " (884) has never hitherto been at all
satisfactorily explained. Lowes shows that it is probably an
allusion to a strange and destructive upheaval of the sea just
after Anne of Bohemia had landed, on her arrival in England in
December, 1381.[3] This indicates 1382 as the earliest possible
date.

Finally, an indication that the *Knight's Tale* was written only
shortly before the *Legend of Good Women* is the often-quoted
couplet which has caused all our pains :

" And al the love of Palamon and Arcyte
Of Thebes, thogh the story is knowen lyte."

We can no longer explain the last clause and the utter disappear-
ance of the supposed older form of the *Palamon* on the ground that
it had been published and failed ; we can explain both on no
ground so reasonably as that Chaucer had never published it at all.
This will explain why he seems to imply that the *Legend* was
written in a new kind of metre, though he had been using the
same in the *Palamon*. When we consider Chaucer's position, and
how simple a matter publication was in his day, it is hard to
imagine any reason for withholding the poem, except that it was
not yet finished.[4] We shall see later that the form of prologue in
which the couplet occurs dates almost certainly from 1386. The
above argument seems to me so cogent that I have little hesitation in adopting the date about 1385 for the writing of the
greater part of the *Knight's Tale*.

In this late date I differ from the only two writers who have as

---

[1] Also alluded to in *N. P. T.*, 4584–6. Cf. Skeat, I. lvi., and Walsingham, *Historia Anglicana*, i. 458, 462.
[2] *Mod. Lang. Notes*, xix. 240–3.
[3] Cf. the Monk of Evesham, *Hist. Vitæ et Regni Ric. II.*, p. 129, for an
odd coincidence when Richard brought home his second bride.
[4] The *Palamon* was scarcely a poem to be voluntarily neglected. I shall
show later good reason for the belief that *L. G. W.* was written in some sense
at the command of the queen. The conjecture seems plausible that Chaucer
broke off his work on *P. A.* in order to write *L. G. W.*

yet abandoned the stanza-theory and discussed the date at length,
Mather and Lowes, who suggest 1381–2. But it will be seen,
I think, that their possible objections to my date can easily be met.
The former[1] puts it very near the *Troilus* because of the verbal
similarities already spoken of. But if the latter was finished in
1377 or so, and the *Knight's Tale* refers to events of 1381, it
is impossible to put them close together. I have already shown
that Chaucer's revision of the *Troilus*, perhaps in 1380 or later,
will help to account for the two having been together in his mind ;
and his permanent and intimate familiarity with the *Troilus* is
accounted for by the fact that he had written it more carefully and
valued it more highly than any other of his works. Mather's belief
that the *Teseide* stanzas inserted in the *Troilus* during the revision
were so inserted while Chaucer was writing the *Knight's Tale* I have
tried to show is highly improbable. I must relegate to a foot-note
what seems to me proof positive that Skeat's calendar method of
dating the *Knight's Tale*, of which Mather and Lowes approve,
cannot possibly work. Mather argues further that if we put the
Knight's Tale in 1381–2, where we know the *Parliament of Fowls*
belongs, "the whole preoccupation with the *Teseide* would have
extended over only a year or so, and certainly this supposition
is better than that of its gradual dismemberment." To say nothing
of the inappropriateness of this last phrase, we know that Chaucer
made some small use of the *Teseide* years before in the first version
of the *Troilus*, so in spite of us his use of the *Teseide* extended
over at least six years or so. This answers, I think, all of Mather's
arguments. Lowes[2] has no arguments not already dealt with
except the reference to the "tempest"; this obviously implies
a date after 1381, but not necessarily just after. The incident
may well have sprung vividly to mind two or three years later.[3]

---

[1] *Furnivall Miscellany*, pp. 308–10.

[2] *Publ. Mod. Lang. Assoc.*, xx. 841, ff.

[3] Professor Skeat has made an ingenious attempt to find the date of what he
considers the revised *Knight's Tale* (*Notes and Queries*, 4th series, ii. 243–4 ;
reprinted with alterations in his *Chaucer*, V. 75–6). Palamon escapes from
prison early in the morning of the 4th May (1462–7), and the woodland
combat therefore occurs the 5th May (1610) ; that the first of these days was
Friday, Skeat thinks is suggested by the fact (according to him, but Chaucer
does not say so) that Arcite goes a-Maying in the first hour, which on Friday
is dedicated to Venus, and by the fact that Chaucer uses Friday as a symbol
for the moods of lovers ; and that the second day was a Saturday, presided
over by the unlucky planet Saturn, by the fact that the duel is interrupted.
(But is not all this reasoning rather too much as if it were history ; would
Chaucer have thought of all this ?) The assembly before the tournament is to

The best conclusions as to the date of the first writing of the
Knight's Tale seem to be these. It is later than the *Troilus*, and
even than the revision of it—hence much later than 1377 ; later
than the *Parliament of Fowls*—hence later than 1381, as is further
indicated by two probable historical allusions. The manner in
which it is mentioned in the *Prologue* of the *Legend of Good
Women* points plainly to its having been written very recently.
Everything seems to harmonize with the date 1384–6.

As to its completion and adaptation to the *Canterbury Tales*, this
probably took place not many years afterwards. It is well known,
or we shall see later, that in the *Tales* of the *Second Nun*, the *Parson*,
the *Shipman*, and the *Merchant* Chaucer neglected to make even
such revisions as appropriateness strongly demanded. Now at the
beginning of the *Knight's Tale* Chaucer made such changes as were
certainly not in the least necessary. This points to a time when the
Canterbury Tales were fresh to him. It is also suggestive that the
Knight's Tale stands first in the series, and that the *Prologue* directly

---

be that day fifty weeks (1850–3) ; no doubt, as Skeat says, a year (though it
is odd that Theseus says, "fifty wykes, *fer ne ner*"), for Boccaccio has "un
anno intero," and it actually occurs not in April but in May (2484). Sunday
(2188), the 5th May if it is a year from the first fight, the knights assemble
for the tournament ; Monday they amuse themselves (2486) ; and the tournament occurs the following day (2491), Tuesday, the 7th. Skeat thinks it not
unnatural to suppose that Chaucer took the scheme of the year in which he was
writing ; and finding (correctly) that the second set of dates fits 1387, concludes
that this may have been the year of revision. The question for us of course
is not the year of revision—that Chaucer should have made such an elaborate
adaptation of course is not to be thought of—but the year of first writing ;
although, risky as the scheme is and as Skeat admits it to be, it might have
some value if it fitted in with the other evidence, ten Brink rejects it as too
conjectural (*Studien*, 189), and I fear we must reject it on other grounds as
well. The striking fact that Chaucer chooses such an unobvious date as 3rd
May for Palamon's escape I have shown to be explained probably by a
reminiscence from the *Troilus*. There are really no striking coincidences to
indicate that Chaucer had in mind from the start an elaborate scheme covering a year, and Pollard shows that he was quite indifferent to the larger time-
scheme of the poem (*Knight's Tale*, 1903, pp. 81–2). The most striking
defect in Skeat's scheme is that it is the *second* of the years in the poem which
he identifies with a current year ; if the scheme is as elaborate as he whom I
fear we must call its author believes, it would be strange that Chaucer should
not have made the *first* year fit the current one. This would give 1380 or
1386. The former of course is impossible, and the latter would inadmissibly
crowd the *Legend of Good Women* and the *Canterbury Tales*. Therefore
Skeat's clever scheme cannot be accepted. This is only one of several cases in
which more recent scholarship has come to see that in the past we have
attributed to Chaucer more care and accuracy in insignificant matters than he
really observed. Many of these tempting methods of dating poems must be
abandoned. In regard to minute accuracy, Chaucer goes with Shakspere, not
with Dante.

introduces it. We shall see later that Chaucer was probably busied
with the *Prologue* about 1387, and that it was perhaps the very first
written part of the whole work. There is much in favour of the
view that the *Knight's Tale* was the first *Canterbury Tale* to be
meant for such, and that it was put into its present position soon
after the writing of the *Prologue*, about 1388–90.[1]

§ 4. *The Anelida and Arcite.*

As to the date and interpretation of that perplexing poem the
Anelida and Arcite we have been left to rather vague conjecture.
Dr. Furnivall[2] dates it between 1374 and 1384. Dr. Koch[3]
suggests 1383, between the demolition of the supposed stanzaic
Palamon and its reconstruction in the *Knight's Tale*. Ten Brink[4]
thinks it may have been begun before the recasting of the *Palamon*
was finished ; he is quite certain that the opening was derived from
the first form of that poem. Mr. A. W. Pollard, in 1893,[5] put it
about 1380, and suggested " that it represents Chaucer's first study
of the *Teseide* before he turned to the *Filostrato*." Dr. Skeat
merely puts it after 1373, and after the *Palamon*, from which he
believes the opening to be taken ; with the added suggestion that
" Chaucer's thoughts may have been turned towards Armenia by
the curious fact that, in 1384, the King of Armenia came to
England."[6] Dr. Lowes dates the poem about 1380–2.[7] The
best treatment of its genesis is that by Dr. Mather,[8] who denies
that the opening was derived from the *Palamon*, and (rather
extremely) regards the *Anelida* as " the necessary middle stage
between" the *Troilus* and the original form of the *Knight's Tale*
(p. 310, note) ; it must therefore have been begun before the
Knight's Tale. He also suggests " that Chaucer having completed

---

[1] Another of the earliest-written tales is probably the *Physician's ;* see
pp. 155–6 below. There is evidence that *Kn. T.* was known to the world
before 1392. Two lines of it (1785–6) are quoted in the *Book of Cupid* (Skeat,
VII. lvii. ff., 347 ff.), which Professor Kittredge shows some reason to believe
was written before that date (*Mod. Philol.*, i. 13–15). This and one or two
other things go to show that Chaucer allowed some parts of the *C. T.* to
become known while he was still working on others.

[2] *Trial Forewords*, p. 16.   [3] *Chronology*, pp. 46–8.

[4] *Geschichte*, ii. 196–8 ; cf. *Studien*, pp. 53–6.

[5] *Primer*, p. 81 ; cf. his *Knight's Tale* (1903), p. xi.

[6] Vol. i., p. 77. Skeat is mistaken as to the date, which was Christmas,
1385 (Walsingham, ii. 142, and cf. p. 151). This would put the poem at
a time already crowded.

[7] *Publ. Mod. Lang. Assoc.*, xx. 861–2.

[8] *Furnivall Miscellany*, pp. 307, 309–10 (note), 311.

Troilus began *Anelida* as a pendant to it" (p. 311), since the plots of the two "are identical, only the main *rôles* being reversed."

Professor Bilderbeck, in *Notes and Queries*,[1] suggests that the poem is an allegory on a contemporary incident. He quotes Thomas Walsingham's *Historia Anglicana* to show that in 1387 Robert de Vere, Earl of Oxford and Duke of Ireland, repudiated his wife Philippa, cousin of the king, and married a Bohemian lady, who had come to England in the train of Queen Anne. Obviously de Vere would be represented by the faithless Arcite, and the forsaken grand-daughter of Edward III. by Anelida, Queen of Armenia. He finds some confirmation for his conjecture in the King of Armenia's visit to England, which may have suggested the nationality attributed to Anelida. Prof. Bilderbeck's conjecture is rather attractive, but cannot possibly be accepted. I have shown elsewhere [2] that only two years before the divorce episode, and a year before the date to which Bilderbeck assigns this expression of reprehension, Chaucer fell under very considerable obligation to the Earl of Oxford; the presumption is strong, therefore, that he would not have undertaken publicly to attack him.

But there is another and a much more conclusive argument against this date. Most of the light which we can expect on the date of the *Anelida* must be derived from its relations with the *Troilus* and the *Knight's Tale*. It must quite certainly have been written before the latter; it was only the stanza-theory that required the reverse order.[3]

The first argument is the presence in it of passages from

---

[1] Eighth Series, ix. 301–2. He might also have referred to the Evesham *Hist. Vitæ et Regni Ric. II.* (ed. Hearne, Oxford, 1729), p. 84; and to C. Höfler, in the *Denkschriften* of the Vienna Academy, xx. 188–91.

[2] *Mod. Philol.*, i. 328. It was de Vere that got Chaucer his deputy at the Custom-house.

[3] Ten Brink's other arguments are nugatory. If it was written early he thinks it inexplicable that Chaucer should have permanently abandoned "ein mit so groszem pomp eingeleitetes, mit so vielem aufwand dichterischer mittel begonnenes werk"; and still more inexplicable that it should be preserved (*Studien*, p. 54). But why may not a poem lie in a chest twenty years as well as ten? Its eventual publication is natural; at his death Chaucer must have occupied much the same pre-eminent position as Dante at his, and somewhat as the last cantos of the *Paradiso*, according to Boccaccio's story, were sought and published, why not any interesting fragments of Chaucer's poetry that were found among his papers? Nor is there any significance in the fact that Lydgate mentions the *Anelida* and not the *House of Fame*.

the *Teseide* some of which were used also in the other poem.
It is natural to use parts of a poem and then decide to adapt
the whole, and unnatural to use where they do not belong stanzas
which had already been used where they do.   Another consideration is that Chaucer is unlikely to have given to the heartless
betrayer of Anelida the name and antecedents [1] of the chief hero of
so important a poem as the *Palamon and Arcite*, if he had already
written it.   Moral indignation, to be sure, is not Chaucer's usual
attitude, and he shows a certain tolerance for the faithless males of
the *Legend;* but the human emotion of his poems he took seriously,
and the other Arcite embodies a high ideal.[2]   Such treatment of one
of his own best poems would show an almost flippant lack of feeling.
He would have been more likely to choose Palamon, whom he puts
in a much worse light.   Finally, Mather points out (p. 307) that
the poem stops with a suggestion that Chaucer was about to describe
a temple of Mars.   Now, considering the intimate connection of this
poem with the *Teseide*, and the imposing description in the latter,
which so impressed Chaucer that he alludes to it in the invocation
which heads the *Anelida*, if certainly looks as if a version of this
were to follow ; otherwise, how could he have walked straight into
such a no-thoroughfare ?   The feeling is hard to resist that the
break in the *Anelida* just here is somehow connected with the
presence of the description in the *Knight's Tale*.   If the break can
hardly come here because he had used the description, nothing
remains except that he meant to use it.

It may be allowable to attempt a conjectural restoration of
Chaucer's procedure.   In the *Parliament of Fowls* he had closely
imitated Boccaccio's description of the temple of Venus, which
almost immediately follows that of the temple of Mars.   This use
of the *Teseide* must have refreshed his memory of the poem, and he
may then have undertaken to use larger portions of it, including
this second fine description.   It may also have occurred to him to
sketch a poem in contrast to the *Troilus*, which he had probably
been revising not long before ; a poem in which the tables should
be completely turned on Arcite's sex.[3]   Whence he got the names

---

[1] It is not quite accurate to say that this Arcite has only the name in
common with the other ; cf. *A. A.* 85.

[2] That Chaucer sketched him with strong liking is suggested by the changes
he makes in Boccaccio's portraiture of the cousins.   See Appendix C,
pp. 231–2.

[3] Cf. *Troilus*, V. 1779–85.

and material for the poem we do not know yet.[1] But it did not proceed well, and the path ahead does not look very straight. At this point Chaucer brought up before the temple of Mars. He may have felt then that a much worthier use for that description and the admirable poem of which it is only one ornament would be a free but complete adaptation. Here therefore he permanently abandoned the *Anelida.*

As to the exact date, we cannot be sure. The above conjecture would put it about 1383–4, to which there are no objections. We cannot doubt that it comes between the *Troilus,* on the one hand, and the *Legend*[2] and the *Palamon,* on the other, which gives the limits 1377 and 1385.

CHAPTER IV.

THE *LEGEND OF GOOD WOMEN.*

§ 1. *The Two Prologues : The Question of Priority.*

THE *Prologue* to the *Legend of Good Women* is extant, as is well known, in two versions, the shorter of which is found in only one MS., and is usually deemed the earlier. This I shall call G, and the other F.[3] The existence of version G was not generally known

---

[1] For Cowell's suggestion that Anelida was originally a Persian goddess, see Ch. Soc. *Essays,* 617–21 ; cf. also Samuel Dill, *Roman Society from Nero to Marcus Aurelius* (London, 1904), p. 556. But there seems little doubt, as Professor J. Schick shows, that an Anelida was a character in the Matter of Britain, and the explanation of the *Anelida and Arcite* may lie in some voluminous Arthurian romance. In the old Italian *Intelligenza* (ed. by Gellrich, Breslau, 1883, st. 75, l. 2 ; cf. Schick, *Temple of Glas,* E.E.T.S., p. cxx.) she appears with Yvain among several pairs of lovers :

"La bella Analida e lo bono Ivano."

Froissart has the same couple (*Dit dou bleu chevalier,* 301 ; ed. Scheler, i. 357 ; cf. ten Brink, *Studien,* 213) :

"Je prenc Tristan pour Yseut le premier, Et en après Yewain le preu pour la belle Alydès."

Just as she is here *bella* and *belle,* so Chaucer frequently calls her "faire Anelida."

[2] It is not mentioned in it, but Chaucer would hardly speak of an abortive fragment, which he had quite given over. Koch makes too much, I think, of what is no real difficulty (*Chronology,* pp. 46–7).

[3] Prologue G is usually called A, and F is called B, designations which I reject because they imply what I believe to be a false view as to order ; this is also implied by the order in which they are printed by Skeat in all his

of [1] till it was printed by the Chaucer Society about 1871.[2] At
first it was usually argued or assumed to be the earlier and rejected
version,[3] and it was not until 1892 that a voice was heard on the other
side. Since then the matter has been much debated, especially in
Germany and lately in America, though something has come also
from both sides of the English Channel ; and even now, in the view
of some, the conclusive word has not been spoken, in spite of the fact
that perhaps never has a scholarly question been settled so many
times to the satisfaction of the settlers.   In 1892, by a keen article
in *Englische Studien*,[4] ten Brink supported the view that version
G is the later, on the ground mainly of its relation to Chaucer's
life and later works.   His opinion was promptly accepted by Dr.
Emil Koeppel,[5] by Dr. Max Kaluza,[6] and by Dr. F. J. Mather ;[7]
attacked by Dr. John Koch in an appendix to his *Chronology oj
Chaucer's Writings ;*[8] defended again by Koeppel in a review of
Koch's book ;[9] and attacked (on more purely æsthetic grounds, yet
with a singularly cocksure manner) by M. Émile Legouis.[10] This last
paper was reviewed unfavourably in a valuable article by Gustaf
Binz,[11] and favourably by Koch.[12] In England, up to this point, the
whole controversy was ignored, and the older opinion supported by
Skeat [13] and Pollard.[14]   But in 1902 Professor J. B. Bilderbeck

---

editions and by Pollard in the *Globe Chaucer*. I follow several other writers
in calling the shorter G, after the unique MS. in which it is found, Camb.
Gg. 4. 27, and the other F, after its best MS., the Fairfax, out of the eight
or so which contain the *Prologue*.

[1] Ten Brink states (*Engl. Stud.*, xvii. 13) that in 1870 he had seen a tran-
script of it, and then became convinced that it is the later version.   It had
been discovered by Mr. Henry Bradshaw and privately printed as early as
1864 (*Trial Forewords*, p. 104).

[2] *Odd Texts of Chaucer's Minor Poems*, edited by F. J. Furnivall,
1868–1880.

[3] As by Furnivall in 1871 (*Athenæum*, Oct. 21, p. 528 ; *Trial Forewords*,
106) ; by Skeat (*Leg. of G. W.*, Oxford, 1889, p. xiii.); by Dr. Siegfried
Kunz, *Das Verhältnis d. HSS. v. Chaucers L. G. W.* (Breslau dissertation,
published in Berlin, n. d.), p. 12.

[4] Vol. xvii. 13–23.

[5] *Engl. Stud.*, xvii., pp. 195–200.   [6] *Ibid.*, xxii. 281.

[7] *Chaucer's Prologue, etc.* (Boston, 1899), p. xxiii., note.

[8] Published by the Chaucer Society and strangely dated 1890 ; see pp.
81–7 of the book.

[9] *Literaturblatt f. germ. u. rom. Philol.* (1893), vol. xiv. 51–3.

[10] *Quel fut le premier composé par Chaucer des deux Prologues de la Légende
des femmes exemplaires ?* In the *Revue de l'enseignement des langues
vivantes*, Paris, April, 1900 ; pp. 58–71.

[11] *Anglia Beiblatt*, xi. 231–7 (1900).

[12] *Engl. Stud.*, xxx. 456–8 (1902).

[13] III., xxi.-xxv. (1894).   [14] *Globe Chaucer*, xlv. f. (1901).

published a careful study of the *Legend,* in which he defended the older view on æsthetic and other grounds.[1] In 1904 the most important contribution to the subject ever made came from the pen of an American, Professor J. L. Lowes, who showed that version F contains borrowings from foreign poetry which prove its priority.[2] In 1905 Dr. J. C. French supported the older view and attacked Lowes' position on æsthetic grounds;[3] his book was reviewed, unfavourably to French's opinions, by the present writer,[4] and was criticized by Lowes incidentally to a fuller discussion of the *Legend.*[5] Lowes' principal conclusions were accepted by Mr. A. W. Pollard.[6] The fact that they are rejected in so good a book as Dr. R. K. Root's recent *Poetry of Chaucer* will excuse my keeping the subject open.

Although the succession of able articles by ten Brink, Koeppel and Binz, together with other evidence, had already thoroughly convinced me of the priority of F, the new evidence introduced by Lowes is particularly important and conclusive. The great service performed by him[7] was the pointing out that Chaucer borrowed from a considerable number of French poems, by Machault, Deschamps and Froissart; besides the verbal parallels in

[1] *Chaucer's Legend of Good Women,* London, 1902 (114 pp.).
[2] *Publ. of the Mod. Lang. Assoc. of America,* xix. 593–683.
[3] *The Problem of the Two Prologues, etc.,* a Johns Hopkins dissertation, Baltimore ; 100 pp.
[4] *Mod. Lang. Notes,* xxi. 58–62.
[5] *Publ. Mod. Lang. Assoc.,* xx. 749–864 (on French, see pp. 749–51, note).
[6] *Academy,* no. 1759, p. 62 (1906).
[7] In his first article, *Publ. Mod. Lang. Assoc.,* xix. 611–58. In my review of French I pointed out one or two other verbal parallels (see *Mod. Lang. Notes,* xxi. 59–60, notes 7 and 12). On the manner of introducing the Balade, cf. the following :

> "So womanly, so benigne, and so meke, . . .
> Half hir beautee shulde men nat finde . . .
> And therfor may I seyn, as thinketh me,
> This song, in preysing of this lady fre " (F, 243–8).

> " Son bel maintien, sa douce vois, . . .
> Me semont fort à ceste fois
> Que une balade je die
> En l'ounour ma dame jolie " (Froissart's *Le joli mois de May,*
> ll. 313–9 ; ed. Scheler, ii., 204).

While in G (89) May is almost past, in F (108)

> "this was now the firste morwe of May ; "

so in Deschamps' *Lay de franchise,* which Chaucer used so much (*Soc. des anc. textes franç.,* ii. 204, line 14) :

> " Le premier jour de ce mois de plaisance."

F 40–65, he shows similarities of plan also to the *Lay de fran-chise* and the *Paradys d'amours*, by the two last (respectively). Not only is this highly interesting in itself ; its chronological signifi-cance lies in the fact that though parallels exist in both F and G, there are far more in F. " The inevitable conclusion must be," to quote earlier-published words of my own, " that Chaucer read his French predecessors just before writing F. Now since their influ-ence on G is also unmistakable, a defender of the priority of G must ask us to believe that he went over these poems before each writing, and in F added to his mosaic with almost inconceivable care and ingenuity ; and, besides this, that he abandoned independ-ence in points where such a procedure was equally injurious and unmotived. " [1] The priority of F, it seems to me, has been shown by Lowes in a very demonstrative way.

But the question is a highly intricate and ambiguous one, more so, it seems to me, than Lowes altogether shows. The puzzle is that F, which he proves to be the displaced version, seems to most readers the better and pleasanter. Legouis believes the æsthetic evidence speaks in favour of version F (p. 59). Even Koeppel characterizes the spirit of G as " ein ganz anderer, kräftigerer, aber auch etwas nüchternerer Geist," with the personal feeling banished and the May scene relegated to the dream —he thinks G seldom improves over F, and more often shows signs of hasty revision.[2] Lowes too is of much the same mind : " that the B [F] version has the note of freshness, of spontaneity, of composition *con amore* to a greater degree than A—that it is even the more delightful version of the two—all will perhaps agree." [3] There are three more or less general and striking differences between F and G which will be thought at first to mark F as the better. These are its more genial and personal tone ; the pleasing suspense as to the identity of the lady of the Balade and the lady who enters with the God of Love, which is wholly given up in G ; and the fact that after she has been repeatedly named in his presence

---

[1] *M. L. N.*, p. 60. Lowes' fuller and more authoritative discussion of this evidence will be found on his pp. 658 ff. French's unfair treatment of Lowes' arguments I pointed out in my review (see his pp. 32, 35–8, 65–6).

[2] *Literaturblatt*, vol. xiv. (1893), col. 52. He attributes the change in spirit to the attempt to adapt part of the *Legend* for use as a *Canterbury Tale*. It is impossible to regard this suggestion with favour.

[3] *Publ. Mod. Lang. Assoc.*, xix. 683, note ; " but these," he continues, " are the very marks of a work written *currente calamo*, as against the firmer touch, the surer craftsmanship, the more compact unity of A " [G]. Why the latter merits should expel the former he does not tell us.

Chaucer in G affects not to know who she is, a blunder almost wholly absent from F. The first is particularly important, for it will be found that most of the detailed points of superiority in F are bound up with it. These matters nobody has adequately explained, especially no advocate of the priority of F. Lowes' attempt at some of them seems very slight and unconvincing,[1] and his entire argument therefore lacking in finality. A perfectly satisfactory and rather illuminating explanation I believe is possible ; but must be deferred till the question of priority has been discussed on other grounds. Except for these three points I believe all of the important æsthetic considerations will indicate that G is the revised version.

All the thorough discussions of the æsthetic evidence, those of Legouis, Bilderbeck, and French, have been by the supporters of the priority of G,[2] so it may be well to show that even on purely æsthetic grounds a good case can be made out for G as the revised version. These three writers have almost confined themselves to æsthetic arguments. But obviously, if others disagree with them as to the value of their arguments, and if Chaucer can be shown to have had a non-æsthetic motive for revision, which accounts for occasional inferiority in the later version, they have no case. Legouis' argument seems much the best ; but it is not surprising that the accomplished critic of Wordsworth comes to Chaucer without the knowledge of the poet and his age requisite to a just estimate, and most of Legouis' points either prove to be connected with the omission of the personal feeling, which subject we are holding in reserve, or seem ambiguous or trivial. The other two writers, as I tried to show at more length, in the case of French, in my review, seem still more to select ambiguous or trivial details ; their standards are singularly arbitrary,[3] and they never seem to see that many of their cases could be used as contrary arguments equally well. The fact that G exists in only one, and that a somewhat corrupt, MS.

---

[1] *Publ. Mod. Lang. Assoc.*, xix. 676, 681.

[2] On the other side, of course, æsthetic considerations have not been wholly neglected. Lowes treats them more or less on pp. 661, 663, 665, 678–80 of his first article.

[3] Notably as to alliteration and grammatical and logical structure. Nor do they seem to recognize how much of the broad and even careless style of mediæval oral poetry still clung to Chaucer. The use which Bilderbeck makes of small peculiarities in G is particularly curious because he admits that it "has to some small extent been edited" by another than Chaucer (p. 47 ; cf. 71); and cf. French, p. 70.

vitiates minute points of evidence ; in particular, the small variations
between F and G from F 426 to 495 are most probably due to
a scribe. Besides this, the more important changes mentioned in
the last paragraph may at times involve lesser changes which are not
for the better. I am fully conscious of the difficulties and dangers of
this kind of argument, and mean to notice every one of their arguments which does not fall under one of the condemnations which I
have mentioned ; and mean to propose none myself which has not a
large objective element. It might seem *a priori* that a thorough
examination of the minuter differences of the two versions should
clearly indicate which is the revised version. I can only state that
after a very careful consideration of the two poems and of the
attempts of the three writers just mentioned, I am convinced that it
does not, partly, no doubt, because of the unsatisfactory MS. tradition.
I am equally convinced that Koeppel, defender though he is of G as
the revised version, does injustice to the merits of G ; and that
apart from the three points held in reserve the more important and
unambiguous æsthetic differences will speak in its favour.[1] There is
also evidence of a different character, which associates G with
a later period in Chaucer's life than F.

We come now to the points in which G is the better. In the
first place, it is more reasonably arranged—more methodical, though
without stiffness. This is notably so in the proem and what leads

---

[1] Two apparent important signs of the priority of G must be remarked on.
The following couplet of F, 143-4, on the birds, is absent from G :

> " Upon the braunches ful of blosmes softe,
> In hir delyt, they turned hem ful ofte."

That these admirable lines were deliberately omitted it is difficult to believe.
But not only is there very considerable chance of accidental omission in
a unique MS., which has suffered serious damage immediately before and after
the place where this couplet should be (as Binz points out, p. 236 ; and French
admits, p. 70 ; Legouis does not see it, p. 67) ; but also, as even the hostile
Bilderbeck shows (p. 45), some such couplet as this is needed to make grammatical connection between lines 130 and 131 of G. So we may conclude that
this omission was accidental. Secondly, in F 551 and G 541 Love declares
that he shall " charge " Chaucer no more ; in G the *Prologue* ends in four more
lines, but in F not for twenty-eight, which contain several instructions. At first
sight it looks as if in F Chaucer had inserted a passage which makes 551 of
none effect, as Koch thinks (*Engl. Stud.*, xxx. 458). But the force of this
argument is destroyed when we observe that in F the instructions do not follow
immediately on line 551 ; while in G, 541 is directly followed by the command
to begin " at Cleopatre." It seems quite as likely that G is the result of
condensation as that F is of addition. To the best of my belief and judgment,
no other signs of the priority of G can be mentioned without including the
trivial and the still more debatable, and also multiplying instances on
the other side.

up to the dream and the entry of the God of Love, as may be made
clear by a brief and bald analysis of F 40–213, and G 40–145.

F	G
His love of the daisy. He visits it in the morning. None ever loved hotter than he loves the daisy. At evening he runs to see it close. It opens in the morning. He would fain praise it worthily, and invokes lovers' aid, but they have already done so better. Hopes he shall incur no ill-will for repeating their words, since he does all in honour of love and in service of the flower. Again declares his love and reverence. Will tell later why he says that we should trust authorities. Love made him rise early to see the daisy; he knelt to watch it unclose. Description of the meadow; the birds' mirth. Allegorical digression on the birds. Sank down to watch the flower all day. Praises it again. But he is no partisan of either flower or leaf. Toward night he goes home, meaning to rise early to see the daisy again. Dreams he is back in the meadow. Entrance of Love.	His love of the daisy. He would fain praise it worthily, but "folk" have already done so better. Hopes he shall incur no ill-will for repeating their words, since he does all in honour of those who serve either leaf or flower. But he is no partisan of either. We should trust authorities. Means to declare old stories. After he has roamed the meadow, goes home to sleep. Dreams. Description of the meadow. The birds' mirth. A lark announces the God. He enters.

I do not mean, of course, that here or anywhere G is pleasanter
than F on a casual reading; rather the contrary, since it omits the
passionate devotion of the other. But in a number of points
here it is more reasonable and pleasing on examination, and closer
to Chaucer's later work. A few of these points may be indicated.
While in G he defends himself from the charge of partisanship
immediately on mentioning the flower and the leaf (70), in F,
though his devotion to the daisy is far more marked, he does not
do so till over a hundred lines later (72, 188 ff.). If G is the
earlier, there is no discoverable reason why he should have made
such a postponement in revising. Secondly, the analysis makes
very clear the extraordinary skipping about in F between morning

and evening; without motive Chaucer would hardly have made order into chaos. Thirdly, after asking in F why men should trust authorities, Chaucer says (101) " That shal I seyn, whan that I see my tyme," and then returns to dilate on his passion for the daisy, and never fulfils his promise. In G (81–8) he explains his attaching such importance to belief in authorities by the fact that he is about to relate tales drawn from them.[1] The passage in F is a good example of the free-and-easy inconsequence of that version; that in G, of its soberer forethought. Which of these characteristics may most naturally be attributed to a first version, and which to a second, is obvious enough. Next, the relation between the dream and the preparation for it seems better in G ;[2] after the essential introduction, his habitual affection for daisies, and the afternoon in the meadow which was the starting-point of the dream, he goes home and falls asleep, and the description of the meadow and the birds is a part of the dream.[3] One advantage of the method of G is that it makes the entrance of the God less abrupt ; in F Chaucer begins to dream in line 210 and in 212 the God appears, when the poet has barely got his eyes shut. But for every reason I do not see how it can be denied that this shortening and clear-marking of the introduction, and this centring of the interest on the dream scenes and incidents is an improvement. Nor, if G preceded F, is it likely that Chaucer would have made the contrary change, which would not have been in the least involved by the introduction of the personal feeling.

But more than this, version F in this point resembles Chaucer's earlier poetry, and G his later. In the *Book of the Duchess* there is a preliminary ramble which forms nearly a quarter of the whole poem, and is not closely enough connected with the main transaction to justify half that length ; in the *Parliament of Fowls* the introduction forms a sixth of the whole, and by no means justifies its length. In both he gives quite otiose accounts of what he had been doing. In the *House of Fame* the proem and invocation,

---

[1] G 81–4 will be seen to be not quite grammatical, a natural consequence of a not very careful change in the form of the sentence. An almost grotesque example of the rambling style of F will be found in the House-that-Jack-built sentence in ll. 103–114.

[2] So Binz, p. 235. Skeat also points out (III. xxiii.) that the proem is more distinctly marked in G (1–88).

[3] Legouis' reasons (see p. 62) for preferring the method of F are hardly intelligible, for the dream is quite sufficiently accounted for in G. Unfortunately the mediæval court-poet needed little excuse for dreaming.

110 lines long, followed by hundreds of lines based on the *Aeneid*, make very little contribution to what follows. It is clear, therefore, that in his earlier dream-narratives Chaucer, unlike his model Guillaume de Lorris, was in the habit of lingering in the world of actuality, even to the point of scattering, if not annihilating, the interest. But compare the fine rapidity with which he breaks into the main narrative in every one of the *Canterbury Tales*.[1] Does not this comparison suggest that G was written not only after F, but long after?

One of the most striking points of superiority in G is in the entrance of the procession and the presentation of the Balade. In F, after the God and the lady have entered together and been described at great length, Chaucer introduces the Balade with the words:

> "And therfor may I seyn, as thinketh me,
> This song, in preysing of this lady fre" (247–8).

After it he continues:

> " This balade may ful wel y-songen be,
> As I have seyd erst, by my lady free" (270–1);

he praises her again, and finally (70 lines after the first two) introduces the rest of the procession, the nineteen ladies, followed by a great multitude, who kneel in honour of the daisy and sing a few lines to her. In G the God is announced by a lark:

> " Til at the laste a larke song above:
> ' I see,' quod she, 'the mighty god of love!
> Lo! yond he cometh, I see his winges sprede !'" (141–3).

After the God and the queen have been described, the rest of the procession enters, and the Balade is sung by the ladies. As to the lark, Dr. Skeat says (III., xxiv.) it "is left out, as being unnecessary. This is a clear improvement."[2] I can only say that the lark seems to me just as necessary, and in the same sense, as the whole poem is. Again, the pause during the entrance of the procession is only about half as long in G as in F, where the Balade intervenes. But the most striking point of superiority in G is the way in which the Balade is presented. In F it has no function in

---

[1] Except the *Pardoner's* and *Canon's Yeoman's*, where the ramble is deliberate.

[2] Similarly French, p. 50 ; cf. my review, *Mod. Lang. Notes*, xxi. 61. Legouis (p. 62), however, says Chaucer had to sacrifice this pretty detail ; why ?

the narrative,[1] and even the ladies have little. I have shown else-where that the artistically unintelligible manner in which it is introduced is clearly one of the points in which at first Chaucer followed his French exemplars.[2] A further disadvantage of the state of things in F is that it makes Love refer (539 ff.) to a poem which he has not heard.[3] Is there any comparison between the two methods as to art and grace ? Could Chaucer have changed the conditions in G to those in F ?[4]

Among many small points in which on examination G appears superior to F, three may be especially mentioned. In F one of Chaucer's crimes is recorded thus :

> " For in pleyn text, with-outen nede of glose,
>   Thou hast translated the Romaunce of the Rose " (328–9) ;

in G thus, of course with the same meaning :

> " For in pleyn text, hit nedeth nat to glose " (254). . . . .

The ambiguity of the F-reading is such that it misled Dr. Koch, who says of the *Romance of the Rose* that this line " implies, though not directly meant in that way, that his rendering was a literal one."[5] Certainly there was no reason for change from the G to the F reading. Another change in the interest of lucidity occurs in G 343–6 :

> " And takth non heed of what matere he take ;
>   Therfor he wroot the Rose and eek Crisseyde
>   Of innocence, and niste what he seyde ;
>   Or him was boden make thilke tweye " ;

in F the passage is practically the same with the omission of the two middle lines. The naming of the two poems is necessary, for even in F *thilke* must go back for its antecedent past thirty-four

---

[1] So ten Brink (*Engl. Stud.*, xvii. 16–17) ; Binz (*Angl. Beibl.*, xi. 235) ; cf. also, on all this, Lowes in *Publ. Mod. Lang. Assoc.*, xix. 655–7.

[2] See *Mod. Lang. Notes*, xxi. 59, and p. 88 above. Lowes did not remark on this point, which seems to me important.

[3] It is curious also that in F Love reproaches Chaucer for not having put Alcestis into the Balade partly on the ground that he is " so gretly in hir dette " for the protection which she has only just given him. On the Balade ten Brink has some rather over-subtle criticisms (*l. c.*, p. 16–17).

[4] The one point of superiority in this part of F, the anonymity of the lady, I have asked to have held in suspense till later.

[5] *Chronology*, p. 13. The first line obviously has the same meaning as the fourth line of the Wife of Bath's spurious " head-link " in the Lansdowne MS., " I will nouht glose, bot saye the text." On this couplet, see also Lowes in *Publ. Mod. Lang. Assoc.*, xx. 855.

lines occupied with other matters.[1]   The third point is the ending ;
after the God's final admonition,

> " with that word my bokes gan I take,
> And right thus on my Legend gan I make " (578–9),

for which G has (544),

> " With that word of sleep I gan a-awake " [*sic*].

That is, in F Chaucer passes from his dream-adventures in the
meadow to working in his own library, without awaking.[2]   These
instances of the superiority of G to F are by no means all ; there
are many more in which most tastes would probably recognize
improvement.   In every case there is a clear motive for the change
if G is the later ; in every case there is none if it is not.

We now come to the cases which show other than æsthetic
evidence that G is the later version.   The " old fool " passages are
the first.[3]   In G (258–62) Love remarks that Chaucer's wit is
full cool, and adds,

> " Wel wot I ther-by thou beginnest dote
> As olde foles, whan hir spirit fayleth " ;

and later that (314–5)

> " thou reneyed hast my lay,
> As othere olde foles many a day,"

for which F has " other wrecches " (337).[4]   Now, so far as I have
been able to find, Chaucer's only other references to his own elderly
years are in the *Complaint of Venus* (76–8), where he says that age

---

[1] Legouis thinks the greater clearness of G a mark of priority, and the
obscurity of F a result of condensation (p. 64, note ; Koch agrees with him,
Engl. Stud., xxx. 457–8 ; cf. his. *Chronol.*, 83, and Binz, p. 236).   But there
is no indication in either prologue that Chaucer was trying to condense—
certainly not at the expense of clearness.   The notion that he was rests only
on the supposition that Love is Richard II., and that F 570–7 is an expression
of the royal desire for brevity.   It is unnecessary to dwell on this, especially
since, instead of being shorter than G, F is 34 lines longer.

[2] Legouis curiously ignores this consideration, and thinks F 578 superior
because it returns to the books mentioned at the beginning of the *Prologue*
(p. 65).   I may compare a similar change in the *Confessio Amantis.*   Though,
in both of Gower's versions of the end, the departure of Venus is mentioned,
that of Genius is ignored except in the revised version (Macaulay, vol. iii.,
p. 467).

[3] The point was first made by ten Brink (*Engl. Stud.*, xvii. 14 ; and see
Lowes, xx. 782–7).

[4] Cf. G 400–1 (nothing corresponding in F) :

> " Whyl he was yong, he kepte your estat,
> I not wher he be now a renegat."

has dulled him and taken away his subtlety ; and in the *Envoy to Scogan* (27, 31–5, 36–42).[1] These two poems there are good reasons for dating between 1390 and 1400.[2] Legouis (pp. 63–4) finds ground for change from the G-form in the fact that here Love falls below the dignity of a god ; but I think this reason would hardly have appealed to Chaucer, who enjoys nothing better than putting down the mighty from their seats as witness the colloquial discourse of the eagle in the *House of Fame*, or of Pluto and Proserpina in the *Merchant's Tale*. Legouis also assumes with Skeat (III. xxii.) that the revision occurred very shortly after the first draft, an assumption which is made very unlikely by the extent of the alterations.[3] Ten Brink points out that when Chaucer wrote the first version (whichever that is) he was not old enough to use such language even in joke.[4] Of course the remarks are jocose ; but since the only conceivable reason for omitting such good and characteristic lines—sensitiveness—is negatived by all that we know of Chaucer's character and practice, the most reasonable inference is that G was written long enough after F for Chaucer to have come to make fun of his own advancing years.

F 537–40 and G 525–7 form a case where the superiority of F actually suggests that G is the later. F reads :

> " Than seyde Love, ' a ful gret negligence
> Was hit to thee, that ilke tyme thou made
> " Hyd, Absolon, thy tresses," in balade,
> That thou forgete hir in thy song to sette ' " ;

for which G has :

> " ' a ful gret negligence
> Was hit to thee, to write unstedfastnesse
> Of women, sith thou knowest hir goodnesse.' "

Negligence is as distinctly the right word in F as it is the wrong one in G. The line in which it occurs is the last of a long passage in which probably only one of the differences between the versions is due to Chaucer ; to alter the word would have required recasting

---

[1] The remark in the *House of Fame* (995) need hardly be considered.

[2] On *Venus*, see Skeat I. 86 ; on *Scogan*, Skeat I. 556–7, and G. L. Kittredge, *Harvard Studies and Notes*, i. 116–7 ; on both in connection with the year of Chaucer's birth, Lounsbury's *Studies*, i. 36–42. In partial answer to Lounsbury, I may point out that January in the *Merchant's Tale* is regarded as an old man at sixty.

[3] See p. 122 below.

[4] *Engl. Stud.*, xvii. 10 ; cf. Koeppel, *Literaturblatt*, 1893, p. 51 ; and Koch, *Chronology*, p. 82.

DEV. CH.

of the whole couplet of which it is one of the rhymes.   If Chaucer
wrote G first, it is strange indeed that the change he made in the
later lines exactly fitted the proper meaning of this word, while if F
is the earlier it is not surprising that he failed to alter it.[1]

In F, among the parting injunctions of Love, is the line (562) :

"Make the metres of hem as the leste."

Is not this assuredly an allusion to the fact that Chaucer is using a
metre new to English poetry ?[2]   I have already shown that this
cannot be the first poem in which Chaucer used the decasyllabic
couplet, but no doubt it was the first one published.   Such an
allusion is certainly less surprising in a first version than in a second ;
if a long interval elapsed between, this line almost proves F the
earlier.

There are several passages which suggest that F is the earlier and
G the later by certain points of connection with earlier or later works
of Chaucer's.   This has already been pointed out in the case of the
introductory portion of the *Prologue.*   But the most important
cases of parallels to earlier and later works are the only two long
passages that are confined each to one version.

In F 153–187, the digression on the birds, the first part is
strongly in the style of the *Romance of the Rose* and the *Parliament
of Fowls,*[3] with its (quite superfluous) characterization of an individual bird, its vows of constancy, and its allegory ; it is a digression
from a digression, with an impertinent quotation from Aristotle.   The
passage is so irrelevant that Mr. Bilderbeck [4] has found it necessary
to fill it with political allegory.   It alone would suggest that the
version which omits it is the later,—it is surely not very likely to
have been added on revision, especially if the revision was made
a considerable time after the first writing, and most especially if in the
Canterbury-period.   But it is less significant than the second passage,[5] G 267–312, where Love asks Chaucer why he has not written
of good women, and declares that he might have found many such

---

[1] Cf. Lowes, in *Publ. Mod. Lang. Assoc.*, xx. 799.
[2] Cf. Lowes, p. 814, whose alternative suggestion seems to me hardly
possible.
[3] Cf. Skeat's notes, III. 295–6.
[4] Pp. 101–3. His interpretation seems to me very unlikely ; it is vague, and
touches the passage at only a few points. It is so easy to construct *ex post facto*
allegories (as witness the procedure of the Shakspere-Bacon fanatics, and, in the
sixteenth century, of Tasso and of the admirers of Ariosto) that it seems to
me they should be submitted to a very austere criticism.
[5] This argument is developed from ten Brink's, in *Engl. Stud.*, xvii. 15–16.

in Valerius, Titus, Claudian, Jerome, Ovid, and Vincent. Only one
reason worth mentioning why Chaucer should have omitted this
passage is suggested by those who think F the later version ;
Legouis (p. 63) thinks this passage a verbose pedantic sermon.[1]
We may like the passage or we may not,—in itself it is not much
better than the verses on the birds which G lacks ; but it forms an
integral part of the poem, which the other does not, by adding
force to Love's rebuke. As to the charge of pedantry, the Middle
Ages took a view different from ours of appeals to authority, even of
a display of learning, and no criticism can do mediæval literature
justice which disregards this fact ; the greatest of all mediæval
poets is full of direct citation of Aristotle and the theologians.
Chaucer uses the practice with humorous effect in the *Nun's
Priest's Tale*, but that he was far from meaning to ridicule it
is shown by the discourse on ancient chaste heroines with which
Dorigen assuages her grief.[2] With this latter passage the one
in question has much in common, in source, tone, and content—
enough to link it rather to Chaucer's later work than to his earlier ;
and it is certainly more in place.

But it is also important to observe the authors whom Chaucer
names here. We may at once disregard Ovid, with whom he shows
familiarity throughout his literary career ; Claudian, to whom he
refers in the *House of Fame ;* and Titus, no doubt Livy, with
whom he had long been familiar through *Le Roman de la Rose*,
and whom he quotes, not necessarily at first hand, in the *Legend of
Lucretia* and in the *Book of the Duchess.* Vincent of Beauvais,[3]
it has been supposed, or else *Jerome against Jovinian*, is quoted on
the use of a hyæna's gall to cure blindness in *Fortune*, 35–6, a
poem of wholly uncertain date ; but it is impossible to be sure
of the source of an idea like this, and moreover this poem may be a
translation.[4] Chaucer possibly quotes Vincent in the *Nun's Priest's
Tale*, 4354, and probably in the *Wife of Bath's*, 1195. So far as
evidence goes, then, Vincent is associated with the period of the

---

[1] See also Koch, *Chronology*, p. 83 ; Bilderbeck, p. 83.
[2] *Frankl. T.*, 1364–456. A similar list and discourse, under not dissimilar circumstances, is to be found in Boccaccio's *Fiammetta* (Moutier,
Florence, 1829 ; vol. vi., pp. 181–99). The whole eighth chapter is
occupied by a soliloquy, in which Fiammetta cites and dwells on two or
three dozen antique heroines, in order to console herself for her disappointed
love.
[3] See Lounsbury's *Studies*, ii. 379–80.
[4] *Ibid.*, p. 296.

Canterbury Tales. As to Valerius, it is not quite certain who is meant, for Chaucer mentions three of the name. It is certainly not Valerius Flaccus, the author of the *Argonauticon*.[1] Skeat thinks it is Walter Map's *Dissuasio Valerii ad Rufinum*,[2] which he mentions or quotes in the *Wife of Bath's Prologue* and the *Merchant's Tale*.[3] Koeppel and Lounsbury[4] think it is Valerius Maximus, who elsewhere is quoted only in the *Wife's Tale* and *Prologue*, and perhaps in the *Nun's Priest's Tale* and the *Monk's Tale*.[5] Though the last has sometimes been thought earlier than the *Legend*, this has certainly not been proved, and later I hope to go very far toward disproving it.[6] Certainly it is fair to say that Valerius Maximus[7] is distinctly associated with a subsequent period. With the work of Map the case is still stronger. *Jerome against Jovinian* Chaucer uses or mentions only here and in the *Canterbury Tales*, so far as present information goes, and except for one or two possible cases. The first is the almost nugatory one mentioned already, in which in *Fortune* he may quote either this work or Vincent of Beauvais ; the second is a quotation from either Jerome or John of Salisbury[8] in *The Former Age* (33),

[1] Cf. *L. G. W.*, 1457–8 ; *T. and C.*, V.·8.
[2] In Map's *De Nugis Curialium* (Camden Society, 1850), pp. 142–52.
[3] See Lounsbury, ii. 367–70 ; Koeppel, *Anglia*, xiii. 181–3.
[4] *Anglia*, xiii. 182 ; *Studies*, ii. 276.
[5] Lounsbury, *Studies*, ii. 273–6. Miss K. O. Petersen (*Sources of the N. P. T.*, Boston, 1898 ; pp. 110, 117) shows that the two *exempla* in *N. P. T.* 4174–4294 may be from neither Cicero nor Valerius directly, but may come from the latter through Robert Holkot's *Super Libros Sapientiæ*. Professor Bright (*Mod. Lang. Notes*, ix. 241) has attempted to show that this Valerius is quoted in *H. F.* 516. The *Elcanor* to whom a marvellous dream is attributed he thinks is Hamilcar, whose dream as to the taking of Syracuse is narrated in a few lines by Valerius in book I. 7, 8. But such a monstrous corruption as this seems hardly probable in late written tradition. I fear that we must agree that this reference is still unexplained. The conjecture that there might be something to explain it in the romance of *Escanor* is negatived by an examination of that poem kindly undertaken by Dr. G. L. Hamilton.
[6] See pp. 164–172 below.
[7] I agree with Koeppel and Lounsbury that Chaucer probably refers to him. In *Valerii Maximi factorum dictorumque memorabilium libri ix.* (Curiae Regnit, 1799), iii. 2, "De fortitudine" praises Portia, wife of Brutus ; iv. 6, "De amore conjugali" again praises her, and also Julia, daughter of Cæsar, and others ; vi. 1, "De pudicitia" praises Lucretia and others, mainly severe-minded men ; vi. 7, "De fide uxorum erga maritos" praises the wives of Scipio Africanus, Q. Lucretius and Lentulus. Cf. French, p. 57, whose treatment of the subject of these authors, however, is very unsatisfactory. The work of Map praises, to be sure, Lucretia, Penelope, and the Sabine women ; but immediately adds, "Amice, nulla est Lucretia, nulla Penelope, nulla Sabina ; omnes time" (p. 145). An allusion to this book by the God of Love could be explained only as a *mauvaise plaisanterie*.
[8] The Rev. W. W. Woollcombe can hardly be said to have proved Chaucer not to have known the *Polycraticus* (Ch. Soc. *Essays*, 295–8).

a poem of unknown date, which cannot be assumed to be contemporaneous with the *Boethius*. What has usually been deemed a third use of Jerome occurs in both forms of this very prologue— the mention of "Marcia Catoun" as a "Good Woman" in the Balade. But I have tried to show elsewhere that such is very unlikely to have been her source, and that she is most likely derived from the *Divine Comedy*, where the poets meet Marcia the wife of Cato in Limbo, and in Purgatory appeal to the husband in her name.[1] There is no evidence, therefore, that Chaucer was familiar with any of St. Jerome's works before the time of the *Canterbury Tales.*[2] But then he quotes from *Jerome against Jovinian* frequently and extensively; twice in the *Pardoner's Tale* (505, 527), once in the *Manciple's Tale* (148), largely in the *Franklin's Tale* (1367–456), and (as Koeppel shows) in the *Wife of Bath's Prologue*, the *Sumner's Tale*, and the *Merchant's Tale, passim.*[3] Now in the G prologue Chaucer betrays great intimacy with the work; otherwise it is the last thing which he would think of making Love quote, and while the other authors are barely mentioned he has twenty-four lines on Jerome's work. Does not this fact point to a period when he was especially familiar with it? Therefore of the six authors mentioned we have found three to be more or less distinctly and emphatically associated with the Canterbury-period.[4]

The only two long passages, therefore, which are each found in only one version are unambiguous in their testimony. That in F is likely to have been written relatively early in Chaucer's poetic career, because it resembles in tone several of his earlier works; and might well be omitted on revision because it is a digression. That in G, on the other hand, performs a function in the narrative, and by its character and by the authors to whom it refers associates itself with Chaucer's later work.

A somewhat similar argument may be based on the mention in G only, among Chaucer's own works, of the book,

---

[1] *Inf.*, IV. 128; *Purg.*, I. 78–81. See *Mod. Philol.*, iii. 368–70.

[2] He quotes him several times in the *Pars. T.*, which may antedate most of the *C. T.*; but it is certainly a translation.

[3] See Skeat's index of authors; Lounsbury's *Studies*, ii. 292–7; Koeppel, *Anglia*, xiii. 174–81. One cannot help fancying that Chaucer first became familiar with this work when he was planning and writing *W. B. P.* See also pp. 202, 209, 212 below.

[4] Of course this is no proof that he did not know some of them earlier, but the inference is justifiable that he was not familiar with all of them.

> " ' Of the Wreched Engendring of Mankinde,'
>   As man may in pope Innocent y-finde." [1]

Professor Lowes [2] is no more assuredly right in rejecting the
biographical reasons for dating this work in the late eighties than
in deducing a late date from the use of it in the *Man of Law's
Prologue* and *Tale*,[3] and the *Pardoner's Tale*, and also in dwelling
on the improbability of Chaucer's mentioning it here unless he had
just produced it.

This finishes the evidence on the question of priority, save
for the three matters which I have been holding in solution.
Aside from them, points of superiority in F are negligible. The
indications that G is the later, on the other hand, are many and
various, and by no possibility which I can conceive, even granted
that individually they are sometimes small, can they be explained
away. Considerations of merit and of literary relations both lend
strong support to the crucial evidence supplied by Lowes' demon-
stration of the closer connection of F with certain French models.
It remains for me to attempt the rehabilitation and extension of the
old and orthodox theory of a personal compliment to the queen
paid through Prologue F, and removed from G ; which I believe
will account for all the respects in which the latter seems inferior
to the former.

§ 2. *Its Connection with the Queen.*

The theory which I propose as to a connection between the
Legend of Good Women and the queen is largely the old one ; but
I can offer new evidence for it, and make a new application of it.
I believe :—That Chaucer uses the daisy and Alcestis expressly as
vehicles for his personal tribute to Queen Anne ; that accordingly
the personal devotion expressed in F was meant and understood as
a compliment to her ; that the writing of the whole *Legend* was a

---

[1] It also seems odd that if F is the later, Chaucer should at once omit this
work and substitute *holynesse* for *besinesse* just before. Legouis takes an
opposite view (p. 68).

[2] *Publ. Mod. Lang. Assoc.*, xx. 790–4. The force of the argument was
admitted by even Koch (*Chronol.*, 86), but later he changed his mind (*Engl.
Stud.*, xxx. 457). And cf. Legouis, 65.

[3] Cf. pp. 181–2 below. I show on p. 214 that the passage in *W. B. P.* is
perhaps due to Gower's *Mirour*. Another connection between G and *M. L. T.*
(pointed out by Koeppel, Herrig's *Archiv*, lxxxiv. 411) is that G 312, 529
parallel *M. L. T.* 701–2.

task imposed, in a light vein, by her;[1] that the revision of the *Prologue* was made after her death; and that all the passages in it which definitely recalled the earlier connection with her were carefully excised, probably out of consideration to her husband's feelings. Put thus baldly, this may well sound rash and gratuitous; but I believe there is excellent evidence for all of it, and that thus alone can the facts be explained.

Tyrwhitt first showed the connection with Queen Anne made by the couplet (F, 496–7) in which Alcestis instructs the poet to present the finished work to the queen, "at Eltham, or at Shene."[2] Ten Brink in 1870 suggested[3] that the queen was celebrated by means of the daisy and Alcestis, and that the whole was a tribute of gratitude to her for having secured for Chaucer in February, 1385, permission to discharge his custom-house duties through a deputy. Till 1903 this view was accepted by everybody (I believe) who expressed himself in print on the subject; by Dr. Furnivall (doubtfully) in 1871,[4] by Professor Skeat in 1894 and earlier,[5] by Dr. Koch in 1890,[6] by Mr. A. W. Pollard in 1901,[7] and by Professor Bilderbeck in 1902.[8] In one of the last articles he ever wrote,[9] ten Brink kept this date for the first version of the *Prologue* and for the legends, and therefore evidently held to the theories on which the date rested. But in 1903 I showed[10] that, since the petition that Chaucer might be allowed a deputy was signed by Robert de Vere, Earl of Oxford, it was he and not the queen who was Chaucer's sponsor in this matter, and that therefore there is no such external reason for connecting the *Legend* with the date 1385, or with the queen. My conclusions have been almost universally accepted.[11] But Professor Lowes,[12] acting in part

---

[1] In this point I slightly modify my earlier article on *L. G. W.* (*Mod. Philol.*, i. 326).

[2] *C. T.* (1830), I. clxi. He pointed out that we must therefore date the poem not earlier than 1382, when Richard II. married.

[3] *Studien*, pp. 147 ff. A list of those who have accepted the identification of Alcestis and Anne is given by Lowes, *Publ. Mod. Lang. Assoc.*, xix. 666; but add Legouis, p. 69. The daisy was always believed to mean some living woman; Speght in 1602 (p. *b. vi. bis*) stated that it typified Princess Margaret.

[4] *Trial Forewords*, pp. 25, 106.   [5] III. xix.

[6] *Chronology*, 44–5.

[7] *Globe Chaucer*, xlv.; cf. *Chaucer Primer*, 95–6.

[8] Bilderbeck, *Chaucer's L. G. W.*, p. 88, note.

[9] *Engl. Stud.*, xvii. 19. Cf. also his *History of English Literature* (1893), ii. 110–13.   [10] *Mod. Philol.*, i. 324–9.

[11] By Lowes, *Publ. Mod. Lang. Assoc.*, xix. 670; (apparently) by French, *The Problem of the Two Prologues* (Baltimore, 1905), p. 21; by Koch, *Engl. Stud.*, xxxvi. 141–2. Root rejects them (p. 141).   [12] *L. c.*, 669–76.

on my evidence, goes so far as to reject all connection between the
queen and the apparent symbolism of Prologue F. Herein I
believe he goes too far, and that his and my opinion that F is the
earlier version is greatly strengthened by the orthodox view as to
the queen and the *Prologue.*

Let us first consider the surface appearance of the two versions.
That some living woman is symbolized by the daisy and by
Alcestis in F, and not in G, seems a plausible and almost inevitable
conjecture. In their treatment of the daisy, the contrast, as to
personal devotion, between the two versions can hardly be
exaggerated. In G this devotion finds distinct expression only in
lines 40–8, 55–60, 92, 511–12; in F, however, in 40–8, 50–9,
60–72, 82–96, 103–111, 115–17, 180–7, 201–2, 211, 523–4.
Again, it is expressed in F with a warmth to which there is no
parallel in the other version. Consider, among others, the following lines peculiar to F:

> " Ther loved no wight hotter in his lyve " (59);

> " The herte in-with my sorowful brest yow dredeth,
>   And loveth so sore, that ye ben verrayly
>   The maistresse of my wit, and nothing I " (86–8);

> " My besy gost . . . .
>   Constreyned me with so gledy desyr,
>   That in my herte I fele yit the fyr " (103–6).

All this language, it must be remarked, is used toward the daisy.
In lines 69–83 he appeals to lovers to help him praise the flower,
and apologizes to them, instead of to the indefinite "folk" of G,
for repeating their words. Three small points may be especially
noted : in F he writes

> " in the honour
> Of love, and eek in service of the flour " (81–2),

in G

> " in forthering and honour
> Of hem that either serven leef or flour " (69–70);

he is kneeling by the daisy in F (308) when the procession enters
and surrounds him—"faste by under a bente" in G (234); and
only in the former does the God of Love call the daisy his flower
(316, 318), or his relic (321). Finally, there is no mistaking in
F the human symbolism of the daisy. This appears first in the
pronouns used in speaking of it. In G, *hit* is used in 49, 52–3,

and *she* only in 95 (which reads practically the same in F); in F
hit is used in 49, 52, 56, 62, 65, 111, 117, 183, but *she* (*hir*) in
53, 63, 64, 84, 186–7, and *yow* (*ye, your*) in 86–7, 89, 92, 93, 94,
95.   Although the change to the second person is due to the fact
that Chaucer is translating here from the *Filostrato*,[1] while
Boccaccio uses the singular *tu*, Chaucer changes to the more
reverent plural.[2]   The personal symbolism shows markedly in the
use of such expressions toward the daisy as *maistresse* (88), *lady
sovereyne* (94 ; cf. 271–5, where similar language is used of
Alcestis, in F only), *erthly god*[3] (95 ; cf. the whole passage, 83–
96), *this flour so yong*,[4] *so fresh of hewe* (104),—all of which
are unparalleled in G.   In contrast to this reiteration, intensity
and unquestionable inner meaning, we have in G only the
minimum of devotion necessary to justify the introduction of the
daisy at all.[5]   As to Alcestis, she is explicitly identified with the
daisy in both versions (G 499–500, 506–7 ; F 511–12, 518–19),
and in gratitude for her protection is highly extolled for her beauty
and goodness ; but in F Chaucer's devotion to her is slightly more
pronounced (cf. 270–5, not in G).[6]   There can be no doubt that
all these differences were deliberate ; either Chaucer introduced
human symbolism and an appearance of warm feeling into a poem
originally without a sign of either,[7] or else he cut them out of a
poem that had had both.

It has seemed worth while to sift out the reasons for the impres-
sion of personal feeling which F gives as opposed to G, because it
brings the issue to a head.   But now how is it all to be interpreted?
Lowes says this feeling is all literary convention, and directed to
Chaucer's ideal mistress Alcestis ; "all these assumed allusions of
Chaucer to the Queen are nothing whatever but translations of such

[1] See Lowes, *Publ. Mod. Lang. Assoc.*, xix. 619.
[2] Evidently he would not *thou* his queen.
[3] Skeat (III. xxiii) glosses this phrase by line 387, where Alcestis says
that lords (Skeat errs in saying *kings*) are "half-goddes in this world here."
[4] The queen was twenty at the probable date of the F prologue.
[5] Chaucer expresses love for the daisy only once (42–4), and in the *plural*
(*these floures*).
[6] In F Alcestis seems to be the vehicle for Chaucer's veneration toward the
queen, and the daisy for his "courtly love."
[7] So Furnivall (*Trial Forewords*, p. 106).   Skeat (III. xxii.) thinks that
even in G the queen was symbolized, but so inadequately that Chaucer at
once rewrote it.   Not only is such a procedure highly improbable, and not
only does it represent Chaucer as singularly helpless and inept, but if we
had only version G we should be unable to detect more symbolism than the
relation between the daisy and Alcestis.

conventional expressions as form the very warp and woof of the French poems he was imitating;"[1] all the personal language, including the *lady sovereyne*, he regards as "commonplaces taken over bodily from the originals" in French and Italian, and the use of *she* or *her* for the daisy is "simply the adoption of the convention of the type." As to this last point, Lowes disregards the obvious fact that while *elle* is required in French by the grammatical gender of *flour* and *margherite*, *she* in English is wholly personal. He is quite justified in saying that Chaucer's other personal and emotional language, and his celebration of the daisy, are paralleled in French poetry; and he has made an important contribution to the subject by showing that this alone cannot prove a connection with the queen. But an examination of all the French poems in question will show that Chaucer altogether outdoes his French exemplars. These poems may be divided into two classes. Of long narratives there are two, Deschamps' *Lay de Franchise*, and Froissart's *Paradys d'Amours*, to which Lowes has shown that Chaucer is deeply indebted for his plan. The lyric poems comprise Machault's *Dit de la Marguerite*, Froissart's *Dittié de la flour de la Margherite, Le joli mois de May*, the 17th Pastourelle and the end of the *Plaidoirie*, and a dozen or so of Deschamps' *balades*. Most of these poems fall far behind Chaucer's in intensity and insistency of feeling. Of all of them the warmest devotion and love is to be found in the first two of the lyrics; elsewhere courtly compliment is paid to the flower, and devotion to the poet's lady, but the two are rarely combined, as in Chaucer. What Chaucer has really done is to combine the lyric warmth of Machault's *Dit* and Froissart's *Dittié* with the narrative schemes of Froissart and Deschamps, introducing also an intensely personal passage from Boccaccio's *Filostrato;* so that he may indeed be said to have outdone his models in strength and personalness of feeling. These French and Italian poems are known to have been addressed to real ladies, and their strong language therefore had point; must we believe that Chaucer even went beyond them, yet had nobody in view nearer than a mythical Greek lady? With the conditions in the later version Lowes' view would perfectly agree; but it attributes to F, it seems to me, tasteless and pointless extravagance. We may well agree with the God of Love that Chaucer's wit is full cool; his manner here would seem very much out of character.

[1] *Publ. M. L. A.*, xix. 670–1: cf. 620–1.

But Lowes believes[1] that some of this language would hardly fit the queen either; that an identification of the daisy and Alcestis with the queen involves offences against taste and reason. The question is, of course, what we mean by identification; it seems to me, though this is a charge that can rarely be brought against Professor Lowes' views, that his conception of it is rather bare and bald. I conceive that Chaucer wished to pay a gallant and delicate tribute to his queen; that he adopted a well-recognized form, poetic praise of the daisy, which at once set people asking who was really meant; his overt answer in the poem is—*Alcestis;* an answer which, considering contemporary custom and the strength of his language, was hardly quite satisfying, yet took the crude edge off the identification with the queen; the more subtle answer is indicated when Alcestis herself says at the end that the whole completed poem is to be laid as a tribute at the feet of Anne. He that had ears to hear, let him hear. A lady is ardently celebrated in the poem, which announces its own dedication and presentation to a lady; must they not in some way be identified? Supposing Chaucer had wished to celebrate the queen in the *Legend of Good Women*, how could he have done it better? Obviously the daisy could not be made to speak, nor could he bring Queen Anne in person into the poem. I shall suggest presently that the poem was probably destined to be read at court; what could be more tasteful and clever than Chaucer's method? There had to be a human understudy and intermediary, and what more suitable one could be chosen than Alcestis, the model queen and devoted wife, who had had for years such a charm for the poet?[2] This tacit understanding secured delicacy, and gave him freedom; he might express as much *latria* for the daisy as he pleased, and by the time it had passed through the hands of Alcestis to those of the queen it had become nothing more than a proper *dulia*. I do not think this is over-subtle, though of course what it makes explicit was in Chaucer's mind in part only implicit; and it makes innocuous the warmth of the affection which Chaucer expresses. Considering that for years poets had applied similar language to ladies whom they had not always a right to address so,

---

[1] Pp. 671-2, note.

[2] Chaucer had already several times, while following a more or less common late mediæval literary custom, foreshadowed his collection of the martyrs of love and his celebration of Alcestis. See *B. D.*, 62-220, 330-1, 726-41, 1080-7; *T. C.*, V. 1527-33, 1777-8; *H. F.*, 239-382, 388-426.

and considering the free manners of the time, the customs of "courtly love," and the familiar sort of relations which we are coming to see more and more clearly had existed for years between Chaucer and the court, why should not the genial poet of forty-five or so have thus addressed his queen of twenty? It seems also to make the identification a little too strict and frank to see a violation of good taste in the bare mention of Alcestis' death and going to hell instead of her husband; was Chaucer to ignore the main element in her story? And the fact that it is Alcestis who bids the poet present the book to the queen seems to me not in the slightest degree to contradict such a vague relation between the two as I have conceived, but rather to strengthen the probability of it.[1] Finally, it seems to me that in one passage of the *Prologue*,[2] quoted earlier for another reason, there is strong evidence for precisely such an ill-defined but close connection of the queen with the poem, and its daisy and lady, as I had conceived before I noted this passage. After highly praising Alcestis,

> " Than seyde Love, 'a ful gret negligence
> Was hit to thee, that ilke tyme thou made
> " Hyd, Absolon, thy tresses," in balade,
> That thou forgete hir in thy song to sette,
> Sin that thou art so gretly in hir dette'" (537–41).

Love believes that the " my lady " of the Balade is another than Alcestis; who is she if not the queen? Chaucer may have landed himself in subtle difficulties[3] by his hypostatic union, but some such union he clearly made. Here he sacrifices a little poetic propriety in order to make his compliment plainer.

A somewhat close connection of the *Legend of Good Women* with the court circle and the queen is made particularly plausible by the close and familiar association with them which we are learning that Chaucer enjoyed. I need only recall his almost life-

---

[1] The substitution in G of *And* in the " *I* al foryeve " in F 450, of which Lowes (p. 672, note) makes much, I have little doubt is a scribal variation; it comes in a long passage in which all the variants appear to be such, as we shall see presently.

[2] Cf. ten Brink's not very satisfactory discussion of this passage in *Engl. Stud.*, xvii. 16–18.

[3] Another one (it may be thought) is that while according to my suggestion it was the queen who had upbraided Chaucer for writing " the Rose and eek Criseyde," Alcestis apologizes for his having done so. Here it is the God of Love that plays the queen's part. But a critic must feel that this cold-blooded analysis rather spoils things. Chaucer's method here is not only intelligible enough artistically, but is notably delicate and clever.

long connection with John of Gaunt, and the familiar relations which Professor Kittredge has shown to have subsisted between Chaucer and other members of the court circle;[1] the fact that probably his wife was sister to Katherine Swynford, John's mistress and finally wife ; that exactly as he fell into misfortune in 1386, when Parliament began to object to the king's appointees, just so his prosperity revived in 1389, with the king's return to authority;[2] that, to say nothing of many other appointments and pensions from the Crown, he had been sent to France in 1378 to negotiate Richard's marriage, and (as I have said elsewhere)[3] perhaps his later trip to Milan may have been not unconnected with the marriage-proposals of Richard and Caterina Visconti ; finally, that he wrote the *Parliament of Fowls* to celebrate the betrothal of Richard and Anne, a poem written in such a light and at times even jocose vein as would have been very unsuitable as coming from the pen of any but a real friend.   I should conceive Chaucer's relations with the royal family, allowing for personal differences, to have been something like those between Sir David Lyndsay and the young James V. of Scotland, which account for the respectful familiarity which the former often expresses in his poems.   There is a parallel to this in the admonitory tone of Chaucer's *balade, Lack of Steadfastness*, obviously addressed to King Richard.

For the connection of Chaucer and the *Legend* with the queen, and certainly with the court circle, there is some evidence in the allusions in the *Prologue* to the Flower and Leaf cult, which Professor Kittredge suggests imply some kind of a court club.[4]   In

---

[1] *Modern Philology*, i. 1 ff.

[2] Within two months in each case.   Cf. Hales in *Dict. Nat. Biogr.*, x. 165 ; *ibid.*, xlviii. 148.   Chaucer's new appointment seems to have been connected rather with this than with John of Gaunt's return to England.

[3] See pp. 41–2 above.   See also *Life Records*, pp. xxviii. 203, 230.   Other connections with the court are his intimacy with the courtier Bukton (pp. 210–11 below), and the fact that the Earl of Oxford got him his custom-house deputy.

[4] *Mod. Philol.*, i. 1–2.   The lines which I quote show, according to him, "that English court society, in the time of Richard II., entertained itself by dividing into two amorous orders—the Leaf and the Flower—and by discussing . . . the comparative excellence of those two emblems or of the qualities they typified.   If we call in Gower's testimony also, we are perhaps justified in supposing that the two orders sometimes appeared in force, each member bedecked with the symbol to which he or she had sworn allegiance."   He refers to Gower's *Confessio Amantis* (ed. by Macaulay, vol. iii., p. 453), and to *L. G. W.* (G), 69–70 ; *T. C.*, I., st. 3; *Sq. T.*, 272.   The Daisy cult, presumably at first independent, of course was readily absorbed by the other.   It is a plausible guess that the queen belonged to the order of the Flower, and therefore, celebrating her as the daisy, Chaucer is anxious to disclaim permanent partisan-

spite of his devotion to the daisy-blossom, he is anxious lest he shall
be thought a partisan of the Flower against the Leaf, which he
denies being (F, 191–6 ; G, 75–80):

> " For, as to me, nis lever noon ne lother ;
> I nam with-holden yit with never nother.
> Ne I not who serveth leef, ne who the flour ;
> Wel brouken they hir service or labour ;
> For this thing is al of another tonne,
> Of olde story, er swich thing was begonne."

This sounds as if there were some jocose mystery about it, and (as
Professor Kittredge points out to me) as if Chaucer had not yet
become a member.   Now the first literary expression of the Daisy
and Flower and Leaf cults are in the works of Machault, Froissart
and Deschamps, and further, one of these poems, Froissart's *Prison
Amoureuse*, written in 1371, is addressed probably to Wenceslas of
Brabant, Anne's own cousin, and Froissart's friend and patron.[1]
The second cult seemingly developed among royal ladies connected
with France, and finally it involved one of John of Gaunt's daughters,
in 1386 or earlier.[2]   May we not even conjecture that it was partly
through Queen Anne that it was introduced into England ?   There
is some countenance for this suggestion in the way in which Gower
mentions the Flower and the Leaf (VIII. 2467–72); the companies
of lovers wore

> " Garlandes noght of o colour,
> Some of the lef, some of the flour,
> And some of grete Perles were ;
> The newe guise of Beawme there,
> With sondri thinges wel devised,
> I sih, wherof thei ben queintised."

He thus connects the Flower and Leaf cult with the new Bohemian
fashions introduced by Queen Anne.

Two or three passages in the poem suggest that Chaucer had in
mind to read it aloud in a circle of his friends, presumably at
court.[3]   At the end of the *Legend of Phyllis*, he says (2559–61):

> " Be war, ye women, of your sotil fo,
> Sin yit this day men may ensample see ;
> And trusteth, as in love, no man but me."

---

ship.   If the Leaf people wish to make him a member, he will not decline.
On all this cf. an article by G. L. Marsh in *Modern Philology*, iv. 121–167.
  [1] See Lowes, in *Publ. Mod. Lang. Assoc.*, xix. 600.
  [2] Kittredge in *Mod. Philol.*, i. 4.
  [3] I find Mather makes the same suggestion (*Chaucer's Prol.*, etc., xxiii.).

In the *Legend of Hypsipyle* he says of Jason (1554-5) :

> " But in this hous if any fals lover be,
> Right as him-self now doth, right so dide he."

I take this as explaining a phrase in G 85 :

> " For myn entent is, *or I fro yow fare,*
> The naked text in English to declare
> Of many a story." [1]

Does not this also account for the informal, colloquial, jocose and even frivolous tone which is more striking in the *Legend*[2] than in almost any of Chaucer's poems, even than in the *Canterbury Tales,* which are represented as orally delivered? Does it not especially account for Chaucer's jocosely classing himself, in G, among " old fools " (262, 315)?

It will be recollected that according to Lydgate it was the queen that dictated the subject of the *Legend:*

> " This poete wrote, at the request of the quene,
> A Legende, of perfite holynesse,
> Of Good Women, to fynd out nynetene." [3]

[1] This passage is Koeppel's chief argument for believing the G-prologue meant to be delivered as a *Canterbury Tale* (*Literaturblatt,* xiv., col. 52). Cf. p. 89 above. But allusions to the practice of reading aloud are not uncommon in Chaucer's works ; see *A. A.,* 165-6 ; *T. C.,* I. 450, II. 30, 43, 1751 ; *Cl. T.,* 1163 ; even *Pars. T.,* 1081 and *Astrolabe,* Prol., 48. Cf. also Lounsbury, *Studies,* i. 228.

[2] Cf. the end of the *Cleopatra* (703-5) :

> " Now, er I finde a man thus trewe and stable,
> And wol for love his deeth so freely take,
> I pray god lat our hedes never ake ! "

See also 863, 1076-7, 1383, 1557, 1887, 1893, 2177-80, 2227, 2490-3. I may ask, by the way, whether the intimacy with Minos as infernal judge which produced the rather superfluous apostrophe to him in one of the above passages, 1886-8, was not due to his prominence in the *Divine Comedy* (*Inferno,* V. 4-24, and elsewhere), rather than to the *Aeneid,* where he is barely mentioned (VI. 431-3).

[3] See *Skeat,* III. xx. "Lydgate can hardly be correct," according to Skeat, for if Chaucer had done so, " he would have let us know it." Why, since by hypothesis he was writing for the queen and not for us ? Lydgate's testimony is also rejected by Pollard (*Globe Chaucer,* p. xlv.), but is accepted by Koch (*Chronology,* pp. 43-4), and Bilderbeck (p. 84 ; cf. 88, note). I have even suggested already the occasion of her (not very serious) request ; see the chapter on the *Troilus,* p. 17, in reply to Lowes' suggestion that *L. G. W.* is the response to a supposed sensation produced by the first appearance of *T. C.* Queen Anne, a foreigner, coming to England in December, 1381, would hardly have been able to read the *Troilus* and the *Romance of the Rose* much before the date of the *Legend ;* after she had done so, what more natural than that she should reproach the poet for his cynical taste, and tell him to write now on the other side—to accomplish his desire of writing on Alcestis

I have shown earlier that Lydgate was in a position to know about the time when the *Troilus* was written, and I see no reason why the above statement, which is very unlikely to have been made up groundlessly, should not be correct.[1] To substantiate it there is very good internal evidence. For one thing, I have said earlier that Chaucer's manner of mentioning the *Palamon* suggests that it was unfinished. Why did he drop it and begin something else (returning to it later), unless on external pressure ? But above all, why did Chaucer, to whom poetry was an avocation, and who was constantly leaving things unfinished, continue this poem long after it had become a burden to him? At times, as we shall see, the style is almost careless, and Chaucer expresses far more sense of haste and weariness than in any other of his works.[2] At the end of Prologue F, 570–7, Love tells him to be brief,[3] which is certainly more likely to be the poet's own excuse than the record of a command by his patron ; so even at first he felt the task to be a large one. At times he seems to be spurred on only by a sense of duty, and shows a sense of the monotony attending his subject. He will not describe Cleopatra's wedding-celebration lest, having undertaken so much else, he should have to omit matters of more consequence (616–23) ; it would be loss of time to say why Dido came to Lybia, and he does not care to (996–7) ; he would to God he had leisure and time to rhyme all Jason's wooing (1552–3) ; Hypsipyle's and Medea's letters in Ovid would be too long to write

---

which he had expressed at the end of the *Troilus?* He says so very much, with such iteration, about the faithlessness and dangerousness of men, that the whole poem is clearly, as Lowes points out, a rejoinder to comment produced by the *Troilus* and the *Rose*, yet I have tried to show that the *Legend* cannot have been written till ten years or so after the *Troilus ;* if it was a rejoinder to the general comment evoked by the latter, Chaucer certainly was, as Lowes says, belated. But if it was the Queen that chaffed him, all is explained. He felt, of course, in duty bound to carry out her suggestion ; the *Prologue* he wrote *con amore*, but the legends without enthusiasm. We may conjecture that after a time the queen "let him off," which accounts for the unfinished state of the work (this in answer to Pollard, *Globe Chaucer*, p. xlv.).

[1] Chaucer rather distinctly suggests in the *Legend* that the writing of the *Troilus* and of the *Romance of the Rose* was encouraged, at least, by some one of high station (F, 366–7 ; G, 346–7) :

          "Or him was boden make thilke tweye
           Of som persone, and durste hit nat withseye."

[2] *Kn. T.* shows a sort of conscious rapidity, because he was always aware of an original five times as long ; so does *M. L. T.*, though without the same reason. But the manner of *L. G. W.* is quite different.
[3] This prosaic and gratuitous passage is omitted in G.

(1565, 1679); in telling of Lucretia he will be brief and " touche but the grete " (1692-3); the tale of Minos and Nisus' daughter would be too long for him (1921); he is weary to tell of Tereus, and it is time he should make an end (2258, 2341, 2383); he says little of the reception of Demophon by Phyllis because he is sick of his subject, and must hasten him in his Legend, which he prays God to help him finish (2454-8); he will rehearse but a word or two of Phyllis' letter, for he will not vouchsafe to " swinke " on Demophon, " ne spende on him a penne ful of inke " (2490-1); he cannot write all of Phyllis' letter, " for it were to him a charge," but will repeat it only here and there where it is good (2513-17); and he fears that the tale of Hypermnestra may be too long (2675). Chaucer, the busy man of the world and of affairs, and in his leisure the easy and graceful poet, was not used to groaning over distasteful literary tasks, like the plodding Lydgate; he simply dropped them. What was it here that aroused his sense of duty, unless somebody was urging him on whom he did not like to disappoint ? [1]

Finally, the poem is dedicated, in a very graceful manner, to the queen.[2] At the very end of the F-prologue (496-7) Alcestis bids him,

"When this book is maad, yive hit the quene
On my behalfe, at Eltham, or at Shene."

This fact throws new light on his references to the Flower and

[1] One more bit of a suggestion as to a close connection between *L. G. W.* and the queen may be worth a foot-note.   It must strike every one at once as odd that Cleopatra should appear as an estimable martyr to love.   The account of her in L. Annaeus Florus (on the sources, see Bech, *Anglia,* v. 314-18), and elsewhere, hardly explains this ; perhaps that in Orosius (VI. 19) is the least unfavourable, but Chaucer's high conception and praise of Antony and Cleopatra are unparalleled anywhere, so far as I know.   His account was clearly written from memory, but he cannot have been unaware of the changes he made.   Furthermore, why does Love make it such a point that Chaucer shall begin with her ?   Now it will be noted that of all the martyrs celebrated, Cleopatra is the only queen, and the only woman except Thisbe (the legend of whom comes *second*), whose lover is quite blameless toward her.   Just as Chaucer highly praises Antony, of Pyramus he says (917-19) :

"Of trewe men I finde but fewe mo
In all my bokes, save this Piramus,
And therfor have I spoken of him thus."

Chaucer may have felt a lack of delicacy in celebrating his own enamoured queen in the *Prologue,* and then immediately recounting the tales of other queens and women basely betrayed by their lovers.
[2] Mr. Pollard (*Acad.,* no. 1766, p. 228) suggests that this no more constitutes a dedication to her than the allusions earlier to the French poets are a dedication to them.   I fail to see the parallel, and can hardly conceive a method of indicating a connection with the queen more worthy the name of dedication than this.

Leaf cult, and his expectation of reading the poem aloud at court,
and lends countenance to the belief that he wrote it, as Lydgate
says, at the request of the queen.   After all this we shall surely
not be unprepared to find evidence that the queen was definitely
celebrated in the *Prologue*.

Lowes himself was the first to make the important observation
that the omission from G of the dedicatory couplet, F 496–7, on the
presentation of the poem to the queen, "at Eltham, or at Sheen,"
is probably due to consideration for the feelings of King Richard
after the death of his dearly-loved wife.[1] To most bereaved persons
it would be a doubtful kindness to remove all references to the
departed, but Richard was emotionally eccentric.   Chaucer's omission of the reference to Anne as alive "at Eltham or at Sheen"
is a perfect literary parallel to Richard's conduct.[2] As Lowes
points out, he caused the manor of Sheen, where she had died, to
be destroyed, though it had been a favourite royal resort.   Furthermore, for a whole year, according to the Monk of Evesham, he
avoided every spot, except churches, associated with her.[3] Will
not this be paralleled if we find that Chaucer omits all reminders
of the queen from the *Prologue*, and will it not explain his doing
so? Is it not possible, for instance, that the *Legend of Good
Women* was a favourite poem of Richard's, but that he could not
endure in it specific reminders of his lost wife?[4] Richard was an
erratic member of an erratic family.

[1] *Pub. Mod. Lang. Assoc.*, xx. 780–1.
[2] Yet Mr. Pollard (in his criticism of Lowes' article, *Academy*, no. 1766,
p. 228) prefers to think Chaucer struck out the couplet because the queen had
not prevented his loss of office in December, 1386, rather than because she was
dead.   He cannot believe that *L. G. W.* was taken up again after the *C. T.*
were begun, and thinks that in encouraging the royal grief Chaucer would
have been childish.   But was this anything like as childish, to say no more,
as omitting the compliment for the reason which Mr. Pollard suggests?
Legouis (p. 63) agrees with Pollard in being unwilling to believe that Chaucer
would concern himself with the abandoned *Legend* when once he was started
on the *C. T.*   But why should he not care to handle again that *Prologue* about
which both these critics are so enthusiastic?
[3] "Set nec in loco [*sic*] aliquem, ubi sciebat illam perante fuisse, per totum
annum sequentem introire dedignabatur, præter in ecclesiam" (*Hist. Vitæ et
Regni Ric. II.*, ed. Hearne, 1729; pp. 125–6).   Richard's grief and demon-
strativeness are illustrated by the fact that beside her recumbent effigy on her
tomb in the Abbey he caused his own to be put, "with their hands clasped
together" (Gairdner, in *Dict. Nat. Biogr.*, i. 422–3).   As Clerk of the Works,
1389–91, Chaucer had had oversight of the manor of Sheen and the "lodge"
at Eltham.   See also Adam of Usk's *Chronicon* (ed. by Sir E. M. Thompson,
1994), p. 9.
[4] Cardinal Manning, after the death of his much-loved wife, would never
mention her to anybody (Purcell's *Life*, i. 123).

What seems to me far the strongest argument in favour of the orthodox view that Chaucer meant to celebrate the queen in the *Legend of Good Women*, and in some sort identifies her with the daisy and Alcestis, is the fact that this theory alone will account for the most puzzling peculiarities of the revision. We have already taken it as proved, especially by Lowes' parallels to the French poems, that version F is the earlier; but we have taken it as proved only on condition that we can account for certain difficulties. These are the abolition in version G of almost all the warm feeling, and with it many excellent passages; secondly, the giving up of the suspense as to who is the lady of the Balade, and the lady who comes with the God of Love; and thirdly, the fact that, although she is repeatedly named in G, Chaucer at the very end affects not to know who she is. Without the connection with the queen, all these I believe to be quite inexplicable; with it, all seems clear.[1]

Now, forgetting all this for a moment, let us examine the facts —the lines peculiar to F, which Chaucer deliberately omitted from G, if that is the later.[2] These lines number 135. Of these, 50 occur in two long passages; *i. e.* 152–77 contain the description of the birds, etc., in the vein of the *Romance of the Rose*, and 552–65 and 568–77 consist almost wholly of directions as to choice of subjects and brevity of treatment; for the omission of both we have seen that Chaucer had excellent reason. Of the remaining 85 lines, 15[3] are of miscellaneous and indeterminate character. The other 70 are connected more or less closely with the hearty personal feeling; the poet repeatedly expresses his pleasure in the daisy, and warm love to it,[4] calls on lovers to help him, describes his eagerness to see it and how he kneels to watch it and reclines there all day, he praises the flower anew, introduces his Balade in

---

[1] The principle on which Legouis based his discussion of the question of priority was æsthetic. "En l'absence de témoignage direct qui tranche la question de priorité, le bon sens dicte la règle suivante : si Chaucer a pris la peine de remanier son Prologue, c'est afin de le rendre plus parfait" (p. 59). This simple principle utterly breaks down under the failure of the critics to agree. The only way in which Lowes makes his study convincing to a reader is by almost ignoring it. To make Chaucer's procedure intelligible, I maintain that a different guiding clue is necessary.

[2] Skeat in his large edition marks them with an asterisk.

[3] I put the following into this class : 101–2, 120, 143–4 (probably omitted by accident), 201, 229–31, 335, 348–9, 357, 368, 380.

[4] Cf. the substitution of G 58, "As wel in winter as in somer newe," for F 56, "And I love hit, and ever y-lyke newe."

honour of his lady, whom he praises; records the women's song
in praise of the daisy, calls it Love's "relik," says that the
book shall be presented to the queen, and is reproached by Love
for omitting Alcestis from his Balade, since she is the model
of lovers.   That is to say, over half of all the lines omitted are
directly connected with the personal feeling in prologue F; or, disregarding two unified passages, the omission of which has already
been easily accounted for, about five-sixths.

Moreover, most of these passages are not only excellent in
themselves, but leave the G-prologue noticeably poorer.   Their
omission is the reason why it is generally regarded as the inferior
version; even of those who believe it is the later, Koeppel, as we
have seen, regards it as less rich and as injudiciously revised, and
Lowes admits that F " is even the more delightful version of the
two."[1]   We miss particularly the beautiful expression of the poet's
love (83–96) which Lowes has shown to have been derived from
the *Filostrato*, the agreeable picture of him as reclining all day
long in the meadows watching the daisy and kneeling by it when
the procession enters,[2] and the deliciously quaint line where Love
says of the daisy:

" Hit is my relik, digne and delytable " (321).[3]

I am quite sure that a candid examination of the two versions will
show that almost all the points of superiority in F, which are not
trivial or debatable, are directly concerned with this matter.

How is all this to be accounted for?   Koeppel thinks Chaucer
revised carelessly and hastily; Lowes thinks that in F he had
" allowed himself to go on, adding for the sake of its beauty detail
after detail as one recalled another, until his lines are like the
costume of the Squyer," that " the omissions in A [G] will then
be amply accounted for if we suppose Chaucer to have come
back to the Prologue, the spell of the *marguerite* songs no longer
upon him, with the unity of his plan the dominant motive in
his mind";[4] that it was a " sterner sense of the subordination
of beauty of detail to the demands of the artistic whole that

---

[1] *Publ. Mod. Lang. Assoc.*, xix. 683, note.
[2] G less picturesquely has him "lening faste by under a bente" (234).
[3] But it had a much less rare poetic flavour in the fourteenth century than
now, just as there was no conscious quaintness in calling the Palladium a
Trojan relic (*T. C.*, I. 153).   Cf. also *L. G. W.*, 1310, 2375–6, etc.
[4] *P. M. L. A.*, xix. 676.

seems to have underlain the excision "[1] and condensation. But where else does Chaucer show any such austerity? Certainly not in the *Canterbury Tales*. Moreover, it seems to me the mere *extent* of the revisions indicates that Chaucer was not simply trying to improve things. The changes are beyond all comparison greater than those in the *Troilus*, which was perhaps not revised till after a number of years. Presumably Chaucer made his first version as good as he was able. Would it not be almost a self-stultification, a confession of weakness, so utterly to recast a carefully studied poem? If there is no personal bearing in F, the feeling which it expresses seems extravagant; but if so, why did Chaucer put it in, we may ask, if his judgment later required him to omit it? A long and elaborate poem, much more than a prose-work, must be a product of prolonged planning and workmanship; however spontaneous it may seem, it only has the art which conceals art. Are we to suppose that Chaucer's taste changed so extensively in a few years? I fully agree with Lowes that the plan of G is improved, and that Chaucer did well to rearrange it; but I do not believe that he was such a tasteless, hit-or-miss and unintelligent critic that, on one of the rare occasions when he revised an older poem, he impoverished it so much and so needlessly that posterity can hardly tell which is the revised version. To my mind all this is a convincing argument that he had a reason other than purely æsthetic to guide him in his revision.[2]

The second of the points of superiority in F, of which I have

---

[1] *Publ. Mod. Lang. Assoc.*, xx. 799, note.

[2] Besides showing consideration for Richard's feelings, Chaucer may have felt that there was no point in thus celebrating Anne after her death; the *Prologue* to the *Legend* was hardly suitable to be turned into an *In Memoriam*. There is ample evidence that mediæval poets sometimes rededicated their works. Gower transferred the complimentary notice in the *Confessio* from Richard II. to the future Henry IV. (cf. Macaulay, II. xxi., ll.), and Froissart that of the *Méliador* from the Duke of Luxemburg to the Comte de Foix (see Kittredge in *Engl. Stud.*, xxvi. 323–4). But these cases lend no countenance to the view that Chaucer may have abolished his laudation of the queen before her death, which I agree with Lowes is inconceivable. Gower, who transferred his compliment during the reign of Richard II., was a landed gentleman, independent of court favour, with uncompromising political and moral convictions; Chaucer, on the other hand, was largely dependent on court favour, for which during the latter part of his life he was more or less suing, and, even had he been such stuff as martyrs are made of, can have had no adequate reason to inflict such a slight on the queen. These considerations do not seem to have struck ten Brink, who dates the poem 1393, or later—possibly, that is, before the queen's death (*Engl. Stud.*, xvii. 20; Koch justifiably objects, *Chronology*, p. 85); or Koeppel, who dates it even earlier (*Engl. Stud.*, xvii. 198).

postponed the discussion, is explained in the same way. In F, the lady escorted by Love, the heroine of the Balade, is anonymous; this, aside from the unintelligible and clumsy way in which the Balade is introduced, is clearly an advantageous bit of suspense.[1] Not till the end of the *Prologue* does Chaucer, with a rush of joyful surprise, learn that she is the lady who has been his ideal for years. In G this advantage is lacking; directly she enters, her name is baldly and ungracefully announced—"Hir name was Alceste the debonayre" (179). Lowes does not try to explain this, and it seems, at first, evidence for the priority of G. But I have shown already that Love's belief that the lady of the Balade is another than Alcestis makes Queen Anne's presence in the poem particularly clear; if Chaucer gives up the suspense, and makes it plain from the first that the lady who enters with Love, and she who is celebrated in the Balade, are both Alcestis and Alcestis only, he removes one of the clearest allusions to Queen Anne.[2]

Connected with this is the third point, which may be called the main *crux* of the whole poem; namely, the fact that after Alcestis has been named in his presence, Chaucer affects not to know who she is.[3] The trouble exists in both versions, but is far worse in G. The passages involved are these:

Version F.	Version G.
241 And by the hande he held this noble quene	173 And by the hande he held the noble quene
	179 Hir name was Alceste . . .
255 "My lady cometh" . . .	209 "Alceste is here" . . .
262 ,, ,, ,,	216 ,, ,, ,,
269 ,, ,, ,,	223 ,, ,, ,,
341 Tho spak this lady . . .	317 Than spak Alceste . . .
432 "I, your Alceste, whylom quene of Trace"	422 "I, your Alceste, whylom quene of Trace"
459–460 "And yeve me grace . . . That I may knowe soothly what ye be."	449–450 "And yeve me grace . . . That I may knowe soothly what ye be."
499 "Wostow . . . wher this be wyf or mayde?"	487 "Wostow . . . wher this be wyf or mayde?"
505 "Nay, sir" . . .	493 "Nay, sir" . . .
510–11 "Hastow nat in a book . . . The gret goodnesse of the quene Alceste?"	498–9 "Hastow nat in a book . . . The grete goodnesse of the quene Alceste?"
518 "Now knowe I hir! And is this good Alceste?"	506 "Now knowe I hir! And is this good Alceste?"

[1] So Legouis, pp. 60–61.
[2] I can see no other possible explanation for Chaucer's giving up what seems to me a great merit in F; I certainly cannot attribute it, as Lowes does (*Publ. M. L. A.*, xix. 681, note), to an "instinct for unity." Where, once more, does he show any such stringent (if not unintelligent) method as this?
[3] Cf. Lowes, *Publ. Mod. Lang. Assoc.*, xix. 653–5.

The inconsistency in F (between 432 and the later passages) is hardly greater than many another slip in Chaucer's poetry,[1] and may as easily have come in a first as in a second version. In G the blunders are so outrageous that whatever we do we cannot reasonably believe that Chaucer made them in straightforward writing. But on my theory I think they can be thoroughly explained.[2] The discords with the first part are all between lines 450 and 506, and there is hardly any variation between the two versions from G 416 to 525; between these limits the only difference between the two prologues for which Chaucer must be responsible is the absence in G of F 496-7 (the direct reference to the queen); of other variants there are nine, but none are greater than scores of variations among the MSS. of version F.[3] There is not the slightest evidence, therefore, that Chaucer made any change between F 426-537 (G 416-525), except to omit the single couplet which directly mentions the queen. This couplet he was sure to think of, on our theory; and it is equally suggestive that the point where he returns to revising is at F 538 ff., where he omits Love's upbraiding of the poet for "negligence" in omitting Alcestis from his Balade. Is not just one explanation of all this obvious and indeed irresistible? When he began to revise he made in the early part of the *Prologue* the extensive changes required by his reason for revision, and took occasion also to make certain improvements; in the latter part his interest may have failed, and at any rate he believed that only one or two scattered

---

[1] *E. g., L. G. W.*, 2075, 2099 ; *Melib. Prol.*, 2154 (the word *wryte*); and cf. several in *Kn. T.*, pp. 69, 70 above, and in the *Legend of Ariadne* (Lowes, *P. M. L. A.*, xx. 811). We moderns were not the first to notice the slip in F 432, for opposite it MS. Fairfax has *nota*. The fact that it survived for years and reappears in G is an illustration of Chaucer's habit of not reading his own poetry much.

[2] Cf. Binz, in *Anglia Beiblatt*, xi. 233-4. Koeppel thinks the inconsistency in G due to haste in revising (*Literaturblatt*, 1893, col. 51). Ten Brink curiously ignores the whole matter. Koch (*Chronology*, p. 84) thinks it indicates the priority of G ; so does Bilderbeck (p. 82).

[3] The lines may easily be found, being the unmarked ones in Skeat's large edition. At times some of the F MSS. agree with G, and several times their common reading looks like the only genuine one. It must always be remembered, also, that version G is in a unique MS. In the most important variant—"I al foryeve" (F 450), "And al foryeve" (G 440)—G is probably corrupt, for Chaucer had not offended Alcestis, and she needed no exhortation to forgive him (cf. French, p. 91 ; Lowes, xix. 672, note). For my view that in these 110 lines there are almost no genuine revisions there is a good parallel in *T. C.*, IV. 953-1085 ; I showed (p. 9) that the absence of important variants here indicates that the passage came in during a revision, and was not revised itself.

changes were requisite, and neglected to read it through. He quite forgot that his having given up the lady's anonymity made some of the latter part of the poem nonsense. I hope I have shown, therefore, that the furious blunder of G, and its almost complete absence from F, so far from being an argument for the priority of G, is one for the contrary view.

And so we seem to find that the belief in the lateness of G and in the close connection in F of Anne with the daisy and Alcestis support each other. If we deny the second, there are such unanswerable arguments against the first that we are completely at sea; but if we believe both, everything connected with the *Prologue* falls logically into place, and nothing remains for us except a discussion of the dates.[1]

---

[1] Starting with the identification of Alcestis with the queen, several writers* have identified the God of Love with Richard II.; except by Bilderbeck, the point has scarcely been argued,† it has been assumed,† quite groundlessly, I am persuaded. Bilderbeck's arguments have been so thoroughly refuted by Lowes‡ that I may be brief, though I believe of course that Lowes errs in denying Bilderbeck's main argument, the connection of Alcestis with Anne. In the first place, there is no presumption in favour of the idea; because a wife is symbolically represented, there is no reason why her husband should be; a symbolizing of real characters is under no obligation to be so complete. It may be noted that Love speaks of and to Alcestis in a distant and almost reverential manner. The sun-crown (see F 230) about his head, not only a sign of royalty, but also a source of brightness, is thoroughly paralleled elsewhere, as Professor W. A. Neilson kindly points out to me. In love-allegory the god is frequently spoken of as a king or prince (see Neilson, *Court of Love*, pp, 74, 84, 105); he always wears a crown in the illustrations to the 1493 edition of the *Roman de la Rose* (see nos. 13, 15–8, etc., at the end of vol. v. of Jules Croissandeau's edition; Orléans, 1880). Much of the description of him is derived from the *Roman de la Rose*, and some details, possibly, (as Child points out, *Mod. Lang. Notes*, xi. 488–90) from Boccaccio's *De Genealogia Deorum.*—But nevertheless, in Alcestis' admonitions to the God of Love (F 373–402, G 353–88) it seems not at all unlikely that Chaucer had Richard partly in mind, somewhat as Bilderbeck believes (pp. 94 ff.) and somewhat as even Lowes admits (xx. 779), though I can hardly accept the former's specific suggestions or believe that Chaucer was so impertinent as to offer indirect advice to Richard through Anne. We can hardly hope to identify any particular incidents which Chaucer had in mind (though there may be something in those which Lowes rejects on pp. 778–9), nor can any chronological conclusions (I think) be based on these passages. But to one who was familiar with his character, even during the years when his government was going well, Richard must often have given occasion for anxiety. One particular point, however, may be mentioned. Two passages are added in G, 360–4 and 368–9, in which

* Skeat (III. xxiv. f.), Legouis (p. 69), Binz (*Angl. Beibl.*, xi. 236), Koch (*Engl. Stud.*, xxx. 457), Bilderbeck (85–7, 103).

† Binz, *e. g.* speaks of "den liebesgott, hinter dem sich offenbar der könig Richard selbst verbirgt."

‡ *P. M. L. A.*, xix. 674–5; xx. 773–9. He also disposes of Bilderbeck's arguments for 1385 and 1390 as the dates of the two prologues.

§ 3. *The Legends and the Date.*

The date of the first or F version of the *Prologue* of the *Legend* I think Professor Lowes has settled definitively. One interesting argument he quotes from Hales. In F 203 Chaucer goes to sleep "in a litel herber that" he had, which implies a house in the country, or at any rate on *terra firma*. Now for many years he had lived in a house on the city wall over Aldgate; but in 1385 he almost certainly left this for Greenwich, where he lived probably till 1399.[1] So unobvious and circumstantial a detail as this of his having a little arbor it is natural to connect with the facts, not only with the poetic fiction. This gives a date at least not earlier than 1385. But in 1903 I showed that there is no reason whatever for connect-

---

(after urging that a lord or king should be righteous, not wilful and tyrannous and cruel, but benign and open-eared to his people, and should "kepe his liges in justyce") the poet says,

> "And therto is a king ful depe y-sworn,
> Ful many a hundred winter heer-biforn;"

he then declares that the lords should be duly honoured but the poor treated with compassion. Did not Chaucer perhaps have in mind certain passages in Richard's coronation-oath? According to Thomas Walsingham (I. 333), he swore: "Tertio, ut non esset personarum acceptor, sed judicium rectum inter virum et virum faceret, et praecipue misericordiam observaret, sicut sibi suam indulgeat misericordiam clemens et misericors Deus." Part of the coronation-oath, between 1307 and 1603, is given thus by L. G. W. Legg (*Engl. Coron. Records*, Westminster, 1901; p. xxxi.): "Facies fieri in omnibus iudiciis tuis equam et rectam iusticiam et discrecionem in misericordia et veritate secundum vires tuas. *Respondebit*, Faciam." Now on June 3, 1388, Richard had been compelled by Parliament to renew his coronation-oath that he would observe the laws of the realm, and follow the counsels of the lords and of parliament, not those of flatterers (see the *Continuatio Eulogii Historiarum*, ed. F. S. Haydon, Rolls Series, 1863; III. 367). It should not be supposed that a side glance at Richard would have been felt to be dangerous or in bad taste. I have already compared Chaucer's relations to the English court with those of Sir David Lyndsay to the Scottish, and Lyndsay was free-spoken enough; Gower is frank enough to Richard in the *Confessio*, and treats Edward III.'s memory with scant respect in the *Mirour*; I shall show later that the *Physician's Tale* seems to contain clear references to two scandals in the family of John of Gaunt, and the *balade Lack of Steadfastness* shows no fear of wounding the royal feelings. I cannot think that Lowes quite makes his point that this passage of the *Legend* is wholly accounted for by the situation in the poem; a few lines on the "natural king or lord" might be used by Alcestis in admonishing the God of Love, but what was the poet's motive for putting in so long and detailed a discourse on the "Regiment of Princes," and even in adding two passages during revision, though this part of the poem is otherwise little changed? I cannot but suspect an extra-æsthetic reason for this addition, as for the omissions early in the poem.

[1] I treat this subject at length in the next chapter, and make some modifications of Hales' suggestion.

ing the *Legend* with the appointment of a deputy in the custom-house, and therefore with the year 1385 ; and now Lowes proves that it quotes Deschamps' *Lay de franchise*, which was written about May, 1385, and further that Chaucer can hardly have had an opportunity to see that poem before the spring or summer of 1386.[1]   A date much later than this we shall presently find to be still more unlikely ; therefore we may accept 1386.

On the date of the second prologue, G, I have little or nothing to add to Lowes' discussion,[2] which shows on various grounds that it must have been produced some years after the first.   One reason (pp. 782–9) is the jocose references in G to Chaucer's old age ; another (pp. 790–6) is the mention among Chaucer's works of the (probably recent) translation of Pope Innocent's *De Contemptu Mundi*, with which work he shows such familiarity in the *Man of Law's Tale*, which I hope to show is late, and in the *Pardoner's Tale*, which certainly is ; a third[3] (pp. 800–1) is the existence of G in but a single MS., since a revised version published immediately after the original would be likely to drive it out.   Another may be added —the mere extent of the alterations, even apart from those involved by the moving cause of the revisions.   We have seen also that in regard to structure, some of its contents and the reading of which it gives evidence, it seems to place itself in the period of the *Canterbury Tales*.   As to the exact date, we have seen that it can hardly have been written before Queen Anne's death, June 7, 1394 ; and since the revisions seem to have been made out of consideration for Richard's overwrought feelings, and since by the latter part of 1396 he had so far recovered that he was willing at any rate to go through the form of marriage again, it was probably written soon after Anne's death.   The date 1394–5 seems to be clearly indicated.

Coming to the question of the time when the *Legends* were written, I find that I must wholly part company with Professor Lowes.[4] It is in this connection, it is true, that he made one of his best

---

[1] *Publ. Mod. Lang. Assoc.*, xx. 753–71. He shows that the relations of France and England were prohibitively hostile, and that Chaucer's and Deschamps' common friends could hardly have served as intermediaries before 1386.

[2] *Ibid.*, xx. 780–801.

[3] And also a rather strong argument, I think, for the posteriority of G.

[4] For his views, which are offered with the greatest open-mindedness, see *Publ. Mod. Lang. Assoc.*, xx. 802–18.

observations.   He shows very convincingly that certain details in the *Legend of Ariadne* (1960–2122) are due to Boccaccio's *Teseide*. "The prison of Theseus is a tower, which is 'joyning in the walle to a foreyne' belonging to the two daughters of King Minos, who dwell in their chambers above.   The two young women hear Theseus complaining as they stand on the wall in the moonlight, and have compassion on the prisoner.   When, their plan for his escape having been formulated, they disclose it to Theseus and the jailor, Theseus proposes to' forsake his heritage at home and to become Ariadne's page, working for his sustenance.   In order that neither Minos nor any one else 'shal [him] conne espye' he declares he will disguise himself in lowly wise :

> ' So slyly and so wel I shal me gye,
>   And me so well disfigure and so lowe,
>   That in this world ther shal no man me knowe.'

The proposition is of course not carried out, and the remainder of the story follows more closely the classical sources" (pp. 804–5). The resemblance is unmistakable to the account in the *Teseide* and the *Knight's Tale* of the imprisonment of Palamon and Arcite, and of the disguise and service of the latter ; it even extends at times to verbal resemblances between the two English poems. But I cannot at all agree with the chronological inference which Lowes has drawn from it,[1] that the *Ariadne* must have been written before the *Tale* because it contains " a decidedly inferior and rather sketchy replica of two motives already fully and artistically worked out " (p. 809).

That Chaucer did not object to repeating motives, any more than Shakspere did, may be proved again and again ; as, for example, by the borrowings in the *Merchant's Tale* from *Melibeus* and the *Troilus*, which will be shown in a later chapter.   We have also seen clearly how little he objects to repeating phrases and lines, a thing still less to be expected.   Moreover, the parallels, though striking enough when pointed out, are so unobvious that it was five hundred years, so far as we know, before any one noticed them. As to the inferiority of the "replica," I do not at all see it—just the contrary, in fact.   In contrast with the pretty but very commonplace picture of Emily walking about the conventional garden,

---

[1] Some of his secondary deductions I have already had to combat in my chapters on the *Troilus* and the *Knight's Tale*.

we have the two princesses upon the wall in the moonlight,[1] look-ing across their courtyard [2] to the donjon whence issue the prisoner's groans, presumably through a loophole; a romantic picture which recalls that in the *Troilus* [3] which so charmed Shakspere's Lorenzo, where the deserted lover

> " mounted the Troyan walls,
> And sigh'd his soul toward the Grecian tents,
> Where Cressid lay that night."

Lowes also thinks that Chaucer would not have superimposed, upon " the very noble and stately figure of Theseus in the *Knight's Tale*," " the despicable traitor of the *Legend of Ariadne*." But Theseus is not a central character in the *Knight's Tale*, nor is there any sign that he regarded him there with such liking that he should shrink from repeating the very familiar story of his youth.[4]

I should go so far as to believe that internal evidence actually favours the posteriority of the *Ariadne*. The intimate familiarity shown with the details of the story of Arcite and Palamon, which Lowes points out (pp. 805–9) more searchingly than I have done, is more likely to have followed than to have preceded the trans-lation of it. One or two of the details look like a reminiscence of the *Knight's Tale* rather than of the *Teseide*. Palamon has been in prison (and in love about) seven years; Theseus declares he has

---

[1] There is a very Chaucerian touch here :

> "Hem leste nat to go to bedde sone."

[2] I have no hesitation in accepting this meaning from Skeat. The question was, how were people in the same thick-walled building to hear the prisoner's lamentations ? The only possible way was across a courtyard, which corre-sponds to Boccaccio's *giardino*. The tower was "joining in the wall" to the "foreyne," which belonged to Minos' daughters; they lived in the large rooms above the dungeon, but when they heard his groans they were outdoors on the wall, across the court from the tower. This meaning of the word is sufficiently supported by the *N. E. D.*, which under the third definition of the noun (in the plural) gives : "The outer court of a monastery; also, the space immediately outside the monastic precincts. *Obs.*, but surviving as a proper name in various places where monasteries existed." Though the earliest quotation given is of 1668, this last sentence proves that it must have been common ; the extension from a monastery to a castle is easy enough. As to the extraordinary interpretation of the word in this passage offered by Mätzner (in his *M. E. Dictionary*) and accepted by Lowes, it seems to me, though such is the commonest meaning of the word, no less repugnant to good sense than to good taste.

[3] *T. C.*, V. 666–79.

[4] Falstaff must have been a greater favourite with Shakspere than Theseus with Chaucer, yet the dramatist did not shrink from covering with ridicule in the *Merry Wives* and at the end of *Henry IV.* him who had always been so finely master of the situation earlier in the latter play.

loved Ariadne seven years, though it is not clear how he has known of her; there is nothing of the sort in the *Teseide* (Lowes, 807 ; cf. 811, note).   The curious blunder which Lowes (808, note) points out in 1966, where Chaucer (according to the MSS.) puts the prison where Theseus is confined in Athens instead of Crete, is more natural as a reminiscence of his own *Knight's Tale* than of the *Teseide*.   On the other hand, the deliberate variations which Chaucer introduces, such as the substitution of the moonlit wall scene[1] for the sunlit garden, show a natural unwillingness to reproduce his earlier *motifs* quite identically.   This is the chief variation from the original ; on the principle which Lowes uses in his treatment of the two forms of the *Prologue*, is not that of two versions which is farther from the original likely to be the later?

For an early date of the *Ariadne* Professor Lowes believes he finds evidence also in its style.   If it was written before the *Knight's Tale*, it was written also before the *Prologue* of the *Legend*, and for this he thinks there is evidence in the versification —a lack of flexibility and variety as compared with that of the *Prologue*.   But in the nature of the case is not a semi-lyrical poem likely to have more melody and variety of verse than a rapid narrative?   So far as the *Ariadne* is needlessly inferior in this respect, I agree with Mr. Pollard[2] that the fact is due, not to lack of skill in the *Ariadne*, but to lack of care.   Chaucer makes repeatedly in the *Legend*, as we have seen, the plainest possible declarations that he is in haste.   " Technique of that sort," says Professor Lowes (p. 813), " is scarcely a thing that can be put on and off at will."   But is it not always rather a matter of pains?   Hasty writing at any date will make poor verse.   The particular peculiarity of style on which Lowes dwells is so striking that I think it can hardly be due to inexperience; when Chaucer began 21 out of 43 lines (2136–78) with *and*, was he unconscious of the fact or unable to remedy it?   I hold that this is simply Chaucer's rapid narrative style.   In the *Knight's Tale*, Lowes believes Chaucer had thoroughly learned the technique which he was practising here; yet in the *Knight's Tale*, 1399–450, out of 52 lines 21 begin with *and* and 7 with *that*.   These *and*-lines are

---

[1] It may have been suggested by an earlier passage in the *Ariadne* (1908–11.)

[2] *Academy*, no. 1766 (1906), p. 228.   For an earlier discussion of Chaucer's verse in its chronological bearings, see my chapter on the *Knight's Tale*, p. 61.

noticeably frequent in the (late) *Canon's Yeoman's Tale;* in 1026–35 there are 6 out of 10, in 1102–15 there are 7 out of 14, in 1228–35 there are 4 out of 8, and in 1308–26, 11 out of 19. In the lively scene at the end of the *Reve's Tale*, 4292–312, out of 21 lines 12 begin with *and.* Granted that the *Ariadne* passage is an extreme instance of what elsewhere is often employed with admirable effect,[1] this seems to me due rather to excess than to defect of ease. I do not at all agree with Mr. Lowes (p. 813) that "it is a fair presumption that the *Ariadne* is unmelodious because the technical difficulties of a somewhat unfamiliar metre had not yet been surmounted." I have pointed out in an earlier chapter that the differences between the stanza and the couplet are hardly so great as to signify in this connection.[2]

So, as I read the matter, there is no evidence for the opinion that the *Ariadne* was written before the *Prologue.* A *fortiori* there is none for Professor Lowes' opinion (p. 816) "that the Prologue was written after most, perhaps after all, of the narratives it introduces." For this view I fail to see the antecedent probability which he sees. It seems to me a prologue, which gives the plan of the ensuing poem, is likely to be written early, while the zeal is still keen; in the next chapter I shall show very good reasons for the opinion that in the *Canterbury Tales* the *Prologue* was one of the very earliest-written parts. When Chaucer had become thoroughly weary of the *Legends,* it is hard to believe that he would have written the *Prologue* with such delight, unless for some external reason, and that which Lowes suggests, that it is a poetic retort to the criticism which the *Troilus* had evoked, I have tried to show on chronological and other grounds can hardly be accepted.

There seems to be evidence, as well as probability, for the

---

[1] Cf. *Kn. T.*, 2925–66; *N. P. T.*, 4565–72.

[2] Rather I should find in the carelessness of the *Ariadne* and the other *Legends* (so far as it exists) an indication that Chaucer was kept at his task by an external motive after his pleasure in it had evaporated. For this there is further evidence in the numerous inconsistencies and blunders in the *Ariadne* which Lowes points out (p. 811, note), and which are much greater than those which I pointed out in the *Kn. T.* (pp. 69, 70). Cf. also the errors in the second part of the *Sq. T.*, which Lounsbury (*Studies*, iii. 318) attributes to lack of revision. If any one should object that Chaucer would have put his best work into a poem written for and at the request of his royal mistress, I reply that the defects (to call them so) are such that nothing can be more unlikely than that she would ever have observed them, considering the kind of reading to which she was probably used. Compared with the extemporaneous style of most mediæval poetry, Chaucer's style at its poorest is finished and polished. Besides, the duty-poems of later poets laureate are rarely among their best works.

opinion that most or all of the *Legends* were written after the
Prologue. In the *Prologue* we are told that nineteen ladies entered
after Alcestis and the God of Love ; and in F 554–60 the latter
clearly refers him to the Balade for their names, and appoints them
to be the heroines of his legends :

> " Thise other ladies sittinge here arowe   ,
> Ben in thy balade, if thou canst hem knowe,
> And in thy bokes alle thou shalt hem finde ;
> Have hem now in thy Legend alle in minde,
> I mene of hem that been in thy knowinge.
> For heer ben twenty thousand mo sittinge
> Than thou knowest."

It is true that in the Balade there are only eighteen women, and
that one or two of them would hardly have been suitable ; of course
when the Balade was written Chaucer had no idea of making it a
table of contents, and when he wrote the above passage he probably
had not carefully considered the details.[1] But if he had already
written the *Legends* and introduced several persons not mentioned
here, it is difficult to see why he should have introduced this perfectly needless passage. Now he follows the list in the Balade till half-
way through the fourth legend, in which, after treating Hypsipyle,
the connection of Jason with Medea leads him to deviate for her ;
and later he devotes the seventh legend to Philomela, also not in
the Balade. When he wrote, in the *Man of Law's Prologue*, 63–75,
the list of ladies whom he states there to have been treated in his
Legend, he had entirely abandoned the list in the Balade ; and
finally, when he came to revise, the passage in question was omitted
from the *Prologue*. How can we avoid attributing this omission to
the fact that the passage did not agree with his changed plan,[2] or

---

[1] Cf. Lowes' sensible remarks (*Publ. M. L. A.*, xx. 817–19); and French,
p. 30. On this passage cf. also Legouis, p. 65.

[2] So ten Brink, *Engl. Stud.*, xvii. 19. By "thise other ladies" Chaucer
clearly means the 19 chief ones. Koch is surely not justified in saying that
Love here gives him permission to write the lives of some of the 20,000
others. (This number is a mere convention for a vast quantity ; cf. *H. F.*
2119, *Sumn. Prol.*, 1695.) Therefore this passage does not relax Chaucer's
bonds, but puts them on. Dr. Koch's whole criticism of the matter is so
confused as to be unanswerable (*Chronology*, p. 85). The same may be said
of Bilderbeck's (pp. 82–3) ; he implies that the indefinite number in G must
be larger than the number 20 in F. But $x > 20$ is not an axiom in algebra.
It may be added that, just as is the case in the *Canterbury Tales*, the *Prologue*
promises so much more than was ever performed, and than Chaucer must have
seen before long was likely to be performed, that he is hardly likely except
at the very beginning to have made a perfectly unnecessary announcement of
his design.

rather his desire not to be held to the original one? The natural conclusion is that the extant *Legends* were written between the two forms of the *Prologue*.

There are some indications that the *Legends* were written in about the order in which they stand in all the MSS.,[1] which is—

Cleopatra,	Hypsipyle and Medea,	Philomela,
Thisbe,	Lucretia,	Phyllis,
Dido,	Ariadne,	Hypermnestra.

If, as we have seen is probable, most or all of the *Legends* were written after the F-prologue, *Cleopatra* must have been written among the first, since at the end of the *Prologue* (566) Love bids the poet begin with it. This is also suggested by lines 616–23 :

> "The wedding and the feste to devyse,
> To me, that have y-take swiche empryse
> Of so many a storie for to make,
> Hit were to long, lest that I sholde slake
> Of thing that bereth more effect and charge."[2]

As to the later *Legends*, the only references which I find from one to another are from *Phyllis*, no. 8, to *Ariadne*, no. 6. If Chaucer rearranged the poems, *Phyllis* should directly follow *Ariadne*, since they are so closely and consciously connected in subject.[3] As it is, the wholly irrelevant legend of *Philomela* is interjected. Again, certainly no method is discoverable running through the arrangement. Finally, the signs of haste and weariness which I have collected above (pp. 112–13) become noticeably more frequent and intense toward the end ; and it is the last legend that is unfinished. All the indications are that the present is the order of writing.

Indications of the chronological *terminus ad quem* of the *Legend* are to be found in the fact that two non-Chaucerian works seem to betray vestiges of its influence. One of these is Gower's *Confessio Amantis*. In book VIII., among lovers, the poet sees a company of unhappy women-lovers, namely (2550–96) :

Dido,	Medea,	Progne and Philomela,
Phyllis,	Deidamia,	Canace,
Ariadne,	" Cleopatras,"	Polyxena.
Dejanira,	Thisbe,	

---

[1] Cf. Bilderbeck, p. 74.
[2] This passage contrasts with the other indications of hurry and distaste noted on pp. 112–13. Miss E. P. Hammond calls my attention to the parallel between the above passage and *Kn. T.* 885–8, also at the beginning of a long task.
[3] Just as *Hypsipyle* and *Medea* are, which form one *Legend*.

Then, after the amorous sorceresses Circe and Calypso, come the best of women-lovers, Penelope, Lucretia, Alcestis and Alcyone. It is true that the tales of all of these except Cleopatra are more or less told in various scattered earlier parts of the poem; but it is suggestive that here occur all but two [1] of the ten heroines treated by Chaucer in the *Legends*, and of the others some entered into Chaucer's announced plan. Cleopatra comes just before Thisbe, as in Chaucer; but it is more important that Chaucer's " Cleopatras " has influenced Gower's in other things besides her name. All that Gower says is (2572–7):

> " I syh also the wofull queene
> Cleopatras, which in a Cave
> With Serpentz hath hirself begrave
> Alquik, and so sche was totore,
> For sorwe of that sche hadde lore
> Antonye, which hir love hath be."

Chaucer, at the end of her *Legend*, says (696–702):

> " And with that word, naked, with ful good herte,
> Among the serpents in the pit she sterte,
> And ther she chees to han hir buryinge.
> Anoon the neddres gonne hir for to stinge,
> And she hir deeth receyveth, with good chere,
> For love of Antony, that was hir so dere :—
> And this is storial sooth, hit is no fable."

The representation of Cleopatra as dying for the love of Antony by leaping into a pit filled with serpents, and as being buried there, is confined to these two accounts,[2] and no one reading the above

---

[1] Hypsipyle and Hypermnestra.

[2] These points are not in any of Chaucer's probable sources as given by Skeat (III. xxxvii.) and M. Bech (*Anglia*, v. 314–8), and are probably original with him. Macaulay (*Gower*, iii. 547) suggests that he may have derived his idea of Cleopatra's death from Vincent of Beauvais (by a very confused recollection). The passage mentioned above seems to be the only case of borrowing between the *Confessio* and the *Legend*, unless two details in their accounts of Ariadne show mutual influence (cf. Macaulay, iii. 503). Bech in one section of his essay on the *Legend of Good Women* attempts to prove a number of borrowings on Gower's part (*Anglia*, v. 365–71); Skeat in a rather confused passage (III. xl. ff.) reduces them to two, but his first seems hardly significant. The only one of Bech's cases rejected by Skeat which is worth mentioning is in *Conf. Am.*, i. 93–202, where the striking thing is the similarity of the *rôles* played by Venus and Cupid to those of the God of Love and Alcestis in the *Legend ;* Cupid is stern to Gower (though without apparent reason), and Venus is kind to him. This evidence, however, is nullified by the fact that the situation is paralleled in other amoristic allegory ; as Professor Neilson points out to me (see his *Court of Love*, pp. 42–3), in *Venus la Deesse d'Amor*, for example, both deities appear, and Venus appeals for the lover. Venus' mediation might easily be derived by any poet from the influence exerted on each

2222222222222

passages can doubt that Gower was the borrower. As to the
date, Macaulay (II. xxi.) has shown that the *Confessio* was
finished in 1390 ; we have evidence therefore as well as probability
that the *Legend* was as much finished as it is now not later
than 1390.

The date will be thrown still further back by the connection
of the *Legend* with Thomas Usk's *Testament of Love.* I believe I
have shown already (pp. 22, 23) that Usk certainly knew the
Prologue of the poem, and probably one or two of the *Legends.*
We have seen that the *Testament* cannot have been written later
than 1387, and almost certainly dates from that year. The *Legend
of Good Women* was therefore presumably brought to an end by
the latter part of 1387.[1] It may well have been not much earlier
than that, for Usk's connection with Chaucer's associate Brembre
would doubtless give him exceptional advantages for procuring
Chaucer's works.

This throwing back of the date is further confirmed by what we
shall find in the next chapter as to the date of the *Canterbury Tales,*
the beginning of which we shall find reason, partly depending
on what we have learned as to the date of the *Legend,* to put about
1387. We can hardly believe that the *Legends* were continued after
the *Canterbury Tales* were once under way. Nor is there need
of thinking that the *Legend* was interrupted by the conception
of the more promising poem ;[2] it has every appearance of having
run down, as it were, of itself. We have seen good reason to think
that it was written rapidly, and we may assume that no more of it was
ever written than is now extant—that Chaucer never told us for just
what " conclusion " the tale of Hypermnestra was said.[3] Therefore

---

other during the Middle Ages by the conceptions of Venus and of the Virgin
Mary. Both Skeat and Bech find a borrowing in *Conf. Am.,* VIII., about
2440–2750, where Cupid comes with a vast train of lovers (2456–8) ; though
this too is somewhat paralleled elsewhere (cf. Neilson, *Romania,* xxix. 87),
the influence of Chaucer is not unlikely, but the passage is really part of the
one I have cited. As to the mention of the flower and the leaf in *Conf. Am.,*
VIII. 2468, Kittredge has shown (*Mod. Philol.* i. 2) that this is an allusion
rather to contemporary life than to literature.

[1] If this view is correct, of course it disposes of Bilderbeck's suggestion that
the *Legends* were produced at the rate of one a year (see his pp. 89–91, 108).
But there are many other reasons to doubt this idea.

[2] Cf. Pollard, *Globe Chaucer,* p. xxiv.

[3] Lydgate's manner of speaking of the poem (quoted in Skeat, III.xx.), and
the colophon put by the scribe of MS. Fairfax at the head of the *Prologue,*
indicate that they at least believed the poem to have been not nearly finished.
The unanimity of the MSS. is further confirmed by a spurious *Cronycle made* ·

the whole period of Chaucer's occupation with the 2723 lines of the *Legend* may have been only a few months.   We have learned from Lowes that the earlier part of 1386 is the earliest likely date for the *Prologue;* and we have just seen that the latter part of 1387 is the latest date possible for the publication of the whole work.   The date 1386–7 for the *Legend of Good Women* may therefore be accepted.[1]

<h1 style="text-align:center">CHAPTER V.</h1>

THE CANTERBURY TALES.

§ 1. The Canterbury Tales as a Whole.

SEVERAL attempts have been made to find a point of departure for dating the *Canterbury Tales* as a whole, but few of the results seem very reliable and some of them are worthless.   The conjectures which have attracted most attention have started with the idea that the basis of the poem is an actual pilgrimage made by Chaucer. This idea seems to be wholly baseless.

It is quite unnecessary, of course, in order to explain the existence of the poem; I need hardly recall the various mediæval

---

y Chaucier, in one of Shirley's MSS. (see *Odd Texts of Chaucer's Minor Poems,* Ch. Soc., 1871, I. vi.–viii.), which treats of the "nyene worshipfullest Ladyes."

[1] Professor Bilderbeck (pp. 32–44) tries to prove that Chaucer revised the first six (but not the last three) legends, and that MS. Camb. Gg contains the earlier version of them as of the *Prologue.*   Since it seems to be quite certain that this MS. contains the later version of the *Prologue,* his view as to priority between his versions of the *Legends* is hardly possible.   When we come to examine the evidence, we find, I think, no reason to change our minds. Of the two or three dozen variants which Bilderbeck quotes, none compares in importance with those in the *Troilus,* or those in the *Prologue* to the *Legend,* even apart from the excision of allusions to the queen.   Even the readings peculiar to MS. Harl. 7334 of the *Canterbury Tales,* which I am convinced cannot be attributed to Chaucer, look far more genuine than these.   The most favourable of Bilderbeck's cases (2008–9):

<blockquote>". . . he shal at (on) him lepe,
And (To) slen hym as (or) they comen . . .,"</blockquote>

is not in the least striking.   In no case does the variation seem to me too great to have been produced by a scribe, even unconsciously.   It is natural that the text of MS. Gg should be notably different from the others, since it probably parted from them very early in the MS.-tradition.   If there were a striking contrast in the number of more important variants in legends 1–6 and 7–9, we might hesitate ; but according to Bilderbeck's account, in the former there is 1 in 53 lines, and in the latter 1 in 100, and I cannot see that they are any less important.   So probability and evidence alike seem to negative the idea of revision.

collections of stories in a frame, of which of course the *Decameron*
is only one, and other things may have contributed their hints.[1]
In the fourteenth century story-telling must have been common on
pilgrimages.[2] Nor is it necessary in order to explain the vividness of
the narrative.[3] Absolutely all the familiarity shown with the external
circumstances of the pilgrimage Chaucer would have gained from
the numerous times he had passed over the same road on his
journeys to the continent,[4] and the two observations on the position
of the sun (*M. L. Prol.*, 1–14; *Pars. Prol.*, 1–11) might have
been taken at home as well as on the road, or have been made up
at any time of year by a little calculation.[5]

---

[1] The assumption that the *Decameron* must have been Chaucer's model was
the mere child of ignorance, and dates from the Dark Ages, the eighteenth century; it is one of the few things which we have to forgive Tyrwhitt (ed. of 1830;
I. clix.). More recently it has been denied with patriotic vehemence; *e. g.*
by Skeat (III. 371; yet in V. 270 he seems to think Chaucer to have been
familiar with the *Decameron*), and Pollard (*Globe Chaucer*, xxviii.). In Italy,
naturally, it is still popular. Peter Borghesi argues very unconvincingly that
Chaucer must have known the *Decameron* (*Bocc. and Ch.*, Bologna, 1903; pp.
50 ff.). Professor Cino Chiarini inclines (though without bigotry) to believe it
(*Nuova Antologia*, lxxii. 334; on pp. 148–65, 325–43, he rather agreeably
introduces the *C. T.* to Italian readers). It will be seen that none of these
writers have any evidence; the argument is always that he *must* have known
the *Decameron*. It seems to me almost certain that he did not. Hales, who
thinks he did, is misleading in his arguments (*Dict. Nat. Biog.*, x. 163). Cf.
also pp. 160–1 below. The germ of *C. T.* is in the house of Rumour in *H. F.*
(lines 2121–36; cf. A. W. Ward, *Chaucer*, E. M. L. Series, 95–6); in *Piers
Plowman* (Seeley, in Skeat, III. 372; ten Brink, *Hist. E. L.*, ii. 140–1—he
rejects a real pilgrimage as unnecessary). Chaucer had already produced an
approximation to the *C. T.* in the *L. G. W.* More than this, the frame-story
might develop spontaneously at any moment out of the mediæval fondness for
anecdotes and *exempla*, as it did in Gower's *Confessio Amantis*. The *H. F.*
illustrates the point, with its sketches of ancient heroines.

[2] Only singing and piping are mentioned in the dialogue between Thorpe
and Abp. Arundell (in 1407; cf. Littlehales' *Road from London to Canterbury*,
51–2); but during the halts, anyway, we may be sure there was "taling."
That it was common on pilgrimages seems to be implied in all versions of
Piers Plowman:

"Pilgrimes and palmers . . .
    Wenten forth in heore wey · with mony wyse tales."

(A, Prol., 46–8; C has *vn-wyse*.)

[3] Cf. Pollard (*Globe Chaucer*, xxvii.): "No one who has read the talks by
the way can doubt that the poet himself had travelled over the ground. . . .
Chaucer's own pilgrimage, then, may have been made in 1385." Cf. *Primer*,
p. 100.

[4] Probably also in going to Canterbury on business connected with his
wardship in 1375; see R. E. G. Kirk in *Life Records* (Ch. Soc., 1900), p. xxv.

[5] Nobody pretends that Dante, from whom as well as from real life Chaucer
may have imitated this way of telling time, must always have just made an
exact observation when he mentions the positions of the heavenly bodies.
This sort of attempt to extract chronological sunbeams from cucumbers is no
more tempting than it is fallacious.

Connected with the idea of an actual pilgrimage is the attempt to discover the year meant in the *Canterbury Tales* from the passage in the *Parson's Prologue* (1–11); at four [1] o'clock

> . . ." the mones exaltacioun,
> I mene Libra,[2] alwey gan ascende."

W. Hertzberg, in his German translation of the *Canterbury Tales*,[3] follows Tyrwhitt (iv. 335) in thinking that *exaltacioun* cannot be used here in the strict astrological sense, since Taurus, not Libra, is the exaltation of the moon, and Libra is that of Saturn,[4] but that it must mean simply *rising;* and he thinks that Chaucer meant here to hint at the year of the pilgrimage[5]—apparently in a cabalistic way. He assumes that the journey occupied but one day, and therefore, on the basis of Tyrwhitt's reading (also the Ellesmere) for *M. L. Prol.*, 5, that the day here was April 28. With the assistance of his "verehrter Freund" Professor Scherk, he announces that on that day within the proper limits as to years the moon could have risen at four in Libra only in 1393. Therefore the date of the imaginary pilgrimage was April 28, 1393.

It is unnecessary to follow this ball as it was tossed back and forth in Germany, with an occasional kick from England. By various changes and corrections in the number of days of the pilgrimage, in the MS. reading and in the astronomy, Koch,[6] Skeat,[7] A. von Düring[8] and C. Ehrhart[9] find (or accept or reject) the years 1393, 1391, 1388 and 1385. This last year was fully accepted by Pollard[10] in 1893.

---

[1] Most of the MSS. read *ten*, which is certainly wrong ; Chaucer cannot have blundered to this extent.

[2] Harl. 7334, and also Laud 600 (in the Bodleian Library), read "In mena Libra," which gives no sense, and is one of the Harleian eccentricities which do not look as if they came from Chaucer. MS. Camb. Ii reads "I meen in libra."

[3] Hildburghausen, 1866 ; pp. 666–7.

[4] See, *e. g.*, Wm. Lilly's *Christian Astrology* (London, 1647), pp. 57, 80.

[5] Similarly A. E. Brae (*The Treatise on the Astrolabe of Geoffrey Chaucer*, London, 1870 ; p. 74). He deduces the year 1388, by emending "I mene Libra alwey" to "In Libra *men alawai*" (the name of a star, which he says could have risen with the moon at the proper time only in that year). In broad daylight !

[6] *Ch. Soc. Essays*, 415–7 ; *Ausgewählte Kl. Dicht. Chaucers* (Leipzig, 1880), 65–6 ; *Chronology*, 49–50, 64–6. His opinion was the same in 1902 (*Pard. T.*, xxii.).

[7] *Ch. Soc. Essays*, 417.

[8] See his German translation of Chaucer, iii. 409.

[9] *Engl. Stud.*, xii. 469–470.

[10] *Chaucer Primer*, p. 100. In the *Globe Chaucer*, however, he ignores this argument (see p. xxvii.).

All this seems to me entirely out of the question. The idea that the passage concerned proves a real pilgrimage supposes that Chaucer either wrote the last link of all immediately on his return, or else that he made notes of such trivialities for use years afterwards. Even if the meaning assumed for *exaltacioun* were possible, it would be infinitely more likely that Chaucer inserted the remark simply as indicating the sort of thing which a star-wise person would have seen if he had been there, than because he remembered seeing it. But the whole idea is practically disposed of by the fact that Chaucer elsewhere uses *exaltacioun* and its adjective only in the correct astrological sense, which is what any fourteenth-century reader would have understood here; and by the fact that the other interpretation really makes Chaucer say " the moon's rising continued to rise," which is almost as bad as Dr. Johnson's "observation with extensive view." The only possible explanation of the passage as it stands seems to be that either the scribe blundered,[1] or Chaucer, through forgetfulness; and I do not see the least improbability in thinking that it was Chaucer, even if he did know his astrology fairly well.[2] Therefore, whether in connection with the pilgrimage idea or not, conjectures founded on this passage are to be rejected[3] without qualification.

[1] Tyrwhitt (iv. 336) suggests that "the mones" is an error for "Saturnes." An error would be the easier because the first 10° of Libra are "the moon's face" (Skeat, V. 445); and the second 10° of Libra are "Saturn's face" (Lilly, *op. cit.*, pp. 58, 81).

[2] Surely Lounsbury has pointed out inaccuracies enough in Chaucer's work, and the list can easily be enlarged. As another astronomical blunder, he puts Ariadne's Crown in the sign of Taurus, to which it is just opposite (*L. G. W.*, 2223-4). But the curious thing about the passage under discussion, which apparently has never been remarked upon, is that what Chaucer seems to imply that he saw, the sign or constellation Libra rising, he could not possibly have seen at four o'clock of an April afternoon. The passage sounds much more like a conscious reminiscence of Dante than like an observation of nature. This manner of telling time occurs again and again in the *Divine Comedy*; cf., *e. g., Inf.* XI. 113-4, XX. 124-6, XXIX. 10; *Purg.* I., 19-21, II. 1-6, 55-7, XXV. 1-3, and E. Moore's *Time-References in the Divina Commedia*, Tables V. and VI. *Purgatorio*, II. 1-6 is particularly suggestive:

> " Già era'l Sole all' orizzonte giunto,
> Lo cui meridian cerchio coverchia
> Gerusalem col suo più alto punto :
> E la notte, ch' opposita a lui cerchia,
> Uscia di Gange fuor con le *bilance*,
> Che le caggion di man quando soverchia."

Cf. also *Man of Law's Prol.*, 1-12, with *Purg.*, IV. 15-16 :

> " Chè ben cinquanta gradi salit' era
> Lo Sole, ed io non m'era accorto.'

[3] So Skeat in 1894 (V. 445).

That Chaucer did make a pilgrimage to Canterbury at some time
or other is likely enough—*religionis erga* perhaps, or he may even
have been so modern as to wish to know how a real pilgrimage felt
while he was writing about an imaginary one.   All that can
be said is that there is not the slightest evidence for it in the
Canterbury Tales.

Some scholars have advanced the idea that by the last decade of
his life Chaucer had aged too much to have written many of the
Canterbury Tales, or at any rate to have planned the whole.   Dr.
Furnivall in 1871 [1] took the years about 1386 as the central period
of the work, when the best tales were written, and assigned the
" dull ones " to times earlier and later ; to the years 1390–1400 he
definitely assigned only small and inferior works, and from a passage in *Venus* and from the supposed inferiority of the minor poems
known to have been written about then he deduces " a slow autumn
of decay." [2]   Dr. Mather agrees with his general idea,[3] mainly because
of the *Retractations.*   Mr. Pollard says : " The short poems written
towards the close of his life show that the not very advanced age
to which he attained pressed heavily on him, and it would be
unreasonable to assign the plan of the *Tales* to his last decade." [4]
Similarly, Professor Hales believes that practically all the *Canterbury Tales* which were not earlier work were written between
1387 and 1392.[5]

As to the *Retractations,* if the poem was never published by Chaucer
as a whole, as I hope to show on a later occasion, they need imply
nothing more than a few weeks of other-worldliness at the very
end, and surely have nothing to say as to a whole decade.   The
remarks in *Scogan* and *Venus* seem to me to have little more significance.   In the former he refers to his portly figure and to the fact

[1] *Trial Forewords,* pp. 16, 25 ; cf. 6 (note), 99.
[2] *Ibid.,* 28, 99.   [3] *Chaucer's Prologue, etc.,* p. xxxiv.
[4] *Globe Chaucer,* p. xxvii.   So also Koch (*Chronol.,* 51–2, 69), who thinks
Chaucer was in poor circumstances during this period.   He does not deny
that some of the tales may have been written then, but in his table (p. 79) he
recognizes the possibility only for the *Parson's Tale.*   Pollard regards "the
scheme of the *Canterbury Tales* as taking form during" 1386–8 (p. xxvii.).
Ten Brink denies (*Studien,* p. 153) that Chaucer has left any works which
show failing powers.   Koch has a quaint conjecture founded on Chaucer's age.
He points out that Chaucer "in the wast is schape as wel as" the Host
(B, 1890), who was "a semely man" (A, 751) ; therefore "we must figure the
poet to ourselves as a stately man of some forty years rather than as one who
already feels old age approaching, and is '*hore and round of shape*' ('Scogan'
l. 31)" (*Chronol.,* pp. 52–3).   But the *Prologue* to *Sir Thopas* is a *Selbstporträt*
in hardly such a photographic sense as this.
[5] *Folia Literaria* (London, 1893), pp. 101–2.

that he is no longer young, and even says that he thinks never
again to wake his muse (l. 38); the date may well be 1393.[1] Yet
the whole tone of the poem is light,[2] and any sense of discourage-
ment which may lie beneath may be accounted for by the appeal
for court-favour in the *Envoy.* In *Venus*, which was probably
written somewhere near this time,[3] he complains that age has dulled
his spirit and nearly bereft his subtlety, and that close translation
of elaborate verse is difficult in English (76–82); yet it certainly
cannot be said to show failing powers. The evidence of these
poems, therefore, is almost negligible; and since they may date
from the same period, possibly one of trouble and ill-health, they
cannot be used to characterize the whole decade. *Bukton*, on the
other hand, certainly written at the end of 1396,[4] obviously is with
the *Canterbury Tales* in spirit, and we shall see later is closely
associated with some of them; it shows a gentle cynicism, somewhat
recalls the *Merchant's Tale*, and refers to the *Wife of Bath's Prologue.* The *Complaint to his Purse*, one of the last things
Chaucer wrote,[5] is full of cheery punning, exaggeration and
flippancy. Neither shows a spirit which was incapable of pro-
ducing any part of the *Canterbury Tales* at the same time. The
sharp contrast in tone among various parts of the *Canterbury Tales*
and other works of this period simply shows what we may be very
ready to believe of Chaucer, that he was a man of moods. It seems
fair, then, to say that there is no evidence here against his having
written any of the undated tales between 1390 and 1400, or even, if
this were not unlikely on other grounds, against his having designed
the poem then. It is rather satisfactory if we can feel under no
necessity of believing Chaucer ever to have had a "decline."[6]

Several scholars have thought the time about 1386–8 so full of
change and trouble as to have been unsuitable for projecting or
even working much on the *Canterbury Tales.* Ten Brink,[7] who
did not commit himself as to exact dates for that work, believed

---

[1] Skeat, I. 556–7 : Lounsbury, *Studies*, i. 36–42 ; Lowes, *Publ. M. L. A.*,
xx. 787, 792.
[2] Cf. G. L. Kittredge, *Harvard Studies and Notes*, i. 116–17.
[3] See Skeat, I. 86.   [4] See pp. 210–11 below ; and cf. Skeat, I. 85.
[5] Skeat, I. 88.
[6] Professor Kittredge has some wise remarks on the injudiciousness of
taking these words of Chaucer's very seriously, in the New York *Nation*, liv.
214 ; he is answering Lounsbury, who is inclined to do so. See also
Kittredge's article on *Scogan*, just mentioned.
[7] *Hist. of Engl. Literature*, ii. 119–20 ; cf. also Koch, *Pardoner's Tale*
(1902), p. xxiii.

that the political unrest of this period must have produced a deep impression on Chaucer's mind, and that his personal troubles (financial and family) may well have produced a time of seriousness; to this time he accordingly assigns some of the more serious works which he thinks were not till later connected with the *Canterbury Tales*.   In 1389, however, he points out[1] an improvement in Chaucer's circumstances, to which he attributes such spirited poems as the *Wife of Bath's Prologue* and the *Merchant's Tale*— still unconnected with the poem as a whole. Not till about 1390, for no very clear reason, does he recognize the proper time for the conception of the whole work.[2] Dr. Koeppel, similarly, in his review[3] of the *Chronology*, thinks that Koch assigns "a feverish poetic activity" to years too engrossed with other things to be poetically productive; he refers to Chaucer's parliamentary career in 1386 and the misfortunes of the succeeding years, and thinks that we may suppose him to have written then little besides *Melibeus*, the *Parson's Tale* and a partial translation of Pope Innocent's *De Contemptu Mundi*, and that the conception of the *Canterbury Tales* came later, beginning with an attempt to recast the *Legend of Good Women* for use in it.[4]

All such arguments as those of these two or three German Chaucerians seem to me such as we commonly use when we have no others. Caution here seems very necessary. We know so little of those details of Chaucer's life which may have had as much effect on his state of mind as weightier matters, so little even of the details of his personality, that it is unsafe to draw conclusions. There is no necessary connection between ill circumstances and solemn literary work, and the leisure perhaps implied by the former might make such a time peculiarly productive of poetry of all kinds. Was not Chaucer just the man to beguile a dreary time, and perhaps occupy his enforced leisure, by working on his art?[5] So out of this whole mass of *a priori* conjecture we seem to have gained nothing reliable.

[1] *Hist. of Eng. Literature*, ii. pp. 123 ff.

[2] He therefore seems to put such tales as the *Miller's* in the very period from which other scholars have excluded all but serious and dull works. He and Koch are diametrically opposed. Such disagreement indicates something wrong with the method.

[3] *Literaturblatt für germ. u. roman. Philologie*, xiv. 54.

[4] Cf. p. 111 above.

[5] Cf. Lowes' wholesome remarks to this effect (*Publ. Mod. Lang. Assoc.*, xx. 792).

I shall begin my consideration of the more important arguments
with one which justifies treatment at length rather because of
its interest than its weight.   Why did Chaucer select a Canterbury
pilgrimage as the frame for his tales?   Even though such amuse-
ments were common on pilgrimages, there is a certain lack of
realism, even as Dean Stanley points out,[1] in representing the tales
as told during the ride, and heard by any considerable number of
people amid the clattering and chunking of one hundred and twenty-
eight hoofs.   This he was willing to overlook for the sake of other
points of fitness, a large and miscellaneous assemblage doing an
everyday thing in common.   But is not this selection especially
natural if pilgrimages to Canterbury were daily under his eyes?
Where was Chaucer living during the planning and writing of the
Canterbury Tales?

On May 10, 1374, Chaucer leased the house above Aldgate for
his whole life, and without the power to sublet ("alicui dimittere");
four weeks later, June 8, he received his formal appointment as
Comptroller of Customs of Wools, etc., in the Port of London.[2]
February 17, 1385, he received the formal permission to discharge
the duties of this office through a deputy which he already had for
those of the Customs office received in 1382.[3]   October 12, 1385,
he was appointed one of the Justices of the Peace for the county
of Kent, apparently to take the place of one of those appointed the
previous year who had died; June 28, 1386, he was one of sixteen
(all but two of whom were in the previous list) to receive a new
commission for the same office.[4]   In August or September, 1386,
he was elected Knight of the Shire for Kent.[5]   October 5, 1386,
the house above Aldgate was leased by the city to Richard Forster,
probably a friend of Chaucer's.[6]   March 12, 1390, he was appointed,
with five others, to survey and keep in repair the bank of the
Thames between Greenwich and Woolwich.[7]   In the *Canterbury*

---

[1] *Historical Memorials of Canterbury* (London, 1900), pp. 213–14.
[2] *Life Records*, pp. 190–1 ; the two records are consecutive.
[3] *Ibid.*, pp. 237, 251.
[4] *Ibid.*, pp. 254, 259.
[5] *Ibid.*, pp. 261–2.   The sheriff of the county who signed the return had
been one of his colleagues as J.P. in 1385 (but not in 1386).
[6] *Ibid.*, p. 264 ; cf. p. 216.
[7] *Ibid.*, pp. 283–5.   Among the commissioners were his friend Sir Richard
Stury, and apparently one of the Culpepper family which had supplied
one of his colleagues as J.P. in 1385 and 1386.   Two of his present
colleagues served also on a similar commission for Middlesex, but Chaucer
did not.

Tales (*Reeve's Prol.*, 3907) there is a curious and unexplained innuendo about Greenwich :

"Lo, Grenewich, ther many a shrewe is inne."

The last stanza of the *Envoy to Scogan* (43–6) addresses the poet's friend thus :

"Scogan, that knelest at the stremes heed
Of grace, of alle honour and worthinesse,
In thende of which streme I am dul as deed,
Foryete in solitarie wildernesse."

The MSS. gloss the first line "Windesore" and the last "Grenewich." Finally, Chaucer did not hire his house near Westminster Abbey till 1399.[1]

The following explanation seems usually certain and always probable. In May, 1374, when he knew that he was to receive the appointment at the Custom-House,[2] he took the house over Aldgate, ten minutes' walk from his office, a little over half-a-mile.[3] But the way in which Chaucer vivifies French conventions in the *Prologue* of the *Legend of Good Women* is alone enough to tell us that he was a lover of nature ; so as soon as his appointment of a deputy rendered his daily presence at the office unnecessary, he moved to an easily accessible spot in the country, Greenwich. The city did not, it is true, lease the house again till twenty months after the deputy was allowed ; but, especially since the new lease was by the city and not by Chaucer himself, he may have left the house long before.[4] We can hardly doubt that he was a resident of Kent when he was appointed J.P.,[5] eight months after the permission to have a deputy. It is almost equally certain that as

[1] *Life Records*, p. 329.
[2] Cf. Hales, in *Dict. Nat. Biogr.*, x. 161; cf. also his *Folia Literaria* (London, 1893), pp. 87–9 (reprinted from *Acad.*, xvi. 410, December 6, 1879).
[3] Aldgate is under half-a-mile north of the Tower. The Custom-House was very near the Tower (*Life Records*, 290 ; cf. xxxix.) ; it obviously would be near London Bridge, the head of marine navigation. At the present day it is between the two, and was there in 1543 (cf. Van den Wyngaerde's *Panorama ; e. g.*, in Sir W. Besant's *London in the Time of the Tudors*, 350–1).
[4] Cf. Skeat (I. xxvi., xxxviii.). Hales (*Academy, Fol. Lit., l.c.*) and Lowes (*Publ. Mod. Lang. Assoc.*, xx. 772) rather assume the contrary, and think it may have been his entering Parliament which led him to move ; Lowes also suggests that his appointment as J.P. may have been the cause. But is not this putting it wrong-end to ?
[5] Cf. Stubbs, *Const. Hist.*, ii. 272–3, and especially D. J. Medley, *Engl. Const. Hist.* (Oxford, 1894), 351–60 ; cf. also *Statutes of the Realm*, I. 364. It is interesting to note that in 1388 J.P.s were required by a re-enacted statute to hold sessions four times a year, and during the session were to be paid 4s. a day (Medley, 354, 358).

Knight of the Shire he was a resident. In the latter part of the
preceding century, those who held that office were clearly residents ;
" the office was not coveted," and at times the sheriff may almost
have had to compel service.[1] By 1413, it is true, apparently non-
residents sometimes had served, for in a statute of 1 Henry V. it is
required that knights shall be residents of their shires; but since
the same statute requires that electors shall also be, it probably does
not imply any frequent deviation from the obvious and original
rule.[2] " It may be said that, with here and there an exception, in
the early days of the representative system the counties were represented by men of landed wealth and social standing, and that the
election of men not possessing land in the counties they represented
was comparatively rare."[3] Since Chaucer must have owned land in
the county outside the cities and boroughs, which sent their own
representatives to parliament, since he was not a rich man and can
have had but little landed property, and since Greenwich was
neither city nor borough,[4] therefore his land was probably his home-
stead in Greenwich. In his responsibility for the south bank of
the Thames from Greenwich to Woolwich there is confirmatory
evidence for his residence in the former place ; and although of
course the Host's remark about the tough characters who lived in
Greenwich might be a well-known local hit, it is natural to take it
as a jocose dig by Chaucer at himself or his friends. Perhaps his
friends and he, the genial man of the world and courtier, were
regarded as *fast* by quiet suburban Greenwich, or he may be chaff-
ing his unsophisticated neighbours. Finally, it is clear that when
he wrote *Scogan* he was living in some small place far down the
river, and there is no reason to doubt that the scribe knew what
he was talking about when he glossed the allusion as being to
Greenwich. Skeat shows good reason to believe that the poem
was written in 1393.[5]

[1] Stubbs, *Const. Hist of Engl.*, ii. 68, 90, 221–3, 232, 433.
[2] *Statutes at Large*, iii. 1 ; cf. Medley, p. 152, and Sir Harris Nicholas' *Life
of Chaucer*, Note S (in Morris' *Chaucer*, 1883 ; I. 102).
[3] E. Porritt, *The Unreformed House of Commons* (Cambridge, 1903), i. 511 ;
cf. 21, 122, 512. Seats did not begin to be in demand till early in the fifteenth
century. Non-residence first came in among the representatives of cities and
boroughs.
[4] See *Life Records*, p. 262 ; T. H. B. Oldfield, *Representative History of
Great Britain and Ireland* (London, 1816), vi. 311, and *History of
Boroughs* (London, 1792), iii. 42 (at the end). Before the nineteenth century, Greenwich itself was represented in Parliament only in 4 and 5 Philip
and Mary.   [5] I. 556–7.

Chaucer's odd calamities of September 6, 1390, afford curious confirmation of the belief that at this time he was living in Greenwich. It may be remembered that on this day he was robbed twice, once at Westminster, of £10, by one William Huntingfield, or Richard Brerelay, and others unknown, and again at "Hacchesham," Surrey, of over £9, by Brerelay with three others (being a gang of professional robbers).[1] Chaucer at this time was Clerk of the King's Works at Westminster, among other places; Hatcham is between Peckham and New Cross, near the Old Kent Road, the direct route from Westminster to Greenwich, about two-thirds of the way. The obvious explanation of all this is that Brerelay, or whoever it was, after the first robbery, knowing or suspecting that Chaucer was to carry a large sum home with him the same night,[2] therefore collected part of his gang and lay in wait for him on the way. If Chaucer was not going home, how did they know where to catch him?[3]

It may be taken as a certainty, then, that from 1385 till well into the nineties (probably till 1399) Chaucer lived in Greenwich. Not only has this some possible bearing on the date of the *Legend of Good Women*, as Professor Hales points out;[4] as Professor Skeat shows, it offers a bit of evidence for dating the *Canterbury Tales*. Since Canterbury pilgrims went past Greenwich, Chaucer's daily familiarity with them probably dated from his residence there; living in Aldgate he would not see them at all. The inference, though by no means necessary, is natural, that the first conception of the *Canterbury Tales* dates from 1385 or later.

The most important element for ascertaining the *terminus a quo* of the *Canterbury Tales* is the date of the *Legend of Good Women*. Lowes has shown us that it cannot antedate 1386, and Skeat has shown reason (independent of the date of the *Tales*) to believe that it was known to the world in 1387. We can hardly doubt that the beginning of the greater work came after the *Legend;* and it may be that impatience to be at it was one reason for the sense of

[1] See *Life-Records* (1875), pp. 8, 9, 15, 19, 28, 30; also (1900) xl.-xlii. The accounts are not wholly consistent, but so much is certain from the indictments.
[2] Possibly in order to pay wages, or the like, at some of the "King's Works" down the river.
[3] For earlier and partial treatments of Chaucer's residence in connection with his poems, see J. W. Hales, *Academy* and *Fol. Lit., l. c.;* Skeat, Chaucer Society *Essays*, 670-1 (cf. *Chaucer*, I. xlii.); and cf. J. L. Lowes, *Publ. Mod. Lang. Assoc.*, xx. 771-3.
[4] *Academy*, and *Fol. Lit., l. c.* See also p. 121 above.

haste betrayed in the other. There is the further consideration
that as, with all proper deductions of parts earlier written, the
Canterbury Tales compose nearly half of Chaucer's known literary
work, so it is not injudicious to allow them nearly half his literary
life. The date 1387 [1] for the commencement of the *Canterbury
Tales* harmonizes with all that we have found already; and also
with the results of our next deliberation, as to the date of the
General Prologue.

§ 2. *The General Prologue.*

Was the *Prologue* written early or late in the *Canterbury* period?
Dr. Furnivall believes that it and the links were written after most
of the tales.[2]   Skeat says,[3] " The Prologue, answering somewhat to
a preface, is one of his very latest works, and in his best manner ;
and before writing it, he had in some measure arranged a part of his

---

[1] An opinion favoured by critics. Tyrwhitt (I. clxii., note) thought the
poem could not have been "much advanced before 1389"; Mather (*Chaucer's
Prologue, etc.*, p. xxxiii.) thinks "the writing and arranging of the *Canterbury Tales* must have proceeded intermittently from 1387 to 1400"; Skeat
(III. 372) thinks the poem "was most likely in hand up to the time of his
death, though he probably neglected it towards the last." Pollard, however,
seems inclined rather to think that Chaucer dropped the *Canterbury Tales* soon
after 1390 (*Globe Chaucer*, p. xxii.).   There is possible confirmation for the
date 1387 in a suggestion of Skeat's ; though I must say that by itself I should
attach little value to it.   Excluding all years except 1386–90, and starting
with the date mentioned in the *Man of Law's Prologue*, April 18, the second
day after the pilgrims assembled, he says (III. 373–4) that the year could not
have been 1389, when that day was Easter ; nor 1390, when April 17 was
Sunday ; nor 1386, when the pilgrimage would have been in Holy Week ;
nor 1388, when April 19 was Sunday, and something must have been said
of the pilgrims hearing mass.   (Skeat sometimes forgets the fragmentary state
of the poem.)   This leaves only 1387, when they would have assembled,
Tuesday, April 16, "and had four clear days before them."   (I should prefer
to say three ; cf. my article in *Publ. Mod. Lang. Assoc.*, vol. xxi., pp. 478–85,
on the number of days of the pilgrimage.)   The confirmation which Skeat sees
in the date 1387 which he had selected for the revised *Knight's Tale* must
vanish if that poem is practically identical with the *Palamon and Arcite ;*
and I have tried to show earlier that his method of arriving at it is hardly
trustworthy.   In writing so protracted a poem as the *Canterbury Tales*,
Chaucer would have involved himself in some inconveniences by choosing a
definite year and carrying it all through, and nothing would have been gained
by so doing.   Dante did, to be sure, but in rigid consistency there is a vivid
contrast between the two poets.   Even if he laid his plan, and wrote the *Man
of Law's Prologue*, at the season of year of which he writes, still more if he
did not, there is no strong ground for thinking that he would have adapted
his poem to the Sundays and movable feasts of the year in which he wrote, or
of any year.   But the coincidence between Skeat's date and that reached by
other routes may perhaps suggest that he did.

[2] *Trial Forewords*, p. 10.

[3] III. 374–5. Yet he quotes Hales' evidence as to the date (to be mentioned
presently).

materials." When Chaucer wrote the end, at least, of the *Prologue*, he had probably planned and perhaps written the first group or so ; the *Knight's Tale* was ready to hand, and Chaucer's apology (725– 42) seems to have reference to the *Miller's* and *Reeve's Tales*. But if a considerable time had passed since the whole work had been designed and begun, he would hardly have announced the immense plan which we find in lines 791–5, almost at the end ; and is not a prologue which lays a ground-plan likely to come early ?[1] I shall present evidence later that several parts of the poem were written after the *Prologue ;* most of the links palpably were, since they take for granted the characterizations presented in it. Therefore, quite apart from other evidence on the date, it certainly appears that the whole *Prologue* was among the earlier-written parts of the poem ; and there is nothing against putting it immediately after the conception of the whole, as I should do.[2]

For dating the *Prologue* exactly, only one piece of evidence has hitherto been found, but happily that, so far as it goes, is conclusive. The Merchant, says Chaucer (276–7),

> " wolde the see were kept for any thing
> Bitwixe Middelburgh and Orewelle," [3]

which makes it plain that those were the ports of entry and departure for the traffic in which he was engaged.

During the fourteenth century, as is well known, there was more or less legislation in England directed to the control of trade for the benefit of the royal exchequer and of English merchants, and one of the items in this legislation was the establishment of the staple. Though the exact history of this institution is not perfectly clear, it

---

[1] This in answer to Lowes on *L. G. W.* (*Publ. Mod. Lang. Assoc.*, xx. 816 ; and cf. p. 126 above).

[2] The *Prologue* may not have been written quite continuously. As Miss E. P. Hammond suggested, I believe, in a paper read before the Modern Language Association of America, in Madison, Wisconsin, December, 1905, lines 542–4 look like a fresh start. No doubt Chaucer left for years a blank between the Prioress and the Monk, where the " Prestes thre " now stand (164) ; it is not impossible that at this point he cancelled descriptions of the Second Nun and the Nun's Priest ; it should never be forgotten, however, that all the evidence shows that cancellation was anything but Chaucer's practice. The " wel nyne and twenty in a companye " (l. 24) Chaucer must have put in after the *Prologue* was practically complete, since it is hardly to be supposed that he settled on this unobvious number at the start.

[3] The former is in Holland, on the island of Walcheren, at the mouth of the Scheldt, and the latter is just across the river Orwell from Harwich. The route was therefore the same as that of the modern North Sea steamers from Harwich to Antwerp.

was an establishment in an English or continental port to which the chief products of England, wool, woolfells and leather, had to be taken before they could be sold to foreigners ; and it was connected not primarily with the collection of customs, but with the attempt to create a forced monopoly.[1] Now Professor J. W. Hales has pointed out,[2] by a reference to Craik's *History of British Commerce* (cited below), that Middleburgh was the staple-port only between 1384 and 1388, and therefore concludes that the *Prologue* must have been written between those years. The matter may be confirmed by reference to more reliable sources of information, David Macpherson's *Annals of Commerce* [3] and contemporary documents.

In 1353 the staple was removed from the continent, where it had been for some time previously, and fixed " for ever " at ten places in England and several in Wales and Ireland ; in 1363 the staple for wool, woolfells and hides was moved to Calais ; in 1369, in consequence of the war with France, it was restored to much the same list of English towns as before; in 1376 it was restored to Calais ; in 1378 merchants from countries in the extreme west of Europe were allowed to come to Southampton or elsewhere instead of Calais.[4] In 1382–3 (6 Ric. II.) there was a prospect of its being moved from Calais, in consequence of a treaty with the Flemings ; in 1383–4 it was arranged to be either at Calais or at some English port.[5] That the staple was still at Calais on September 22, 1383, is probably indicated by the fact that on that date the King promised to repay a loan, which the mayor and commonalty of London had made him, by abating their subsidies, etc., to him, " and by grant hereby made that when the 2000l. for the safe keeping of Calais has been fully discharged by the subsidy of 23s. 4d. a sack of wool, the collectors of that subsidy shall deliver the same to the said mayor," etc.[6] It was at Middleburgh April

---

[1] See Hubert Hall in the *Gentleman's Magazine*, cclv. (1883), 255–75, especially p. 257 ; R. H. I. Palgrave, *Dictionary of Political Economy* (London, 1901), iii. 460–2 ; George L. Craik, *History of British Commerce* (London, 1844), i. 120 (the account here, however, is not quite accurate). For information and references on this whole subject I am much indebted to the kindness of Professor E. F. Gay, of Harvard University.

[2] In a letter to the *Athenæum*, April 8, 1893 (no. 3415, 443–4), reprinted in his *Folia Literaria*, 99–102. See Craik, i. 123.

[3] London, 1805.

[4] Macpherson, i. 546–7, 566, 576, 582, 587–8.

[5] *Rotuli Parl.*, iii. 136b, 159a.

[6] *Calendar of the Patent Rolls: Richard II.* (London, 1895–1902), ii. 307.

20, 1384, as is shown by the [1] "appointment of William Brampton, of London, governor of the merchants of the staple of wools kept at Middelburgh, to search" for money illegally exported; and several references show that it was still there at least in 1386 and 1387.[2] In February, 1388, the Commons prayed that the staple of wool might be moved from "Mideburgh" to Calais on or before the next Michaelmas (September 29); the king granted that it should be moved to Calais or to a port in England before the next Parliament (which was held in January, 1390).[3] According to other authorities, Parliament ordered that the staple should be moved from Middleburgh to Calais by December 1, 1388.[4] It had been moved to Calais before January, 1390.[5] On December 3, 1390, certain wools, woolfells and hides were declared forfeit to the crown "because shipped in Newcastle on Tyne for the staple of Calais and taken to Middelburgh in Seland contrary to the king's prohibition thereof." [6] In November, 1390, it was ordered to be moved from Calais to England by the following January.[7] In December, 1390, it was still in Calais; in November, 1391, it was ordered to be within the realm.[8] From 1388 to 1390, according to Macpherson,[9] the staple was at Calais, and during the remainder of the century it was sometimes at Calais and sometimes at English towns. It is certain, then, that during the latter part of the fourteenth century the staple for wools, etc., was at Middleburgh from late in 1383 or early in 1384 till 1388, and then only.[10]

---

[1] *Cal. Pat. R., Rich. II.*, ii. 397. Of this says Macpherson (i. 596, note): "This is probably the first establishment of the staple at Middleburg."
[2] See note 10 below.   [3] *Rot. Parl.*, iii. 250b.
[4] Knighton's *Chronicle* (Rolls Series, 1895), ii. 298, 308. Cf. also Walsingham, ii. 177; *Statutes of the Realm*, ii. 60; Macpherson, i. 600.
[5] *Rot. Parl.*, iii. 268b. The Monk of Evesham is therefore clearly mistaken or misleading in implying that as late as 1392 the staple had been at Middleburgh (*Hist. Vitæ et Regni Ric. II.*, ed. Th. Hearne, p. 123).
[6] *Cal. Pat. R., Rich. II.*, iv. 355.
[7] *Stat. of the Realm*, ii. 76; *Rot. Parl.*, iii. 278a.
[8] *Rot. Parl.*, iii. 279b, 285a.
[9] i. 600, 602, 604, etc.
[10] I give here certain further items about Middleburgh and Orwell as ports. Before the establishment of the staple at Middleburgh some persons had been allowed, by royal patent, though it was against the ordinance of Parliament, to carry wools, etc., to Middleburgh and elsewhere. The right was guaranteed by Parliament, with reference to Middleburgh, in 1372 (*Rot. Parl.*, ii. 315b). But that both Middleburgh and Orwell were relatively unimportant for English commerce except when the staple was at the former place is indicated by the fact that, while both appear frequently in the *Cal. Pat. Rolls*, beginning at the end of 1383, neither is mentioned during the years 1377–82 (see indexes), and each only twice between 1388 and 1392. The staple at Middleburgh is

From all this, two interesting deductions may be made. In the
first place, it is natural to find that the Merchant was probably one
of the merchants of the staple,[1] and dealt in the commodity with
which Chaucer was best acquainted—wool. But much more
important is the fact that the description of the Merchant (and
therefore, we may infer, most of the *Prologue*) cannot have been
written earlier than 1384. That it was written some little time
after this is suggested by the fact that the Merchant

" wolde the see were kept for any thing " ;

it had therefore proved to be dangerous. This is confirmed by
actual incidents in 1385 and 1387.[2] Therefore for two or three
years there may have been agitation for a safer route, which may
have been one reason for the petition of the Commons to have the
staple transferred. It is not quite certain, perhaps, that the passage
was written in 1388 or earlier, for Chaucer may have had in mind
a definite year, or vaguer period, a little further back than the time
when he wrote. But since there is not the slightest evidence

---

mentioned July 1, 1386, and January 15, 1387 (iii. 190, 253) ; on the latter
date the king orders vessels of war to convoy certain ships laden with wool
from the port of Orwell to the staple of Middleburgh. This and the next
item explain the Merchant's desire that the sea should be "kept for any
thing." Under date October 2, 1385, we learn (iii. 86) that a ship belonging
to Florentine merchants, laden at Middleburgh and bound for England, was
chased by the king's enemies, beached and abandoned at Orwell, and her cargo
plundered. (See also *Essays on Chaucer*, Ch. Soc., pp. 470–1. According to
Walsingham, ii. 217, Danish pirates greatly harassed merchants and seamen,
especially the men of Norfolk, in 1395.) The fact that several contemporary
authorities mention the transfer of the staple back to Calais, and all ignore the
previous change, suggests that the dangers of the North Sea passage had caused
considerable agitation for removal. During the session of Parliament in October,
1385, there was agitation for restoring the staple to an English port ; where it
was then is not stated, but it is implied that it was at some port, other than
Calais, outside of England (*Rot. Parl.*, iii. 203a, 204b, 214a). For other
references to Middleburgh and Orwell in these years see *Cal. Pat. Rolls,
Rich. II.*, vols. ii., iii., iv., indexes. Under date of February 20, 1388,
Orwell is shown to have been a terminus of the wool-traffic (iii. 470). I may
add here a little note on the Shipman, who for aught Chaucer knew was
from Dartmouth, and was in the habit of stealing wine. On December 6, 1386
(*Cal. Pat. R.*, *Rich. II.*, iii. 247), the bailiff of Plymouth, John Hanley of
Dartmouth and others were appointed to compel restitution by five men
of Plymouth, Hugh de Weston of Dartmouth, and three men of Kingswear
(" Kyngeswere ") for the theft of four tuns of wine from the "Cristaven"
of Middleburgh. But, unfortunately, we have no information that the master
of the ship "Maudeleyne," hailing from Dartmouth, was ever named Hugh
de Weston (cf. Ch. Soc. *Essays*, 484–5).

[1] He even wears a "Flaundrish bever hat."
[2] See note 10 above.

of this,[1] we may conclude that the probabilities are strong for 1387–8 as the date of this passage, and therefore presumably of the entire *Prologue*.

Striking confirmation for a date no later than this is afforded by a probable other contemporary allusion.   The Squire

"had been somtyme in chivachye,
In Flaundres, in Artoys, and Picardye,
And born hym wel, as of so litel space" (85–7).

On this Dr. Mather[2] remarks: "The English under Edward III. made numerous descents upon the Low Countries.   Chaucer may well be thinking particularly of the campaign of 1359–60, in which he himself was taken prisoner."   But this campaign did not take place in Flanders at all; the English army went through Artois and Picardy, but only *en route* to Rheims, near which[3] Chaucer was made prisoner, and to Paris; the peace was signed at Bretigny, near Chartres.[4]   Chaucer no doubt did think of his own maiden campaign, but it can hardly have supplied him with his geography. Moreover I find in Walsingham no record whatever of an English campaign in Flanders between 1359 and 1383, or between 1383 and 1395.

But in 1383 there was one which exactly fits the conditions.[5] In May of that year, Henry le Despenser, the militant Bishop of Norwich, with the benediction of Pope Urban VI., and to the indignation of John Wyclif, led from England an expedition, which he gave all the airs of a Crusade, against the schismatic

[1] If there is internal evidence of adaptation to any year, that year, as we have seen, is 1387.

[2] *Chaucer's Prol., etc.*, p. 5.

[3] At "Retters," according to the contemporary account; *i. e.* at Réthel, as Lounsbury seems to have been the first to point out (*Studies*, iii., 452). J. W. Hales (*Dict. Nat. Biogr.*, x. 157) says "Retiers in Brittany," which is certainly wrong.   *Réthel* and *Réthers* were different forms for the same name (see Kervyn de Lettennove, *Froissart*, xxv. 228).

[4] See Walsingham's *Historia* (Rolls Series, 1863), i. 287–90.

[5] The best early account is Walsingham's, ii. 71–104.   Froissart gives a very detailed one in book II., chaps. 207–14 (ed. by J.-A. Buchon, *Coll. des Chron. Nat. Franç.*, Paris, 1826; vol. xxxii. pp. 413–71; see also the translation by T. Johnes, pt. II. chapters 131–45).   See also *Eulogium Historiarum a Monacho Malmesburiensi* (ed. by F. S. Haydon, Rolls Series, 1863), iii. 356–7; Malverne, in Higden (Rolls Ser., 1886), ix. 15–26; *Chronicon a Monacho S. Albani* (R. Ser., 1874), pp. 355–7.   The fullest modern accounts are *The Crusade of 1383*, by G. M. Wrong (London, 1892); and *Der Kreuzzug des Bischofs Heinrich von Norwich im Jahre 1383*, a dissertation by Gerhard Skalweit (Königsberg, 1898).   For a fuller bibliography, see *Dict. Nat. Biogr.*, xiv. 412; and Skalweit, pp. 5–7, 75–83.

French adherents of the antipope Clement. For political reasons, the greater part of the campaign was in Flanders, though the Flemings were as good Urbanists as the English, especially about Gravelines (Gravénynge), Dunkirk, Ypres and Bourbourg (Burburgh), all of them in that province.[1] But in August the bishop, hearing that the King of France was come to Amiens with an army, entered Picardy [2] with a part of his force, and defied the king to battle; his defiance not being accepted, he returned to Gravelines. He must have passed through Artois going each way. He ended his short "chivachye" by surrendering Bourbourg, retreating, and destroying Gravelines; his reception in England shortly afterwards was not cordial.

In discussing the characters in the *Prologue* there is always danger, of course, that we may attribute to Chaucer a more detailed and realistic conception than he had; but at any rate everything here fits with great nicety the strikingly circumstantial account given by Chaucer. The Squire had been on a "chivachye"[3] which had not lasted long (l. 87), in exactly the region which had been covered by the Bishop of Norwich's expedition, and which had not been the scene of such events for a generation or more. His father's campaigns had all been semi-religious, of the nature of Crusades, and the Knight was just the sort of man to be imposed on by the ecclesiastical zeal of the bishop into thinking his cause a sacred one. These events created a great deal of talk and scandal, and must have been fresh in every one's mind when Chaucer wrote the passage. The account of the Squire's experiences is as detailed and specific, so far as it goes, as that of his father's, which have all been identified with real events within the lifetime of such a man. Surely the inference is not forced that Chaucer meant the Squire to have been in this expedition.

But we have now ample grounds for believing that the *Prologue* cannot have been written before 1387. Professor Lowes has shown that the *Prologue* to the *Legend of Good Women* cannot

---

[1] Cf. *Atlas de Géographie Historique*, ed. by F. Schrader (Paris, 1896), plate 28; or the Spruner-Mencke historical atlas. Nearly all the places mentioned in the sources may be found in the *Atlas des Baillages en 1789*, by Armand Brette (Paris, 1904).

[2] See Wrong, p. 77, and Walsingham. Froissart passes over this episode, but Skalweit shows (pp. 71–4) that his account of the Crusade is neither complete nor very valuable.

[3] Froissart constantly uses in his account the verb *chevaucher*. The campaign hardly outlasted the summer.

well have been written before 1386, and Chaucer can hardly have
been at leisure to begin a new poem before the following year.
Yet the Squire at the time of the pilgrimage was only about
twenty, which would make him only sixteen or so on his
campaign. It may be attributing too much exactness to Chaucer's
conception to argue the matter thus, but at any rate this objection
will prove to have no weight. It will be noticed that the Squire
has not just returned—it was " somtyme," "at one time;" similarly,
the Crusade was not over till the fall, and this is April. Moreover,
if this is not pushing realism too far, while his father has just
arrived, all travel-stained, from a journey, the Squire is in most
exquisite order. But, most interesting of all, sixteen does not
seem to have been an exceptionally early age for the fourteenth-
century soldier to enter his profession.[1] In the fourteenth century
people certainly matured earlier than under modern social conditions,
and at a time when the military class was not expected to have
very much education, what should a squire be at, when once he
had got his growth? The hero of the romance of *King Horn* is
ripe for warlike exploits and is knighted soon after he is fifteen.[2]
Much evidence to bear me out is also supplied by the royal families
of England and France, the members of which are no more likely
to have been precociously military than others of the fighting class.
On Chaucer's campaign in 1359 Edward III. was accompanied by
his four eldest sons, of whom Lionel was twenty-one, John nineteen
and Edmund eighteen.[3] At the age of seventeen Lionel was
knighted, and went on a military expedition to France. At the
Battle of Crécy (August, 1346) Edward the Black Prince com-
manded one of the two main divisions of the English army, and
was left quite independent by his father in order that he might
win his spurs; yet he was only sixteen.[4] Most striking of all, at

[1] Which should not be too surprising to a generation which has allowed
preparatory-school boys to kill each other in playing university football.

[2] MS. Laud, l. 18 (Herrig's *Archiv*, vol. l., 41) ; MS. Harl. (in Ritson) ;
omitted in MS. Camb. (E. E. T. S., 1866). In the description of the Squire
there are some possible reminiscences of the romance of *King Horn ;* compare
83-4 with *Horn* 93-4, 899-900 (Cambridge MS., E. E. T. S.), and 100 with
233-4 and indeed the whole account of Horn and his education. (But
cf. also Mill's *History of Chivalry*, i. 36 ; *Life Records of Chaucer*, Ch. Soc.,
1876, p. xiii. ; Furnivall's *Manners and Meals*, E. E. T. S., 1868, pp. 137-9,
369). With *Horn* 133-4 (MS. Harl., in Ritson) compare also *Nun's Priest's
Tale*, 4391-2.

[3] *Dict. of Nat. Biog.*, xxxiii. 336, xxix. 417, xxxii. 109.

[4] *Ibid.*, xvii. 90 ; Green's *Short History* (New York, 1890), p. 226.

the Battle of Poitiers (September, 1356) King John of France was accompanied by his four sons, of whom Charles was nineteen, Louis was seventeen, Jean under sixteen and Philippe only fourteen ; and though the three older ones fled, Philippe stood by and aided his father in his last stand, and was taken prisoner with him.[1]

So there is nothing whatever against our believing that Chaucer deliberately represented his twenty-year old Squire as having campaigned in 1383.   But to have done so much later than 1387 would have been a real oversight, and probably would never have occurred to him.   We have here, I think, genuine confirmation for the belief that at least the first part of the *Prologue* was written in 1387.[2]

§ 3. *The Physician's Tale.*

The *Physician's Tale* has been little regarded in Chaucer criticism, for the obvious reason that it is short and not of the first merit.   It has usually been put in the early part of the *Canterbury* period, but for almost valueless reasons.[3]   I hope to show others, conjectural but respectable, for the same opinion.

That it comes after the first *Prologue* of the *Legend of Good Women* may be inferred on several grounds.[4]   The argument, used more than once elsewhere, must be used here also, that it is precisely such a story as Alcestis should have scored up to Chaucer's credit, had it existed.   We have also seen that the more poems in

[1] Michaud, *Biographie Universelle,* vii. 531, xxv. 297, iv. 102, xxxiii. 118 ; Guizot's *History of France* (N. Y., 1885), ii. 104.   In connection with Chaucer's own 1359 campaign, this opens the door to the belief that he may have been born later than 1340, for which I believe there is not a little to be said ; at least it would make the earlier part of his life somewhat more intelligible.

[2] Possibly a little more evidence for a date in this neighbourhood may be found in the *Prologue.*   In August or September, 1386, Chaucer was elected Knight of the Shire for Kent (*Life Records,* Ch. Soc., pp. 261–2) ; and of the Franklin he says :

"Ful ofte tyme he was knight of the shire " (356).

Of course this might be a coincidence, but Chaucer's own office makes the detail especially natural.   Moreover "at sessioun ther was he lord and sire," and his friend and companion the Man of Law was justice in assizes by patent and by "pleyn commissioun."   Chaucer was appointed J.P. for Kent in 1385, and received a full commission in 1386.

[3] Cf. my Introduction ; and also p. 155 below, and J. Koch, *Pardoner's Tale,* p. xxii.

[4] Of course it followed the *Troilus.*   For one thing, it may be worth noting that in *T. C.,* IV. 414 Chaucer represents "Zanzis" as a writer ; and in *Phys. T.,* 16, correctly, and following *Le Roman de la Rose,* as a painter.   Cf. T. R. Lounsbury, *Studies,* ii. 411–12.

10-syllable couplets we put before the *Prologue* of the *Legend*, the
stranger becomes the metrical allusion in F, 562. Doubtless, therefore, it was written later than 1386.[1]

A date not far from this, near the *Legends of Good Women*, is
suggested by its general similarity to them in treatment. Here, as
in them, Chaucer is singularly bald in his account and slavish
toward his source. There is none of the warmth and expansive-
ness which characterizes most of the *Canterbury Tales*. Chaucer
here observes the respectful and pupillary and frigid treatment of
classical story which appears in the *Legend*, but which he wholly
got over in such a poem as the *Manciple's Tale*. The *Physician's
Tale* in every respect is harmonious with the *Legend of Good Women*.

On the other hand, it probably preceded the publication of
Gower's *Confessio Amantis*, 1390.[2] I hope to show strong reason
to believe that Chaucer had read and remembered Gower's version
of the story of Constance when he wrote the *Man of Law's Tale*;[3]
now there is not only no evidence that he had read Gower's story
of Virginia[4]—there is striking evidence that he had not,[5] but

---

[1] It may seem as if we should put *Phys. T.* after the translation of Innocent's
De Contemptu Mundi. We shall see in the case of *M. L. T.* (see p. 182),
the peculiarly strong probability that works which quote this book followed
Chaucer's version of it, which there is reason to date (probably late) in the
period 1387–94; Chaucer certainly shows no sign of having known the
original before this time. *Phys. T.*, 280,

> " The worm of conscience may agryse,"

seems at first sight to repeat a phrase from the pope's work : " vermis enim
conscientiæ nunquam moritur " (I. 19) ; " vermis conscientiæ tripliciter lacer-
abit" (III. 2). But the phrase "Li vers de conscience" occurs in Jean de
Meun's *Testament*, 1939, as is shown by Koeppel (*Anglia*, xiv. 266) ; he shows
also that Chaucer certainly quotes this poem in *W. B. Prol.*, and probably
elsewhere in the *C. T.* Considering his intimacy with *Le Roman de la
Rose*, he is likely at any time to have known Jean's *Testament*. On the
possible connection of Chaucer's phrase with Innocent, see Skeat, V. 264 ;
and K. C. M. Sills, *Journ. Compar. Lit.*, i. 390–1 (1903–4, the only year it was
published), in connection with a possible borrowing by Wyatt from Chaucer ;
both Sills and Koeppel declare the phrase to be common, but each quotes
only three passages. All I can find are the one in Chaucer, the two in
Innocent, the one in Jean de Meun's *Testament*, and finally one in *Richard
III.*, I. iii. 222. Shakspere is no doubt quoting Chaucer ; of course the ultimate source of the phrase is " Vermis eorum non moritur," St. Mark ix. 43,
45, 47, perhaps through some patristic or scholastic allegorization.

[2] The date is fixed by Macaulay, II. xxi.

[3] See pp. 183–6.   [4] *C. A.*, VII. 5131–306.

[5] So Skeat, III. 437 ; O. Rumbaur, *Die Geschichte von Appius u. Virginia
in der engl. Litt.* (Breslau, 1890), pp. 12–15. The latter is certainly correct
in believing also that Gower's account shows no influence of Chaucer (p. 16).
Lounsbury (*Studies*, ii. 281–4) shows very convincingly that Chaucer did not
use Livy.

merely expanded the bald and crude account in *Le Roman de la Rose*.[1] Had he read a better account, in a large number of points he could not have failed to show its influence.[2] One small detail is especially significant. Chaucer always calls the judge "Apius," and the accomplice "Claudius," and is even very emphatic about the names.[3] Gower makes particularly conspicuous the fact that the former was named "Apius Claudius," and the latter "Marchus Claudius."[4] It is hardly a risky inference, therefore, that the *Physician's Tale* is not only later than 1386, but antedates 1390.

But this may be further confirmed. To begin with, Professor Kittredge points out[5] a probable and very interesting contemporary allusion in the tale. " It is now generally admitted that Chaucer's wife was the sister[6] of Katherine Swynford, who was for some time governess of John of Gaunt's daughters,[7] and whose career as the Duke's mistress[8] and subsequently his wife is well known. Is it possible that Chaucer put the following verses into the Doctor's mouth without thinking of his own sister-in-law?" Then he quotes *Physician's Tale*, 72–85, verses in which the poet reminds the mistresses in charge of *lord's daughters* (note that he and *Le Roman de la Rose* call Virginius only a *knight*, and lay

---

[1] 5613–82 (Méon); conveniently given by Skeat, III. 435–7.

[2] *E. g.*, the fact that Virginia was betrothed (to Ilicius in Gower, Icilius in Livy, III. 44), heightens the pathos. All this is by no means parallel to such a bit of forgetfulness as is mentioned in connection with the *Monk's T.* (see p. 169 below).

[3] . . . "The cherl, that highte Claudius.
This false Iuge, that highte Apius,
So was his name (for this is no fable)" (153–5).

Chaucer follows the error of *R. R.* For a similar blunder, cf. *House of Fame*, 177–8; and for the opposite kind, *Monk's T.*, 3887.

[4] " At Rome whan that Apius,
Whos other name is Claudius " (5131–2);

" Which Marchus Claudius was hote " (5167).

[5] *Modern Philology*, i. 5, note.

[6] In the Chaucer Society's *Life Records* (London, 1900; pp. xv.–xix.) will be found all the evidence, which makes it practically certain that if Philippa was not Katherine's sister she was her sister-in-law. See also, among other references, J. W. Hales, *Athenæum*, no. 3153 (1888), pp. 404–5, on Thomas, Philippa and Elizabeth Chaucer. Even if she was neither, Chaucer must have been so familiar with the affairs of the Lancaster family that the allusion, to be noted shortly, seems obvious.

[7] From before 1369 to 1382, when she retired to the country with her illegitimate children, the Beauforts. See S. Armitage-Smith, *John of Gaunt*, Westminster, 1904; pp. 390–1.

[8] Beginning about 1371–2; in 1396 they were married. See Armitage-Smith, pp. 196, 433.

no stress on his rank) that they owe their positions to the fact that either they have kept their virtue, or through having formerly lost it are peculiarly fitted to safeguard that of others.[1]

But the whole first part of the tale has a singularly actual effect, where, after a long and detailed account of Virginia's beauty and goodness, the poet addresses "maistresses" and parents, and recommends judicious strictness. Any one who carefully reads it, I think, will grant that it has every appearance of having been inspired by personal feeling or reminiscence; it has much more the air of having been written with interest than anything which follows in the tale, it is not even remotely suggested by anything in *Le Roman de la Rose*, and is not a particularly obvious outgrowth of the story itself. More than this, no such serious, overt and practical criticism of life is to be found anywhere else in the *Canterbury Tales*.[2] We shall not be unprepared, therefore, if we detect another contemporary allusion, closely connected with the other.

One of Virginia's virtues was that she avoided company too old and too dissipated for a girl of fourteen :

> " And of hir owene vertu, unconstreyned,
> She hath ful ofte tyme syk hir feyned,
> For that she wolde fleen the companye
> Wher lykly was to treten of folye,
> As is at festes, revels, and at daunces,
> That been occasions of daliaunces.
> Swich thinges maken children for to be
> To sone rype and bold, as men may see,
> Which is ful perilous, and hath ben yore.
> For al to sone may she lerne lore
> Of boldnesse, whan she woxen is a wyf" (61–71).

Then comes the warning to duennas. Now one of Katherine

---

[1] Line 79 in this passage—

> "(Or elles ye han falle in freletee,)
> And knowen wel y-nough the olde daunce,"

at once suggests the last line of the description of the Wife of Bath in the *Prol.* (476), and a line at the end of the account of her original in *R. R.*, La Vieille, who acts as jailor over the imprisoned Bel-Acueil :

> "Qu'el scet toute la vielle dance" (4078, ed. Marteau).

Clearly, the Wife of Bath and La Vieille were not absent from Chaucer's mind when he wrote this passage in *Phys. T.* ; but, clearly also, it was this passage which recalled them to him, not *vice versa.* Cf. pp. 209–210.

[2] Except, perhaps, in the beautiful passage on connubial conduct in *Frankl. T.*, 761–86 ; and possibly the ironical digression at the beginning of *Merch. T.*

Swynford's young charges had been all that Virginia was not.[1]
Elizabeth, second daughter of John of Gaunt and Blanche of
Lancaster, born about 1368,[2] solemnly betrothed in 1380 to the
young Earl of Pembroke, and of marriageable age in 1386,[3] was
then introduced to society and had her first taste of "chere of
court." "Altera vero fuit desponsata," according to Malverne's
continuation of Higden, " comiti Penbroke puero immaturæ ætatis ;
sed illa viripotens tunc effecta, in regalem curiam est delata ad con-
spicandum gestus aulicos et mores eorum. Quam ut aspexit domi-
nus Johannes Holand, frater domini regis nunc ex parte materna,
vehementer captus est ejus amore, propter quod die noctuque eam
sollicitavit, tamen per temporum intervalla tandem tam fatue illam
allexit, sic quod tempore transitus domini ducis patris sui ad mare
per eum extitit impregnata. Unde illam incontinenti postea duce
acceptante, duxit in uxorem ante prolis exortum transivitque in
Hispaniam cum illo."[4] Elizabeth and her husband returned to
England in June, 1388, or earlier.[5] The whole episode is the more

[1] This is not the first time that the people concerned in this affair have
been brought in to explain a *Canterbury Tale.* In 1889 Professor A. Brandl
tried to show that the *Squire's Tale* is an elaborate historical allegory (*Englische
Studien*, xii. 161–74). Professor G. L. Kittredge (*E. S.*, xiii. 1–24 ; he gives a
large amount of valuable information), as Brandl himself admitted, promptly
and utterly overthrew his opinions. It will be seen that the incident to be quoted
is the most complete possible confirmation of Kittredge's position (if such were
needed) ; as he conjectures from Knighton's language, Elizabeth, instead of
wearing the willow, conferred it ; this also explains why the Earl of Pembroke
refused to confirm his marriage with her (see Kittredge, p. 21, and cf. p. 12).
Brandl would have to change his sexes ; the tercelet would be Elizabeth, the
peregrine falcon young Pembroke and the kite John Holland. One authority
for the matter is Knighton's *Chronicle* (ed. J. R. Lumby, Rolls Series, 1895),
ii. 208, but he omits the scandalous inner history, perhaps out of good feeling
(see Kittredge, p. 13, n. 2) ; the authority for this is John Malverne's continuation of Higden's *Polychronicon* (ed. Lumby, Rolls Series, 1886 ; who
wrongly gives the date of the incident as 1387, p. xvii.), ix. 96–7. Armitage-
Smith (p. 459) says that " he is usually so full and accurate that there can be
little hesitation in accepting the story, especially as it squares with everything known of John Holland's character and the manners of the English
court at the time." He was a contemporary (died about 1415, according to
Gross, *Sources and Literature of English History*, p. 289). The only dis-
crepancy between Knighton and Malverne is that according to the former the
marriage of Elizabeth and Holland took place after her departure to Spain,
and according to the latter just before, in which he is supported by Froissart
(cf. Kittredge, pp. 12–14). An earlier intrigue of Holland's, according to
Shirley's testimony, is the subject of Chaucer's *Complaint of Mars* (see
Skeat, I. 65).
[2] Cf. Kittredge, *Engl. Stud.*, xiii. 19.
[3] The marriageable age for women, according to canon-law, was twelve (see
Kittredge, *l. c.*, p. 20) ; of course she was long past this, but Malverne implies
that she had been kept away from court.
[4] Malverne's continuation of Higden's *Polychronicon* (Rolls Series, 1886),
ix. 96–7 ; also quoted by Armitage-Smith, *John of Gaunt*, p. 459, and cf. 310.
[5] Kittredge, *l. c.*, pp. 14–15.

likely to have impressed itself on people because Elizabeth had
been really married to Pembroke, in 1380,[1] so far as legally she
could be to so young a boy.[2] He secured a divorce either just after,
or shortly before, her departure for Spain ; it is pretty clear, therefore, if we compare the accounts of Malverne and Knighton, that
she was still bound to Pembroke when her *liaison* with Holland
began, and the inference is obvious that it was at least one cause
for the divorce. The suggestion of the passage in the *Physician's
Tale* is clear; Virginia avoided just the dangers that had led
Elizabeth (only four years older than she) into ruin. Everything
fits so well the passage in the *Physician's Tale* that, considering
Chaucer's relations with the Lancaster family, even if he had been
writing such a passage ten years later, he could hardly have failed
to think of his sister-in-law and the then Duchess of Exeter. Yet
the reference is not direct enough to have given offence in a rather
coarse age ;[3] besides which, directly after (or just before) the
marriage, which would then have been thought to make everything
right, all concerned went to Spain and France for two years.

The bearing of all this on the date of the *Physician's Tale* is
plain. If the allusion is admitted, the date is 1386 or later.
But such a long and serious discourse as Chaucer's is likely to have
been written when the incident was fresh in his mind ; and perhaps
he is a little more likely to have so delivered himself when the
persons whom he had in mind were out of the country. A further
suggestion of about this date is afforded by ten Brink, who believes
that the strong interest which Chaucer shows here in the bringing
up of young girls, and his warning to parents (93–104), indicates
the time just after the death of his wife, between June and
Michaelmas of 1387.[4] This is not unlikely, though he is plainly
thinking in the main of people of much higher station than his
own, or even that of Virginius. But we certainly have tolerable
grounds for dating the *Physician's Tale* between 1386 and 1390,
probably about 1388. Since we have found reason to believe that
the *General Prologue* was written about 1387, the *Physician's*

---

[1] Armitage-Smith, p. 459.

[2] Kittredge, *l. c.*, 18–23. He was born in 1372.

[3] I have suggested already, in connection with *L. G. W.*, that Chaucer did
not have to be as careful as some have supposed about exciting royal resent-
ment. Cf. also the *balade, Lack of Steadfastness*.

[4] *Hist. of Engl. Lit.* (London, 1893), ii. 121, note. We know nothing,
however, of any daughter of Chaucer ; Elizabeth Chausier, who entered
religion in 1377, cannot have been, as Hales assumes, his daughter (see *Life-
Records*, 337–8) ; she was probably a sister, or niece, or cousin.

Tale may very well be the first story written expressly for the *Canterbury Tales*.

§ 4. *The Clerk's Tale.*

On the date of the *Clerk's Tale* opinions have varied rather widely. While Koch, ten Brink and Mather regard it as dating from the period of the *Canterbury Tales*, Pollard and Skeat date it immediately after Chaucer's first journey to Italy. The latter[1] believes that Chaucer learned the tale directly from Petrarch. According to Pollard[2] we have "Chaucer's distinct statement that he learnt the story of Grisilde at Padua of 'Fraunceys Petrak,'" whom he "may have met on his Genoa mission of 1373, when Petrarch was living at Arquà, near Padua"; Mr. Pollard is also somehow conscious of a "general agreement" that he wrote his Englishing of the Griselda story soon after his return.

The supposed early date of the *Clerk's Tale* partly rests on the idea of a meeting between Chaucer and Petrarch, though it should not be forgotten that the one by no means proves the other. On the other hand, if the meeting is disproved, a date for the tale earlier than 1378 or so goes with it, as will be seen later. Pleasant though the thought may be of an interview between the two most distinguished literary men of their time, it must (I think) be relegated to the *Imaginary Conversations;* as Dr. F. J. Mather has done so much to show us in his admirably thorough and judicious article.[3]

It must be clearly recognized at the outset that there is not a shred of evidence for such a meeting. It is not in the least needed, of course, in order to account for Chaucer's obtaining the Latin version of the Griselda story. Considering the reputation both of the *Decameron* and of Petrarch, MSS. of his cultivated Latinization of its last tale are likely to have been speedily multiplied. His version and its authorship were known in France as early as 1392–4, for

---

[1] III. 454–5.

[2] *Globe Chaucer*, p. xxv. ; cf. *Chaucer Primer*, pp. 66–8, and *Knight's Tale* (1903), p. xvi.

[3] *Mod. Lang. Notes*, xii., coll. 1–21. Besides other more obvious references see the following : *Pro.* : J. J. Jusserand, *Nineteenth Century*, xxxix. 923–1005 ; C. H. Bromby, *Athenæum*, no. 3699 (1898), pp. 388–9 (and later); Peter Borghesi, *Boccaccio and Chaucer*, Bologna, 1903, 71 pp. (thinks probably Boccaccio introduced Chaucer to Petrarch, pp. 17–18) ; J. W. Hales, *Dict. Nat. Biogr.*, x. 160. *Con:* S. C. Baddeley, *Athenæum*, no. 3710, p. 791 (and earlier) ; P. Bellezza, *Engl. Studien*, xxiii. 335–6 ; Sir Harris Nicholas, in Morris's *Chaucer*, I. 7–17.

it is the avowed source of a part of the *Ménagier de Paris*.[1] Again,
it is pleaded that the Clerk tells us he had learned the tale at
Padua from Petrarch's mouth; we have equally strong evidence in
the *Canon's Yeoman's Tale* that Chaucer had known a roguish
canon who cheated chantry priests.[2]   It seems highly probable, as
Mather suggests, that this dramatic touch is due to two passages,
near the beginning and end of the letter to Boccaccio [3] which contains Petrarch's Latin version of the Griselda story, and which we
know to have been Chaucer's source; in these passages Petrarch
tells how he had communicated the tale to many of his friends,
how it had been praised and sought after, and how profoundly it
had affected one of them.   This anecdote, and the familiarity with
Petrarch which Chaucer no doubt gained by hearsay, makes such
a fiction as the Clerk's meeting him absolutely natural, and even
obvious.[4]   At first sight a rather striking coincidence suggests
intimate knowledge on Chaucer's part of Petrarch's movements;
during Chaucer's first visit in Italy, because of war between Padua
and Venice, Petrarch was living at Padua, where the Clerk says he
saw him, instead of at Arquà, his home.   But the strangeness
disappears when we reflect that to the western Italian Petrarch
must have passed as a Paduan; the two places are under twenty
miles apart, and Petrarch had often lived in the larger, where he
held ecclesiastical preferment.   But, what is especially important,
Mather has shown that it would have been no easy matter to crowd
a long winter journey, across the Apennines, through districts full
of wars and tumults, into the short time which Chaucer had in
Italy, certainly less than four months,[5] with king's business to
attend to in Genoa and Florence.

[1] Ed. by Jerôme Pichon, Paris, 1846 ; see vol. i., pp. 99–125, and on the
date of the work, p. xxii. There is not the least evidence, as a brief comparison will show, that Chaucer ever saw this version ; it is striking, however,
that he uses the French forms of some of the proper names, such as *Saluces*.
The *Ménagier* contains also the French version of *Melibeus*, which was the
source of Chaucer's tale.

[2] Skeat's arguments seem singularly nugatory (III. 454, note), if not worse.
Were not poor travelling clerks one of the most characteristic classes of the
Middle Ages ? And how much realism does he feel justified in demanding of
the *Canterbury Tales?*

[3] *Originals and Analogues* (Ch. Soc.), pp. 152, 170–1.

[4] Professor G. L. Hendrickson of Chicago shows in *Modern Philology* (iv.
179–88) that a similar method of making citations is a literary convention as
old as the Ciceronian dialogue (though he does not show how Chaucer became
acquainted with it).

[5] See *Mod. Lang. Notes*, xi. 419–25 ; and cf. my article in *Mod. Phil.*, i.
319–21. On the duration of the journey to Italy, cf. *Chronicon Adae de Usk*
(ed. by Sir E. M. Thompson, 1904), pp. xxii.–xxvi.

One piece of negative evidence against the meeting I think has never been allowed sufficient weight. Can any Chaucerian doubt that Chaucer would have made a rather considerable impression on Petrarch? It was late in April, 1373, that Petrarch wrote the letter to Boccaccio which includes the Latin version of Griselda,[1] and if Chaucer met Petrarch it must have been in February or March. Now in his letter Petrarch tells much, as we have seen, of

[1] The most difficult point of all is the date when Petrarch composed his version of the Griselda story. Dr. F. J. Mather's reconstruction, following M. Jusserand's lead, of Petrarch's procedure in regard to his last three or four letters to Boccaccio is a clever and usually satisfactory treatment of a puzzling tangle (see *Mod. Lang. Notes*, xii., columns 1–21). Late in June, 1373, it seems quite certain, Petrarch wrote a short letter to Boccaccio in which he said that two months earlier he had written and begun to copy a long letter to him, evidently of rather impersonal character; relieved of the labour of copying by a friend, he wrote another, nearly as long as the first, and more personal. That one of the two letters contained the Griselda story we know from a letter of Boccaccio's. In the *Epistolæ de Rebus Senilibus,** which Petrarch himself edited, the first-mentioned of the above three letters stands first in the 17th book, followed by two longer ones; of these the first has every appearance of being the second he mentions, and the second the first. This latter is the one which contains the Griselda story. We cannot doubt, therefore, that the Petrarch had the Griselda letter copied about the end of April, 1373. When the Griselda part was composed is a more difficult question. It is clear that the *Decameron* had not been long in Petrarch's hands : " Librum tuum . . . ad me delatum vidi. Nam si dicam legi, mentiar, siquidem . . . tempus angustum erat ; idque ipsum, ut nosti, bellicis undique motibus inquietum, a quibus et si animo procul absim, nequeo tamen fluctuante Republica non moveri."† The reference is to the war between Padua and Venice, which began about the middle of 1372 ; Venetian troops "penetrated into the Padovano (November, 1372), and spread desolation through the entire district."‡ By November 14 Petrarch had taken refuge in Padua.§ It is clear that the *Decameron* came into his hands at a time of great anxiety over the war ; not earlier, therefore, than the middle of 1372. He goes on to say that he had gone through the book in a cursory way, and read more particularly the beginning and the end ; the last novel so charmed him that he learnt it by heart and used to repeat it to his friends. "Quod cum brevi postmodum fecissem gratiamque audientibus cognovissem," it occurred to him that those who knew no Italian would also enjoy it. "Itaque die quodam . . . calamum arripiens, historiam ipsam tuam scribere sum aggressus. . . . Quæ licet a multis et laudata et expetita fuerit, ego rem tuam tibi non alteri dedicandam censui." It is clear from all this, especially the last sentence, that the translation must have been made at least some weeks before the end of April, when the copy was made ; Mather seems to overlook this fact when he thinks April a possible date. The earliest possible date of Petrarch's Latin version of the Griselda story is therefore the end of 1372, and the latest is March, 1373. Since Chaucer, if he went to Padua, must have been there not later than March, nor earlier than February (cf. *Mod. Lang. Notes*, xii. 11), it is perfectly possible, so far as concerns the date of the story, that Chaucer got it immediately from Petrarch. But obviously there is no evidence here that he did ; and I have tried to show evidence that he did not.

* See the Italian translation by Giuseppe Fracassetti (Firenze, 1870), vol. ii. 523–566).
† *Originals and Analogues* (Chaucer Soc.), p. 151.
‡ *The Venetian Republic*, W. C. Hazlitt, i. 653.
§ *Petrarca's Leben und Werke* (Leipzig, 1878), by Gustav Koerting, p. 444.

how the story had been admired and sought after in both Boccaccio's
and Petrarch's versions, and in particular how deeply it had affected
a Paduan friend, and how differently a Veronese had taken it. If a
month or two earlier Chaucer had heard it, and begged a copy, it is
strange indeed that we know nothing of the fact'; that Petrarch
says nothing of "quidam advena ultimæ Thulæ," or "viator a
partibus barbarorum adhuc profectus." He missed an admirable
chance to compliment his friend. And Petrarch's own vanity is
sufficiently well known ; he was surely not proof against such a
compliment as Chaucer would have paid him by taking such a
journey to see him, nor was he too modest to mention the fact.
It seems to me this argument from silence is peculiarly strong.

A few other pieces of evidence may be given that Chaucer
did not meet Petrarch. He was never at all familiar with his
works. Besides this story he shows knowledge only of a single
sonnet. In another point he shows strange ignorance. It is
well known that Petrarch's father was named Petracco,[1] and that
the poet's name would naturally have been Francesco Petracchi ;
but that for some unknown reason he changed it.[2] The earlier
form of the name is, however (even at times in autograph), often
found in Latin and Italian MSS. of the fourteenth century,[3] and
must have been familiar. Now according to the great preponderance
of MS. evidence,[4] this is the form which Chaucer uses in the three
passages in which the name occurs—*Monk's T.* 3515, *Cl. Prol.* 31,
Cl. T. 1147.[5] *Petrak* (with variants, once *Patrik*!), instead of
Petrark, is the reading, in the first passage, of 12 MSS. out of 16,
including the best (El, Hn, Cm) ; in the second, of 17 out of 24,
including all the *S.-T.* MSS. ; in the third, of 14 out of 17, including all the *S.-T.* The spelling with two *r*'s later of course became
universal, in England[6] as well as elsewhere, so its occurrence in late

---

[1] Cf. G. Koerting, *Petrarca's Leben und Werke* (Leipzig, 1878), p. 49.

[2] There are facsimiles of three autograph signatures, "Petrarca" and
"Petrarcha," dated 1338–1341, in Ugo Foscolo's *Essays on Petrarch* (London,
1823), frontispiece.

[3] Fracassetti, *Lettere Familiari*, i. 216, note. "Pétrac" is the form used in
the introduction to the story of Grisélidis in the *Ménagier de Paris*, of date
1392–4 ; see vol. i., 99, 124.

[4] As Pollard, in the *Globe* edition, seems to have been the only editor to
recognize.

[5] In the two latter cases fortunately we can consult sixteen MSS. ; see
Spec. of all the Access. Unpr. MSS. of the "C. T." ; parts vi. and vii. (Ch.
Soc., 1899, 1900). I have further supplemented by nine unprinted MSS., the
four in Cambridge, those in the Lichfield and Lincoln Cathedral libraries, and
MSS. Harl. 1239, 1758 and 7333.

[6] Cf. the entry "Petrarchæ quædam" in Ritson's list of Lydgate's works

MSS. is natural.   The older form would never have come into the
earliest MSS., in all these passages, at the hands of scribes; yet if
Chaucer knew Petrarch, he certainly must have known his name.

Another rather strong piece of evidence, far stronger than his
speaking of Petrarch, seems to me Chaucer's constant silence as to
Boccaccio and his obligations to him.   I do not propose to go
into the Lollius problem, or record his various wrong attributions
of Boccaccio's works, but I will recall the fact that in the passage
of the *Monk's Tale* just mentioned he assigns to Petrarch the *De
Casibus*, a work really by Boccaccio, just as in the *Clerk's Prologue*
he implies as distinctly as possible that Petrarch was the author
of the Griselda story.[1]   If he had met Petrarch, and obtained
a copy of the Griselda story from him, he could not have
failed to learn who was the author of it as well as of the *De
Casibus*, and something of his personality and other works as well.
It seems to me nearly certain that Chaucer did not know the
Decameron,[2] and quite certain that he did not know it well or
own it, yet Petrarch had just obtained a copy.   If he met Petrarch,
his attitude toward Boccaccio is utterly inconceivable.[3]   On the

---

(*Bibl. Poet.*, p. 80).   "Petir Petrarke" is mentioned by Lydgate (Halliwell,
Minor Poems, Percy Soc., p. ix.).   L. Einstein (*The Italian Renaissance in
England*; see index) indicates that Petrarch was becoming fairly well known
in England by the second quarter of the fifteenth century.

[1] It has been pointed out before now that Pierre de Beauvau, author of the
old French translation of Boccaccio's *Filostrato*, attributed the original without hesitation to "ung poethe Florentin nommé Petrearque" (Moland et
d'Héricault, *Nouv. Franç. du xivᵉ Siècle*, Paris, 1858, p. 120).

[2] Professor Cino Chiarini (*Nuova Antologia*, lxxii. 333) argues conversely
that *since* Chaucer met Petrarch, he *must* have known of the *Decameron*.
In the complete absence of perfect evidence in regard to either matter, the
a priori argument for the negative view of both is incomparably stronger than
for the positive.

[3] As to Chaucer's silence as to Boccaccio's name, I do not see how it can be
attributed to any cause but ignorance.   Probably all the works of Boccaccio
which he possessed were in one or two MSS., which lacked the author's name.
Boccaccio was almost certainly not in Florence during Chaucer's short visit
there in 1373.   In the first part of 1373 Boccaccio seems to have been in
Certaldo, where he had been extremely sick during the latter part of the
preceding year.   [See Gustav Koerting, *Boccaccio's Leben u. Werke* (Leipzig,
1880), p. 322.]   He was not appointed to lecture in Florence on Dante till
August, 1373, and did not begin till October 23.   [See Paget Toynbee,
Athenæum, no. 4034 (1905), p. 210.   Mr. Toynbee might have much more
vehemently denied Hales' guess that Chaucer may have heard Boccaccio
lecture, and must have become familiar with his name, if he had known of
Mather's proof that Chaucer was back in England in May.   I should point
out that this fact was known to Furnivall as long ago as 1875-6; see Thynne's
Animadversions (Ch. Soc.), p. 22, note.]   Certaldo is twenty miles from
Florence.   Chaucer's short visit in Florence must have been in February

whole, therefore, these arguments, coupled with the total absence
of evidence in its favour, perhaps warrant us in dismissing the
idea of a meeting between Chaucer and Petrarch.

If they did not meet, of course it is absolutely out of the
question that he learned the story on his first visit to Italy.   The
letter containing it, of which it is certain that Chaucer had a copy,
cannot have got into general circulation before the middle of
1373, and probably not before a year later, after Petrarch's death.
What can be plainer, therefore, than that Chaucer first came upon
the story during his second visit to Italy, in 1378 ? So far, therefore, this seems to be the earliest possible date for the *Clerk's Tale.*

But it is very difficult to believe that Chaucer made his translation before the *Prologue* of the *Legend of Good Women* was
written,[1] that is, before 1386.   There is not one of the works
mentioned there which offsets the *Romance of the Rose* and the
Troilus and Criseyde so capitally as the story of Griselda would
have done.   If he pleads the *House of Fame,* the *Boethius,* and
(though it was unpublished and very probably unfinished) the
Palamon and Arcitê, could he conceivably have passed over such
a story of feminine patience and devotion?   This brings us to
the very verge of the period of the *Canterbury Tales,* and I think
we shall find that there is not the least evidence that it does not
date from that period.   Professor Skeat's discussion[2] of the subject
is one of the most unsatisfactory parts of his edition.   The
evidence of the metre as to date is wholly nugatory, and to plead it
arrantly begs the question; that "the closeness of the translation also
proves" the earliness of the tale is just as gratuitous.   It is also

---

or March.   He is therefore most unlikely to have seen the old invalid.   Prof.
Hales (*D. N. B.*, x. 160), like Mr. Borghesi, suggests that Chaucer met
Petrarch through Boccaccio ; if he knew neither of them, how, asks Hales,
did he obtain a copy of the Griselda story ?   To this I reply—how did the
French writer of the *Ménagier de Paris* get a copy of it (see pp. 156–7 above),
no later than 1392–4 ?   On Chaucer's second visit to Italy, both Boccaccio and
Petrarch were dead.   Chaucer's failure to learn more of the personality and
works of the distinguished Italians illustrates vividly the degree to which he
must have been preoccupied with business during his two very brief visits in
Italy ; which makes it the more unlikely that he undertook the long and
arduous journey to Padua.   It must be remembered, too, that he went to
Italy only as a diplomat, and at the time was still obscure as a literary man ;
he was little over thirty, and had written no poem of importance, and none of
any length except the *Book of the Duchess.*   Boccaccio was sixty and Petrarch
sixty-nine, and Chaucer had no claim upon them.   It defies chronology to
picture two laureled forms rushing into each other's arms.

[1] Cf. Mather, *Mod. Lang. Notes,* xii., col. 16.   [2] III. 453 ff.

difficult to see how the excellence of verses 995–1008 indicates that they were written at a different time from the rest of the poem.

The chief reason, no doubt, why many persons have felt disposed to put the *Clerk's Tale* comparatively early in Chaucer's career is its thoroughly mediæval character—its want of harmony with the modern spirit and with that of the more advanced and realistic of the *Canterbury Tales*.[1] May I be permitted to say here, as I say elsewhere, in the cases of the *Man of Law's Tale*, the *Monk's Tale* and *Melibeus*,[2] that there seems to me something radically erroneous in this point of view? Was Chaucer so far beyond the most modern of the Italians, Boccaccio and Petrarch? Chaucer's feeling in the matter seems thoroughly intelligible and characteristic. He, like the two Italians, and like many men since, was profoundly touched by the ideal beauty of the story, and reproduced it with perfect sympathy ; then, like Petrarch, but unlike the less reflective Boccaccio, he disclaimed literal approval of Griselda's conduct, and drew an obvious mediæval moral ; and finally, unlike either of his predecessors, he became somewhat frivolous and ironical in the *Clerk's Envoy* at the expense of the modern woman. The fact that the Greek tragedian completed his serious and elevated trilogy by a mocking and farcical satyr-play does not prove that it must have been written long after the trilogy, or that he had come to think lightly of the earlier plays. This is not the only time that Chaucer shows indisposition to take himself too seriously ; nor is he the last man who has covered sensibility by a little cynicism. His literary taste can hardly have changed so much between the ages of forty and fifty that he came to scoff at what had once affected him. I cannot believe that the *Envoy* implies any more aloofness from the tale than would have been as natural just after writing it as ten years later.[3] It seems to me also

[1] Professor Lounsbury (*Studies*, iii. 344) thinks Chaucer inserted it in the *C. T.* because he wished them to contain something which would appeal to all kinds of people. This is by no means the most striking case where that scholar seems greatly to exaggerate Chaucer's modernness.

[2] I point out elsewhere that *Cl. T.*, *Monk's T.* and *Mel.* are the only ones of the *C. T.* which Lydgate thinks worth specific mention in his list of Chaucer's works in the *Falls of Princes* (see Lounsbury's *Studies*, i. 421). There is also evidence in the MSS. that *Cl. T.* was one of the most popular of the *C. T.* The popularity of the Griselda story in England lasted for centuries.

[3] The *Envoy* is no doubt egregiously out of character for the Clerk ; but I cannot in the least see why this should indicate that it was written long after the tale (this in answer to Koch, *Beiträge zur neueren Philologie, Jakob Schipper dargebracht*, Wien, 1902 ; p. 284). Chaucer would always rather

proper to deprecate the practice of regarding the *Canterbury Tales* as a dumping-ground for Chaucer's old outgrown literary work.[1]

A specific date for the *Clerk's Tale* seems impossible to arrive at for the present. Ten Brink [2] believes he finds internal evidence for a date after 1387, for he sees in 995–1008, where the narrator exclaims over the warm greeting given Walter's second wife by his people, a reference to the hearty reception given Richard II., on November 10, 1387, by the citizens of London, who both before and after sided with his opponents. But the conjecture carries no conviction.[3] There was apparently a more gorgeous reception on a similar occasion in August, 1393.[4] Or the reminiscence might equally well be of the events of 1381. But the closest parallel that can be found in contemporary history to the situation in the poem is the reception given the little Isabelle of France, in 1396, on her arrival in London to be Richard's second bride, by the citizens who had been so attached to the first; "multi de civitate exierunt per pontem ad videndam eam," insomuch that in returning some were "oppressi et ad mortem conculcati."[5]   But without further evidence

---

lose his dramatic propriety than his jest.   Compare the self-exposure of the Pardoner.

[1] It may be asked if any evidence for an early date for the *Cl. T.* is to be found in the MSS., especially in the two or three which contain it alone (and thus testify to its popularity). There is not the slightest evidence in any MS. that the tale ever existed in Chaucer's day apart from the *C. T.* Of printed MSS. there are sixteen, of which one (MS. Longleat) contains only *Kn. T.* and *Cl. T.*, and two contain only *Cl. T.* (MSS. Phillipps and Naples; on this latter see Koch, in the Schipper *Festschrift* just mentioned, pp. 257–85). All these three naturally omit the *Cl. Prol.*, and MSS. Longl. and Ph. omit a little at the end, including the reference to the Wife of Bath (Ph. omits 1163–76, L. omits 1170–6; MS. Petworth also omits 1170–6); but all three have the *Envoy*, and MS. Naples has the whole end, the *Envoy* and the "Host-Stanza" (given by Skeat in a note at the end of the tale). It is clear, therefore, that these MSS. are all derived from more complete ones of the *C. T.*, and are not survivors from an earlier version. I have also examined 32 unpublished MSS., being all that exist in public libraries in England and France, except MS. Sion (published). They completely bear me out. To the above-mentioned three fragmentary MSS., which testify to the especial popularity of *Cl. T.*, I may add MS. Harl. 1239, which contains only *Kn. T.*, *M. L. T.*, *W. B. T.*, *Cl. T.* and *Frankl. T.*

[2] *Hist. of Engl. Lit.* (London, 1893), ii. 123.

[3] See H. Wallon, *Richard II.* (Paris, 1864), i. 330; Knighton's *Chronicle* (Rolls Series, 1895), ii. 241. Walsingham says nothing of the incident. The Monk of Evesham, to whom ten Brink refers, certainly does not dwell on it, and his account of the fickleness of the Londoners is in another connection (see Thomas Hearne's edition of the *Hist. Vit. et Regni Ric. II.*, p. 85).

[4] Höfler dwells on this more than on the other; see his monograph on Queen Anne, in the *Denkschriften* of the Vienna Academy (*Phil.-Hist. Classe*), xx., pp. 193, 218. See also *Hist. Vit. et Regni Ric. II.*, p. 124.

[5] *Hist. Vit. et Regni*, p. 129.

it will hardly do to use any of these possible references as arguments
for dating the *Clerk's Tale ;* for the passage in the poem explains
itself without them.　For the present we must be contented with
the certainty that it was written after 1378, and the strong probability that it was written after the *Legend* and in the *Canterbury*
period, after 1387.

§ 5.　*The Monk's Tale.*

There cannot be the least doubt that the *Monk's Tale* dates from
later than Chaucer's first journey to Italy.　It is not merely that
more or less of the poem is derived from Boccaccio's *De Casibus
Virorum Illustrium* and *De Claris Mulieribus,*[1] works which
Chaucer is much more likely to have found in Italy than in England ; or that the account of "Hugelinus Comes de Pize" is derived
avowedly from Dante,[2] since some regard this as a later insertion.
He quotes Dante also in the account of Nero ;[3] and the Italian
influence is also plain in the form of the names which he gives to

---

[1] Cf. certain passages, especially, in the account of Zenobia (Skeat, V. 236–
238), and the rubric at the beginning of the poem in MSS. El, Cp, Ln, and
Cm Dd.　It seems at first as if we could prove that Chaucer could not have
seen, and certainly not have secured a copy of the *De Casibus* until his second
journey to Italy ; for Hortis (*Studj sulle opere latine del Boccaccio*, Trieste,
1879 ; p. 134, note), Koerting (*Boccaccio's Leben und Werke*, Leipzig, 1880 ; p.
730), and others, declare with a good apparent show of reason that the work
cannot have been published till 1373–4.　But Henri Hauvette (*Soc. des
anciens élèves de la Fac. des Lettres de l'Univ. de Paris*, 1901　279–97) shows
not only that this conclusion is not necessary, but also that there is strong
evidence against it and in favour of the date 1356–9 for the composition of the
De Casibus, and about 1363 for its publication (p. 296).　One of the most
promising Chaucerian subjects still to be investigated seems to be the sources
of the *Monk's Tale*, which have been left somewhat at loose ends.
[2] Possibly Chaucer used also Villani ; see Paget Toynbee, *N. and Q.*, 8
ser., xi. 205 f. (and cf. S. C. Baddeley, *ibid.*, 369 f.).　But cf. *M. T.*,
3651–2.　J. W. Hales (*The Bibliographer*, i. 37–9) argues for a knowledge on
Chaucer's part of Italian and Dante before his first journey to Italy ; he has
no evidence, and his *a priori* considerations are not in the least convincing.
For the same view cf. also, among other places, Lounsbury's edition of the
Parliament of Fowls (Boston, 1877), p. 7, and Francesco Torraca (*Journ. of
Compar. Lit.*, i. 82–4) ; the latter's argument is completely disposed of by
J. L. Lowes, *Mod. Philol.*, iii. 1–46.　At the same time it is wholesome to
remember that the belief, on which so much Chaucer chronology is based,
that the Italian influence cannot antedate 1372, supported though it is by
probability and what evidence we have, is not quite a certainty.
[3] "His lustes were al lawe in his decree" (3667); cf. "Che libito fe' licito
in sua legge" (*Inf.*, V. 56).　This borrowing, along with many others, was first
pointed out by Cary, in his translation of the *Divine Comedy ;* see vol. i., p.
201 (London, 1831).　Cf. my article in *Mod. Philol.*, iii. 371, note.　Skeat
and Lounsbury curiously ignore this borrowing.

Zenobia's sons (3535).[1] So far we have 1373 as the earliest possible date, on which all will probably agree.

A date not earlier than 1379–81 [2] is suggested by a probable quotation from Gower's *Mirour de l'Omme*. At the end.of the account of Alexander, the Monk apostrophizes him thus:

"Thy *sys* fortune hath turned into *as*" (3851).[3]

Speaking at some length of the uncertainties in the life of potentates, Gower says:

> " Fortune leur changa le dée[4]
> Et desmontoit ce q'ot monté " (22024–5);

continuing, he apostrophizes Fortune for her instability, speaks of her wheel, compares her to the winds, tells of her two trumpets of fame,[5] and relates the career of Alexander (22051–68), how Fortune made him king and then poisoned him. Addressing the goddess, he says:

> " Le dée du quell tu jueras
> Ore est en sisz, ore est en as " (22102-3).[6]

An even closer parallel is to be found in 23399:

> "Dieus changera tes sis en as."

Chaucer and other poets not infrequently derive figurative language from dicing, but no such cases as these have been found.

It is necessary now to examine carefully the prevalent view that the *Monk's Tale* was written not long after Chaucer's introduction to

---

[1] Apparently Chaucer did not like the Latin fashion of the names (see Skeat, V. 236); he says they are Persian (3536), but has really changed them to an Italian form. It is remarkable that he has done the same thing in many other cases, either because the Italian form pleased his ear better or because it afforded more rhymes. In Skeat's index of names I find the following instances, omitting those in poems of directly Italian origin (*i. e.*, *T. C.*, *K. T.*), and *H. F.*, 1229 :—Cambalo (*Sq. T.*, 31, 667 ; but cf. 656); Danao (*L. G. W.*, 2563, etc.) ; Hermanno (*Monk's T.*, 3535) ; Iulo (*H. F.*, 177); Lino (*L. G. W.*, 2569, etc. ; cf. Skeat, III. xl.) ; Myda (*W. B. T.*, 951, 953 ; possibly from *T. C.*, III. 1389) ; Parnaso, Pernaso (*passim*) ; Sitheo (*L. G. W.*, 1005); Thymalao (*Monk's T.*, 3535) ; Vulcano (*H. F.*, 138).

[2] See Appendix A, pp. 220–5, on the date of the *Mirour*.

[3] I cannot deprive my readers of a "jewel five words long " afforded by the scribe of the Lansdowne MS., who reads :

> "Þin suster fortune haþe torne in-to an as."

[4] Cf. *K. T.*, 1238.

[5] In this part Gower seems to have borrowed from *H. F.*; see pp. 38–40 above.

[6] Cf. also ll. 11 600–1.

things Italian, at any rate before the period of the *Canterbury Tales*.[1]
The ground on which this position rests appears to be that the tale
to us is dull, and very inferior in merit to the tales which we know
date from the period of the whole poem ; and further that in the
Nun's Priest's Prologue the Host and Knight show somewhat the same
opinion.   It is presumed, therefore, to have been Chaucer's, as the
Host's opinion of the *Tale of Thopas* no doubt is, and the history
of the tale to have been parallel to that of the *Second Nun's*.   The
subject has never been thoroughly overhauled, however, nor the
evidence all collected or carefully treated.   By doing this I think
I shall establish a strong probability that the *Monk's Tale* was
written for the *Canterbury Tales*.

In the first place, I must protest against the slur on Chaucer's
literary conscience cast by this opinion ; if the tale is too poor to
date from his heyday, he must have been conscious of its inferiority,
and could hardly have been so slack and slovenly as to embody it
permanently in his masterpiece.   *Sir Thopas* and *St. Cecelia* are
not parallel cases ; the use of the former, an unmistakable parody, is
doubtless due to Chaucer's tactful wish to avoid seriously competing
among his pilgrims, and the latter is by no means so poor a poem,
to our way of thinking, as the *Monk's Tale*, and the reasons for dating
it early are quite different.   Nor is there the least evidence that
Chaucer thought ill of it.   But I must also refer to what I have said
elsewhere in connection with the *Man of Law's Tale*,[2] as to the
caution necessary in discussing Chaucer's taste.   He was not wholly
beyond his age, or beyond the sort of thing which appealed to men
as advanced as Petrarch and Boccaccio.   Though it was tempera-
mentally impossible for him (if not for anybody) to write *con amore*
a poem like the *Monk's Tale*, yet it is not without a certain
impressiveness, even for us, and its subject, the mutability of
fortune, had a peculiar interest for Chaucer to the end of his life.
The stories are too brief to be interesting, and he was never good at
vitalizing material derived from ancient sources.   But is there any
difficulty in putting the *Monk's Tale* not long after the *Legend
of Good Women ;* or, allowing for the difference of plan, is it greatly
inferior to the *Physician's Tale*, which perhaps dates from about
1388 ?[3]   And could a man who had quite grown beyond the

[1] Cf. *e. g.*, Pollard, *Knight's Tale* (1903), p. xvi., and Skeat, III. 427–431.
For a fuller statement of this view, see Lounsbury, *Studies*, iii. 332–4.
[2] See p. 176.   [3] See pp. 155–6.

Monk's Tale have translated and inserted in his masterpiece the interminable dreariness of the *Tale of Melibeus* without a sign of emotion ?   Moreover, sufficient stress has never been laid on the nicety with which the tale is adapted to the teller.   The Monk, though a sportsman and a *bon vivant*, was a man of position and dignity ; of these he would be particularly conscious in a large and miscellaneous company, especially after the impudent familiarity of the Host in his prologue.   Accordingly he searches his memory for something safe, monastic and improving ; if not the life of St. Edward, then tragedies, some biblical and all other-worldly in their tendency.

Professor Lounsbury, who is always, if I may be permitted to say so, much inclined to take Chaucer out of his age, with which he himself appears hardly to be in sympathy, it seems to me takes a very mistaken view of the *Monk's Tale*.   It belongs to a "species of composition to which," he says, " the men of Chaucer's age were exceedingly addicted";[1] he refers to Boccaccio's *De Casibus*, to Lydgate's *Falls of Princes*, and to the *Mirror for Magistrates*. Though Chaucer, he thinks, "fell at first under the influence of the dominant taste," "his clear critical perception put him speedily in advance of his contemporaries " ; and in the *Canterbury Tales* "the Monk's tale is introduced as a specimen of these collections of stories, and largely and perhaps entirely for the sake of satirizing, or at least of censuring, the taste that created and enjoyed them."   Now the first sentence which I have quoted is absolutely misleading.   There is no question that the *genre* represented in the *Monk's Tale* was wholly the creation of Boccaccio,[2] both in conception and form, though hints are of course traceable to other mediæval works. If the *De Casibus* was the first work of the species, the "taste" was certainly not widely popular in Chaucer's age anywhere in Europe, and was doubtless wholly unknown in England.   So Chaucer's procedure in introducing the species in order to censure it would be something like that of a prohibition agitator who should debauch an innocent community with strong drink in order to secure the diversion of preaching against it.   The *Monk's Tale* certainly could not be taken as a parody, and there cannot be the least question that

---

[1] *Studies in Chaucer* (New York, 1892), iii. 332–4.
[2] See Attilio Hortis, *Studj sulle opere latine del Boccaccio* (Trieste, 1879), pp. 117, 120.   A forthcoming dissertation by Professor K. C. M. Sills will doubtless throw much new light on the subject.   I am already bound to him for information and much generous assistance.

it would have been thoroughly enjoyed by serious-minded readers. That the *genre* was likely to become popular in England is indicated by its harmony with mediæval taste ; by its later vogue due to Lydgate's *Falls of Princes* (often printed in both the fifteenth and sixteenth centuries), and (nearly two centuries later than the *Monk's Tale*) to the *Mirror for Magistrates ;* and by the fact that the *Monk's Tale, Melibeus,* and the *Clerk's Tale* are the only individual *Canterbury Tales* deemed worthy of separate mention by Lydgate in his long list of Chaucer's works in the *Falls of Princes.*[1] On the whole, therefore, instead of first following and then scorning a " dominant taste," it seems probable that Chaucer constantly shared it and was in the head and front of its creation.

The attitude of the Knight and Host toward the tale seems to me more worthy of attention than any other adverse argument ; it does seem at first a trifle odd that Chaucer should put into their mouths such disrespectful language toward the subject and even the phraseology of a poem seriously intended. But to this I reply that he may have had a revulsion of feeling when he wrote the *Nun's Priest's Prologue,* and have felt that a moderate amount of this sort of thing certainly *was* sufficient.[2] After a time he may have wearied of its gloom and monotony, as he did in the *Legend of Good Women ;* but this does not mean that he came to regard the whole thing with alienation and scorn. A bantering manner is characteristic of Chaucer, even toward things which he really respected, and (if I may be allowed to say so) it is perfectly possible to take his humour too seriously. Moreover, the attitude of the two critics is thoroughly good dramatically. Neither the Knight nor the Host was likely to care for such a tale. I can hardly grant Lounsbury that the Knight, who had passed his life campaigning, was representative of " the highest cultivation of the community " ; nor was he especially likely to welcome a recent literary departure. As for the Host, he was disappointed as well as bored. He deserved some reward for his patience through *Melibeus ;* it is evident, by his banter, that he expected something merrier from the Monk, and after the interruption he pleads for a tale of hunting (cf. 3114-5, 3995). But, once more, the presence of *Melibeus* just before,

---

[1] Lydgate was surely no unfavourable example of contemporary cultivation (cf. pp. 162, 190-1, and Lounsbury's *Studies,* i. 421).

[2] Boccaccio and Lydgate, who were far more lengthy than Chaucer, express over and over again (as Mr. Sills points out to me) a sense of effort and exhaustion. But they certainly did not think ill of their work.

uninterrupted and uncondemned, seems to me a sufficient refutation of the notion that the Host and Knight voice Chaucer's serious and permanent opinion.

So far there is nothing like proof of the earliness of the tale. Three other arguments adduced by Professor Skeat [1] seem to be of still less value. The canon that poems in stanzas are early is useful for general classification, but has no weight in argument. The *Prioress' Tale* is universally granted to be late, and I have shown elsewhere reason to think that the *Man of Law's* and *Clerk's* are also. The *Monk's Tale* is Chaucer's only narrative poem in the 8-line stanza, but of the half-dozen other poems written in it two at least (*Bukton* and *Venus*) date from the last decade of his life. Skeat also deduces from Chaucer's confusion of Busiris with Diomedes (3293–4), who are properly distinguished by Boethius, that he had not yet produced his translation of that philosopher; it is hardly necessary to say that the lapse of fifteen or twenty years may produce forgetfulness of a trivial matter as dense as original ignorance. Dr. Skeat also tries to prove the greater part of the poem earlier than the so-called Modern Instances, [2] which are known to date from 1386 or later; " the difference in style between the tragedy of Ugolino and such a tragedy as that of Samson or Hercules, must strike the most careless reader." Skeat ignores the fairly obvious fact that in the *Ugolino* Chaucer is closely following one of the greatest poets of the world. The question of excellence is of course a purely subjective matter; I can only say, however, that after many careful readings I can see no difference or superiority in the Modern Instances, except so far as the *Ugolino* is indebted to Dante. They seem as bald as any part of the poem, and even in the *Ugolino* the want of congruity and feeling at times (*e. g.* 3619–20, 3635–6) is the more striking because of the moving horror of the original. [3]

---

[1] III. 427, 430. Ten Brink also has another argument. He thinks (*Sprache*, p. 23) the imperfect rhyme of close with open *o* characteristic of Chaucer's earlier work, and points to one in *M. T.*, 3510-2-3-5. But, to say nothing of the excuse here in the number of rhyme-words required, ten Brink himself shows that the same rhyme (*to, tho*) occurs in the *W. B. Prol.*, 369–70. Was this one reason for his extraordinary opinion that the *Wife's Prologue* was an early work? We certainly need a more thorough chronological study of Chaucer's rhyme and verse usage; it will be highly valuable negatively if not positively. Where is the Quintus Curtius?

[2] The quaint and convenient term applied by Bradshaw to the tragedies of the two Pedros, Ugolino and Bernabò Visconti.

[3] I find that the late Professor Francis Palgrave expressed exactly the same opinion of the Ugolino passage (for his interesting essay on Chaucer and the

The least significant of the contrary evidence seems to me weighty compared with this. We may note, in the first place, the manner of address in line 3429, at the end of the account of Balthasar:

"Lordinges, ensample heer-by may ye take";

lordings as a vocative Chaucer seems to use only in the *Canterbury Tales* and toward people physically present; usually in the links, but sometimes in the tales[1] as well it is used to the pilgrims. Here, clearly, Chaucer has in mind oral delivery. Again, Professor Koeppel[2] has detected a probable borrowing from Pope Innocent's *De Contemptu Mundi* in the account of Adam (3199):

"With goddes owene finger wroght was he,
And nat bigeten of mannes sperme unclene";

compare "formatus est homo . . . de spurcissimo spermate." The pope's work is freely quoted, it will be remembered, in the *Man of Law's* and the *Pardoner's Tales*, and Chaucer's translation of it was produced between his two versions of the *Prologue* to the *Legend of Good Women*, 1387–1394. Considering its exceedingly uncongenial character, it is hard to doubt that his familiarity with it dates from the time of his own translation.[3] Next, at the beginning and end of the *Monk's Tale* a colloquial style, an absence of formality, may be detected:

"I wol biwayle in maner of Tragedie";

the definition of tragedy, echoing that in the *Monk's Prologue*, is casually introduced in the third line of the last stanza, a strange place for it if the poem was originally independent and unconnected with the *Monk's Prologue;* we should rather have expected it in the first stanza. Of course Chaucer might have made these changes in adapting the poem to the *Tales;* but they are so unnecessary as to be wholly improbable. Elsewhere in reassigning tales he usually neglects highly necessary revisions.[4]

But the most important evidence relates to the position of the

---

Italian Renascence, see *The Nineteenth Century* for 1888 ; xxiv. 340–59). He even goes so far (p. 350) as to think such a passage as 3620, compared with its original, enough to make one doubt the authenticity of the whole *Monk's Tale;* which can hardly represent a mature conviction.

[1] *Pard. T.*, 573 ; *Cl. T.*, 1163 ; *Manc. T.* 309. In *Melibeus* it is used occasionally by the characters in addressing each other (*e. g.* 2212, 2228).

[2] Skeat, V. 228.

[3] See pp.181–2. Cf. also Lowes, *Publ. Mod. Lang. Assoc.*, xx. 794.

[4] As in *Kn. T.*, *Sh. T.*, *S. N. T.*

Modern Instances. Bernabò Visconti died December 18, 1385,[1] and thereby supplies us with the latest acknowledged allusion in any part of the *Canterbury Tales*. Clearly, this passage cannot have been written before 1386 at the earliest, so if the tale was early, this passage was a later addition; this is generally assumed, and also that the three contiguous passages came in with it. But I think it can be shown conclusively that these passages were not a later addition. Out of 41 MSS. which I have examined, in 10[2] the Modern Instances come at the end of the tale; in 22[3] they come about the middle. If they were added later, the natural place for them was at the end; not only would this carry out the chronological order which is generally observed, but to put them in the middle would require MS.-readjustment, no small matter. But it is clear that when Chaucer put the *Monk's Tale* into the *Canterbury Tales* they were where they are now in the majority of MSS. The life of Crœsus was clearly meant to come last, for it ends with a definition of tragedy, just as another precedes the whole poem at the end of the *Monk's Prologue;* and the last line of *Crœsus* is alluded to in the *Nun's Priest's Prologue*, 3972.[4] Another thing, the Monk in his prologue (3174–80) apologizes at some length for departing from the chronological order, of which to a mediæval reader there is no violation worthy such apology if Bernabò and his associates are at the end.[5] So when the tale was put in its place, it was certainly arranged in a strikingly incorrect order. The only way in which we can make Chaucer responsible also for the order in the Ellesmere group is to suppose that, presumably in preparing the poem for the *Canterbury Tales*, he first added the Modern Instances at the end, that the poem in this form got into independent circulation, that

---

[1] Skeat, V. 240 ; Froissart, *Chronicles* (tr. by Thomas Johnes, London, 1839), ii. 32.

[2] MSS. El, Hn, Cm, Hodson (*Second Supplement to the S.-T.*, Pard. Prol. and T., Ch. Soc. 1900), Linc, R. Coll. Phys., Ad 5140, Haist, Ch.Ch., Seld.

[3] MSS. Hl, Cp, Pt, Ln, Cm Dd, Lich., Cm Ii, Cm Mm, TC 3. 15, TC 3. 3, Hl 1758, Sl 1686, Roy. 17 D, Roy. 18 C, Sl 1685, Rawl. 141, Laud 600, New Coll., T C 49, Bodl. 414, Hatt., Parl. 20. They (together with all or almost all the tale) are lacking in 8 MSS., Hl 1239 and 7335, Ad. 25718, Paris, Rawl. 149 and 223, Laud 739, and Bodl. 686. In MS. Hl 7333 they occur in both positions, a good example of scribal meddling.

[4] Cf. Skeat, III. 429 ; his whole argument is unintelligible.

[5] Omitting them, the order is Lucifer, Adam, Samson, Hercules, Nebuchadnezzar, Belshazzar, Zenobia, Nero, Holofernes, Antiochus, Alexander, Cæsar, Crœsus.

here these ten MSS. go back to a MS. that originated thus, that
he afterwards distorted the tale and placed it in the *Canterbury
Tales*, and that most of the MSS. are descended from this form.
It would require an enormous alternative difficulty to make one
accept such an improbability as this; yet there is no alternative
difficulty whatever.   Therefore I do not see how we can avoid the
conclusion that the arrangement with the Modern Instances at the
end is due to a stupid and pedantic scribe;[1] that the other arrangement is the only genuine one, that therefore the whole second half
of the poem was written not earlier than 1386.[2]   But that it was
not written so immediately after Bernabò's death is suggested by
the fact that his "tragedy" is preceded by those of the two Pedros,
who died in 1369; we should expect that Chaucer would have
begun with the modern potentate whom he had known, if he had
just died.   Finally, Professor Lowes has shown that Chaucer
must have been occupied with the *Legend* in 1386, and we have
seen that this and the following year were pretty well occupied
with that and with the zealous beginning of the *Canterbury Tales*.
Everything therefore indicates that the *Monk's Tale* was written
when the *Canterbury Tales* were already well under way.

§ 6. *The Man of Law's Tale.*

The materials for dating the *Man of Law's Prologue*[3] and *Tale*,
aside from their connection with the *Canterbury Tales*, are their
relation, on the one hand, to Gower's *Confessio Amantis*—an allusion to it in the *Man of Law's Prologue*, and the connection between
Chaucer's and Gower's versions of the story of Constance; and, on
the other, to the *Legend of Good Women*.

The *Man of Law's Prologue*, as I am not the first to point out,
was certainly written after the *Confessio Amantis*.   After giving a
sort of programme of the *Legend of Good Women*, the Man of Law
declares that Chaucer has written no word of the wicked example

---

[1] It was pointed out long ago by Bradshaw that these MSS. show signs of
"editing" (see Furnivall's *Temp. Pref.*, pp. 23-4).   I am simply enlarging
upon the opinion of these two scholars.
[2] Of course it is open to any one to believe that the earlier part was written
long before, but I do not see what will be gained by so doing.
[3] I use this term for the *Man of Law's Headlink* (Furnivall), or *Introduction
to Man of Law's Prologue* (Skeat); and for the stanzas on poverty the term
Proem.

of Canacee or of Apollonius of Tyre, and expresses the strongest
abhorrence of such stories.   When we find these two [1] the only
really objectionable stories (and both related at length) in a contemporary poem the author of which Chaucer knew well, and in the
first of them the author's good taste so perverted that he throws
blame on the father's violence and condones the corruptness of the
children, it cannot be doubted that the reference is to that poem.[2]

[1] *Canacee* is in the *Confessio Amantis*, III. 143–336, and *Apollonius* in VIII.
271–2008 (Macaulay, vols. II. and III.).

[2] Dr. Bech (*Anglia*, v. 375–6) offers the extraordinary explanation that it
was the Man of Law's soul which was horrified by the illegality of the conduct
of Canacee and Apollonius ; "bei dieser auffassung wird zugleich die annahme
einer invective Chaucer's gegen Gower beseitigt." Could the force of perversity
further go ?   Dr. Root has an over-facile note on the subject (*Poetry of Chaucer*,
p. 184).   It is neither here nor there to urge that the pavement-detail (l. 85)
is not in Gower ; neither is it in the half-dozen other versions of the Apollonius story which I have examined, including Godfrey of Viterbo's, Gower's
source.   Chaucer must have had a confused recollection either of another
horrible touch in the original Latin version (ed. Riese, p. 2), or of a passage in
Gower's Canacee story (III. 307–320).   I do not see how we can deny the existence of some ill-feeling, perhaps temporary and mild, between Chaucer and
Gower ; who may be said, therefore, to supply us with one of the earliest bits
of literary gossip in our history.   Macaulay (I. xxvii.) may be right in thinking
that Chaucer, conscious of his own occasional lapses from decorum, could not
resist the temptation to make a humorous dig at the moral Gower (cf. Karl
Meyer, *John Gower's Beziehungen zu Chaucer u. K. Richard II.*, Bonn, 1889,
p. 12).   It is true that Professor Hales points out (*Dict. Nat. Biogr.*, x. 166)
what looks like a complimentary reference (or is it sarcastic ?) to the *Canterbury Tales*, of the character of which work Gower would be cognizant years
before it was published, in the revised prologue of the *Confessio* (ll. 81–2) :

> "Bot for my wittes ben to smale
> To tellen every man his tale"

(cf. *Pars. Prol.*, 25).   This prologue dates from 1392–3.   But the passage in
the *Man of Law's Prologue* certainly gives an impression of perfect seriousness.
It surely must also be more than a coincidence that the complimentary reference to Chaucer which Gower had inserted in 1390 (probably) at the end of the
Confessio he omitted before the middle of 1391.   I must agree with Dr.
Heinrich Spies (*Engl. Stud.*, xxxv. 108) in rejecting Macaulay's suggestion
(II. xxviii.) that Gower removed the lines merely in order to make room for
something else.   In 1387 Gower highly disapproved of the Earl of Oxford, to
whom Chaucer was bound by a great favour ; so the alienation of the two
poets may possibly have had political connections (see Gower's *Cronica
Tripertita*, I. 63–76 ; Wallon, *Richard II.*, I. 484 ; *Mod. Philol.*, i. 328).
Very tentatively I will offer a further possible contribution to the evidence.
There is certainly something a little odd about the *Man of Law's Prologue*.
Almost half of it is quite irrelevant.   After admitting his obligation to tell a
tale, the Man of Law laments :

> "'I can right now no thrifty tale seyn,
> But Chaucer, though he can but lewedly
> On metres and on ryming craftily,
> Hath seyd hem in swich English as he can
> Of olde tyme, as knoweth many a man.

And when we consider further that the story of Apollonius is the
last in the whole of Gower's work, it is tolerably clear that that had

> And if he have not seyd hem, leve brother,
> In o book, he hath seyd hem in another.
> For he hath told of loveres up and doun
> Mo than Ovyde made of mencioun
> In his Epistelles, that been ful olde.
> What sholde I tellen hem, sin they ben tolde?
> In youthe he made of Ceys and Alcion,
> And sithen hath he spoke of everichon,
> Thise noble wyves and thise loveres eek.' "

Here follow seventeen lines describing the *Legend*, and then in thirteen lines
he reprehends the tales of Canacee and Apollonius, ending :

> " ' And therfor he, of ful avysement,
> Nolde never wryte in none of his sermouns
> Of swiche unkinde abhominaciouns,
> Ne wol I noon reherse, if that I may.' "

Chaucer nowhere else in the *C. T.* names himself, and he appears to be
incognito when he tells his own tales. Why does he speak so modestly of his
own versification, one of the points in which everybody knew he was most in
advance of contemporary standards ? If he wished to give a list of his earlier
works, why does he mention those alone which relate classical love-stories,
thereby naming the *Book of the Duchess* only by a minor episode in it?
Why is this whole passage such an echo of the latter part of the *Prologue* to
the *Legend?* I will venture to commit the following conjecture to fine print.
Chaucer may have been more or less seriously nettled at a continuation
or revival of the criticisms of him for misogyny and cynicism which had
evoked the *Legend of Good Women.* These criticisms may have been echoed
by Gower or accompanied by contrasting praise of him. Now he was the one
contemporary poet with whose versification Chaucer had any reason to fear
comparison ; much as we may prefer Chaucer's, Gower's is the most regular and
accurate verse from Orm to Surrey (cf. Macaulay, II. xvi.–xix.), and some contemporary taste may have preferred it, as Gascoigne and other mid-sixteenth
century poets probably would have done, had they known how to read it.
Chaucer declares that lewd though his metres and uncrafty though his rhymes
may be, every one knows that he has done his best, in more books than one, to
exalt lovers, and has written a whole large volume (here he stretches the truth)
of legends of Cupid's saints ; but one thing he has not done, "of ful avyse-
ment," he has told no such tales as have defaced the *Confessio*, nor will the
Man of Law do so. This explanation will account for his mentioning the
Book of the Duchess as he does ; he needed its testimony in his favour, but
perhaps did not care to recall the tears which he had shed for John of Gaunt's
first wife after the bereaved husband's twenty years of domestic vicissitudes
and his relations with Chaucer's own sister-in-law. Though Chaucer was not
very far from thirty when he wrote it, that was twenty or twenty-five years
before, so that the phrase " in youthe " is not surprising, and we are not
forced to the opinion that *Ceyx and Alcyone* was an independent work ; any-
one who will read critically Professor Bilderbeck's note in his edition of the
Minor Poems will see how little there is to be said for this view. One would
hesitate to suggest such an explanation as this of the *Man of Law's Prologue* if it implied anything like pettiness or malice or ill-temper on Chaucer's
part, which it is impossible to attribute to him ; but there is nothing here
that is not perfectly just, and even delicate and good-humoured. It seems
also to suggest rather vividly how much to the same " set " the two poets
belonged.

been already finished. Professor Macaulay shows, on the clear
evidence of dates in the MSS., that the second version of the
epilogue to the *Confessio* was written in the last half of 1390 or
the first half of 1391 ; and that the first form of prologue was
written in 1390, therefore after the poem was finished.[1] This plainly
assigns to the *Man of Law's Prologue* the date 1390 or later.[2]

As to the *Tale* of the *Man of Law*, it is necessary to notice
first the view of Skeat, Pollard, Hales, Professor W. P. Ker and
others that it was written somewhat early in Chaucer's literary
life.[3] Skeat's belief that in his story of Constance Gower borrowed
from Chaucer's will be noticed later, but its evidential value in this
connection disappears at the same time with Pauli's early date for
the *Confessio*. Nor can the fact that the *Man of Law's Tale* is in
stanzas be used as evidence, for not only is the stanza particularly
well adapted to a remote, lyrical and rhetorical poem like this, but
Dr. Skeat himself admits that the stanzaic *Prioress' Tale* was
written late.[4] All that is left, then, is the subject, treatment and
style.

---

[1] Macaulay's *Gower*, vol. ii., pp. xxi., xxii. and 13, and iii. 468.

[2] According to ten Brink (*Engl. Stud.*, xvii. 19–20), *M. L. P.*, 60–76
indicates that Chaucer was purposing a continuation of the *Legend of Good
Women ;* since the list of heroines there said to be treated in the *Legend*
is larger than the correct list, and otherwise different. He associates this
project with the revision of the *Prologue* to the *Legend*, and attributes
both to the year 1393 or a later time. Little can be built, I think, on
this argument, simply because we cannot be sure that Chaucer had not
intended all along to continue the *Legend* at some time ; as to the revision
of the *Prologue*, we have seen that it was probably due to a special cause.
Koeppel (*Engl. Stud.*, xvii. 199) and Lounsbury (*Studies*, i. 418) drop a couple
of other chronological hints which can hardly be taken up.

[3] Hales (*Folia Literaria*, p. 101 ; cf. also *Dict. Nat. Biogr.*, x. 161–2) dates
M. L. T., *Cl. T.*, *Pri. T.*, "and possibly other pieces," "many years before " the
C. T. Skeat says (III. 409 and cf. 413) : "We can easily see, from the style
and by the metrical form, that this Tale is a piece of Chaucer's early workmanship, and was revised for insertion among the Tales, with the addition of
a Prologue and four stanzas, about 1387." Mr. Pollard says : "There are
many blots in the story : the monotony of the parts played by the two
mothers-in-law—one in Syria, the other in Northumberland—the unreasoning
prodigality of time, and the refusal of Constance to declare who she is, being
the most obvious. Chaucer . . . . had not yet learnt to reconstruct a story
for himself, or to clothe his characters in flesh and blood " (*Primer*, p. 69).
"The *Man of Lawes Tale*, once more a curiously inappropriate one, is cast in
the same seven-line stanza as the *Seint Cecyle* and the *Griselde*, and from its
subject, style, and tone appears to have been written towards the close of the
same period " (1369–79 ; Pollard, *Globe Chaucer*, p. xxvi.). The remarks of
Professor Ker are not dissimilar (see his discriminating *Essays on Mediæval
Literature*, London, 1905 ; pp. 96–7). Cf. also my Introduction, for other
opinions.

[4] The "quod she " of line 1644 of course shows that the proem at least was

The idea that Chaucer is not quite as likely to have written a poem on such a subject after 1390 as in 1380 seems in a measure to disregard two facts—that at earliest he was a middle-aged man when he wrote it, and that as a poet he was always a mediæval as well as a modern. In the first place, we are not justified in assuming that a kind of subject which attracted Chaucer at thirty-five or forty he would have despised at fifty because meanwhile he had begun writing on others which happen to please us better. I do not forget that Chaucer experienced a reaction against allegory, which is absolutely out of harmony with the concreteness which is his ideal in the *Canterbury Tales,* but there is no reason to suppose that in ten years of middle life his taste changed so completely that pleasure in the *Nun's Priest's* or *Miller's Tale* drove out pleasure in the story of Constance. He must have enjoyed reading both at forty; at fifty, why not writing both? Besides, is the tone of the *Man of Law's Tale* so very different from that of the *Franklin's Tale,* for example? Moreover, the fact that Chaucer turned his back on the Middle Ages in some respects cannot be held to show that he did so in all. Even the poet who, because his peculiar genius was for realism, was capable of so miraculously modern a touch as where the friar in the *Sumner's Tale* drives the cat off the bench—even he could express himself only in such ordinary mediæval *genres* as religious and moral legends, or in Boccaccio's new invention, tales of fallen great ones, when he turned in a more serious mood to a subject which greatly interested him, the mutability of fortune, and to admiration of the Christian virtues. Chaucer's sympathy was catholic enough to embrace them all; there were other Chaucers besides him of the May mornings or of the "merry tales." And is there any reason to suppose that he ever quite grew beyond the sort of thing which was written by the very Italians from whom he had learned so much? [1]

written for the Prioress (and cf. also line 1653). The passionate indignation against the Jews is exquisitely in character for her; and lines 1832-3,

"This abbot, which that was an holy man,
As monkes ben, or elles oghten be,"

suggests her disapproval of the worldly Monk.

[1] Does not Professor Brandl commit the error of taking Chaucer too much out of his age by pairing the *Prioress' Tale* with *Sir Thopas* (Paul's *Grundriss,* 1893; ii. 680): "Auf die unmittelbar vorhergehende Verspottung kindi-

The element in the story and its conduct to which critics have especially objected is a certain crudity in the plot. We may admit that several *motifs* are a little overworked—the treacherous mother-in-law, the caitiff lover, and the divinely-guided voyage; but the mediæval reader, and writer, was used to such repetition of good things.[1] As to what Mr. Pollard calls " the unreasoning prodigality of time," he himself has pointed out exactly the same thing as existing to an unusual extent in the *Knight's Tale*,[2] which is certainly neither crude nor early, and which Mr. Ker uses as a standard of comparison for the *Man of Law's Tale*. The lack of intelligible motivation in Constance's conduct I shall speak of later; her refusal to declare her identity is more or less necessary to the plot, and, at any rate, is dismissed more briefly by Chaucer than by either Trivet,[3] his source, or by Gower.[4] It must not be forgotten that Chaucer was relating a story already made well known by Trivet and by Gower (as I hope to show shortly), and that in the Middle Ages history and fiction had not yet made the declaration of mutual independence which to their common advantage they have made since. He did not care by deviating markedly from the received version to make his readers open their eyes in amazement; in one or two minute points among those where he does deviate, as we shall see, he comments on the fact. Wherever we can

scher Legenden setzt er die der vulgarisierten Romanzen"? Professor Gummere has an admirable paper on the mediæval and the modern in Chaucer, in *Publ. Mod. Lang. Assoc.*, XVI. xxxvii.–xl., Appendix ; and Professor Lounsbury makes some judicious remarks on the unwisdom of attempting to date poems merely according to their excellence, and illustrates his point from other poets (*Parl. of Fowls,* Boston, 1877 ; pp. 7–8).

[1] It is much more striking in one of the gems of Middle English romance, *King Horn ;* which introduces a Saracen invasion three times, and twice Horn's coming to a foreign court and having a princess thrust on him, twice his arrival just in time to stop a fatal wedding, twice his entrance in lowly disguise and his slaughter of the guests, and twice a veridical dream. Reynild is an understudy to Rymenhild, and Arnoldin to Athulf. In that other Middle-English gem, *Sir Gawain and the Green Knight*, the unaccountable and the unmotived are far more prominent than in the *Man of Law's Tale*. With how many mediæval narratives would *M. L. T.* suffer by comparison ? If we compared Chaucer with our contemporaries less, and with his own more, we should get a truer estimate of him.

[2] See his edition of it, pp. 81–2.   Though one would hesitate to construct a time-table for a fairy ship, the allowance of several years (the same in Trivet and Gower) for drifting from Syria to Northumberland, and thence to Spain and Italy, seems rather a concession to realism than the reverse. A similar voyage in the lay of *Emare* takes only "a full seuene-nyght and more" (l. 674).

[3] See the passage from Nicholas Trivet's Anglo-French *Chronicle*, edited by Edmund Brock, in the Chaucer Society's *Originals and Analogues*, pp. iii.–53.

[4] *Confessio Amantis*, II. 587–1598.

see Chaucer at work (especially on well-known originals) we never find him making such radical changes; he is well content with his data as he finds them, and confines himself, in the main, to adding, illuminating, and vivifying. Nor can I grant Mr. Ker that the story seriously lacks unity or is unwieldy. Few of the *Canterbury Tales* are more free from disproportionate and overgrown passages. If we compare some of the discourses and soliloquies in the *Tales* of the *Knight*, the *Franklin*, the *Wife of Bath* and the *Nun's Priest*, the *Man of Law's Tale* will not suffer greatly. It seems to me that Pollard and Ker make quite too much of a relatively small matter.

As to its conduct and style, the *Man of Law's Tale* seems quite harmonious with Chaucer's best period. In spite of the remote and fragile character of the subject, here and there are gleams of humour; after esoteric discussion the soldan's counsellors can find no remedy for his woe but marriage (217), and the soldaness is of the opinion that if they are baptized (352),

> "Cold water shal not greve us but a lyte."

The poet smiles again, for better or worse, in lines 272–3 (" Housbondes been alle gode "), 355–7, 709–14, and 789. In vividness and realism of detail (except as regards Constance herself) the poem compares not unfavourably with any of the non-humorous tales. We may note the conferences of the soldan (204–31) and the soldaness (326–57) with their councils (in neither Trivet[1] nor Gower) ; in both the other writers the traitor knight is confounded directly after his accusation of Constance for the murder, but in Chaucer there is a highly vivid judgment-hall scene (617–86) ; there is a lifelike and wholly original touch in the embarrassment of the pagan official at hearing Christianity openly taught by his wife (568–9). No one can miss what Mr. Ker calls the "nobility of temper" in the poem ; or its magnificently rhetorical character, especially in its use of astrology and in its occasional passages of melancholy, pathos and devoutness,[2] a character which led ten Brink[3] for some reason to conjecture that Chaucer originally meant to deliver this tale himself on the pilgrimage. It is hardly just to pick out a few of these finer passages which are not found in Chaucer's source, as Dr. Skeat does

---

[1] In whose version the soldaness merely hires seven hundred ruffians.
[2] *E. g.*, ll. 295–315, 421–7, 449–62, 631–58.
[3] *History of Engl. Literature* (London, 1893), ii. 157.

(III. 410), and explain them as later additions, especially since we
have at least the tales of the *Second Nun*, the *Shipman* and the
Parson to show that Chaucer's practice was not to revise works
which he transferred to the *Canterbury Tales* or from one teller to
another.   Many of the best passages,[1] sometimes contiguous with
those which Skeat points out as possible additions, are so intimately
connected with the rest of the story as to forbid the conjecture that
they were written at a different time.   And finally the *Man of Law's
Tale* shows an ease, a mastery and an artistic aloofness in Chaucer's
attitude toward his material which is far different from his earlier
manner.   The style of the poem is remarkably unified and harmonious;[2] the original and splendid passages are not jewels stuck
in a plain setting, but as it were flowers growing out of a plant
which naturally produces them.[3]

   This attitude toward his material may help to account for
Chaucer's treatment of Constance, the chief puzzle of all and
probably the main thing which has led some critics to put the
tale early in Chaucer's literary life.   In Chaucer she has, it is true,
more human feeling than in Trivet; she pities her child when they
are about to be cast adrift (853–61), and is not without sense
of her husband's cruelty (863, 1055–7), which accounts for her
slowness to make herself known to him in Rome ; none of this is in
Trivet.[4]   But though she says far more than in Trivet or Gower, she
acts less ; except for her religious duties, she can be said to come
out of her passiveness only three times, when she tells her son to
stand before Alla, proposes to her husband a feast for the Emperor,
and alights from her horse to make herself known to him (1013,
1079, 1104).   Her concealment of her identity from the Constable
and the Senator (524–7, 972–3) is more complete in Chaucer than
in Trivet ; it is probably for the sake of brevity as well as mystery

[1] *E. g.*, ll. 211–7, 270–87, 351–7, 811–19, 1052–78.
[2] With the sole exception of the position of Constance in it.
[3] This air of mastery and aloofness shows especially in the religious and
astrological passages, and is even the cause of some of the imperfections which
strike a modern reader.   Without being at all perfunctory, Chaucer greatly
condenses, especially towards the end, and omits many minor circumstances.
This accounts for the obscurity where the blind man appeals to Hermengild
for his sight (561–2), without apparent reason or explanation ; in Trivet he is
taught by the Holy Ghost to do so.   The *Tale* is far shorter than Trivet's
version, and (save for Chaucer's lyrical additions) even than Gower's.   No
other of the *Canterbury Tales*, unless it is the *Knight's*, has so many references
to the fact that the poet was condensing.
[4] Nor in Gower, except for her attentions to her child (*C. A.*, II. 1061–83).

that Chaucer refuses to dwell on it.[1] Chaucer's Constance, as compared with Trivet's and Gower's more commonplace figure, is marked by vividness without intelligibility, and against Chaucer's far more realistic background she passes about, attended by miracles, like a being from another world (which perhaps she is). It is impossible to be sure of Chaucer's motive for the change which he made in her relation to the story, of which he can hardly have been unconscious, but the following suggestions may come somewhere near the truth. He was probably interested in the story chiefly for its possibilities of rhetorical poetry and impersonal feeling, and in its heroine chiefly as a decorative figure, an embodiment of suffering and constancy. To rationalize her would have been to make yet more incongruous than it is a story which is incurably miraculous. Therefore, though giving her more human feeling than Trivet does, in order to enhance her pathos, he leaves her in the nimbus of conservatism which is the proper surrounding of a religious figure, while he draws forward the rest of the story into a more modern light. To all this there is a general parallel in the *Clerk's Tale ;* and just as by disclaiming an intention to hold up Griselda as a model to other wives he shows his consciousness of her remoteness, so here by affecting to attribute to all wives the sanctity of Constance (708–14).[2]

Whether all this was quite deliberate we cannot say, and it does not free Chaucer from the imputation of occasional bad art, but his method is the best possible with such an intractable subject. It is

[1] In both cases, in Trivet's version, she does explain who she is, in very general terms ; but for no intelligible reason refuses to mention names, even to the Senator at Rome, whom she recognizes (pp. 13–15, 41). Gower's treatment of her reticence is odder than that of either of the others. Though she explains herself vaguely to the Senator (1148–69), she utterly refuses to do so to the Constable (738–9) ; and will not reveal her history to her husband either when they are married or when they are reunited in Rome (910–11, 1450–5 ; neither of these two points is in Trivet or in Chaucer). Constance's reticence is paralleled in the lay of *Emare,* which of course is nearly related to *M. L. T.* (ll. 358–60 ; in Ritson, vol. ii., and edited by A. B. Gough, London, 1901), and the heroine of which changes her name. Dr. Gough shows that it is a primitive and wide-spread element in the story ; see *The Constance Saga* (*Palaestra,* xxiii. ; Berlin, 1902), pp. 13, 17. Is not this silence perhaps the relic of the *tabu* frequently found in tales of fairy-lovers, which doubtless Constance originally was ? (Cf. Schofield, *English Literature from the Norman Conquest to Chaucer,* pp. 191–2.)

[2] On the similarity of Constance to Griselda, compare :

" And she sorwe as domb stant as a tree " (*M. L. T.,* 1055).

" And she ay sad and constant as a wal " (*Cl. T.,* 1047).

a delicate matter to know just how much new wine can be safely poured into old bottles. Chaucer is a positive, not a negative realist; that is, he constantly adds reality, but does not remove unreality. At times he becomes the more incongruous, therefore, by the very reason of his greatness. Though this may somewhat mar the perfection of his art, it adds greatly to its interest from a historical point of view. That his sense of congruity did not keep him from sounding, even in his best days, notes that jar on our ears, we shall see if we remember Troilus' long soliloquy (IV. 958–1078), Dorigen's long list of heroines on an agitated occasion (*Frankl. T.*, 1367–456), and the introduction into the *Canterbury Tales* of *Melibeus* and the *Parson's* and *Monk's Tales*. Even if in a sense the *Man of Law's Tale* is more incongruous than the *Second Nun's*, chiefly because of its superior realism, it is certainly a far better poem and bears every mark of a much later period in Chaucer's development. In a word, can any one deny that Chaucer might choose such a subject late in his life? And if he did, in what regard have we a right to expect the *Man of Law's Tale* to be different from what it is?[1] It seems to me, therefore, that in the plot of the tale, still more in its style and subject, there is nothing whatever against putting it late, even in the last decade of his life.

One piece of evidence that the *Man of Law's Tale* is later than the first *Prologue* to the *Legend of Good Women*, and perhaps not much earlier than the second, is to be found in the presence in it of five passages[2] translated from the *De Contemptu Mundi* of

---

[1] *Emare* is an example of a similar story completely rationalized, and thereby made (save for two or three life-like touches) utterly prosaic.

[2] Lines 99–121 in the Proem and 421–7, 772–7, 925–7 and 1134–8. See Skeat, III. 407–8, or Koeppel in Herrig's *Archiv*, lxxxiv. 405–18. Comparison with the Latin will show that only the lines which I have indicated are taken from it. The passage in the Proem was first pointed out by A. von Düring in 1885 (see his translation of Chaucer, iii. 352); the others simultaneously by Koeppel and Lounsbury. Skeat thinks (III. 307, 408) that all five passages are fragments rescued from Chaucer's own poetic version of the Latin work, which he dates 1373–7 (*Chaucer Canon*, p. 154), and that they were inserted here on the revision of the *Tale*. Thus the evil communications of ten Brink on the stanzaic *Palamon* continue to corrupt the world. Koeppel also thinks these passages derived from Chaucer's version of Innocent (*Engl. Stud.*, xvii. 196–7, 199); which is the more odd because he (like ten Brink) believes that this work was in prose, and that, when Chaucer wrote the G-prologue, it had not advanced beyond the first few chapters of the pope's treatise; while all the passages quoted in the *Man of Law's Proem* and *Tale* and in the *Pardoner's Tale* are from the last chapters of the first book or from the second. I find no evidence that these passages are in any sense quoted from Chaucer's translation. In the first place, the manner in which the work is mentioned in the *Legend* (G, 413–15) certainly seems to imply that

Pope Innocent III. It will be remembered that Chaucer's lost translation of this is mentioned in the *Prologue* to the *Legend*, but only in the second version, and is the only addition which the latter makes to the list of Chaucer's works given in the earlier version. Disregarding the use of it here, it is quoted only in the *Pardoner's Tale* and perhaps the *Monk's*, both late. On this and other grounds, fully set forth by Professor Lowes, the probabilities are overwhelming that it was written not long before 1394, certainly later than 1386.[1] There is no impossibility, of course, in the idea that Chaucer made these quotations before he had made his translation; yet one cannot but feel that the pope's work was so foreign to Chaucer's disposition that it could hardly have been one of his favourite books, and that he is not likely long before he translated it to have acquired such familiarity with it that he could readily have made these not very striking excerpts.[2] It is not a forced inference, then, that these passages were written after (and probably a good while after) 1386.

But Skeat would have us believe "that the Prologue [Proem] and the four inserted stanzas were placed where they now are at the

---

it was in prose. Secondly, there is not the least reason to believe that it ever advanced very far; if there ever was excuse for Chaucer's habit of dropping things in the midst, it was here. His way of speaking of it,—

"And *Of the Wreched Engendring of Mankinde,*
As man may *in pope Innocent* y-finde,"—

strongly suggests that the translation included only the early part of the work. The second of the above lines seems to imply only a partial version; and very much as Koeppel points out, while the title of the original is *De contemptu mundi, sive de miseria conditionis humanæ,* Chaucer's title corresponds only to the first five chapters of the first of the pope's three books; they alone deal with conception and gestation, which, according to the pope, are very wretched indeed. This is an odd subject for Chaucer to treat, but so is the whole book, which may explain his getting no farther. Koeppel's only reason for thinking he did get farther is the presence of these quotations in the *Man of Law's Tale* and elsewhere; which is amazingly like reasoning in a circle. Dr. Koeppel, in one of his admirable source-studies (*Anglia*, xiii. 175), affords us one more warning illustration of the orthodox view as to Chaucer's "economy" in cutting out purple patches from cast-off poems; Koeppel carries it to such a point that, in speaking of St. Jerome's "good women" mentioned in the G-prologue of the *Legend*, he says that Chaucer transferred them, after he had revised the *Prologue*, to Dorigen's lament in the *Franklin's Tale.*
   [1] See Lowes' discussion in *Publ. Mod. Lang. Assoc.*, xx. 790-4; and pp. 101-2, 170 above.
   [2] Why did he translate it at all? One cannot help guessing that Chaucer's rendering was done by request. As Lowes suggests, it may also have been not unconnected with Deschamps' version of a part of the *De Contemptu;* see *Publ. Mod. Lang. Assoc.*, xx. 795, note.

time of the revision of what was once an independent tale" (III.
408). How it may have been with the proem we cannot tell, except
that is far more closely connected with the *Tale* than with the
Prologue; but in the other four passages the evidence is all against
Skeat's opinion. In only one case (421–7) do the lines from
Innocent form a complete stanza. In the last case (1134–8) one
line is in one stanza and four in another, both of which stanzas
form an integral part of the narrative; somewhat the same is true
of lines 772–7. It is therefore incorrect to speak of "the four
inserted stanzas." At worst, none of the passages shows any more
sign of being a later addition than any of the exclamatory stanzas
in the poem, and I have pointed out several times elsewhere that
in reassigning tales it was Chaucer's practice rather to neglect
necessary revisions than to make unnecessary ones. These passages
therefore seem to have been written at the same time as the rest of
the *Tale*, and hence to afford a respectable amount of evidence that
the *Man of Law's Tale* was written well within the *Canterbury*
period, certainly after the first *Prologue* to the *Legend*.[1]

But an almost conclusive argument against putting the *Man of
Law's Tale* before the *Legend of Good Women* seems to me, as in
the case of several others of the *Canterbury Tales*, the fact that it
is not mentioned in the *Prologue* to that poem,[2] where Alcestis is
dragging in everything to Chaucer's credit which she can find, and
omits nothing of any length except the *Anelida and Arcite*, which
was unfinished and doubtless unpublished. If the tale of Constance had been written as a separate work before the first version
of the *Prologue*, where *Boethius*, the *House of Fame* and *Origen
on the Magdalen* are duly recorded, nothing seems more unlikely
than that Chaucer should have ignored it.

The relation between Chaucer's and Gower's versions of the story
of Constance has been studied by Dr. Emil Lücke,[3] incidentally

[1] Koeppel (Herrig's *Archiv*, lxxxiv. 411) points out another more
trifling link between the *Tale* and the second *Prologue* to the *Legend;* with
M. L. T., 701–2 cf. *L. G. W.*, prol.-G, 312, 529. I must say, however, that
corn as a symbol for learning and poetry occurs also in *Parl. of Fowls*, 22–3,
and *L. G. W.*, prol.-F, 74–6 (G, 62–4).
[2] Cf. Koeppel, *Engl. Stud.*, xvii. 198, who thinks the omission shows
that the *Tale* followed even the second version of the *Prologue*. But the
reply will serve here, as in the case of other *Tales* of pious women, that
Chaucer might not wish to mention a poem which he was reserving until the
C. T. should appear as a whole.
[3] *Anglia*, xiv. 183–5; whole article, pp. 77–122, 147–85.

to an investigation of the obligations of both to Trivet's Anglo-French *Chronicle.* He proves beyond cavil that Trivet was the main source in each case, but also finds twenty-seven small resemblances, founded on nothing in Trivet,[1] which convince him that the two English versions cannot be mutually quite independent. Skeat agrees with him, and quotes (III. 415–17) the more striking parallels. Even though some of them are trivial, the cumulative effect is irresistible, especially when we consider the complete absence of parallels between the two poets' versions of the story of Virginia, and the almost complete absence of them between the *Wife of Bath's Tale* and the story of Florent in the *Confessio.*[2]

On the question which of the two was written first opinions differ. Lücke, says Skeat (III. 413), " draws what is, in my opinion, the erroneous conclusion, that it was Chaucer who copied Gower ; which seems like suggesting that Tennyson was capable of borrowing from Martin Tupper." I cannot feel, however, that there is the slightest presumption one way or the other. Literary borrowing in the fourteenth century was quite a different matter from what it was in the nineteenth, and at any time a poet may " prendre son bien où il le trouve." Chaucer frequently borrows from writers far inferior to Gower, and it is most unlikely that he had at all as low an opinion as modern critics have of a poet whom their contemporaries and successors constantly put beside him. Flügel has pointed out [3] that in the best of all his works, the *General Prologue,* Chaucer was not above frequently drawing phraseology from Gower's *Mirour de l'Omme.*

As to evidence, it seems to me nearly convincing that Chaucer borrowed from Gower [4]—not that he wrote with the *Confessio*

---

[1] A few others may be recorded. Constance's prayer and her pity for her child, as she goes aboard ship (825–68), resemble the episode in Gower after they are at sea (1055–83 ; in Trivet scarcely in germ). In both Chaucer (904 ff.) and Gower (1084, ff.), when Constance runs aground in Spain, she is not brought before the Spanish admiral (as in Trivet), but remains in the ship. There is an analogy between their ways of mentioning the death of Alla :

"Deeth, that taketh of heigh and low his rente " (*M. L. T.*, 1142) ;

" Bot he which hindreth every kinde
And for no gold mai be forboght,
The dethe comende er he be soght " (*C. A.*, 1572–4).

[2] Cf. pp. 151–2 and 217.
[3] *Anglia*, xxiv. 437–508.
[4] Ten Brink favours this view (*Hist. E. L.*, ii. 156).

Amantis open before him, but that he had read Gower's story attentively, and, perhaps not always knowing that he did so, reproduced some of his ideas and phrases.   It certainly does not look as if Gower borrowed from Chaucer.   There is no point among the agreements of the two as against Trivet [1] which must have emanated from Chaucer, and which is beyond Gower's not inconsiderable abilities.   Moreover, while in every point of any consequence [2] where Gower differs from Trivet, Chaucer agrees with Gower, there are many other and more important places where Chaucer adds to, or otherwise differs from, Trivet, and where Gower does not follow him.   I say nothing of Chaucer's rhetorical additions, which Gower might have wilfully disregarded, or of his more subtle touches, which he might have missed.   But such matters as the following are worth attention.   At the beginning, while both the English poets say nothing of Constance's learning, the only point on which Trivet dwells, Gower has none of Chaucer's eloquent praise of her beauty and goodness (155–68) ; he says nothing of her submissive grief at leaving home for the oriental marriage (264–87) ; nothing of the conferences of the soldan and his mother with their councils (204–31, 326–57) ; nor of Constance's prayer on being cast adrift the first time (449–62) ; nor of her mingled emotions toward her husband when they are reunited (1055–78).[3]   Such omissions on Gower's part could not be explained by an effort at condensation, for which he shows in this tale (as usual) much less disposition than Chaucer does : nor by unwillingness to take hints, since if he was the latter he took many small points and one or two larger. To review the evidence here adduced, I say that since one of the English poets was so familiar with the work of the other as to reproduce even details of language, since where Gower departs (except for the worse) from their common source Chaucer departs also, and since in many more important points where Chaucer departs from or adds to their source Gower does not, the probable conclusion is that not Gower but Chaucer was the borrower.

---

[1] See *Orig. and Anal.*, pp. vi.–x.

[2] Except for a few changes for the worse, as where the miraculous and unaccountable element is increased.   See numbers 3, 5 and 7, *Orig. and Anal.*, p. vi. ; and *Conf. Am.*, II. 910–11, 1450–5, where Constance twice refuses to tell her husband who she is.

[3] Cf. also the three writers' accounts of her rescue by the Roman Senator after her second solitary voyage (T., pp. 39, 41 ; G., 1126, ff. ; C., 967–74). Here Gower reduces her toing and froing, just as he does when she runs aground in Spain, but not as much as Chaucer does.

One thing more will clinch the matter.   Speaking of Maurice at
Alla's feast, Chaucer says (1009–10) :

> " Som men wolde seyn, at requeste of Custance,
>   This senatour hath lad this child to feste " ;

and of the invitation to the emperor (1086–7) :

> " Som men wold seyn, how that the child Maurice
>   Doth this message un-to this emperour ;
>   But, as I gesse, Alla was nat so nyce." [1]

Tyrwhitt [2] thought that Chaucer was alluding to Gower, from
whom he believed him to have taken the whole story ; Skeat
(V. 162–4) thinks the allusion only to Trivet.   It is not Chaucer's
practice, or that of mediæval writers generally, to mention their
departures from authority—rather to plead precedent where they
have none. [3]   There was no reason why Chaucer should call attention to a deviation from Trivet, who was not an especially well-
known writer.   But if the reference is to Gower, all is explained ;
conscious that he was differing from a poem which had (probably)
but just appeared, and was being widely read in the very circles
into which he expected his own poem to go, he suggests that his
predecessor may have been mistaken.   I find it impossible to doubt,
therefore, that Chaucer had carefully read Gower's story of Constance, and therefore that the *Man of Law's Tale* was written after
at least the early part of the *Confessio Amantis*.

The testimony which this conclusion bears as to the exact date

---

[1] Both Trivet and Gower represent the invitation as being carried by
Maurice, but Chaucer thinks it would hardly have been court-etiquette
to send a boy, as Professor Child used to say, with the message, " Papa wants
you to come to dinner."   But in the former case it is curious that Chaucer's
memory played him false, for neither of the others says that Constance asked
that her son might go, but both merely say, as Chaucer does, that she
instructed him to keep in the king's sight.

[2] Edition of 1830, I. clxxxvii. f.

[3] Cf. an example of the usual attitude toward a source (at least as avowed)
in lines 904–5 of this very poem :

> " . . . . . an hethen castel . . .
>   Of which the name in my text noght I finde."

We may notice also the definiteness of "som men " as compared with such
more usual expressions as " but-if that bokes lye."   The nearest parallel
to these passages which I find in Chaucer is that in speaking of Criseyde
and Diomed he says (*T. and C.*, V. 1050) :

> " Men seyn, I noot, that she yaf him hir herte,"

where the independence is less and the motive for it greater.

of the *Man of Law's Tale* unfortunately is not perfectly definite.
It is quite possible that Chaucer read Gower's tale, on a " private
view," soon after it was written, and when this was we have no
means of knowing.   Professor Macaulay thinks the plan of the
Confessio was laid about 1386, " under the combined influence of
Chaucer's *Legend of Good Women* and of the royal command ; " if
we admit the influence of the *Legend*, we must bring the date
a year or two later, but that influence is by no means clear (unless
at the very end), and such a date would involve extraordinarily
quick writing, since the poem was finished in 1390.   The *Confessio*
was certainly written after the *Vox Clamantis*.   This was probably
begun soon after the peasant rising in 1381, and a third of the way
through the writer refers to an event of 1383.[1]   It may fairly be
supposed that before beginning his elaborate English poem Gower
would spend some time in planning and collecting materials.   It is
difficult to believe that he could have reached the second book
of the *Confessio* before 1386–7, the verge of Chaucer's *Canterbury*
period, and the earliest possible date, therefore, for the *Man
of Law's Tale*.   It seems much more likely, however, that Chaucer's
knowledge of Gower's tale dates only from its publication, especially
since his knowledge of it seems to have been so intimate.   Therefore if an almost certain date is after 1386, a highly probable one is
after 1390.

As to the meaning of the way in which the *Man of Law's
Prologue*, *Proem* and *Tale* are put together, it is impossible to come
to any certain conclusion.   Ten Brink,[2] Skeat[3] and others have more
or less ingenious and unacceptable suggestions.   We may be quite
sure, however, that the tale of Constance was not written for the
Man of Law—one of the most unworldly and poetic of tales for one
of the shrewdest and most prosaic of the pilgrims.   It is far more
inappropriate to its teller than the *Shipman's Tale*, the only other
one which is at all unsuitable, and that was certainly written for a
different person.[4]   For whom the story of Constance was written it
would be idle to guess.   But it is certainly noteworthy that the
manner of its assignment to the Man of Law is more ambiguous
and clumsy than that of any other of the *Canterbury Tales*.   In

[1] The Bishop of Norwich's Crusade ; see bk. III., chap. vi.
[2] *Engl. Stud.*, xvii. 22 ; *Hist. of Engl. Lit.*, ii. 156–9.
[3] III. 406–8 ; cf. also Koch, *Chronology*, p. 68 ; Koeppel, *Engl. Stud.*,
xvii. 196.   [4] Cf. pp. 205–6 below.

fact, the unanimity of the MSS. in putting it after the *Man of Law's Prologue* is the only thing that assigns it to him at all. Though the proem on poverty has no connection of content with the *Tale*, granted that Chaucer wished to present it he has effected a rather clever mechanical connection. But connection of any kind between the proem and the *Prologue* is totally lacking; more than this, they absolutely contradict each other. Though the Man of Law announces that he shall "speke in prose" (96), three lines later he begins his lyrical outburst. Moreover, as seems never to have been remarked, this derelict tale is no more anchored aft than forward. The following Link begins :

> " Our hoste up-on his stiropes stood anon,
> And seyde, ' good men, herkneth everich on ;
> This was a thrifty tale for the nones ! ' "

and then proceeds to address the Parson. The only thing to which this passage is linked is the *Prologue* of the *Man of Law* (46), by this word *thrifty*, which the Host uses to assure the teller that he has been better than his word. *Thrifty* is surely a most non-committal, if not highly inappropriate, epithet to apply to this tale, and there is not a single other end-link in the whole of the *Canterbury Tales* which is not indissolubly connected to the preceding tale or its teller. We are therefore forced to the conclusion that, when the *Prologues* of the *Man of Law* and the *Shipman* were written, the story of Constance had not yet been assigned to the Man of Law. As to Chaucer's original plan for him we may find some light when we come to consider the *Tale of Melibeus*.[1]

§ 7. *The Tale of Melibeus.*

Before presenting evidence that Chaucer's *Tale of Melibeus* was written late, it is necessary to take up some *a priori* considerations. The dates of the individual *Canterbury Tales* have been so little discussed that one is sometimes compelled rather to anticipate than to answer objections. But there is one here which is quite certain to be raised. If the *Tales* of the *Monk*, the *Clerk* and the *Man of*

[1] See pp. 195-7 below. The problems connected with "Group B" are more interesting and puzzling than any others involved by the growth of the *Canterbury Tales*. The splitting of Group B in all the MSS. but one, the reassignment of the first two tales, and the variety of the readings in *Shipm. Prol.*, 1179, are all elements in the puzzle. I must reserve further discussion for my book on the evolution of the *Canterbury Tales*, and for p. 218 below.

Law have been thought to have been written early, before the period of the *Canterbury Tales,* because of their unmodern character, *a fortiori* such an opinion is sure to be advanced of *Melibeus.* Indeed it has already been advanced, casually and tentatively, even by so judicious a critic as Dr. Mather,[1] who is "inclined to place" the composition of *Melibeus* between 1373 and 1378, "foi it is difficult to believe that Chaucer would have included this rather stupid piece among the *Tales* were he not working in old material"; he even seems to suggest a motive for its inclusion— "Chaucer, cut off in the middle of his *Rime of Sir Thopas,* avenges himself by telling the very dull prose tale of Melibeus." May I be permitted again to deprecate what seems an unwise, though very natural, tendency to exaggerate Chaucer's modern side and take him too much out of his age ; and the still worse tendency to regard the *Canterbury Tales* as a kind of foundling asylum for the waifs and strays of his earlier begetting? I shall endeavour to point out both probability and evidence that when Chaucer put *Melibeus* in the *Canterbury Tales* the value he set on it was such that he may perfectly well have just written it.

To us *Melibeus* is dull because its human element is thin and crude and its general truths are commonplaces. Is it impertinent to suggest that to the mediæval reader neither was so? The interest of the earlier Middle Ages in creative literature had been chiefly for lyric feeling and for action ; they had produced little analysis of human motive and shown little knowledge of the human heart. At a certain stage in the intellectual development of a people, these become intelligible and attractive ; witness the rise of literary allegory into popularity in the thirteenth century. Now *Melibeus* offers both ; strange as the statement may seem at first, *Melibeus* really shows insight. We, the heirs of all the ages, do not readily perceive it ; but is not the case of Richardson's *Pamela* somewhat parallel, allowing for the fact that it is more than three times as near us as *Melibeus* is? Can most of us at present at all understand the *furore* which it excited all over Europe? Again, though the sayings of dead wiseacres in *Melibeus* seem to us unspeakably trite and dry, all the literature of the Middle Ages proves that they took a different view of such things. There was a time when every commonplace was fresh and startling ; the

[1] *Chaucer's Prologue, etc.* (Boston, 1899), xiv., xv., xxxi.

Middle Ages found mental stimulus in very obvious truths, and a perpetual relish in the gnomic style.[1] Does not Chaucer's constant use of it, notably through the mouths of Pandarus and others in the *Troilus*, but everywhere else as well, prove that he could enjoy it? Moreover, we shall see later that Chaucer's extreme familiarity with the "plot" and contents of *Melibeus* during the middle of the *Canterbury* period is proved by its strong influence on the *Merchant's Tale*. Why did he become familiar with it unless he admired it?

But we are not wholly left to inference. In the *Prologue* to *Melibeus*, of course written after the tale, there is proof that Chaucer regarded it with no alienated eye. He alludes to the fact that more than one version of the work was already extant[2] (2131-42), and apologizes for diverging from his original (2143-54). He thus shows solicitude as to the opinion of his readers. Can we believe, then, that as Mather seems to suggest, he deliberately afflicted his real readers in order to punish his imaginary auditors for their interruption of *Sir Thopas*? A prose tale of 16,000 words forms a pretty extensive practical joke. More than this, the *Monk's Prologue* does not show a sign that the pilgrims regarded *Melibeus* as a penance. In the insertion of it there was no doubt some irony and amused sense of contrast with the former attempt (cf. *Mel. Prol.*, 2127-30, 2154); Chaucer in his own tales deliberately goes to the two extremes. But the fact that he apologizes, not for the tale, but for deviating from another version of it, and actually admits that he tells

"som-what more
Of proverbs, than ye han herd bifore" (2145-6),[3]

proves that he derived, and expected others to derive, serious pleasure from reading it.[4] Is not the other view something like an

[1] The scribes constantly call attention to adages or other pithy sayings in their texts ; MS. Harl. 7334 repeatedly has *nota* in the margin, MS. Arch. Seld. has *A proverbe* opposite *Mill. T.*, 3391.

[2] Therefore now, if not before, he knew both the French and Latin versions (cf. p. 216). His intimate familiarity, shown here and elsewhere, with two earlier versions of the work certainly proves that he regarded it with serious interest.

[3] This is very odd, considering the character of Albertano's version, to which he is alluding.

[4] The popularity of the French version seems to have been considerable from the end of the fourteenth to the early sixteenth century (see Skeat, III. 426-7). It is not a little striking, moreover, that of all the individual *Canterbury Tales* the only ones which John Lydgate thinks worthy of mention in

unconscious survival of the older view of Chaucer's relation to the
English language ; and to represent him as a man aloof from his
age, and taking a patronizing or improving attitude toward it ?
Nor will it do to attribute the insertion of such works as *Melibeus*
and the *Parson's Tale* to a sudden whim or late aberration, for their
prologues, which presuppose the decision, contain as good writing
as there is in the whole poem. A frank recognition of Chaucer's
mediæval side, it seems to me, will promote both a more faithful
estimate of him and also that intellectual breadth and that power
of sympathetic insight which are among the best things one can
gain from the study of mediæval literature.

But to turn now to evidence as to the date. The *Tale of
Melibeus* is in general translated very faithfully from its French
original,[1] as I find after a complete detailed comparison. Chaucer
very seldom adds anything of consequence, and hardly ever omits
anything, except a mere phrase or two, or a longer passage plainly
skipped by accident : that is, when two neighbouring passages end
in the same word, Chaucer or a scribe, glancing up after tran-
scribing the first, confused the end of the second with it, and went
on from that point.[2] In the whole work I find just three passages

the *Falls of Princes* are *Melibeus, Clerk's T.* and *Monk's T.* (see the passage in
Lounsbury's *Studies,* i. 421). Lydgate was no unfavourable specimen of the
cultivated man of the next age.

[1] Attributed sometimes to Jean de Meun, sometimes to Renaud de Louens. It
is most accessible in *Le Ménagier de Paris* (ed. by Jerôme Pichon for the
Société des Bibliophiles Français, Paris, 1846), vol. i., pp. 186–235. This
work, which was written 1392–4 (*ibid.*, p. xxii.), there is no evidence that
Chaucer ever saw. The Latin original, *Liber Consolationis et Consilii,* by
Albertano of Brescia, was edited by Thor Sundby, and issued by the Chaucer
Society in 1873.

[2] This is very frequent, of course, in MSS., especially those in prose. But
of such passages omitted in *Melibeus* there are not more than half-a-dozen as
long as two lines in the French. For one of the passages in Chaucer and not in
the French text see pp. 193–4 below. Another is in l. 2157 ; neither the Latin
nor the French names the daughter. These are about the most important of
twelve or so worth mentioning. Some of these passages were probably in the
MS. which Chaucer used. The longest addition is at the end, 3074–8.
Chaucer so constantly, however, adds unimportant or synonymous words and
phrases (generally of an explanatory nature) that the translation is extremely
verbose and dilatory ; the French contains about 12740 words, and the
English about 16320. Mätzner calls the translation "entschieden wörtlich"
(*Altengl. Sprachproben,* ii. 373 ; his introduction and notes are excellent).
Some idea of its character may be gained by examining Zupitza's quotations
from the original in Koeppel's article in Herrig's *Archiv,* lxxxvi. 30–8.
Chaucer's MS. of the French was rather different from that published in
the *Ménagier,* and better ; see *Mel.* 2177, 2185, 2235–8, 2408–10, 2581–2
(*Ménagier,* pp. 187, 188, 192, 203, 212), but in 2252–3 and 2515, *e. g.,*
Chaucer's readings are less good. The French version, on the other hand,

of two lines or more in the French, the omission of which by
Chaucer is not clearly due to this cause. Two of these (between
2702 and 2703, and 2776–7 ; see the *Ménagier*, pp. 218, 222) are
unimportant, and there is no visible reason for their omission. But
the third is in quite a different category ; it is more than twice as
long as any other omitted, there is not the least chance for such a
skipping as I have described, and there is an obvious reason for its
intentional omission. Prudence is instructing her helpless husband
as to what sort of advisers he is to avoid, and ends in the English
thus : " Thou shalt also eschewe the conseilling of yong folk ; for
hir conseil is nat rype " (2389). But the French text continues :
" De quoy Salemon dit : dolente est la terre qui a enfant à seigneur !
Et le philosophe dit que nous n'eslisons pas les jeunes en princes
car communément ils n'ont point de prudence ; et dit encores
Salemon : dolente est la terre de quoy le prince ne se lière
matin ! " [1] The meaning of this omission cannot be mistaken.
Chaucer was thinking of Richard II., and was anxious not to
annoy him and his family. *Melibeus* must, therefore, have been
written after June 8, 1376,[2] when Edward the Black Prince died,
and Richard became heir-apparent. More definite than this we
cannot be with equal certainty, except that in the later nineties, till
the very end, Richard was neither so young nor so imprudent that
the cap would have fitted. In the earlier nineties the memory of past
unpleasantness would still be fresh. The fit would have been particularly exact, of course, in the middle eighties, but at any time
from 1376 to (say) 1395 a tactful and courtierlike person would not

---

departs widely from the Latin, and should really be called a paraphrase. It
is much shorter, and makes important omissions, some additions, odd mistrans-
lations, and other changes. In particular, on p. 202 (between *Mel.* 2389 and
2390) it omits almost two pages (Sundby, 53–5) ; and on p. 203 (between *Mel.*
2400 and 2401), about a page (Sundby, 57–8). In this latter passage is the
quotation from the pseudo-Seneca on the virtue of prudence mentioned in my
article on *Chaucer and Dante* in *Mod. Philol.* iii., p. 368 ; therefore this
can hardly have been the source of *T. C.*, V. 746–9. It is rather to be
regretted that the Chaucer Society published the ultimate instead of the
immediate source of *Mel.* We may hope that before long some one will give
us a critical edition of the French version, perhaps in parallel-columns with
Mel., at any rate with line for line references ; and with a discussion of the
character of the MS. which Chaucer used.

[1] *Ménagier*, i. 202, and cf. the foot-note. Apparently one MS. substitutes
for everything after *seigneur* the clause : " et de laquelle le prince se desjusne
matin." This and the end of the alternative reading seem to be due to
Albertano's " et cujus principes mane comedunt " (Sundby, p. 53).

[2] See *e. g.* Armitage-Smith, *John of Gaunt*, p. 129 ; Richard was born
January 6, 1367 (*ibid.*, p. 44).

have hesitated to make the omission.[1] Somewhere between these dates, therefore, *Melibeus* probably falls; certainly after 1376.

One argument for a late date for *Melibeus* is the fact that none of Chaucer's works which show its influence seem to be early, as is shown by Dr. Koeppel's[2] article. Of the parallels which he quotes between the *Troilus* and *Melibeus* I shall speak in a moment. The parallels between *Melibeus* and the *Wife of Bath's Prologue* (itself late) we shall see are probably of no consequence. Besides these, the only works in which Koeppel finds parallels are *Chaucer's Proverbs* (of unknown date), the *Nun's Priest's Prologue* and *Tale*, the *Man of Law's Tale*,[3] the *Pardoner's Tale* and the *Merchant's Tale*. Considering the quotable character of the work, and Chaucer's fondness for pithy "sentence," this is a considerable argument.

That *Melibeus* was written after the *Troilus* is not only proved by the date 1376, or later, already arrived at, but is of course strongly probable *a priori;* for one thing, the proverb-loving Pandarus[4] would have been so particularly likely to show the influence of the work that probably, when he wrote the *Troilus*, Chaucer was not even familiar with the original.[5] But there is strong positive evidence for the priority of the *Troilus*. In one of his characteristic sententious speeches (I. 956) Pandarus says:

"He hasteth wel that wysly can abyde."

As Skeat and Koeppel point out,[6] the same words occur in *Melibeus*, 2244: "The proverbe seith: 'he hasteth wel that wysely can abyde'; and in wikked haste is no profit."[7] Chaucer went

[1] Walsingham frequently comments on Richard's youth and folly; see, *e. g.*, ii. 69, 70, 97, 113 (Rolls Series). He even quotes (under date 1383) the same words of Solomon which Chaucer omits: "Væ terræ, cujus rex puer est" (p. 97). One of the authors of *Piers Plowman*, also, who was restrained by no courtiership, quotes the same passage in the B-text in 1377 (Prol. 191; ed. Skeat, I. 16), and it remains in the C-text, about 1393.

[2] *Archiv*, lxxxvi. 30–9.

[3] I have tried already to disprove the view that this is an early work.

[4] It should be remarked that the use of proverbs is characteristic of the poem in general rather than of this particular person in it; Troilus and Diomed use them as well.

[5] Koeppel cites two parallel passages in the two works (Herrig's *Archiv*, lxxxvi. 30), but of course believes that *T. C.* antedates *Mel.* (p. 32). The first of them is so commonplace as to be nugatory (cf. W. Haeckel, *Das Sprichwort bei Chaucer*, Erlangen, 1890; pp. 24–5). The other, quoted above, proves *Mel.* to be the later.

[6] *Oxford Chaucer*, v. 206; Herrig's *Archiv*, lxxxvi. 30.

[7] With the last clause cf. *Pars. T.*, 1003; Skeat, Haeckel and Koeppel also refer to *T. C.*, IV. 1567–8. A poem containing similar sentiments is attributed to Lydgate by Ritson (*Bibl. Poet.*, p. 73; and is therefore probably not by him).

out of his way to insert this passage, for it is in neither the Latin
nor the French original.[1] Moreover, though there are plenty of
parallels for the sentiment of the proverb,[2] none have been found
for the form.   But the striking thing is that not only are the
words in *Melibeus* identical with those in the *Troilus*—they form
a complete metrical line, which stands out as conspicuously from
Chaucer's amorphous prose as a flint in a mass of clay.   Can any
one doubt that the poem which contains the proverb preceded the
prose work ?

That *Melibeus* followed the *Knight's Tale* there is similar evidence.   Not only is there not the least suggestion of the influence
of *Melibeus* on it, but of this poem, too, there appears to be a line
embedded in the prose work.   In Arcite's farewell to Emily, he
speaks of lying in the grave,

"Allone, with-outen any companye" (2779).

In her discourse on poverty, Prudence says : "And if thy fortune
change that thou wexe povre, farewel freendshipe and felaweshipe ;
for thou shalt be allone with-outen any companye,[3] but-if it be the
companye of povre folk " (2749–50).   This would put *Melibeus*
after 1384–6.[4]

Though I do not wish to use excessively the argument from
the silence of the *Legend of Good Women*, I must point out that
Melibeus, had it been written then, would have been a much more
suitable work to mention in the first version of the *Prologue* than
Boethius, the *House of Fame*, and perhaps some others.   This
would date it after 1386.   Of course there is no reason why it
should be mentioned in the revised *Prologue*, if it was destined for
inclusion in the *Canterbury Tales*.   That it comes from their period
is clear from this date, and the busy fulness of the next year or two
perhaps justifies us in putting it forward to 1388 at earliest.

Next may be noted a bit of evidence that *Melibeus* was written
before the *Man of Law's Tale*.   There is no reason to doubt that
the *Man of Law's* proem on poverty was written about the same

---

[1] See Albertano in Thor Sundby's edition (Chaucer Society), p. 12 ; and
Le Ménagier de Paris, I. 192.   I have said that Chaucer very rarely adds
anything of importance.

[2] See Haeckel, *Das Sprichwort bei Chaucer*, p. 25.

[3] For the whole passage from *farewel* to *folk* the French has only "tu
demoureras tout seul" (*Ménagier*, I. 221 ; or Zupitza's note in Koeppel's article,
Archiv, lxxxvi. 34).   The *Teseide* has nothing corresponding.

[4] See p. 82 above.

time as the rest of the poem. Both draw largely on Pope
Innocent's *De Contemptu Mundi*, and I have shown in my
discussion of the tale that the Innocent passages within it cannot
be a later addition.[1] Besides this, the Innocent part of the proem
grows into an apostrophe to rich merchants (120–6), which leads
skilfully into the main narrative; the proem has not all the air of
having been added when the poem was assigned to the *Man of
Law*. Now a part of the passage in the proem, lines 99–121,
which is (somewhat freely) translated from Innocent's Latin,[2]
appears also in *Melibeus*, 2758–61, attributed to Innocent and
still more closely translated from the free French version of
Albertano's Latin, which quotes the pope fairly accurately.[3] There
is not the least suggestion of mutual influence between the two
Chaucerian passages. If the Man of Law's proem had preceded
Melibeus, we should expect that, in writing the latter, Chaucer
would have recalled his former direct and much more extensive use
of Innocent, and that at least a phrase or two of his neat and
harmonious poetic version would have stuck in his memory, so
retentive of words, and come forth in his prose.[4] We have just
seen that a few lines before in *Melibeus* he does quote the *Knight's
Tale verbatim*, and elsewhere the *Troilus*, departing from his
original in so doing.[5] On the other hand, there is less probability
that a prose version should affect one in verse, since verse requires
more manipulation of the material, and Chaucer's prose is always
less polished than his verse. Besides, in the poem he is translating
from Innocent directly, and in *Melibeus* only from a small, and by
no means literal, excerpt in French. If this evidence is allowed
some weight, which I believe it deserves, a relatively early date
is suggested for *Melibeus*.

Now can we form any plausible conjecture as to the original

---

[1] Cf. pp. 181–3 above. Professor Lowes seems hardly to recognize the
arguments for this view (*Publ. Mod. Lang Assoc.*, xx. 796) ; see below.
[2] For which conveniently see Skeat, III. 407.
[3] For Albertano's Latin see Sundby's edition (Ch. Soc.), p. 100 ; for the
French see *Ménagier*, I. 221–2, or Zupitza's note in Koeppel's article, Herrig's
Archiv, lxxxvi. 33. In a neighbouring passage there is a possible verbal
reminiscence between Chaucer's two works ; cf. *Mel.*, 2749 and *M. L. P.*, 116
(not in either original).
[4] *E. g.*, *Mel.*, 2761, and *M. L. P.*, 114 : "bet it is to dye than for to have
swich poverte," "bet is to dyen than have indigence." *
[5] See p. 213 for a possible similar case of reminiscence from *Wife of Bath's
Prol.* to *Mel.* and then to *Merch. T.*

purpose of *Melibeus?* Lounsbury,[1] I believe, first suggested that the *Man of Law's Prologue*, 96, indicates that Chaucer had intended a prose tale for the Man of Law.[2] Skeat makes the same suggestion, though without conviction, and also the further one that this tale was *Melibeus.* He then proceeds to reject both ideas.[3] Dr. Lowes[4] takes up the first suggestion, and on the basis of the *Man of Law's Prologue*, especially ll. 46, 90–6, seems to make it quite clear that Chaucer intended for the Man of Law not his present tale but something in prose, of a pedestrian character; I need not rehearse his arguments, which of course are obvious enough.

It is impossible to regard with as much favour his very tentative suggestion that what Chaucer meant for the Man of Law was his prose translation of Pope Innocent's *De Contemptu Mundi.* The *Man of Law* is nowhere represented as being of a "sombre" turn of mind, as Lowes seems to think. And could Chaucer conceivably have ever meant to have such a thing recited as a tale? The only thing which even approaches it in character is the *Parson's Tale*, which is suitable to the teller, and for the insertion of which he fully accounts in its prologue. Certainly the *Man of Law's Prologue* does not prepare us for any such extraordinary selection as Innocent's work. Moreover, if he wrote *Innocent* for a *Canterbury Tale*, and just before the second *Prologue* of the *Legend,* as Lowes believes,[5] how came he to mention it in that poem? The obvious explanation of his omitting to mention such infinitely more appropriate works as *Physician's Tale, Melibeus* and perhaps others, is that he was holding them in

---

[1] *Studies in Chaucer* (N. Y., 1892), iii. 436.

[2] "'But of my tale how shal I doon this day?
Me were looth be lykned, doutelees,
To Muses that men clepe Pierides—
Metamorphoseos wot what I mene :—
But nathelees, I recche noght a bene
Though I come after him with hawe-bake ;
I speke in prose, and lat him rymes make.'
And with that word he, with a sobre chere,
Bigan his tale, as ye shal after here" (*M. L. P.*, 90–8).

[3] Vol. III., 406. His idea that "I speke in prose" refers to the lawyer's pleading in the courts seems to me very unlikely ; for one thing, the Man of Law has been just speaking of the character of the tale he is about to tell, contrasting it with those which Chaucer habitually writes. Mr. A. W. Pollard (*Primer*, 123–4) also suggests *Melibeus* for the Man of Law, with more conviction than Skeat.

[4] *Publ. Mod. Lang. Assoc.*, xx. 794–6.   [5] *L. c.*, p. 793.

reserve for the *Canterbury Tales*. Finally, Lowes points out that
the actual *Man of Law's Tale* begins with a quotation from
Innocent, and suggests that this and other bits of Innocent were
derived from his own version and worked in when he was adapting
the Constance-story to the Man of Law. But I point out elsewhere
that the evidence is clear against any of those passages having been
added on revision. Therefore, from the first, Innocent was quoted
in the present *Man of Law's Tale*. Therefore the connection
between Innocent and the *Man of Law's Prologue* is *via* the
present *Man of Law's Tale* and not the earlier. Therefore all the
evidence and an enormous weight of probability is against the
opinion that Chaucer meant *Innocent* for the Man of Law.

We have seen, then, that at one time Chaucer probably meant
a prose tale for the Man of Law, but that it was not his version of
Innocent. If the tale was ever written, and has not disappeared
without leaving the slightest trace, we must return to Skeat's
suggestion and conclude that Chaucer originally meant *Melibeus*
for the Man of Law.[1] In this view I think there is great
probability. From beginning to end *Melibeus* is one series of
arguments, and formal ones at that, with constant appeal to
precedent and authority. There is not a single other pilgrim to
whom it would have been half so appropriate as to him of whom
it is said :

"Discreet he was, and of greet reverence :
He semed swich, his wordes weren so wyse.

.   .   .   .

In termes hadde he caas and domes alle,
That from the tyme of king William were falle."

It is perfectly prepared for by the talk of the Man of Law in his
prologue, where, after answering the Host in legal phraseology,
he deprecates comparison with Chaucer's mythological and poetic
tales. It seems to me that therefore we have excellent reason
to believe that *Melibeus* was at one time intended for the Man of
Law, and was perhaps written for him.

[1] It does not necessarily follow, of course, though it is very likely, that
he composed it for him, nor is there the slightest sign that he composed it to
recite himself.

§ 8. *The Wife of Bath's Prologue and Tale, the Shipman's*
Tale, the Merchant's Tale.

On the dates of the poems to be discussed in this section, the
Wife of Bath's Prologue and *Tale*, the *Shipman's Tale*, and the
Merchant's Tale, hardly anything has been written.   Ten Brink [1]
dates the first and the last, whose general resemblance he
recognizes, about 1390, earlier, however, than the conception of the
Canterbury Tales.   The name of the Wife of Bath, he thinks, " had
probably been a sort of proverb before the poet undertook to make
it immortal " (p. 126).   For these strange and unparalleled views
he gives no reasons which need be discussed here.[2]   We have
therefore a clear field before us, for research and for conjecture.

There is something about the *Merchant's Tale* which more than
calls for comment, which demands explanation.   Every one knows
that Chaucer was no cynic.   We can throw ourselves heart and soul
into accord with his moods of mockery and his flings of derision,
as we cannot with those of such a man as Swift or Byron, because
we can see that under his severity and contempt are inexhaustible
stores of good-humour and tolerance and charity.   But with the
Merchant's Tale, if we read it with understanding, we cannot do so.
Its spirit is anything but agreeable.   Its satire on woman and on
marriage is the bitterest that Chaucer has anywhere permitted
himself, on this or any subject.   The fact that it is somewhat
covered[3] only makes it the bitterer.   The poem certainly does not
strike one as an overflowing of jollity, or as a *tour de force*.   The
satire has a serious air, the emphasis is not at all on the brutal

[1] *History of English Literature* (Engl. tr., London, 1893), ii. 126–32.
[2] See *Hist. E. L.*, iii. 267, and *Chaucers Sprache*, § 31, but cf. p. 169 above.
His only important points I treat later.
[3] One or two writers on Chaucer have actually been misled into thinking
the first part of the poem (1245–1392) sincere praise of woman and marriage.
To say nothing of the caustic lines which are interspersed, it is astonishing
that any one should imagine he finds sincere domestic sentiments in the
preface to such a story.   We must choose between bitter intentional sarcasm,
or still bitterer and very stupid unintentional sarcasm.   The ironical con-
cessions which Chaucer makes in this passage, and which depend for their
antidote on the tacit criticism supplied by the tale which follows, are wholly
paralleled by the pillorying of men, ostensibly for the benefit of the female
sex, in *Manc. T.*, 187–95.   *Merch. T.* is, however, well offset by some
beautiful passages at the beginning of *Frankl. T.*; note that *M. T.*, 1260 =
F. T., 805, *verbatim*, and with *M. T.*, 1379 cf. *F. T.*, 751–2.

humour of the situations; the teller even apologizes[1] for his indelicate speech :

> " Ladies, I prey yow that ye be nat wrooth ;
> I can nat glose, I am a rude man " (2350–1);[2]

> " it may nat ben expressed,
> But if I wolde speke uncurteisly " (2362–3).

Not only is the coarseness less light-hearted and naturalistic than in the *Miller's*, *Reeve's* and *Sumner's Tales*, and the cynicism inherent in the story heightened in every way ;[3] there is an occasional touch of earnestness and almost pathos, and the dangerousness of woman and the folly of marriage, especially when the husband is old, are dwelt on at extraordinary length and with a notable air of feeling.[4]   The openly satirical flings are peculiarly frequent and keen ; the following passages may be especially noted :

> " ' Wedlok is so esy and so clene,
> That in this world it is a paradys.'
> Thus seyde this olde knight, that was so wys " (1264–6) ;

> " A wyf wol laste, and in thyn hous endure,
> Wel lenger than thee list, paraventure " (1317–8) ;

> " They been so knit, ther may noon harm bityde,
> And namely up-on the wyves syde " (1391–2) ;

> " ' And elles god forbede, but he sente
> A wedded man him grace to repente
> Wel ofte rather than a sengle man," (1665–7) ;

> " Whan tendre youthe hath wedded stouping age,
> Ther is swich mirthe that it may nat be writen ;
> Assayeth it your-self, than may ye witen
> If that I lye or noon in this matere " (1738–41).[5]

---

[1] The only other apology in a coarse story is in *Manc. T.*, 205–11. Cf. also, of course, Chaucer's own apology in *Prol.*, 725–42 ; and *Mill. Prol.*, 3167–86, and *Reeve's Prol.*, 3917.

[2] Of course the last phrase must not be taken too seriously. The imprecation on " the cursed monk dan Constantyn " (1810) is another suggestion of the refinement and seriousness of the teller.

[3] Cf. especially 1967–76, where the narrator leaves God to decide why May fell so easily ; 1987–94, where he affects to praise her for her " franchyse " and soft-heartedness ; 2185–218, where in one breath she declares with tears her honour and fidelity, and coughs to Damian.

[4] Cf. especially 1263–71, 1634–56, and the speeches of Justinus and Pluto.

[5] Here and elsewhere one is almost inclined to feel that Chaucer was writing somehow from his own experience. If not, the intensity of *Merch. T.* is a little hard to account for, even with my explanation, to be mentioned later.

Even Chaucer's own "favourite line"[1] appears in a connection
which turns its milk of human kindness sour : it is when May has
resolved to grant her love to Damian that the narrator comments :

> " Lo, pitee renneth sone in gentil herte " (1986).

It is specially noteworthy that when the poem is barely begun the
narrator makes a long and quite independent discourse, unparalleled
elsewhere in the *Canterbury Tales*,[2] 126 lines of veiled and grave
irony. And as to the gist and upshot of the story, January's
expectations and their outcome are a perfect commentary on the
words of the *Epistola Valerii :* "Amice, nulla est Lucretia, nulla
Penelope, nulla Sabina ; omnes time." The anti-feminine quality
of the tale is the more striking because the character of the " olde
dotard holour " January (as the Parson would call him) has been
such that we cannot but regard his cuckoldry as poetic justice ;[3]
the emphasis with which Chaucer reads the story contradicts its
natural emphasis.

Now how is all this to be explained ? An amount of it greatly
less in quantity and intensity might be accounted for by the conventional misogyny of the Middle Ages, as a passing allusion to
Chaucer's own experience or observation, as an excuse for the
following story, or as mere wanton humour. But the discourse at
the beginning and the tone all through suggest, it seems to me, if
they do not imply, a definite purpose. We should not like to
believe that it is to set forth Chaucer's own convictions,[4] and we
cannot if we read the first part of the *Franklin's Tale*. Nothing
remains except that the tone of the *Merchant's Tale* is a dramatic
device. Yet in the description of the Merchant in the *General
Prologue* there is not a syllable to account for it. Nor should we
seek an explanation in the *Merchant's Prologue* or *Epilogue*. The
latter was certainly written after its tale, and the former, like

---

The poem comes to strike one as occupying somewhat the same puzzling and
graceless position in Chaucer's works as the *Troilus and Cressida* does in
Shakspere's, though of course the explanation must be quite different.

[1] It occurs four or five times in Chaucer's poetry ; see Skeat, V. 383.
[2] The only abstract digressions elsewhere are of about a fourth the length ;
see *Phys. T.*, 67–104, and *Frankl. T.*, 761–86.
[3] No doubt because Chaucer wished to keep the story well within the limits
of comedy.
[4] In one of Chaucer's poems he does set forth, with every appearance of
seriousness, an unfavourable view of wedlock—*Lenvoy a Bukton ;* it refers to
W. B. P., and is full of parallels to its phraseology, but it is utterly unlike
Merch. T.

almost all the prologues, most likely was. With its improbable exaggeration, its account of his wife's " passing crueltee" after only two months of marriage, it has every appearance of having been written to account for the extravagant animosity of the tale which follows. So we are still left with an inviting field for conjecture to run riot in.

We may get some light on the subject if we observe the affiliations of the *Merchant's Tale*. The parallel passages in it and the *Wife of Bath's Prologue* are numerous and important; especially is the precept of the former constantly supported (or refuted) by the Wife's example in the latter :

"For she wol clayme half part al hir lyf" (*M. T.*, 1300 ; cf. 1343).

But tel me this, why hydestow, with sorwe,
The keyes of thy cheste awey fro me ?
It is my good as wel as thyn, pardee (*W. B. P.*, 308-10).

". . . She that waiteth ay After thy good, and hath don many a day"[1] (1303-4 ; cf. 1270).

They hadde me yeven hir gold and hir tresoor ;
Me neded nat do lenger diligence
To winne hir love, or doon hem reverence (204-6 ; cf. 197, 526).

She seith not ones "nay" whan he seith "ye" (1345).

For by my trouthe, I quitte hem word for word
(422 ; cf. 425 and 379-92).

Suffre thy wyves tonge, as Caton bit ; She shal comande, and thou shalt suffren it (1377-8).

Suffreth alwey, sin ye so wel can preche (437).
. . . Sith a man is more resonable
Than womman is, ye moste been suffrable (441-2 ; cf. 434).

For sondry scoles maken sotil clerkes; Womman of manye scoles half a clerk is (1427-8).

Diverse scoles maken parfit clerkes,
Divers praktik, in many sondry werkes,
Maketh the werkman parfit sekirly.
Of fyve husbondes scolering am I (between 44 and 45).[2]

---

[1] The first two passages in *Merch T.* are from Theophrastus.

[2] These lines, with two more, are to be found in only a few MSS.; besides the three mentioned by Skeat, they are in MSS. Trin. Coll. 3.15, Royal 17 D, Christ Ch., New Coll. and Arch. Seld. They are in no other MS. in any public library in England or Paris (but I have not examined MS. Sion). No one can doubt their genuineness, but Tyrwhitt and Skeat regard them as rejected on revision. The fact that they resemble the lines in *Merch. T.* seems to be no reason whatever for this opinion ; Chaucer is particularly unlikely to have rejected the more for the less elaborate version. The connection between the including lines, 44-5, is so perfect that we may well believe the extra lines to have been inserted later, and their presence in some of the MSS. to be due to contamination with a separate copy of *W. B. P.* There is other evidence that it circulated, somewhat, apart from the rest of the *C. T.* These lines should certainly, I think, be restored to the text.

But sires, by your leve, that am nat I (1456).[1]	And lordinges, by your leve, that am nat I (112).
But I wot best wher wringeth me my sho (1553).[2]	Whan that his shoo ful bitterly him wrong (492).
Paraunter she may be your purgatorie ! (1670 ; cf. 1647).	By god, in erthe I was his purgatorie, For which I hope his soule be in glorie (489–90).
He was al coltish, ful of ragerye, And ful of Iargon as a flekked pye (1847–8).	And I was yong and ful of ragerye, Stiborn and strong, and Ioly as a pye (455–6).
And whan he wolde paye his wyf hir dette (2048[3] ; cf. 1452).	That man shal yelde to his wyf hir dette (130).

Though such reminiscences are frequent in Chaucer, we have found some significance in such numerous parallels as connect the *Troilus*, the *Knight's Tale*, and the *Legend*, and are justified in finding it here.

    Another link is to be found in the works which are quoted in the two poems. The *Parson's Tale* is quoted in the *Merchant's* more frequently than in any other of Chaucer's works except the *Pardoner's Prologue* and *Tale*, and next most frequently in the *Wife's Prologue*.[4] He uses St. Jerome's work against Jovinian, and the extract from Theophrastus which it contains, more extensively in the *Wife's Prologue* than anywhere else ;[5] next to this and the *Franklin's* and *Sumner's Tales* he uses them oftenest in the *Merchant's Tale*, where he also refers explicitly to Theophrastus (1294–5, 1310).[6] Walter Map's *Epistola Valerii ad Rufinum* he mentions and quotes in the *Wife's Prologue ;* elsewhere he quotes it only in the *Merchant's Tale*.[7]

    Certain other points of contact between the *Wife of Bath's*

---

[1] Cf. *Melibeus*, 2278. See p. 213 below. The order of composition is perhaps *W. B. P.*, *Mel.*, *Merch. T.*

[2] From *Jerome against Jovinian*.

[3] Cf. *Pars. T.*, 940.

[4] See Koeppel in Herrig's *Archiv*, lxxxvii. 39–46. Some of the passages are biblical, but the more one investigates Chaucer's reading, the more convinced one becomes that his familiarity with the Bible (and other quotable literature, like Cato and Seneca) was largely at second-hand.

[5] See Koeppel in Herrig's *Archiv*, lxxxiv, 414–15 ; and in *Anglia*, xiii. 175–6 ; W. W. Woollcombe in Chaucer Society *Essays*, 297–304. The use of Theophrastus is the reason for the resemblance between some of the remarks at the beginning of the *Merch. T.* and those quoted by the Wife from her old husband, as is noted above ; cf. 1294–310 with 248–378.

[6] *Anglia*, xiii. 178–80.

[7] The "Valerie" referred to in *L. G. W.*, G-prol. 280, is doubtless Valerius Maximus. See *Anglia*, xiii. 181–3 ; and also, on all this, Skeat's index and notes.

Prologue and the *Merchant's Tale* make it difficult or impossible to doubt not only that the two were written near together, but also that the latter was written after the former; further, not only that Chaucer had the Wife of Bath and her prologue in mind when he wrote the *Merchant's Tale*, but also that he meant his readers to have them in mind.   January is remarkably like the Wife of Bath's old husband.[1]   It is noteworthy that of the dozen or so of analogues to the story[2] none seem to have anything about difference of age between the husband and wife except Boccaccio's, which barely mentions it (*Decameron*, VII. 9); it is natural that the only two great mediæval writers who treated the story should develop this dramatic contrast, but Chaucer lays much stress on it.   May has striking points of similarity to the Wife of Bath (with *M. T.*, 2187–206, 2368–415, cf. *W. B. P.*, 443–50, 226–34); she certainly follows the Wife's principles, and does rather more than bear her husband " on hond the cow is wood."[3]   Again, just as Pluto's talk is suggestive of Jankin's,[4] Proserpina's is a curious reminiscence of the Wife of Bath's; women, she says, shall never lack the power of facing out their offences,[5] and she flouts the authority of Solomon.[6]   Another suggestion of the *Wife's Prologue* is that January will have none of an elderly wife :

> " And eek thise olde widwes, god it woot,
> They conne so muchel craft on Wades boot,
> So muchel broken harm, whan that hem leste,
> That with hem sholde I never live in reste.
> For sondry scoles maken sotil clerkis ;
> Womman of manye scoles half a clerk is " [7] (1423–8).

[1] Cf. one external touch :

> " The slakke skin aboute his nekke shaketh " (1849) ;
> " Mote thy welked nekke be to-broke !" (*W. B. P.*, 277).

[2] See *Originals and Analogues* (Ch. Soc.), pp. 177 ff., 341 ff. ; and Varnhagen in *Anglia* vii., Anzeiger, p. 163.

[3] Unless this was a by-word, it shows that Chaucer knew the version of the Tell-tale Bird story which occurs in the romance of the *Seven Sages ;* cf. particularly *W. B. P.*, 233–4. If he did, it is odd that he used for the *Manciple's Tale* the vastly inferior and less Chaucerian version found in Ovid.   See Skeat's note, and *Academy*, vol. xxxvii. p. 239.

[4] With *Merch. T.*, 2237–53, cf. *W. B. P.*, 641–785.

[5] It is true, of course, that the way in which May allays her husband's indignation is one of the traditional elements in the story.

[6] With *Merch. T.*, 2264–2310, cf. *W. B. P.*, 226–234, 35–43, and the whole early part.   It is striking that whenever Chaucer portrays a sceptic, it is as a woman.   His four sceptics are the Wife of Bath, Proserpina, Partlet, and Criseyde.

[7] Cf. *W. B. P.*, 601–6, 44c–44f, and *passim*.

It is true that Chaucer along here is using Albertano's *Liber de Amore*, but all that the latter says is : " Et uxorem accipias potius . . . puellam quam viduam ; dixit enim quidam philosophus : ' Accipe puellam in uxorem, quamvis sit vetula.' " [1] January's remarks sound very much like a deliberate dig at the Wife of Bath, and certainly reflect her language.   Clearly, then, the *Merchant's Tale* was written with one eye on the *Wife of Bath's Prologue*, and Chaucer must have known that his readers would be aware of the fact.

But finally the allusions to the Wife of Bath became explicit. Justinus, at the end of his temperate and comparatively optimistic advice, some of which contains reminiscences of her prologue, openly appeals to her.   Skeat tries to make the lines an interpolation of the narrator's, and prints the passage thus :

> " ' My tale is doon :—for my wit is thinne.
> Beth nat agast her-of, my brother dere.'—
> (But lat us waden out of this matere.
> The Wyf of Bathe, if ye han understonde,
> Of mariage, which we have on honde,
> Declared hath ful wel in litel space).—
> ' Fareth now wel, god have yow in his grace ' " (1682–8).

In this endeavour to save Chaucer from himself I think the editor makes two mistakes.   For *we* (1686) all the eight published MSS. except the Camb. Dd and the Hengwrt read *ye ;* [2] and, therefore, though Dr. Skeat would doubtless explain it as caught by a scribe from the line above, I think we should accept it.   Secondly, at a time when there was no such paraphernalia of dashes, parentheses and quotation-marks as Dr. Skeat needs to bolster up his interpretation, it is certain that any reader would have understood these lines to be a part of Justinus' speech, as any one will be convinced who will glance at the passage in the *Six-Text ;* what the reader would have understood we may be sure Chaucer meant, even if he had been capable otherwise of such a piece of monstrously and gratuitously bad style as the editor attributes to him.   Chaucer therefore deliberately perpetrates so gross a dramatic impropriety as

---

[1] Koeppel, in *Archiv*, lxxxvi. 42.
[2] *Ye* is the reading of eight others, in London and Oxford (Laud 600 and 739, Harl. 1758 and 7333, Royal 17D and 18C, and Sloane 1685 and 1686) ; *we*, of six others (Bodley 686, Arch. Seld., Barlow 20, Rawl. 149, Egerton, Addit. 5140 ; passage imperfect in Harl. 7335).   Mr. George Stevenson has kindly given me this information.

to make a character in one of the tales refer to one of the people on the pilgrimage; why, unless she had been in his mind all along, and he wished to make the connection explicit?[1]

The *Shipman's Tale* must now be brought into the discussion. To begin with, two verbal parallels may be noted between it and the *Merchant's Tale* (1199 and 1315, apparently taken from *Parson's Tale,* 1068; and 1559 and 2322, apparently from *Le Roman de la Rose*).[2] The two plots in outline are also more alike than either is to any other except the *Miller's Tale.*[3] They stand together and quite apart from any other of the coarse tales[4] in their higher literary and (if I may so put it) social tone. They are more refined, and more cynical. Between the *Shipman's Tale* and the *Wife of Bath's Prologue* there are one or two rather striking parallel passages; compare *Sh. T.,* 1194–209 with *W. B. P.,* 337–56 (on the extravagance of wives in dressing, and its perils), and 1363–7 with 257–62 (on the six good points of a husband and those of a wife).[5] Besides these there is the general congeniality between the woman in the tale and the Wife of Bath in her prologue.

If these points of contact between the *Shipman's Tale* and the other two poems do not seem very significant, there is another which is quite conclusive. The *Shipman's Tale* was certainly written not for the Shipman but for a woman; six times the speaker classes himself among wives (1202–9, 1364).[6] The Shipman no

---

[1] Another reference to the Wife of Bath, which is almost as plain, and which in a manner makes a connection between *Merch. T.* and *W. B. P.*, is in *Merch. Epil.,* 2433–40. The Host regrets that he is bound to a shrewish wife, but will say no more of her, for fear his words should be reported to her by some woman in the company. It is as plain as possible that 2437–8 mean the Wife of Bath.

[2] Cf. Koeppel in *Anglia,* xiv. 257.

[3] As long ago as 1877 Mr. Fleay noted their resemblance to each other, and to the *Wife of Bath's Tale* (apparently), and suggested that they were written in the order, *W. B. T., Merch. T., Sh. T.* (*Guide to Chaucer and Spenser,* pp. 56, 62). In general, however, Fleay's little book is a blind guide.

[4] Unless perhaps the rather slight *Manciple's Tale.*

[5] For similar or complementary passages, see *W. B. T.,* 925–50; *N. P. T.,* 4102–7. With *Sh. T.,* 1417, also compare *W. B. P.* 312 (also *Reeve's T.,* 4264, and *Sumn. T.,* 1943).

[6] First pointed out by Tyrwhitt (London, 1830; iv. 280): "Which would lead one to suspect that this Tale was originally intended for a female character." The matter was noted also by A. J. Ellis (*Early English Pronunciation,* i. 244), Hertzberg (German translation of the *C. T.,* p. 644), Furnivall (*Temp. Pref.,* p. 10), Fleay (*Guide to Chaucer and Spenser,* 54), Lounsbury (*Studies,* iii. 435), and Skeat. Skeat seems to be referring to this confusion of sexes in *Sh. T.,* but in a manner still more confused, when he mentions the *Wife of Bath's Tale* in *The Chaucer Canon,* p. 110. Furnivall and Skeat suggest that *Sh. T.* may have been meant for the Wife of Bath's second tale (*Temp. Pref.,* 10, note; v. 168).

doubt had his faults, but muliebrity was not one of them.   Nor is
the subject, drawn from trivial social life, appropriate to him.
And there cannot be the smallest doubt that the woman is the
Wife of Bath, since the only other women in the party are nuns.
Two or three passages in the tale, already mentioned, are especially
appropriate to her—those on dress and " society," and on the six
good points of a husband.   Considering the way in which the
Canterbury Tales grew, it seems to me much less likely to have
been meant for her second, than to have been displaced from the
position of her first tale.

But to recapitulate.   We have seen that the *Shipman's Tale* was
certainly written for the Wife of Bath.   We have found many
points of connection between it, the *Merchant's Tale* and the *Wife
of Bath's Prologue;* strong probability that the *Merchant's Tale*
was written near the *Wife's Prologue,* and irrefragable proof that
it was written after it.   Next, it is plain that the Merchant's
attitude toward the Wife of Bath, and " al hir secte," is by no
means an amicable one; that he betrays a deep-seated and cynical
animosity toward the latter, and pretty clearly also toward the Wife
herself, which is by no means accounted for.

Now we must observe that the victim in the *Shipman's Tale* is a
merchant, who has considerable points of resemblance to him of the
Prologue.   We may note three things especially.   The French
merchant has business in Flanders (1245, 1490, etc.); so has
Chaucer's (272, 277; cf. p. 146 above).   The former says (1479):

> ''We may creaunce whyl we have a name";

of the latter Chaucer says (279–82):

> "This worthy man ful wel his wit bisette;
> Ther wiste no wight that he was in dette,
> So estatly was he of his governaunce,
> With his bargaynes, and with his chevisaunce."

This statement that, in spite of appearances, Chaucer's Merchant *was*
in debt, and his presence on the pilgrimage, are illustrated by some
of the other merchant's remarks to his wife (1420–4):

> " We may wel make chere and good visage,
> And dryve forth the world as it may be,
> And kepen our estaat in privitee,
> Till we be deed, or elles that we pleye
> A pilgrimage, or goon out of the weye."

Though it would be too much to say, perhaps, that the personality of the merchant in the tale is imitated from him of the *Prologue*, in the former Chaucer certainly followed the type of the latter.[1] My main point, however, is that in the *Shipman's Tale* it is a merchant who is put in a pitiable and ridiculous situation by being cuckolded and cheated of his money. The Merchant on the pilgrimage therefore had as much and the same reason to take offence at this tale as the Reeve had to take offence at the *Miller's Tale*, and nearly as much as the Sumner had to take offence at the *Friar's*.

What I propose is that here we have the vestiges of Chaucer's original design for an exchange of hostilities, a polite quarrel, between the Wife of Bath and the Merchant, somewhat like those which we actually have between the Miller and Reeve, and between the Friar and Sumner. If the two tales were a part of the same design—*i. e.*, if Chaucer had not changed the assignment of one before he wrote the other, some such explanation seems inevitable. If such a tiff was intended, there is point in the direct reference to the Wife of Bath in the *Merchant's Tale*, 1685; what is lost in dramatic propriety within the tale is gained if we consider it as a part of a larger whole; the impropriety of the reference in Justinus' mouth vanishes before its exquisite appropriateness in the Merchant's. If we reject such an explanation the passage becomes an extraordinary aberration.[2] And I think also that my suggestion helps to account for the earnest, disagreeable and cynical character of the *Merchant's Tale*.

Chaucer's procedure, I think, can be restored with both plausibility and completeness. He first wrote the *Shipman's Tale* for the Wife of Bath, following out more or less the characterization of her which he had given in the *Prologue*, and perhaps without intending any particular allusion to the Merchant. He then went on to write a prologue for the tale; and, becoming more interested in

---

[1] On the whole, Chaucer deals throughout his works in vivid types rather than individuals. As another illustration of the fact, in some points there is a resemblance also between the Monk on the pilgrimage, and him of the *Sh. T.* Though the former is the older man, stress is laid on the good looks of both of them (A, 165, 167; B, 1215, 1218); both are "outriders" (A, 166; B, 1255-6), and highlivers (A, 200, 205-6; B, 1260-4); both are masculine, prudent and worldly.

[2] As Lounsbury deems it (*Studies*, iii. 435); but is it not a little too extraordinary, like the blunders as to Alcestis' identity in the G-prologue of *L. G. W.*, to be a mere slip produced in straightforward writing?

her personality, proceeded to far greater length and elaboration than he had intended.[1]   It then occurred to him, perhaps not immediately, to write a sort of masculine rejoinder to her prologue ; and the *Merchant's Tale* is the result.   The whole gist of the poem, when it is read after the *Wife's Prologue*, is : " Now just look at it from the man's point of view ; not only are elderly widows untrustworthy—even young girls are."[2]   And into whose mouth should the retort be put but his who had suffered most from her tale ?

But why did Chaucer change his plan ?   It is natural that, in the course of time, he should have come to see that the *Shipman's Tale* was not wholly suitable to put into the Wife of Bath's mouth after she had recited her prologue.   Her tone in the latter is one of bold self-vindication, it is true, but she is a little on the defensive,[3] and was by no means so bad a woman as the wife in the *Shipman's Tale.*   To tell such a story would have exposed her to damaging retorts.   Chaucer's change of plan may have been hastened by the striking appropriateness of the story which he has used in her actual tale, the gist of which, the sovereignty of woman, has often been pointed out as exactly that of her prologue.   There was now no longer any occasion for the Merchant to take personal umbrage against her, and for some reason Chaucer gave up the idea of any direct answer to her prologue ; therefore the Merchant-Wife-of-Bath unpleasantness was cancelled.   But the idea of an exchange of hostilities, beginning after the *Wife's Prologue* or *Tale,* being still in Chaucer's mind, he transferred it from her and the Merchant to the Friar and the Sumner.   The separately-rubricated part of her prologue (829–56), containing this quarrel, would therefore be much later than the rest of it.[4]   After cancelling the original

---

[1] The self-revelation of the Wife of Bath comes near, at times, to being as impudent as the Pardoner's ; or that of Placebo in *Merch. T.*, 1491–505, or the Friar in *Sumn. T.*, 2074–8.   May we not regard this sort of thing almost as a conventional device to show the speaker's state of mind and character, like the stage soliloquy, as, *e. g.*, those of Iago and Richard III. ; and therefore not to be tested too strictly by realism ?   The source of Chaucer's conception of the Wife is discussed by Professor Mead, in *Publ. Mod. Lang. Assoc.*, xvi. 388–404.   I find that he makes a remark similar to the one above, that *W. B. P.* and *Pard. P.* belong to a well-marked literary form ; they "are alike in that they are, in a sense, confessions—a popular mediæval type, by the way" (p. 388).

[2] Cf. 1393–1468.   [3] Cf., *e. g.*, 229–30, 485, 825.

[4] It will be observed that the Friar's tolerant attitude toward the Wife of Bath and her prologue is admirably characteristic, and wholly different from that which I have postulated of the Merchant.   At the beginning of the actual *W. B. T.* (865–81) she gets in a little dig at the friars.

assignment, he had to transfer the *Shipman's Tale* to some other
of the less refined pilgrims; the Shipman is by no means appropriate, but for the more suitable persons probably he had made or
planned other arrangements.[1]   In order to account for the feeling
with which the Merchant speaks of woman and marriage, *ex post
facto* domestic infelicity was manufactured for him, of which
there is not a hint in the *General Prologue*.   Chaucer's failure to
adapt the tales to the new conditions[2] of course agrees with his
general carelessness of such things in the *Canterbury Tales*.

This whole theory I advance quite tentatively, as a conjecture.
But it seems to me natural, to contradict no facts, and to explain
some things which call for explanation.

And now what light have we on the dates of these poems?   The
early limit is fixed, with a fair amount of positiveness and exactness,
by the certainty that the *Wife of Bath's Prologue* was written after
the *General Prologue*.[3]   Whatever antecedent probability there may
be in the case is decidedly in favour of this view, but there is good
evidence as well.   The Pardoner's interruption, 164–8, is a clear
allusion to a passage in the *General Prologue*.[4]   But besides this,
the *Wife of Bath's Prologue* was surely developed and modified
from her description in the *General Prologue*.[5]   It is rather
suggestive that of St. Jerome's treatise against Jovinian, to which
so much of the *Wife's Prologue* is due, there is not a trace in the
General Prologue.   One of the bits derived from *Le Roman de la
Rose*[6] is also suggestive; in the *General Prologue* we are told:

[1] There is good reason (in the so-called *Shipman's Prologue* in at least five
MSS.) to believe that he meant at first to reassign it to the Sumner, before
the Friar-Sumner quarrel was arranged.   See p. 218 below.

[2] So the Shipman classes himself among women, and Justinus still makes
his strange reference to the Wife of Bath.   Another revision neglected in
Merch. T. is in 1305–6.   Chaucer probably wrote of this couplet only the
words, "And if thou take a wyf," and the MS. readings for the rest are
all spurious.   Some of the MS. readings are given by Skeat, V. 354–5; a
large number are to be found in some copies of the *Six-Text* (Introd., pp. 70 ff.,
between F and G), but (oddly) not in others.   Chaucer's neglect here is
another illustration of his habit of rarely reading his own works.

[3] I have already mentioned ten Brink's wholly unsupported opinion that it
was written before it.

[4] Ll. 688–91.

[5] One or two points, it is true, may seem to suggest the opposite conclusion.
Prol., 446, on her deafness, may seem to be an allusion to the incident narrated
in *W. B. P.*, 634–6, 788–810.   But it may equally well be a casual and arbitrary
detail, like the Cook's mormal, and not have been developed till later; if
Chaucer had already written *W. B. P.* this is hardly the point with which he
would have begun his second description.

[6] The use of *Le Roman de la Rose* in the two poems is interesting (see on this

> " Housbondes at chirche-dore she hadde fyve,
> Withouten other companye in youthe ;
> But therof nedeth nat to speke as nouthe " (460–2),

but in her own discourse she pretty much contradicts this :

> " For lordinges, sith I twelf yeer was of age,[1]
> Thonked be God that is eterne on lyve,
> Housbondes at chirche-dore I have had fyve ;
> For I so ofte have y-wedded be " (*W. B. P.*, 4–7).

Obviously she could not have had much " companye in youthe " before she was married ; so probably the passages were written in this order.[2]   Finally, all the proportion and emphasis of her personality are other and lighter in the *General Prologue* than in the *Wife's Prologue*.   In the former she is merely a capable and ambitious housewife, who excels in making cloth ; there is no suggestion whatever of her relations with her husbands, and almost nothing about her character.   This description is a little more individual and less typical than most of those in the *Prologue*, but otherwise does not differ from them.   Can we doubt, then, that it was written before the most vivid and detailed piece of character-drawing that Chaucer ever did ?   This gives, as the earliest possible date for the *Wife of Bath's Prologue*, 1388.

For the later limit of the *Wife of Bath's Prologue* the most reliable evidence has been pointed out by Skeat.   In *Lenvoy a Bukton*, after warning his friend[3] of the risks of matrimony, Chaucer says, in words which strikingly resemble those in the *Merchant's Tale :*

Skeat's notes, Mead in *Publ. Mod. Lang. Assoc. of America*, xvi. 391–404, and Koeppel in *Anglia*, xiv. 250–5) ; in *W. B. P.* it is very extensive, and in *Gen. Prol.* two lines are due to its account of La Vieille, who guards Bel-Acueil. Line 461, on her "other companye in youthe," is due to " Car j'avoie autre compaignie " (13369, ed. Pierre Marteau, Orléans, 1878 ; she is recalling her youth) ; and 476 is translated from " Qu'el scet toute la vielle dance " (4078 ; the phrase also occurs in the *Troilus*, III. 695, and in *Phys. T.*, 79). Chaucer's first conception of the Wife of Bath was partly due to La Vieille. It was the last two lines of her description in the *General Prologue* that he took as his point of departure, almost his motto, for the later and fuller portraiture ; they may have led him back to *Le Roman de la Rose*, whence he now drew also largely on its account of Le Jaloux (9697 ff., Marteau's edition ; cf. Mead, *l.c.*, pp. 398–403).

[1] Twelve was the marriageable age for females according to canon law.   Cf. p. 154 above, note.

[2] On her pilgrimages, cf. *Prol.* 463–7 with *W. B. P.*, 495, 557 ; and on her teeth, 468 with 602–4.   The tone of easy allusion in the passages in *W. B. P.* rather suggests that they were the later.

[3] Tyrwhitt was mistaken in identifying him (edition of 1830, I. xlviii.) with Peter de Buketon ; among several Buktons of whom there is word in the re-

" The Wyf of Bathe I pray you that ye rede
Of this matere that we have on honde " (29–30).

In his introduction, Skeat declares the allusion to be to her tale; in his note, to her prologue.[1] We cannot doubt that the latter is the case ; but it will not matter, for the tale we shall see must be later than the prologue. The date of *Bukton* may be fixed with great exactness and certainty. The reference in line 23 to the dis-advantages in being taken prisoner " in Fryse " is amply explained by Froissart's [2] account of the expedition against Friesland between August 24 and the end of September, 1396; therefore the poem cannot have been written before October, 1396. Nor later than January, 1397, since, as I have shown in my note, Robert Bukton must have been married by that time. So the date which Skeat assigns to *Bukton*, " about the end of the year 1396," is absolutely and exactly established. At latest, then, by the end of 1396, a copy of the *Wife's Prologue* was in the hands of Chaucer's friend Bukton, and may have been sent as a gift with the *Envoy*.

---

cords, it is easy to make a choice. Queen Anne, by letters patent of December 1, 1391, granted for her lifetime " to her esquire Robert Bucton " " a quantity of pasture and wood called ' Gosewold ' in her lordship of Eye "; October 6, 1393, this benefaction was enlarged " into a grant of the same to him and his heirs by the yearly grant of the rent of a rose as of the honor of Eye ; " and September 29, 1394, a few months after her death, grant was made, " for life, to the king's esquire Robert Bucton of the constableship of the castle of Eye, co. Suffolk " (*Cal. Pat. Rolls*, 1391–6, pp. 324, 495). He may have been the same Robert who had been appointed in October, 1390, one of four king's justices for South Wales (*ibid.* 1388–92, p. 435).   The queen's grant of Goosewold was confirmed by Henry IV. in 1399, and Bukton was still constable of Eye in September, 1401 (*ibid.*, 1399–1401, pp. 16, 540).   In July, 1402, and Sep-tember, 1403, he was given a Commission of Array for the county of Suffolk, but his militia glories seem not to have prevented his being sued for debt in 1402 or 1403 (*ibid.*, 1401–5, pp. 114, 149, 288, 291).   Chaucer himself was still called " king's esquire " in 1394, and may have frequently seen Bukton before the latter retired into the provinces. But for our most valuable intelli-gence we must go to the *Calendar of Papal Registers ; Papal Letters*, vol. v. (pp. 57, 63).   March 14, 1397, indults were granted in Rome to " Robert Bukton, donsel, nobleman, and Anne his wife, noble woman, of the diocese of Norwich," in which Eye was, and is, situated, to have a portable altar and to have mass celebrated before daybreak. Obviously the young man cannot have been married later than January, 1397 ; nor earlier than October, 1396, since the *Envoy* was written not earlier than that time, and shows that he was still unmarried then.   It is curious to see that, like Lord January, he lost no time in flouting Justinus-Chaucer's advice.   In spite of the intense piety of the Lady Anne Bukton, we can imagine what kind of a welcome Chaucer would receive in the castle of Eye.

[1] I. 85, 559.

[2] Ed. by J.-A. Buchon (*Chroniques françaises*, vol. xxxvii. ; Paris, 1825), vol. xiii., 376–7 (book iv., ch. 50); tr. by Thomas Johnes (J. Winchester, N. Y., n.d.), p. 585 (bk. iv., ch. 79).

But there are also some grounds, rather ticklish it is true, for dating it before the G-prologue of the *Legend of Good Women*, which we have found good reason for putting about the latter part of 1394. We have seen how extensively Chaucer uses *Jerome against Jovinian* in the *Wife of Bath's Prologue*, far more than in any other of his works; it is not unnatural to infer that his great familiarity with it dates from his writing of that poem. Now the manner in which he refers to and uses it in the *Legend*, G-prol., 281–304, implies great familiarity; the other five authors mentioned in the G-prologue are dismissed with a word, and Jerome's work is hardly one to be referred to for laudation of women except by one who knew it well, a fact which is illustrated by the surprise of some of Chaucer's critics at its occurrence here.[1] We have already seen that there is no evidence, at any rate, that he even knew the work before he wrote these poems.[2] In the absence of contrary evidence, this may perhaps justify us in tentatively putting the *Wife of Bath's Prologue* not later than 1394.

But we may be able to push it still further back, for I think the indications are that it was written before *Melibeus*, which there is some slight reason for dating earlier than 1394.[3] At first sight the arguments seem weak, for they are mainly *ex silentio*, and not even, some one may at first think, dead silence. Between the *Wife's Prologue* and *Melibeus* there are two, and only two, parallel passages.

---

[1] Skeat, *Legend of Good Women* (Oxford, 1889), p. 141 (but cf., of course, his larger edition, III. 302–3); Koch, *Chronology*, p. 83. Koch does not seem to see any difference between writing against women and against marriage. Neither did most of Chaucer's contemporaries, but Chaucer and the Fathers did. It is worth noticing, however, that here in praising women Chaucer praises virginity, and that the *Legend of Good Women* in general is rather against men than in favour of women; so that its general tendency is at least as much against love and marriage as in favour of them. If the comparison will not be thought impious, Chaucer here is not free from the fluctuating point and purpose which is the main fault of Gower's *Confessio*. That characteristic mediæval quality, incongruity, is frequently present in Chaucer, as in other mediæval poets; the more, many times, for the very reason of his literary greatness. Often enough, too, it adds more to his interest than it detracts from his perfection. This incongruity is sometimes due to his failure quite to unify material of diverse origins, as here in the *Legend* and in Dorigen's lament in the *Franklin's Tale*.

[2] See pp. 100–1 above. The belief that he knew it rather early depends on the belief that Prologue G is the earlier; cf. *e. g.*, Mead in *Publ. Mod. Lang. Assoc.*, **xvi**. 401. See also my article in *Modern Philology*, iii. 368–70.

[3] Besides its omission of the reference to young kings, we may perhaps put *Mel.* before *M. L. Proem* and *Tale*, these about the same time as Innocent, and that certainly no later than 1394, the probable date of *L. G. W., G-Prol.* Of course all this is exceedingly risky.

In speaking of Christ's precept of virginity, the Wife of Bath says :

> " He spak to hem that wolde live parfitly ;
> And lordings, by your leve, that am nat I " (111–12).

Prudence, in her self-defence, is speaking of " jangleresses " ; " of whiche wommen, men seyn that 'three thinges dryven a man out of his hous ; that is to seyn, smoke, dropping of reyn, and wikked wyves ' ; and of swiche wommen seith Salomon, that ' it were bettre dwelle in desert, than with a womman that is riotous.' And sir, by your leve, that am nat I ; for ye han ful ofte assayed my grete silence and my gret pacience " (2276–9).   The French original runs : " femmes jengleresses desquelles on dit : trois choses sont qui gettent homme hors de sa maison, c'est assavoir la fumée, la goutière et la femme mauvaise.   Et de telles femmes parle Salemon quant il dit : il vauldroit mieulx habiter en terre déserte que avec femme rioteuse et courrouceuse.   *Or scez-tu bien que tu ne m'as pas trouvée telle*, ains as souvent esprouvé ma grant silence et ma grant souffrance. . . ."[1]   Now the indications are that the phrase which Chaucer repeats was used for the first time in the *Wife's Prologue*.[2]   One noticeable point is that in *Melibeus* it is as nearly metrical as it can be, and we have seen that twice elsewhere in *Melibeus* he quotes lines from his own poetry.[3]   Secondly, Chaucer quite wantonly departs from the French in using it, a thing which I have said he rarely does ; the timid and literal character of his translation, of which any one may soon convince himself by a comparison, is well illustrated by the remainder of the passages quoted above.   His independence at this point is natural enough. The phrase which he repeats is a neat, forcible, and striking one ; that it stuck for some time in his memory is shown by its recurrence in the *Merchant's Tale*,[4] and I have known modern students of Chaucer in whose memory it has also strangely stuck.

The other parallel passage in the *Wife of Bath's Prologue* corre-

---

[1] *Le Ménagier de Paris*, p. 195 ; the italics, of course, are mine.

[2] It is true that it is not quite as strictly grammatical there as in *Mel.*, but it is perfectly good Chaucerian style.

[3] See pp. 193–4 above.

[4] Where it is less apt :

> " Or for that ech of hem sholde helpen other
> In meschief, as a suster shal the brother ;
> And live in chastitee ful holily.
> But sires, by your leve, that am nat I " (1453–6).

sponds, curiously enough, to the first part of the passage just quoted from *Melibeus :* [1]

> " Thow seyst that dropping houses, and eek smoke,
>   And chyding wyves, maken men to flee
>   Out of hir owene hous ; a ! *benedicite !* " (278–80).

This cannot be held to prove a connection simply because it is an extremely common saying. Without the " smoke " it occurs in *Parson's Tale,* 631, and many other places ; smoke and all, it can be found at least in four Latin works (including Innocent's *De Contemptu*),[2] two French and one non-Chaucerian English work.[3] Of these the most likely source is Gower's *Mirour de l'Omme,* 4117–22 :

> " Trois choses sont, ce dist ly sage,
>   Que l'omme boutent du cotage
>   Par fine force et par destresce :
>   Ce sont fumée et goute eauage,
>   Mais plus encore fait le rage
>   Du male femme tenceresse."

We know that Chaucer often quotes the *Mirour* in the *General Prologue* and elsewhere.[4] Therefore of the two passages common to the *Melibeus* and the *Wife of Bath's Prologue,* one proves nothing, and the other rather indicates that the latter is the earlier.

This view is confirmed by the complete absence of other parallels. The argument from silence is strong because of the frequency with which Chaucer borrows elsewhere from *Melibeus* and the works of Albertano,[5] especially in the *Merchant's Tale,* which we have seen was written about the same time as the *Wife's Prologue ;* and by the obviousness of quoting such a work as *Melibeus* in such a work as the *Wife of Bath's Prologue.* Would not Jankin have been

---

[1] Possibly his recollection of the first passage in *W. B. P.* suggested the use of the second.

[2] Which is suggested as Chaucer's source by Koeppel, in Herrig's *Archiv,* lxxxiv. 414 ; but cf. lxxxvi. 31.

[3] *Piers Plowman,* B, xvii. 315–22 ; C, xx. 297–304. See Skeat, V. 207 ; cf. also *How the Wise Man Taught his Son,* Ritson's *Anc. Pop. Poetry* (1833), p. 94. It is composed out of several passages in the *Book of Proverbs.* There is obviously not the same reason for expecting the influence of Chaucer's poetic on his prose version (if the second is the later) which we found in the case of the *Man of Law's Tale* and *Melibeus ;* the passage is much shorter, and in the poem he is not quoting the original sources.

[4] See Flügel in *Anglia,* xxiv. 437–508. *W. B. P.* 727–32 is doubtless from St. Jerome ; but cf. also *Mirour,* 4165–88.

[5] Koeppel in Herrig's *Archiv,* lxxxvi. 29–46.

likely in such a passage as 775–87 to have shown the influence of such a passage as *Melibeus* 2245–301, which is several times quoted in the *Merchant's Tale;* and the Wife herself to have borrowed at times from Prudence? The two works must have been written near together; I find it hard to believe that the more original fails to show the influence of the translation for any other reason than that it was written earlier. Therefore it may have come even some years before 1396, when Bukton had a copy.

As to the date of the *Merchant's Tale*, the only evidence aside from its connection with the *Wife's Prologue* is the certainty that it was written after *Melibeus*,[1] probably just after. Of the many parallel passages in the two works, all in the *Merchant's Tale* are poetic paraphrases of Chaucer's own prose, as Koeppel's article makes perfectly clear.[2] If he had borrowed in the poem directly and only from the original, his language in the prose translation would hardly agree with the poetic passages so closely, yet always without rhythm, except where it is inevitable; in contrast with the cases already shown where he embalmed a bit of rhythm in the very cloudy amber of his prose. But more than this, though curiously enough it seems never to have been observed before, *Melibeus* has even affected the plot and characterization of the *Merchant's Tale*. It can hardly be doubted that the whole first part of the *Merchant's Tale* is Chaucer's own addition to the story; there is not the least suggestion of it in any of the analogues which have been found, and Professor Varnhagen, who has investigated the history of the story, attributes to Chaucer all but the pear-tree episode, the bare kernel.[3] Now when January has resolved to marry he sends for his friends (by no means an obvious thing to do), states the case, and calls for their advice, but in such a way that they know what advice he desires (1397–468). Just so, after his family misfortunes, Melibeus called a conclave (2194 ff.), "shewed hem his cas" and then "axed he hir conseil upon this

---

[1] If any evidence were needed that *Merch. T.* was written after 1378, we should have some little, in the fact that in lines 1245–6 Chaucer tells us that January was a worthy knight born in Pavia and living in Lombardy, local details which were probably not in his source. His first Italian journey had not led him at all into those parts; but his second took him to Milan, the capital of Lombardy, and only twenty miles from Pavia.

[2] Herrig's *Archiv*, lxxxvi. 34–43. It is plain, from his article, that the connection of *Mel.* with *Merch. T.* is far closer than with any other of Chaucer's works.

[3] *Anglia*, vii., Anzeiger, p. 163.

matere," though "by the manere of his speche" he showed what
counsel he wished (2198–200). In the *Merchant's Tale*, after other
speeches, the flattering Placebo[1] advises Lord January to follow his
own wishes, discoursing on the wisdom of "working by counsel"
and, very undramatically, on the folly of giving lords unwelcome
advice. *Complaisant* advice similar to Placebo's is given, also after
others have spoken, by Melibeus' flatterers (2208–10). Placebo's
two specific points just mentioned are based on *Melibeus* 2193 and
2340–3, and even the idea of his character is drawn from the
latter passage. The indebtedness in its plot of the *Merchant's Tale*
to *Melibeus* is unmistakable.[2] Therefore, considering the strong
influence of *Melibeus* in general and in detail, the conclusion is
irresistible that when he wrote the *Merchant's Tale* he had made
his translation, and probably just made it. Koeppel finds no
evidence, it is true, that Chaucer used Albertano's Latin at all when
he wrote *Melibeus;* while one or two passages in the *Merchant's
Tale* which are taken from the Latin, and are in neither the
French nor *Melibeus*, show that by that time he had procured a
copy.[3] This does not necessarily imply that any considerable
time elapsed between *Melibeus* and the *Merchant's Tale.*[4] He
may have owned the Latin all the time; when he had elected to
translate the shorter French version, there was no reason why he
should consult the original; or it may have been the admiration
which led him to translate the French version that finally brought

[1] The name seems drawn from *Pars. T.* 617, but Skeat gives other
parallels. Of course it is a joke on the vespers for the dead, and may be
proverbial. Placebo's discourse recalls the similarly undramatic self-revelations
of Chaucer's Pardoner and of the friar in the *Sumner's Tale.*
[2] And is so extensive that the latter deserves to be called one of its sources.
Another bit of the plot apparently borrowed from an earlier work of Chaucer's
own is where lovelorn Damian takes to his bed and May pays him a visit
(1932–5). This strikingly recalls the scene where Criseyde makes a similar
visit to Troilus (III. 64–75), which is Chaucer's own addition to the *Filostrato.*
There is a suggestion of irony in making January play the part of Pandarus.
[3] See Herrig's *Archiv*, lxxxvi. 29, 38–9. I have shown conclusive evidence
that when he wrote *Prol. to Mel.* he knew the Latin of Albertano, and
expected that his readers also would know it. In lines 2131–42 he alludes
to the fact that two versions were extant already, and in 2143–54 apologizes
for diverging from his original—Albertano, since he does not diverge from
the French version. In the same volume with the *Liber Consilii* was very
likely Albertano's *Liber de Amore Dei*, which he also quotes in *Merch. T.* and
probably only there (Koeppel, *l. c.*, pp. 40–4; the parallel passages in *T. C.*
are from Solomon and Seneca); and possibly also Albertano's *De Arte
Loquendi*, used in *Manc. T.* This may have a bearing on the date of that
poem.
[4] Skeat, for no very visible or good reason, puts several years between
(V. 353).

the original to hand, too late to be used in the translation. Therefore there is nothing to contradict the obvious conclusion that the *Merchant's Tale* was written shortly after *Melibeus*, very probably not later than 1394.

The theory which I have advanced of course implies that the *Wife of Bath's Tale* was written for the Wife of Bath and after her prologue. This nobody doubts, and the evidence for it is quite conclusive. Lines 925–50 and 1258–64 are full of parallels to the *Wife of Bath's Prologue*. Certain passages (it is true) in the *Shipman's Tale*, 1194–209 and 1363–7, which also parallel the *Wife of Bath's Prologue*,[1] yet were written earlier, are a natural enough comment on the ensuing tale and development from the characterization of the Wife of Bath in the *General Prologue*. But these lines in the *Wife's Tale* are in quite a different category ; they contain very numerous detailed resemblances which show that her character was already fully developed.[2] As to her *Tale* and the *Merchant's*, there is no internal evidence to show which came first. The *Wife's Tale* contains, it is true, no parallels to *Melibeus ;* but the abstract topics on which there is discourse in it, gentility and the advantages of poverty and of old and homely wives, are not treated in the prose work. Therefore, especially if it was written some time after *Melibeus*, we should expect no influence. There is nothing, accordingly, against the requirement of my theory that the *Wife of Bath's Tale* shall have been written after not only her prologue but also the *Merchant's Tale*.[3]

[1] Cf. p. 205 above.
[2] We should observe particularly 928, 929–34, 937 (cf. *W. B. P.*, 662–3), 950 (*W. B. P.*, 531–42), 1027, and all of 1258–64.
[3] It may be asked whether there is any visible relation between Gower's tale of Florent (*C. A.*, I. 1407–861 ; published in 1390) and *W. B. Tale*, such as we have found between the two poets' stories of Constance, which might aid us to date the *Wife of Bath's Tale*. It is quite clear that neither of the poems was the source of the other (see Dr. G. H. Maynardier, *The Wife of Bath's Tale*, London, 1901; pp. 128–46). The only verbal resemblance which I find describes the knight's distress over his ill-looking bride :

> " Bot as an oule fleth be nyhte
> Out of alle othre briddes syhte,
> Riht so this knyht on daies brode
> In clos him hield, and schop his rode
> On nyhtes time " (*C. A.*, 1727–31) ;

> "For prively he wedded hir on a morwe,
> And al day after hidde him as an oule " (*W. B. T.*, 1080–1).

It seems to be the general view that Chaucer's poem followed Gower's, which is confirmed by the probabilities as to its date. But here there is no reliable

The question may now arise as to the temporal relation of these poems to some of the minor parts of the *Canterbury Tales.* We can squeeze out a few more inferences, though they do not all depend on the foregoing. The *Prioress' Prologue* was not written till after the *Shipman's* and *Merchant's Tales* and the *Wife of Bath's Prologue*, and after the change of plan in regard to them, since it refers to the tale of the Shipman as already assigned to him. Lines 829–56 of the *Wife's Prologue*, containing the beginning of the Friar-Sumner squabble, I have shown would be later than the change. So, no doubt, with the present *Shipman's Prologue;* [1] so also with the *Merchant's Prologue* and *Epilogue.* [2] The same is probably true of the *Monk's Prologue*, since it seems to have been written after the *Merchant's Epilogue.* In the latter the Host says (2427–30) :

' I have a wyf, though that she povre be ; [3]
But of hir tonge a labbing shrewe is she,
And yet she hath an heep of vyces mo ;
Ther-of no fors, lat alle swiche thinges go."

___

evidence. *W. B. T.* offers another parallel to Gower. On the ubiquity of the friars, cf. *W. B. T.*, 865–81 with *Vox Clamantis*, IV., cap. xxiii. Note especially 867–8 (but cf. the whole contexts):

"That serchen every lond and every streem,
As thikke as motes in the sonne-beem":

"Iudeos spersos fratrum dispersio signat.
. . . .
Nescio si supera sibi clauserit ostia celum ;
Dat mare, dant ampnes, totaque terra viam" (1113, 1123–4).

The Protestant *Pilgrim's Tale* (ed. Furnivall, in Appendix to Thynne's *Animadversions*, Ch. Soc., 1875 ; see ll. 88–100, pp. 79–80) makes interesting quotations from this part of the tale. A partial analogue to *W. B. T.* is suggested by a passage in Miss Edgeworth's *Modern Griselda*, chap. ix.: ". . . the Princess Rhezzia, in the Persian Tales ; who was blooming and charming, except when her husband entered the room . . . doomed to this fate by a vile enchanter."

[1] Hence it was probably later yet (see p. 188) that *M. L. T.* was assigned to the Man of Law. Modern editions obscure the puzzling problems connected with *Sh. P.*, which I hope to treat more fully at another time. The indications are, I think, that Chaucer meant at first to reassign *Sh. T.* to the Sumner, to whom it would have been far more appropriate than to the Shipman, and that he wrote the present *Sh. Prol.* for the former. The reading "Sompnour" in line 1179 found in five MSS. would therefore be the original one. The unification of Group B made by Bradshaw, modern editions and MS. Arch. Seld., I believe was intended by Chaucer, but never actually accomplished. To treat this subject further would anticipate a future book on the evolution of the *C. T.*

[2] The latter still maintains the allusions to *W. B. Prol.*, a work which is striking enough, even without the intended tiff, to be in mind during the later part of the *C. T.*

[3] Did Touchstone remember this line (*As You Like It*, V. iv. 55) ?

This conspicuously ignores the far more detailed and vivacious account in the *Monk's Prologue* of the manners and customs of Mistress Bailey. Surely, therefore, it must have been written before it.[1]

This concludes the present discussion of the chronology and development of the *Canterbury Tales*. It is hardly necessary to say that the evidence presented has differed in value, and the conclusions accordingly in certainty. They are presented for what they are worth, because the publication of plausible conjecture, founded on investigation and recognized as conjecture, leads in the long run to the most fruitful and reliable results. Up to the present time surprisingly little investigation has been done on the *Canterbury Tales*, considering that they have been recognized for five centuries as the greatest work of our first great poet. The reason, no doubt, is the complexity of the problem, and the inaccessibility of much of the evidence. Chaucer students await with deep interest the publication by Mr. George Stevenson of a full description and analysis of all the sixty-odd MSS. of the *Canterbury Tales*. We may then be in a position to show that the very puzzles which make the study of the work perplexing, such as the different readings in the *Shipman's Prologue*, 1179, and the presence in some MSS. of the "Host-stanza" after the *Clerk's Envoy*, help to provide the solution of the whole problem. In putting the poem together, Chaucer did not cover his own tracks. By painstaking examination of all the evidence, and by harmony among reasonable guesses as to separate problems, we may hope to arrive at something like certainty as to the way in which the *Canterbury Tales* came into being and into their present form. But the time has not quite come yet for putting results together.

[1] Several other parts of *C. T.* are more or less closely connected with *Sh. T.*, *W. B. P.*, or *Merch. T.*, either by parallel passages, by showing the influence of the same reading or by some striking correspondence in subject ; these are *Pard. Prol.* and *T.*, *Mill. Prol.* and *T.*, *Reeve's Prol.* and *T.*, *Frankl. T.*, *Summ. T.*, *Manc. T.*, *Pars. T.* It must be said, however, that the evidences of connection are much slighter than in the cases which I have discussed. I advance nothing as to the dates of these poems ; I simply raise the query whether the connection means anything. Mr. George Shipley (*M. L. N.*, x. 275-6) shows some reason to believe that *Frankl. T.* directly alludes to *W. B. T.*, and perhaps even *Cl. T.* ; cf. F 745-7, 751-2, 764-6, 792-3 with (*e. g.*) D 1038-41.

APPENDICES.

APPENDIX A.

The Date of Gower's Mirour de l'Omme.

THE date of Gower's *Mirour de l'Omme* is of no little importance in Chaucer investigation, for it will aid in ascertaining the dates of more than one of Chaucer's poems, especially the *Troilus.* Professor Macaulay determines it to be about 1376–9,[1] but the matter is so important that it is worth while to discuss and strengthen his evidence.

Macaulay points out that lines 22801–24 refer to the conditions at the end of Edward III.'s reign, especially to the domination of Alice Perrers:

> " Voir dist qui dist femme est puissant,
> Et ce voit om du meintenant. . . .
> Qe femme in terre soit regnant
> Et Rois soubgit pour luy servir.
> Rois est des femmes trop deçu, . . .
> Dont laist honour pour foldelit."

This implies a date some time later than August, 1369, when Queen Philippa died, after which the *liaison* became more open than before;[2] and very likely a good deal later, since things gradually became worse. In 1376, Parliament had to legislate against the Perrers woman.[3] But the passage may quite well have been written after Edward's death, June, 1377. It may reasonably be doubted whether Gower would have cared to express himself so fully and frankly on the king's shortcomings, before the king's death, in a poem meant for publication; his other two great works were clearly meant to reach the royal eye. The passage simply expressed generally contemporary conditions, and may well denote a foregone conclusion.

---

[1] *Complete Works,* I. xlii.–xliii.
[2] *Dict. of Nat. Biogr.,* xvii. 66.
[3] Stubbs, *Const. Hist.* ii. 431 ; Th. Walsingham, i. 320.

Lines 22225–359 were almost certainly written by or after 1371. At the very beginning of Gower's discourse addressed to kings, he devotes himself to a king's duties to the Church and to the prelates and dwells with especial disapproval on excessive taxation or pillaging of the Church (22242–5, 22276–8, 22297–359 ; here comes a long lacuna). Now in 1371 the action of Parliament was more strongly anti-clerical than for many years before ; very heavy taxes were laid on the Church, there was even talk of confiscation, and several bishops were ousted from civil offices, a movement which, according to Stubbs, King Edward may even have instigated.[1] There can be little doubt that this passage was written not earlier than 1371, and since Gower was a strong and conservative supporter of the Church, his feelings may well have been keen for some little time after that date.

In several passages it is difficult not to see the influence of Gower's friend Chaucer's journey to Italy, which gives 1373 as the earliest date possible. All are agreed that Gower knew no Italian. Yet lines 3831–4 run :

" Sicomme ly sages la repute,
Envie est celle peccatrice,
Qes nobles *courtz* de son office
Demoert et est *commune pute*,"

which cannot be independent of Dante's words on envy :

" La meretrice, che mai dall' ospizio
Di Cesare non torse gli occhi *putti*,
Morte *comune*, e delle *corti* vizio "
(*Inf.*, XIII.[2] 64–6).

The phrase *ly sages* Gower frequently uses to introduce quotations from various sources. We can hardly avoid believing that Chaucer read or repeated the passage to Gower.[3]   Secondly, the reference of

[1] Stubbs, *Const. Hist.*, ii. 420–4 ; Green, *Short History* (N.Y., 1890), 234 (chap. v., sec. 2).

[2] *Ufizio*, curiously, occurs in line 62, and *peccatrici* (the only time in the *D. C.*) in XIV. 80.   Chaucer of course quoted the same passage, less exactly, in *L. G. W.*, Prol. F, 358–60.   Gower quotes it again, far less exactly and many years later, in *Conf. Am.*, II. 3095 ff.   By this time he had forgotten its origin, and attributed it to " Senec," but Haase's exhaustive index shows, as indeed we should expect, that it is not in Seneca's writings ; nor do Fraticelli, Scartazzini, Moore, or Paget Toynbee attribute Dante's words to Seneca or to any one else.

[3] This is the only clear case of Dante's influence on Gower.   But *M. O.* 11953–6 sounds Dantesque.   The anecdote of Dante in *C. A.*, VII. 2329* ff., seems more likely to have come through Chaucer than through a work of Petrarch's or otherwise.

"la geste de Troÿlus et de la belle Creseide" (5253–5) seems to me quite certainly to Chaucer's poem, and therefore postdates 1373, presumably by some years.[1]

For lines 2142–8 the date of 1377 or earlier is quite certain, as Macaulay shows;[2] for as an example of the sin of Inobedience Gower speaks of the French as in rebellion

"A celluy qui de sa nescance
Le droit depar sa mere prent."

This can only refer to Edward III. and the Hundred Years' War, and must have been written before June, 1377, when he died. But it may well have been written only shortly before; from 1360, just after the Treaty of Brétigny, to 1369 "peace was fairly preserved," but during 1374 Aquitaine revolted from England and joined France, and during the ensuing years hostile relations were only partly interrupted.[3]

For lines 18817–40 the date 1378 or later is equally certain, as Macaulay also shows; Gower, in addressing the Court of Rome, speaks of the monstrous birth in the Church of one body with two heads, obviously referring to the Great Schism, which began in September, 1378.[4]

This date may seem inconsistent with a somewhat later passage. In discoursing on emperors, and addressing Rome and speaking of her spiritual head, Gower says:

[1] Two doubtful points may be added. In 23233–68 Gower discourses on the excesses and outrages of tyrants of Lombardy, in a rather hearsay style ("ascuns diont," "om solait dire"). One thinks immediately of *L. G. W.*, *Prol.* F, 374, and wonders if Chaucer was not the reporter, in 1373 or perhaps after his mission to the Milanese Visconti in 1378. In 18697–732 the Court of Rome is reproached for neglecting to make peace between England and France; the reasons for its neglect are said to be lack of charity and of impartiality, and the fact that it has wars of its own in Romagna. The two latter reasons would apply to pretty much any of the Avignonese popes; but Milman tells us (*Lat. Christianity*, N.Y., 1862, vii. 201, 218, 219–220) that about 1352, 1370, and 1370–77 Innocent VI., Urban V., and Gregory XI. (especially the last) did try more or less sincerely to make peace. But the humiliating failure of the negotiations of 1374–5 might well be attributed to the Roman Court by an Englishman irritated by the diplomatic victories of the Papacy over England in "the negotiations which were carried on at Bruges for a concordat with the pope," under the shadow of which, according to Stubbs (*Const. Hist.*, ii. 427), the peace-conference met. There were also unsuccessful negotiations for peace in 1376 and 1377, but the war of course lasted on for years.

[2] I. xlii.

[3] Thomas Walsingham, i. 317–18; Green, *Short History*, pp. 233–4.

[4] Macaulay (p. xlii.) suggests that this passage may be a later addition, not seeing that the passage about Alice Perrers may well have been written after Edward's death.

> " S'il avient qu'il t'est prochein,
> Lors tolt de toy le flour et grein,
> Et laist la paile deinz ta bonde,
> Et puis se tient de toy forein " (22195–8).

This seems to be an equally certain allusion to an earlier state of
things, the Babylonish Captivity, 1305–1377, but stands more than
3000 lines later than the reference to the Schism.   Yet it is not at
all necessary to believe that it was written before the discourse on
the Roman Court.   Urban V., elected in 1362, had been zealous to
restore the Papal See to Rome, but did not do so till 1367, and
returned to Avignon in 1370.   Gregory XI., elected in 1370,
permanently restored the Papacy to Rome in January, 1377, but at
his death in 1378 he also was meditating a return to Avignon.[1]
For some years the permanency of the Papacy in Rome must have
seemed highly doubtful, and such words as Gower's quite natural·
This passage is the only suggestion that the Papacy had ever been
anywhere but in Rome, though over 600 lines are devoted to the
Curia, and though the abuses of the Avignonese court were particularly obvious to the English.   On the contrary, it is implied or stated
again and again that the seat of the Papacy is Rome, and Avignon
is never mentioned in the poem.   A bull comes " du Romanie "
(18995) ; of the upright clerk in contrast with the simoniacal
" provisour " it is said :

> " N'a Rome s'en vait pas serchant " (16109) ; [2]

cf. 3330, 7360, 18450, 18502, 18421–19056 *passim*, 20349, 21445.
In many of these cases the mention of Avignon would have barbed
the shaft.   And in many cases Gower's omission to mention the
domination of the Papacy by the Crown of France would be strange
indeed if it was so dominated.   So there is nothing against the
opinion that most of the *Mirour* was written after the termination
of the Babylonish Captivity.

At first sight, the mention of " Innocent " [3] in 18783 suggests the
pontificate of Innocent VI. (1352–62).   Yet this passage stands but

---

[1] Milman's *Latin Christianity*, vii. 209–26.
[2] Cf. *Vox Clam.*, III. 1551, 1575 ; he calls the provisors "Romipetæ."

[3] " L'estat du pape en sa nature
    Ne porra faire forsfaiture
    En tant comme pape, ainz Innocent . . .
    Cil puet mesfaire d'aventure."

thirty-four lines before the mention of the Great Schism. Macaulay
is doubtless correct in thinking the name " only a representative
one," and this allusion may as well denote a foregone conclusion
as that to Edward and Alice Perrers, both alike being used to
illustrate general truths. Gower may have meant some irony in the
use of the name Innocent, he may have thought it less disrespectful
to use the name of a dead rather than of a living pontiff, and
was doubtless glad of the rhyme in a stanza which requires six
of each.

So early a date as 1362 is contradicted, and the other evidence
confirmed, by the fact that, as no one who has toiled through the
Mirour needs to be told, it cannot be the work of a very young man.
This is also clear from specific internal evidence;[1] formerly, he
says (27337 ff.), he abandoned himself to " foldelit," and wrote
" fols ditz d'amours," but now all is changed. He has come late to
repentance (27300). But he lived till 1408, and about 1390 produced the *Confessio Amantis*, the liveliest of his works. Macaulay
conjectures that he was born not far from 1332,[2] which fits all the
conditions. So for the *Mirour* some time about the seventies would
seem to be indicated.

Finally, it seems fairly certain that the poem was finished before
or by 1381. As Macaulay points out, the Peasant Revolt of 1381
produced a profound effect on Gower's mind; in the *Vox Clamantis*
it forms the subject of the whole first book, and the rest of the work
is devoted to ascertaining the causes of it. That Gower dimly foresaw such troubles is shown by a number of remarkable passages in
the *Mirour*, which Macaulay points out (p. xlii.); but of the events
of 1381 there is not a word. The *argumentum ex silentio* seems to
me convincing.[3]

Everything indicates that the composition of the *Mirour* must
have fallen wholly or almost wholly in the seventies. The effect of
all this may be more convincing if put in tabular form :

[1] Cf. Macaulay, I. lxii.
[2] I. lxii. Cf. Macaulay's note in the *Athenæum*, no. 3856, p. 385
(September 21, 1901).
[3] It is worthy of remark also that there is not a word of the Bishop of
Norwich's Crusade against the Flemings, 1383, which is dwelt on in the *Vox*,
III., cap. vi.; yet a mention of it would have given peculiar point to some of
the remarks in the *Mirour* on the bishops and the regular clergy. Another
matter ignored which is prominent in Gower's later work is the growth of the
Lollards; it was in 1382 that Archbishop Courtenay began his campaign
against Wyclif, and that the Lollards may be said to have first risen to a bad
eminence.

Rebellious French, l. 2142...................... 1377 or earlier.
Dante quoted, 3831............................. 1373 or later.
Troilus mentioned, 5254......................... after 1373.
? (Pope's neglect to make peace, 18700   ... 1374–5 or later.)
Great Schism, 18817 .... 1378 or later.
(Bab. Capt. alluded to, 22195 .... 1377 or thereabouts.)
Anti-clerical movements, 22297 .... 1371 or later.
Alice Perrers, 22807 .... 1369 or later.

Gower not a young man........................ hardly before 1365.
Bab. Capt. almost ignored..................... 1377 or later.
Peasant Revolt ignored .... 1381 or earlier.

If my arguments are accepted, it will be seen how perfectly satisfactory and consistent this all is. Everything supports the two crucial arguments adduced by Macaulay—that 2142 ff. was written in 1377 or earlier, and 18817 ff. in 1378 or later; and the practical ignoring of the Babylonish Captivity indicates that the middle of the poem must have been reached not earlier than 1377. There is not the smallest reason for believing that the poem was not written in about the order in which we have it, or for postulating interpolations. My conclusion reaffirms Macaulay's, except that, considering the great length of the poem, I should extend the limits to about 1375–81.

The passage (5245–56) in which the *Troilus* is mentioned must have been written, in all probability, by 1377, since 18817–30000 was written between 1378 and 1381. If we accept the reference as being to Chaucer's poem, we may, without reasoning in a circle, declare that it cannot have been made much earlier. So it seems to me that for Gower's reference to the *Troilus* the date about 1377 may be accepted with considerable confidence.[1]

[1] A recent and rather extensive thesis on French and Latin sources of Gower's treatment of the vices and virtues (unimportant for my purposes) is by Miss R. E. Fowler, submitted for the doctorate of the University of Paris (Macon, 1905). In a MS. in the British Museum (Addit. 15606, ff. 6¹–35¹) is an allegory on the Seven Deadly Sins and the contrary virtues, which may be worth mentioning as a parallel to Gower's. The allegory is military, based on the siege of Jerusalem by Nabugodonosor.

APPENDIX B.

The Knight's Tale and the Teseide : A Table of Parallels.

On this table is based much of the reasoning in chapter III., section 1, which will explain its peculiar form; but it is believed that the contents of it may prove otherwise useful to Chaucer students. Each column corresponds to one line of the *ottava rima.* The number before the sign of equality always indicates a line of the *Knight's Tale,* according to the Chaucer Society's numbering; and the numbers after represent the book and stanza of the *Teseide,* the column indicating the line of the stanza. Parentheses show that one English line corresponds to two or more Italian lines, or a considerable part of them, but it has not always seemed necessary to take account of a very trivial part of a line. Therefore a line-number in parentheses always appears in at least two columns. I have meant to include every Italian line to which an English line is clearly due, even though there may be no verbal agreement.   Italics indicate that the translation is very close. Where two lines in the English answer to one in the Italian, occasionally one is a close translation and the other not; this is indicated thus—*2385*-6.

In preparing this table I have been very materially aided by Mr. Henry Ward's marginal references to the Italian in the Chaucer Society's *Six-Text* edition. It is proper to say that these notes are somewhat deficient in both extent and accuracy; but, so far from wishing to reflect on the labours of their author, I must add that my own may not be faultless, though they have been prepared with the utmost care, and thoroughly verified. Very nice cases constantly arise, and not only would the tables of no two men agree perfectly, but any man would possibly revise his own every time he reviewed them. What errors there may be, however, cannot be serious, for it will be seen that the question at issue is always one of proportion.

LINE 1.

- 905 = 2, 26
- 966 = 2, 50
- 1011 = 2, 86
- 1028 = 2, 97
- 1191 = 3, 47
- 1214 = 3, 54
- 1285 = 3, 78
- (1362 = 4, 27)
- (1363 = 4, 28)
- 1371 = 4, 29
- 1402-3 = 4, 38
- (1455 = 5, 3)
- 1476 = 5, 37
- 1551 = 4, 81
- 1668 = 5, 77[1]
- 1814 = 5, 92
- 1881 = 5, 96
- 1856-9 = 5, 98
- (1890 = 7, 110)
- 1893 = 7, 109
- 1982 = 7, 32
- 1994 = 7, 33
- 1999 = 7, 34
- 2011 = 7, 35
- 2017 = 7, 37
- (2102 = 6, 71)
- 2138-9 = 6, 21
- (2140 = 6, 22)
- 2163 = 6, 16

LINE 2.

- 906 = 2, 26
- 965 = 2, 50
- 1049 = 3, 10
- (1191 = 3, 47)
- 1194 = 3, 47
- 1215 = 3, 54
- (1362 = 4, 27)
- (1363 = 4, 28)
- (1455 = 5, 3)
- 1638 = 7, 106
- 1659 = 5, 77
- (1829 = 5, 96)
- 1860 = 5, 98
- 1874 = 5, 100
- 1889 = 7, 108
- (1890 = 7, 110)
- (1982-3 = 7, 32)
- 1993 = 7, 33
- 2022 = 7, 33
- (2140 = 6, 22)
- 2164 = 6, 16
- 2182 = 6, 65

LINE 3.

- 911 = 2, 26
- (917 = 2, 27)
- 945-6 = 2, 31
- 967 = 2, 50
- 1005 = 2, 85
- 1040 = 3, 10
- 1060 = 3, 11
- (1194 = 3, 47)
- 1406 = 4, 38
- 1507 = 4, 62
- 1829 = 5, 96
- 1887 = 7, 108
- 1894 = 7, 109
- 1977 = 7, 31
- (1983 = 7, 32)
- 1985 = 7, 33
- 2003 = 7, 34
- 2012 = 7, 35
- 2105 = 6, 71
- 2129 = 6, 14
- 2140 = 6, 22
- 2162 = 6, 17

LINE 4.

- 898-9 = 2, 25
- 907 = 2, 26
- (917 = 2, 27)
- 1454 = 5, 1
- 1640 = 7, 106
- 1739 = 5, 90
- 1888 = 7, 108
- 1986 = 7, 33
- (2003 = 7, 34)
- (2105 = 6, 71)
- 2142 = 6, 22

LINE 5.

- 908 = 2, 26
- 932 = 2, 28
- 1010-1 = 2, 85
- 1018 = 2, 86
- (1021 = 2, 87)
- 1053 = 3, 10
- 1292 = 3, 78
- 1407 = 4, 38
- 1409 = 4, 40
- 1439-40 = 4, 59
- 1553 = 4, 85
- 1563 = 4, 82
- 1641 = 7, 119
- 1643-6 = 7, 106
- 1710 = 5, 83
- 1978 = 7, 31
- 2004 = 7, 34
- 2141 = 6, 22

LINE 6.

- 934 = 2, 28
- 1009 = 2, 85
- (1021 = 2, 87)
- 1054 = 3, 10
- 1102 = 3, 14
- 1294 = 3, 78
- 1448 = 4, 59
- 1554 = 4, 85
- 1564-5 = 4, 82
- 1642 = 7, 119
- 1711 = 5, 83
- (1851 = 5, 97)
- 1983-4 = 7, 32
- (2140 = 6, 22)

LINE 7.

- 900 = 2, 25
- 928 = 2, 28
- 1016 = 2, 86
- 1023 = 2, 89
- 1081 = 2, 98
- (1078 = 3, 17)
- 1273 = 3, 75
- (1364 = 4, 27)
- 1370 = 4, 29
- 1391 = 4, 37
- (1504 = 4, 64)
- 1567 = 4, 82
- (1569-71 = 4, 87)
- 1625 = 5, 13
- 1785 = 5, 90
- 1826 = 5, 93
- 1839 = 5, 95
- 1979 = 7, 31
- 1990 = 7, 32
- 1997 = 7, 33
- 2009 = 7, 34
- (2130 = 6, 21)

LINE 8.

- 904 = 2, 25
- 947 = 2, 31
- 1022 = 2, 87
- 1032 = 2, 98
- 1055 = 3, 10
- 1075-6 = 3, 11
- (1078 = 3, 17)
- 1120-2 = 3, 21
- 1274 = 3, 75
- (1364 = 4, 27)
- 1392 = 4, 37
- (1504 = 4, 64)
- 1557-8 = 4, 84
- 1568 = 4, 82
- (1569-71 = 4, 87)
- 1626 = 5, 13
- 1705 = 5, 82
- 1828 = 5, 93
- 1850 = 5, 98
- 1892 = 7, 110
- 1976 = 7, 81
- 1991-2 = 7, 32
- 1998 = 7, 33
- 2041 = 7, 37
- (2130 = 6, 21)
- 2135 = 6, 21

[1] Line 1663, which looks like a translation of *Teseide*, VI., 1, 1, I have elsewhere shown to be probably due to Dante (*Mod. Philol.*, iii. 371-2).

LINE 1.	LINE 2.	LINE 3.	LINE 4.	LINE 5.	LINE 6.	LINE 7.	LINE 8.
2198 = 6, 70	2203 = 6, 70	(2173 = 6, 30)	(2173 = 6, 30)	(2173 = 6, 30)	2193 = 6, 65	(2204-5 = 7, 99)	2175 = 6, 41
2219-20 = 7, 43	2222 = 7, 43	2223 = 7, 43	2191 = 6, 65	2194 = 6, 65	2202 = 6, 70	2242-3 = 7, 46	2190 = 6, 65
2227 = 7, 45	2228 = 7, 45	2281-2 = 7, 45	2195 = 6, 69	2196 = 6, 69	(2205 = 7, 99)	(2250 = 7, 46)	(2250 = 7, 46)
2238-9 = 7, 46	2246 = 7, 47	2240 = 7, 46	2225 = 7, 43	2204 = 7, 99	(2241 = 7, 46)	2257 = 7, 49	2258 = 7, 49
2244-5 = 7, 47	2255 = 7, 49	(2247 = 7, 47)	(2239 = 7, 46)	2224 = 7, 43	2278 = 7, 71	(2292 = 7, 74)	2296 = 7, 76
2251 = 7, 48	2279 = 7, 71	2256 = 7, 49	(2247 = 7, 47)	(2241 = 7, 46)	(2283 = 7, 72)	(2317 = 7, 84)	2337 = 7, 91
2254 = 7, 49	2297 = 7, 79	2291 = 7, 74	2252 = 7, 48	2253 = 7, 48	(2292 = 7, 74)	2321 = 7, 84	2356-7 = 7, 89
2261 = 7, 67	2299 = 7, 77	2300 = 7, 79	2302 = 7, 79	2277 = 7, 71	(2317 = 7, 85)	2347-8 = 7, 88	2372 = 7, 23
2275 = 7, 71	2308 = 7, 81	2309 = 7, 81	2310 = 7, 81	(2283 = 7, 72)	(2325 = 7, 85)	2355 = 7, 89	2392 = 7, 25
2281 = 7, 72	(2313 = 7, 80)	(2313 = 7, 80)	2325 = 7, 85	2303 = 7, 79	2336 = 7, 91	2371 = 7, 23	2406 = 7, 27
2290 = 7, 74	2323 = 7, 85	2324 = 7, 85	2334 = 7, 91	2327 = 7, 78	2346 = 7, 88	2400-1 = 7, 26	2424 = 7, 39
2295 = 7, 75	2351 = 7, 89	(2353 = 7, 89)	(2353 = 7, 89)	2335 = 7, 91	2389 = 7, 25	2417 = 7, 28	2433 = 7, 40
2298 = 7, 77	2359 = 7, 90	2381 = 7, 25	2360 = 7, 90	(2343 = 7, 92)	(2398 = 7, 26)	2423 = 7, 39	2446 = 7, 67
2307 = 7, 81	(2365 = 7, 93)	2394 = 7, 26	(2399 = 7, 26)	2385-6 = 7, 25	2415-6 = 7, 28	2445 = 7, 67	
2312 = 7, 80	2374 = 7, 24	(2410 = 7, 28)	2431 = 7, 40	(2398-9 = 7, 26)	(2431 = 7, 40)	2516-20 = 7, 98	
(2323 = 7, 85)	2380 = 7, 25	2429 = 7, 40	2509 = 7, 96	2413 = 7, 28	2440-1 = 7, 67		
2331-2 = 7, 88	2394 = 7, 26	2506 = 7, 97	2514 = 7, 98	(2431 = 7, 40)	2515 = 7, 98		
2339-40 = 7, 92	2404 = 7, 27			2438-9 = 7, 67			
2349-50 = 7, 89	2411 = 7, 28			(2514 = 7, 98)			
2358 = 7, 90	2427 = 7, 40						
(2365 = 7, 93)	(2513 = 7, 99)						
2373 = 7, 24							
2879 = 7, 25							
2393 = 7, 26							
2402-3 = 7, 27							
2407 = 7, 28							
2425-6 = 7, 40							
2435 = 7, 41							
2511 = 8, 5							

LINE 1.

(2513 = 7, 99)
2533 = 7, 96
2561 = 7, 14
2626 = 8, 26
2652 = 8, 123
2689 = 9, 8
2696 = 9, 13
2697 = 9, 49
2701 = 9, 39
(2721 = 9, 58)
(2739 = 12, 83)
(2743-4 = 10, 11)
(2768 = 10, 64)
2773 = 10, 103
2781 = 10, 65
2800 = 10, 111
2831 = 11, 7
2837 = 11, 9
(2839 = 11, 10)
2844 = 12, 6
2853 = 11, 13
2865 = 11, 14
2870 = 11, 15
(2880 = 11, 16)
(2881 = 11, 30)
2889 = 11, 35
2899 = 11, 38
2907 = 11, 37
2913 = 11, 18

LINE 2.

(*2525 = 7, 96*)
2529 = 7, 100
2562 = 7, 14
2603 = 8, 7
2627 = 8, 26
2691 = 9, 8
2702 = 9, 39
(2721 = 9, 58)
(2739 = 12, 83)
(2743-4 = 10, 11)

2770 = 10, 64
2799 = 10, 111
2839 = 11, 10)
2843 = 12, 6
2854 = 11, 13
2856 = 11, 13

2866 = 11, 14
2871 = 11, 15
(2880 = 11, 16)
(2881 = 11, 30)
2885 = 11, 31
2890 = 11, 35
2900 = 11, 38

LINE 3.

(2525 = 7, 96)
2530-1 = 7, 100
(2559 = 7, 12)
2563 = 7, 14
2588 = 7, 19
2722 = 9, 58
(2735 = 12, 80)
(2739 = 12, 83)
2761 = 10, 12
(2768 = 10, 64)

2775 = 10, 103
2801 = 10, 111
2832 = 11, 7
2840 = 11, 10
2845-6 = 12, 6
2855 = 11, 13
(2865 = 11, 14)

2872 = 11, 15
(2879-80 = 11, 16)
2891 = 11, 35
2906 = 11, 40
2926-7 = 11, 25
(2949 = 11, 51)

LINE 4.

(2559 = 7, 12)
2564 = 7, 14
(2735 = 12, 80)

2774 = 10, 103
2802-3 = 10, 111
2828 = 11, 8

(2873 = 11, 15)
(2879 = 11, 16)
2892-3 = 11, 35
2930 = 11, 21
2935 = 11, 27
2950 = 11, 51

LINE 5.

2540 = 7, 7
2587 = 7, 19
2680 = 8, 124
2694-5 = 9, 48

2804 = 10, 111
2841 = 11, 11
2860 = 11, 13

(2873 = 11, 15)
2882 = 11, 30
2884 = 11, 30
2910 = 11, 40
2928 = 11, 25
(2929 = 11, 21)
(2938 = 11, 28)

LINE 6.

2551 = 7, 131
(2571 = 7, 113)
2584-5 = 7, 118
2683 = 8, 124
2717 = 9, 62
2765-6 = 10, 54

2861 = 11, 13

2877 = 11, 15
(2928 = 11, 25)

LINE 7.

(2571 = 7, 113)
2581 = 7, 113
2686 = 9, 7
(2736 = 12, 80)

2789-91 = 10, 62
2805 = 10, 111
2868 = 10, 112
2863 = 11, 13

2868 = 11, 14
2875 = 11, 15
(*2883 = 11, 30*)
2895-6 = 11, 35
2911 = 11, 40
(2928 = 11, 25)
2932 = 11, 21

LINE 8.

2554 = 7, 131
2582 = 7, 114
2678 = 8, 130
2687 = 9, 7
(2736 = 12, 80)
2752-4 = 10, 13

2806 = 10, 111
2864 = 11, 13

2869 = 11, 14
(2883 = 11, 30)
2912 = 11, 40
2931 = 11, 21

LINE 1.	LINE 2.	LINE 3.	LINE 4.	LINE 5.	LINE 6.	LINE 7.	LINE 8.
2915 = 11, 19	2905 = 11, 40					*2987 = 11, 27*	
2918 = 11, 27	*2908 = 11, 37*						
2933 = 11, 27	2916 = 11, 19						
(2949 = 11, 51)	2925 = 11, 25						
	(2938 = 11, 28)						
2953 = 11, 53	2947 = 11, 56	(2955 = 11, 54)	(2969 = 12, 3)	2954 = 11, 53	(2985 = 12, 5)	(2985 = 12, 5)	2980 = 12, 4
2967 = 12, 3	(2949 = 11, 51)	(2969 = 12, 3)	*2978 = 12, 4*	*2968 = 12, 3*	(3023 = 12, 7)	*3024 = 12, 7*	2986 = 12, 5
2975–6 = 12, 4	*2952 = 11, 53*	*2977 = 12, 4*	*3021–2 = 12, 7*	2979 = 12, 4	(3030 = 12, 8)	(3030 = 12, 8)	(3029 = 12, 8)
(2981 = 12, 5)	(2955 = 11, 54)	2982–3 = 12, 5	3028 = 12, 8	(3023 = 12, 8)	3102 = 12, 83	3033 = 12, 10	3034 = 12, 10
3077 = 12, 7	(2981 = 12, 5)	3020 = 12, 7	*3070 = 12, 19*	(3029 = 12, 9)			3040 = 12, 6
(3027 = 12, 8)	*3019 = 12, 7*	(3031 = 12, 10)	*3101 = 12, 83*	*3049 = 12, 9*			
3042 = 12, 11	(3027 = 12, 8)	(3068 = 12, 19)					
3047 = 12, 9	(3031 = 12, 10)						
	3041 = 12, 11						
	3048 = 12, 9						
	(3068 = 12, 19)						

Total number of English lines taken from the Italian :
498

Total number of Italian lines translated, according to their positions in the stanza :

I.	II.	III.	IV.	V.	VI.	VII.	VIII.
98	80	69	47	56	44	55	55

Grand total:
504

Total number of Italian lines closely translated :

I.	II.	III.	IV.	V.	VI.	VII.	VIII.
26	20	8	9	7	4	17	5

APPENDIX C.

Chaucer's Treatment of the Teseide.

READING the *Knight's Tale* with the *Teseide*, one is frequently struck with the preternatural condensation of the *Tale*, and wonders how Chaucer could have left out so much, sometimes such fine touches and passages, of Boccaccio's admirable poem. In the *Teseide* the portraiture of Emily is far more vivid and complete than Chaucer's. In book III., for example, she hears Palamon's " Omè ! ", becomes perfectly aware that the prisoners are in the habit of watching her from the window, and shows a little harm-less coquetry; when Arcite has returned to Athens (book IV.) Emily recognizes him at a feast, wonders about him but discreetly holds her peace. Emily is the first to see the cousins fighting in the wood, stands *stordita*, then cries to Theseus (V. 81). In her attitude towards her suitors there are many nice touches ; in spite of her desire to remain single, she feels a certain attraction towards them (VII. 85), and her soliloquy during the tournament is extremely good—she is not worthy, she says, of the courage which is being dis-played (VIII. 97). Elsewhere, too, Chaucer omits good passages. He manages less plausibly Palamon's escape and meeting with Arcite, in books IV. and V. of the *Teseide*, where the detail " by helping of a frend " is fully accounted for ; he says not a word of Palamon's devoted squire Panfilo, and wholly omits Arcite's triumphal procession after the tournament, which Boccaccio strikingly portrays, and which we should suppose would at least be mentioned—Arcite has to be carried, and for his pleasure the vanquished knights follow voluntarily (IX. 30–4).

One characteristic change, however, Chaucer does make, in the treatment of the characters of Palamon and Arcite. In the *Teseide*, though Arcite cuts slightly the better figure,[1] they are hardly distinguished, and both are valorous and honourable young knights

---

[1] When he is released from prison (III. 74–6), Arcite takes a tender farewell of Palamon ; and is very pathetic and regretful (V. 45 ff.) when Palamon demands a combat.

full of all worthy emotions.[1] But Chaucer draws such a sharp distinction between them that it can hardly have been unconscious. Arcite is very highly praised by the poet and by his own associates for his physical development (1422–5) and for his character (1429–32). He is an agreeable spectacle, like Chaucer's own Squire, in his cheeriness and youthfulness over his ramble on May-day (1500 ff.), and in his falling into lover's dumps (1530). He is judicious in his retorts to Palamon's reproaches (1162–86, 1606); honourable and generous (1608–16), modest and manly (2393–9); and shows the last magnanimity in commending Palamon to Emily (2783–97).   Palamon, on the other hand, is more jealous and less affectionate toward his cousin (1281–1333); despairs readily when discovered by Theseus (1715 ff.); is ungenerous towards Arcite (1722–31, 1740 [2]); has no desire for victory, but only cares for the possession of Emily (2234 ff.) ; and cares no more what becomes of her after his death than the Pardoner about the souls of his dupes after theirs.   With this passage it is curious to compare the Italian lines from which it is altered :

> " Thanne rekke I noght, whan I have lost my lyf,
>   Though that Arcita winne hir to his wyf " (2257–8) ;

> " Che non sarebbe senza lei la vita,
>   Vedendola non mia, ma sì d'Arcita " (VII. 49).

Such a change as this must be the result of a purpose.   Palamon's only amiable traits are his courage (1591–5), and his grief after Arcite's death, and that seems to be only conventional (2882–4, 3062).

Yet it is he who after all wins Emily.   Here is an example of the subtle and perhaps only half-deliberate satire which runs through the *Knight's Tale*.   Poetic justice itself shows in a rather ironical light where Chaucer reverses Boccaccio's order and gives Palamon the better claim to Emily by letting him fall in love with her half-a-minute before Arcite.   A tone of levity and even of gentle ridicule rises here and there all through above the state and pathos of the poem, and contrasts with Boccaccio's perfect

---

[1] Kissner, in his excellent dissertation, *Chaucer in seinen Beziehungen zur italienischen Literatur* (p. 63), says that Chaucer misses the point of the *Teseide*, which is the conflict between friendship and love.

[2] In the *Teseide* (V. 86) it is Arcite ("Penteo") who first speaks when Theseus discovers them ; he does not accuse his cousin, as Palamon does in *Kn. T.*

gravity. Satire is easier to suspect than to prove, especially in a poem written when ideas of what is ludicrous and the connotations of words were so different from what they are now. It may perhaps be purely modern to see a slight lack of seriousness in the account of Palamon's tears wetting the fetters on his great shins, and of the tower resounding " of his yowling and clamour;" and in the description, condensed yet exaggerated, of the sylvan combat. But levity is impossible to mistake in the passage about Emily's bathing (2282–8).[1] In what Chaucer says of the experiences of Arcite's soul there is certainly a lack of seriousness; after the piercing pathos of Arcite's death there came a reaction. The remarks of the old Egeus, who Professor Child used to say was " delicious," read like a satire on commonplace consolation, and after his beautiful thought that just as nobody dies without first living, so nobody lives without dying, Chaucer adds (it would seem with a little irony) "over al this yet seyde he muchel more to this effect." These are the most striking passages, but they are not the only ones.

The light and satirical tone of the *Knight's Tale* seems to me to favour the view that it was written near the time of the *Canterbury Tales;* just as the omission of so many of Boccaccio's good touches suggests that he greatly condensed from the first, and that, therefore, the *Knight's Tale*, as we have it, is practically identical with the *Palamon and Arcite*.

---

[1] Dryden attributes the narrator's hesitation about speaking freely to the fact that the rites were pagan but sacred. This is only one of many cases where Dryden misses Chaucer's point, and tries to make more imposing what Chaucer meant to be light. Two others are his expansions of the two last passages mentioned in the above paragraph. See *Palamon and Arcite*, III. 197–206, 844–53, 883–90.

THE END